Collaborative Software Engineering

Ivan Mistrík · John Grundy · André van der Hoek ·
Jim Whitehead

Editors

Collaborative
Software
Engineering

 Springer

Editors

Ivan Mistrík
Independent Consultant
Werderstr. 45
69120 Heidelberg
Germany
i.j.mistrik@t-online.de

John Grundy
Centre for Complex Software
Systems & Services
Swinburne University of Technology
Faculty of Information and
Communication Technologies
PO Box 218
Hawthorn, Victoria
Australia 3122
jgrundy@swin.edu.au

André van der Hoek
University of California, Irvine
Donald Bren School of
Information & Computer Sciences
5029 Donald Bren Hall
Irvine CA 92697-3440
USA
andre@ics.uci.edu

Jim Whitehead
University of California, Santa Cruz
Dept. Computer Science
Santa Cruz CA 95064
USA
ejw@cs.ucsc.edu

ISBN 978-3-642-42431-1   ISBN 978-3-642-10294-3 (eBook)
DOI 10.1007/978-3-642-10294-3
Springer Heidelberg Dordrecht London New York

ACM Computing Classification (1998): D.2, K.6

Cover design: KuenkelLopka GmbH, Heidelberg

Printed on acid-free paper

Springer is part of Springer Science+Business Media (www.springer.com)

Foreword

While many empirical studies over the years have shown that software development skills and aptitude vary between individuals, the reality is that the size, complexity and longevity of software development projects and artefacts far exceed what any individual software developer can manage on her own. Collaboration among individuals – from users to developers – is therefore central to modern day software engineering. Collaboration takes many forms: joint activity to solve common problems, complementary activity to solve diverse problems, and both social and technical perspectives impacting all software development activity.

The difficulties of collaboration are also well documented. For example, when managerial instinct in dealing with a problematic software project was to add more developers to the development team, Fred Brooks observed and argued in his classic book *The Mythical Man Month* (Addison-Wesley, 1975) that such additions impaired rather than speeded up development. Reflecting on Brooks' observation, one could argue that it is not the addition of developers *per se* that is problematic, but the lack of effective means by which they are able to *collaborate effectively* that is crucial. Indeed the grand challenge of effective collaboration is not only to ensure that developers in a team deliver effectively as individuals, but that the whole team delivers more than the sum of its parts.

Enabling effective collaboration of course is easier said than done. As this book shows, there are many dimensions of collaboration, and many different development contexts in which different forms of collaboration are necessary and effective. The many tools and techniques that work in one context may not work in another. Collaborative software engineering therefore provides a fertile ground for empirical research on collaborative practices and collaboration tools, for technology research on developing tools and techniques for supporting collaboration, and operational research to understand organisational structures, processes, and experiences that impact, or are impacted by collaboration. This book is a welcome contribution to the research discourse in all these areas of study.

As a doctoral student some 20 years ago, I was very interested in understanding and supporting multiple software development stakeholders, as they articulated their differing perspectives of software problems and solutions, developed some shared understanding of their problem and solution worlds, and crucially important in my view, as they agreed to disagree about the parts of the world where their perspectives differed. Acknowledging, understanding and tackling disagreements head on was and is, in my view, fundamental to effective collaboration, and remains at the heart of collaborative software engineering research. While much progress has been made in the area of conflict management research, I believe that it remains a key area for tackling the challenges of supporting effective collaborative software engineering.

The editors of this book have assembled an impressive selection of authors, who have contributed authoritative body of work tackling a wide range of issues in the field of collaborative software engineering. The book will be of tremendous value to practitioners grappling with managing multi-person software development activity, as well as researchers and students interested in the state-of-the-art and the many research directions in this area. The volume is not simply a collection of papers, but a thoughtful assembly of contributions, suitably structured and introduced by the editorial team. Many of the chapters reflect on a body of research and practice that spans many years gone past, while other chapters pose research questions and describe research problems that are fundamental and long-standing. The result is a reference book, a research resource, and a pleasurable read.

Milton Keynes, UK   Bashar Nuseibeh
June 2009

Preface

Software engineering is almost always a collaborative activity. This book brings together a number of recent contributions to the domain of Collaborative Software Engineering (CoSE) from a range of research groups and practitioners. These range from tools and techniques for managing discrete, low-level activities developers engage in when developing parts of software systems; knowledge, project and process management for large scale collaborative software engineering enterprises; and new ways of organizing software teams including outsourcing, open sourcing, highly distributed virtual teams and global software engineering. We believe that all practitioners engaging in or managing collaborative software engineering practices, researchers contributing to advancement of our understanding and support for collaborative software engineering, and students wishing to gain a deeper appreciation of the underpinning theories, issues and practices within this domain will benefit from most if not all of these contributions.

Introduction

Ever since people began to create software there has been a need for collaborative software engineering. At some point people need to share their code and designs with others. Software frequently grows large and complex, thus requiring a team of multi-talented experts to work together to tackle the project. Such a team must adopt suitable processes and project management to ensure the myriad of tasks are completed; to keep track of what each other is doing; and to ensure the project advances on-time, on-budget and with the software meeting appropriate quality levels. The team must share both low-level artifacts and higher-level knowledge in controlled, consistent ways, be proactively informed of changes others make, and co-ordinate their work "in the small" as well as "in the large". Various studies have demonstrated that peer review of designs and code improve them, leading to collaborative testing and quality assurance practices. Recent trends have moved software across organizational and country boundaries, including virtual software teams and open source software development. Agile methods have brought bottom-up, human-oriented processes and techniques to bear that are very different from traditional, centralized and hierarchical development practices.

Our understanding of and support for collaborative software engineering has advanced tremendously over the past forty years. We understand that team formation and management is not a straightforward task. However we are still learning about formation, management and evolution in domains such as agile teams, projects with substantive outsourcing, open source software, virtual software teams and global software engineering domains. Knowledge management is critical in software engineering and we have developed as a community many approaches to representing knowledge about software as well as tools to facilitate its capture. However, shared, evolving knowledge and appropriate tools and techniques to support this is less well-understood from both theoretic and practical standpoints. How do we best represent and collaboratively manage knowledge about requirements, architecture, designs, quality assurance measures and software processes themselves? Social influences on software engineering and teams have become more important as have organizational implications. How do team members relate to one other and how to we build effective team relationships for communication, co-ordination and collaboration? How do we set up a successful multi-site software project? A successful open source project? A successful outsourcing project?

The actual act of collaborative software creation has received much attention over many years. But what are the right sets of tools and work practices to deploy on a collaborative software engineering project to best-support engineers and ensure quality? What are the unsolved issues around co-ordination especially in large or highly distributed teams? Configuration management remains one of the most challenging activities in collaborative software engineering.

Book Overview

We have divided this book into four parts, with a general editorial chapter providing a more detailed review of the domain of collaborative software engineering. We received a large number of submissions in response to our call for papers and invitations for this edited book from many leading research groups and well-known practitioners of leading collaborative software engineering techniques. After a rigorous review process 17 submissions were accepted for this publication. We begin by a review of the concept of collaborative software engineering including a brief review of its history, key fundamental challenges, conceptual models for reasoning about collaboration in software engineering, technical, social and managerial considerations, and define the main issues in collaborative software engineering.

Part I contains five chapters that characterize collaborative software engineering. This includes characterizing global software engineering via a process-centric approach, requirements-driven collaboration using requirements/people relationships, decoupling in collaborative software engineering, agile software development and co-ordination, communication and collaboration, and applying the concept of ontologies to collaborative software engineering.

Part II contains five chapters that examine various techniques and tool support issues in collaborative software engineering. This includes an analysis of awareness support in collaborative software development teams, an overview of several approaches and tools to supporting continuous co-ordination, a maturity model for outsourcing offshore, an architectural knowledge management platform, and a set of design principles for collaborative software engineering environments.

Part III contains three chapters addressing the issue of organizational issues in collaborative software engineering. This includes supporting the concept of collaborative software analysis and making analysis tools widely accessible, open source software project communication and collaboration analysis and visualization support, and a review and critique of multi-site software development practices.

Part IV contains four chapters looking at a variety of related issues in the collaborative software engineering domain. These include key open source/free software development collaboration issues, configuration management and collaborative development, knowledge sharing to support collaborative software architecting, and rationale management to enhance collaborative requirements engineering. We conclude with a summary of current challenges and future directions in collaborative software engineering.

What Is Collaborative Software Engineering?

Collaboration has been a necessity ever since software engineering began. The early days of software engineering saw very limited process, technique and tool support for collaboration. Early efforts to support collaboration were limited to structured, waterfall-based processes, early version control tools, rigid team role specialization, and centralization of software activities. The advent of Computer-Aided Software Engineering tools and Integrated Development Environments introduced a wider, more accessible range of collaboration support mechanisms including awareness support, collaborative analysis and reviews and iterative, rapid applications development processes. More recently has seen the growth of distributed teams, outsourcing, open source software projects, global software engineering processes and highly decentralized team support tools.

Fundamental challenges in collaborative software engineering remain the same: the need to share artifacts, communicate and co-ordinate work. These occur across a spectrum of low-level to high-level. Low-level challenges include making shared artifacts like code, tests and designs accessible in a timely manner to team members while controlling access, ownership, integrity and quality. Large software projects require effective version control and configuration management techniques and tools. Knowledge management is fundamental especially around design rationale, architecture and processes. Software development has changed dramatically over the past 10 years. This is evidenced by new organizational and team dynamics including open source software, software outsourcing, distributed teams, and global software engineering. Choice of processes, project management, tools and evolution of software in these domains is still an emerging field of research and practice.

Key technical considerations in collaborative software engineering revolve around process, project management, knowledge and configuration management and tool platform selection and operation. A software process and project management regime must be chosen that supports collaboration appropriate to the team, project and organizational circumstances. These range from small, single-site/single-project teams, to large team/multi-project/multi-site domains. The later may include outsourcing and open source components. Complex software systems require effective knowledge management approaches and support tools. They also require scalable configuration management tools. Tool platforms and collaboration-supporting components have become very diverse. These range from small-team, homogeneous IDEs with awareness and collaboration plug-ins to highly diverse platforms where software engineering is part of a larger systems engineering activity. Communication support between engineers often becomes a crucial component of the team support infrastructure.

Being an inter-personal and–often–inter-organizational activity, collaborative software engineering introduces a number of social and managerial challenges. Teams may be homogeneous or highly diverse in terms of culture, language and location. This introduces many challenges to supporting collaboration at high levels (process, project management) and low-levels (artifact sharing, consistency). Teams may be comprised of many generalist's e.g., agile methods or highly specialized individuals or sub-teams whose efforts must be coordinated. An organization needs to ensure appropriate management of teams and between teams. In particular, global software engineering domains introduce very new and challenging problems, such as in contracting and quality control in outsourcing, ownership and "group dynamics" in multi-site projects, and overall project direction and co-ordination in open source software projects.

Part I – Characterizing Collaborative Software Engineering

The five papers in this section identify a range of themes around the characteristics of collaborative software engineering. There has been a dramatic increase in interest in the concept of "global software engineering" over the past 10 years. This has included the increasing number of distributed, multi-site software engineering teams; outsourcing of software engineering activities, often in search of cost savings and capacity limits, and open source software development. Each of these trends brings with it added complexity to the engineering process—software engineers are no longer co-located, are no longer in regular face-to-face contact (if at all), and different time zones, cultures and languages enter the mix.

A number of studies have been undertaken to better-understand the issues of collaboration challenges in such "virtual" software team environments. A key aim is to understand factors that adversely impact on collaboration practices and factors that support communication, co-ordination and collaboration in such domains. Studies have focuses on a range of organizations, projects and team sizes. One area of particularly detailed study has been requirements engineering. A distributed team develops and shares a set of requirements and a crucial factor impacting quality of these is communication strategies.

Knowledge engineering has become important in collaborative software engineering. One aspect is the development of ontologies, or shared semantic meanings, of software artifacts and processes. These enable co-ordination of activities along with improved communication about shared concepts in domains ranging from requirements engineering to software architecture.

Agile methods have become popular in many domains of software engineering. A characteristic is their focus on people-centric aspects of software engineering tasks, including communication and co-ordination. Pairing is one aspect of several agile methods that offers a tangible way to encourage improved collaboration outcomes.

Part II – Tools and Techniques

Software engineering requires a number of complex, interleaved activities to be carried out. These must be organized into logically correct teamwork and be supported by appropriate tools. Because of the challenges of supporting collaborating in an already complex engineering process, a multitude of techniques and tools have been developed to support almost all activities of collaborative software engineering.

Traditionally software engineering had been a co-located activity where team members could expect some degree of face-to-face communication and collaboration and co-ordination were important activities but discrete and compartmentalized. Outsourcing parts of a software engineering project and highly iterative agile processes have led to an increased interest in how to best support virtual, distributed collaboration and communication and co-ordination for team activities that repeat in days rather than months.

A range of support mechanisms and associated tool support have appeared in recent years to address concerns in both traditional but more particularly these newer domains of collaborative software engineering. Social networking-style support such as tagging, shared knowledge repositories and communication support have become popular. New search-based support and associated visualization support have become more important as developers are less familiar with large tracts of software systems. These include mining of software repositories and context-aware filtering mechanisms in IDEs. Event-based support mechanisms have always been popular in collaborative support environments. These have been explored further in the context of both same-place and distance-located teams to support proactive notification and various levels of group awareness.

Developer-centric software engineering tools are crucial and this includes support for collaboration. Areas of particular interest in these tools are knowledge management and expertise communication. Knowledge management requires use of shared ontologies and supporting authoring tools, but as importantly the development of true "virual communities" where informal knowledge sharing is supported and encouraged. Expertise communication is one aspect where the collaboration environment allows increasingly geographically dispersed team members to better communicate both knowledge and expertise relating to knowledge and tasks.

Part III – Organizational Experiences

Multi-site, or geographically distributed software development, has introduced a range of unknowns into software engineering practice and research. Of particular note is the lack of guidance around process selection. When running a multi-site, geographically distributed software project, what is the "best" software process to choose to organize this activity, quite apart from tool, project management and team selection issues? How can organizations make process choices, in particular, to best exploit multiple time zones, team expertise, out-sourced and open-sourced parts of a product, and ensure quality, cost and timeliness thresholds? Two fundamental ways of organizing a distributed project are centralized control of overall process and distribution of scoped design/code/test, compared with distributing different phases e.g. requirements team, design and build team, testing team in different locations.

Open source software projects are an increasingly common model of distributed, virtual software teams. Many studies have looked at collaboration aspects of such projects, in particular the evolution of the code base and team communication and co-ordination patterns. Recovering such information is challenging–often via bug reports, detailed code analysis and informal interviews of key team members. It is still an unsolved research problem how to best set up an open source project to achieve high quality communication and co-ordination.

Software artifact analysis has been used extensively for many years. This includes static analysis of source code, tests, designs and requirements and dynamic analysis of execution traces, side-effects and formal models of code. Collaboration around analysis has often been informal and poorly structured. Given the increasing complexity of code and analysis tools and techniques, an open challenge is how to share analysis processes and techniques, and also the tools supporting these, particularly across organizations.

Part IV – Related Issues

A number of socio-technical issues arise in collaborative software engineering. In free and open source software development projects these are particularly challenging. Key issues include overall project ownership and co-ordination, task de-composition, trust, accountability, commitment and social networking. Collaboration affordances in the individual and group development ecosystem must support both the range of collaboration activities but take into account the free and open source domain of work.

Knowledge sharing is crucial in all domains of software engineering. Particular domains of interest include requirements engineering and software architecture where commissioner, engineer, manager and end user constraints intersect and often must be balanced. Knowledge sharing in collaborative software architecting supports better decision making, surfacing of assumptions, and reasoning about design decisions. In product line engineering, variability management is a key challenge, particularly when faced with multi-site software teams. Rationale management can be used to augment the variability management process to improve collaboration support in this context.

Configuration management has long been a challenge in software engineering particularly as systems have grown enormously in size and complexity. As configuration management requires integrating many software artifacts and ultimately impacts all phases of proceeding development, configuration management support systems have been an early contributor to collaborative software engineering infrastructure. They provide a shared space, awareness support, record and enable tracing of team actions, and support both knowledge sharing and communication. Many outstanding research and practice issues exist in each of these areas of configuration management systems support, however, leading to next generation collaborative software engineering tools.

Current Challenges and Future Directions

Collaborative software engineering has been a very heavily researched area and almost all practicing software teams will need to engage in it. However, many challenges still present both in terms of adopting collaboration practices, processes and tools and improving the state-of-the-art. Many of these challenges are long standing, and hence are fundamental to the act of working together to engineer shared artifacts. These include assembling teams, dividing work, social networking within and between teams, choosing best-practice processes, techniques and supporting tools, and effective project management. Others have arisen due to new organizational practices and technical advances, including open-sourced, out-sourced, multi-site and agile software engineering contexts. We still do not know the ideal way to share knowledge, facilitate the most effective communication, co-ordinate massively distributed work, and design and deploy support tools for these activities.

Auckland, New Zealand   John Grundy
Heidelberg, Germany   Ivan Mistrík
Irvine, CA, USA   André van der Hoek
Santa Cruz, CA, USA   Jim Whitehead

Acknowledgements

The editors would like to sincerely thank the many authors who contributed their works to this collection. The international team of anonymous reviewers gave detailed feedback on early versions of chapters and helped us to improve both the presentation and accessibility of the work. Finally we would like to thank the Springer management and editorial teams for the opportunity to produce this unique collection of articles covering the very wide range of areas related to collaborative software engineering.

Contents

Contributors

Ban Al-Ani Department of Informatics, University of California, Irvine, CA 92697-3440, USA, balani@ics.uci.edu

Paris Avgeriou Department of Mathematics and Computing Science, University of Groningen, 9747 AG Groningen, Netherlands, paris@cs.rug.nl

Alberto Avritzer Siemens Corporate Research, Inc., Princeton, NJ, 8540, USA, alberto.avritzer@siemens.com

Stefanie Betz Institute of Applied Informatics and Formal Description Methods, Universität of Karlsruhe, 76128 Karlsruhe, Germany, stefanie.betz@aifb.uni-karlsruhe.de

Jan Bosch Intuit Inc., Mountain View, CA 94043, USA, jan@janbosch.com

Petra M. Bosch-Sijtsema Helsinki University of Technology and Stanford University, Stanford, CA 94305, USA, Pbosch@stanford.edu; petra@petrabosch.com

John Burton Vitalograph Limited, Ennis, Co Clare, Ireland, john.burton@vitalograph.ie

Valentine Casey Software Systems Research Centre, Bournemouth University, Poole, Dorset, UK, vcasey@bournemouth.ac.uk

Viktor Clerc VU University Amsterdam, 1081 HV Amsterdam, Netherlands, viktor@cs.vu.nl

Isabella A. da Silva Department of Informatics, University of California, Irvine, CA 92697-3440, USA, bellinha@gmail.com

Daniela Damian Software Engineering Global interAction Lab, University, of Victoria, Victoria, BC, Canada, danielad@cs.uvic.ca

Remco C. de Boer VU University Amsterdam, 1081 HV Amsterdam, Netherlands, remco@cs.vu.nl

Prasun Dewan Department of Computer Science CB 3175, University of North Carolina, Chapel Hill, NC 27599-3175, USA, dewan@cs.unc.edu

Jacky Estublier Université de Grenoble (LIG/CNRS), 38400 Saint Martin, France, Jacky.Estublier@imag.fr

Rik Farenhorst VU University Amsterdam, 1081 HV Amsterdam, Netherlands, rik@cs.vu.nl

Harald C. Gall Software Evolution and Architecture Lab, Department of Informatics, University of Zurich, 8050 Zürich, Switzerland, gall@ifi.uzh.ch

Giacomo Ghezzi Software Evolution and Architecture Lab, Department of Informatics, University of Zurich, 8050 Zürich, Switzerland, ghezzi@ifi.uzh.ch

John Grundy Electrical & Computer Engineering, University of Auckland, Auckland 1142, New Zealand, j.grundy@auckland.ac.nz

Hans-Jörg Happel FZI Research Center for Information Technology, 76131 Karlsruhe, Germany, happel@fzi.de

Anton Jansen Department of Mathematics and Computing Science University of Groningen, 9747 AG Groningen, Netherlands, a.g.j.jansen@cs.rug.nl

Irwin Kwan Software Engineering Global interAction Lab, University of Victoria, Victoria, BC, Canada, irwink@cs.uvic.ca

Patricia Lago VU University Amsterdam, 1081 HV Amsterdam, Netherlands, patricia@cs.vu.nl

Peng Liang Departmentt of Mathematics and Computing Science, University of Groningen, 9747 AG Groningen, Netherlands, liangp@cs.rug.nl

Walid Maalej Technische Universität München, 85748 Garching, Germany, maalejw@in.tum.de

Juho Mäkiö Forschungszentrum Informatik FZI, 76131 Karlsruhe, Germany, juho.maekioe@gmx.de

Sabrina Marczak Software Engineering Global interAction Lab, University of Victoria, Victoria, BC, Canada, smarczak@cs.uvic.ca

Fergal McCaffery Stokes Lecturer, Dundalk Institute of Technology, Dundalk, Co Louth, Ireland, fergal.mccaffery@dkit.ie

Ivan Mistrík Independent Consultant, 69120 Heidelberg, Germany, i.j.mistrik@t-online.de

Leonardo Gresta P. Murta Instituto de Computação, Universidade Federal Fluminense, Niterói, RJ 24210-240, Brazil, leomurta@ic.uff.br

Kumiyo Nakakoji Research Centre for Advanced Science and Technology, University of Tokyo, Japan; SRA Key Technology Laboratory Inc., Japan, kumiyo@kid.rcast.u-tokyo.ac.jp

Bashar Nuseibeh Department of Computing, The Open University, Milton Keynes MK7 6AA, UK, B.Nuseibeh@open.ac.uk

Andreas Oberweis Institute of Applied Informatics and Formal, Description Methods, Universität Karlsruhe, 76128 Karlsruhe, Germany, andreas.oberweis@aifb.uni-karlsruhe.de

Daniel J. Paulish Siemens Corporate Research, Inc., Princeton, NJ 08540, USA, daniel.paulish@siemens.com

Martin Pinzger Software Engineering Research Group, Delft University of Technology, Netherlands, M.Pinzger@tudelft.nl

David Redmiles Department of Informatics, University of California, Irvine, CA 92697-3440, USA, redmiles@ics.uci.edu

Ita Richardson Department of Computer Science & Information Systems, Lero – the Irish Software Engineering, Research Centre, University of Limerick, Ireland, ita.richardson@ul.ie

Hugh Robinson Centre for Research in Computing, The Open University, Milton Keynes, MK7 6AA, UK, h.m.robinson@open.ac.uk

Anita Sarma Department of Computer Science & Engineering, University of Nebraska, Lincoln, NE 68588-0115, USA, asarma@cse.unl.edu

Walt Scacchi Donald Bren School of Information and Computer Sciences, Institute for Software Research, University of California, Irvine, CA 92697-3455, USA, Wscacchi@ics.uci.edu

Stefan Seedorf University of Mannheim, 68131 Mannheim, Germany, seedorf@uni-mannheim.de

Helen Sharp Centre for Research in Computing, The Open University, Milton Keynes, MK7 6AA, UK, H.C.Sharp@open.ac.uk

Roberto S. Silva Filho Department of Informatics, University of California, Irvine, CA 92697-3440, USA, rsilvafi@ics.uci.edu

Anil K. Thurimella Harman/Becker Automotive Systems, 76307 Karlsbad, Germany, anil_98ee601@yahoo.com

Erik Trainer Department of Informatics, University of California, Irvine, CA 92697-3440, USA, etrainer@ics.uci.edu

André van der Hoek Department of Informatics, University of California, Irvine, CA 92697-3440, USA, andre@ics.uci.edu

Hans van Vliet VU University Amsterdam, 1081 HV Amsterdam, Netherlands, hans@cs.vu.nl

Claudia Maria L. Werner Programa de Engenharia, de Sistemas e Computação, COPPE – Universidade Federal do Rio de Janeiro, Rio de Janeiro 21941-972, Brazil, werner@cos.ufrj.br

Jim Whitehead Department of Computer Science, Jack Baskin School of Engineering, University of California, Santa Cruz, CA 95064, USA, ejw@soe.ucsc.edu

Yasuhiro Yamamoto Research Centre for Advanced Science and Technology, University of Tokyo, Tokyo, Japan, yxy@kid.rcast.u-tokyo.ac.jp

Yunwen Ye SRA Key Technology Laboratory, Inc., Shinjuku, Tokyo 160-0004, Japan, ye@sra.co.jp

Chapter 1
Collaborative Software Engineering: Concepts and Techniques

Jim Whitehead, Ivan Mistrík, John Grundy, and André van der Hoek

Abstract Collaboration is a central activity in software engineering, as all but the most trivial projects involve multiple engineers working together. Hence, understanding software engineering collaboration is important for both engineers and researchers. This chapter presents a framework for understanding software engineering collaboration, focused on three key insights: (1) software engineering collaboration is model-based, centered on the creation and negotiation of shared meaning within the project artifacts that contain the models that describe the final working system; (2) software project management is a cross-cutting concern that creates the organizational structures under which collaboration is fostered (or dampened); and (3) global software engineering introduces many forms of distance – spatial, temporal, socio-cultural – into existing pathways of collaboration. Analysis of future trends highlight several ways engineers will be able to improve project collaboration, specifically, software development environments will shift to being totally Web-based, thereby opening the potential for social network site integration, greater participation by end-users in project development, and greater ease in global software engineering. Just as collaboration is inherent in software engineering, so are the fundamental tensions inherent in fostering collaboration; the chapter ends with these.

1.1 Introduction

Software projects are inherently co-operative, requiring many software engineers to co-ordinate their efforts to produce a large software system. Integral to this effort is developing shared understanding surrounding multiple artifacts, each artifact embodying its own model, over the entire development process [97].

J. Whitehead (✉)
Department of Computer Science, Jack Baskin School of Engineering, University of California, Santa Cruz, CA 95064, USA
e-mail: ejw@soe.ucsc.edu

I. Mistrík et al. (eds.), *Collaborative Software Engineering*,
DOI 10.1007/978-3-642-10294-3_1, © Springer-Verlag Berlin Heidelberg 2010

Software engineers have adopted a wide range of communication and collaboration technologies to assist in the co-ordination of project work. Every mainstream communication technology has been adopted by software engineers for project use, including telephone, teleconferences, email, voice mail, discussion lists, the Web, instant messaging, voice over IP, and videoconferences. These communication paths are useful at every stage in a project's lifecycle, and support a wide range of unstructured natural language communication. Additionally, software engineers hold meetings in conference rooms, and conduct informal conversations in hallways, doorways, and offices. While these discussions concern the development of a formal system, a piece of software, the conversations themselves are not formally structured (exceptions being automated email messages generated by SCM systems and bug tracking systems).

In contrast to the unstructured nature of conversation, much collaboration in software engineering is relative to various formal and semi-formal artifacts. Software engineers collaborate on requirements specifications, architecture diagrams, UML diagrams, source code, and bug reports. Each is a different model of the ongoing project. Software engineering collaboration can thus be understood as artifact-based or model-based collaboration, where the focus of activity is on the production of new models, the creation of shared meaning around the models, and elimination of error and ambiguity within the models.

This model orientation to software engineering collaboration is important due to its structuring effect. The models provide a shared meaning that engineers use when co-ordinating their work, as when engineers working together consult a requirements specification to determine how to design a portion of the system. Engineers also use the models to create new shared meaning, as when engineers discuss a UML diagram, and thereby better understand its meaning and implications for ongoing work. The models also surface ambiguity by making it possible for one engineer to clearly describe their understanding of the system; when this is confusing or unclear to others, ambiguity is present. Without the structure and semantics provided by models, it would be more difficult to recognize differences in understanding among collaborators.

These twin threads – the appropriation of novel communications technologies for project work, and the model-centric nature of collaboration – are what give the study of software engineering collaboration its unique character. Focusing just on communication, the low cost and global reach of email, web, and instant messaging technologies created the potential for global, multi-site software engineering teams. This made it less expensive to globally distribute closed source projects, and created the technological conditions that supported the emergence of open sourceopen source software. In turn, understanding how best to structure and support this communication-afforded collaboration within distributed software engineering has been the focus of sustained study. Much traditional collaborative work research has focused on the use of novel communication technologies in a variety of work settings, viewing them as artifact-neutral co-ordination technologies. What distinguishes the study of collaboration within software engineering from this more general study of collaboration is its focus on model creation. Software engineers are not just collaborating in the abstract – they are collaborating over the creation of a series of artifacts that, together, provide a multi-faceted view of the behavior of a complex system.

1.2 Defining Collaborative Software Engineering

Collaboration is pervasive throughout software engineering. Almost all non-trivial software projects require the effort and talent of multiple people to bring it to conclusion. Once there are two or more people on a software project, they must work together, that is, they must collaborate. Thus, a simple ground truth is that *any software project with more than one person is created through a process of collaborative software engineering.*

There is an old story, running through many cultures, about six blind men and an elephant. One man touches the elephant's trunk, and says the elephant is a rope. Another touches a leg, and says the elephant is a tree trunk. The remaining four describe the elephant as a snake (tail), spear (tusk), wall (body), or brush (end of tail). A large software system is like the elephant in the story, with each software engineer having their own view and understanding of the overall system. Unlike the story, a software system under development lacks the physical fixedness of the elephant; one cannot simply step back and see the shape of the entire software system. Instead, a software system is shaped by the intersecting activities and perspectives of the engineers working on it. Software is thought-stuff, the highly malleable conversion of abstractions, algorithms, and ideas into tangible running code. Hence software engineers shape the system under construction while developing their understanding of it.

Human minds are enormously flexible, approaching problems from unique experiential, cultural, educational, and biochemical conditions; developers have widely varying backgrounds and experiences, come from different cultures, have different types of educational backgrounds, and have varying body chemistry. Somehow, through the imperfect instrument of language, the vast pool of variable outcomes inherent in any software system needs to be reduced to a single coherent system. In this view, *software engineering collaboration is the mediation of the multiple conflicting mental conceptions of the system held by human developers.*

Collaboration takes the form of tools to structure communication and lead to consensus, as in the case of requirements elicitation tools. Other tools mediate conflicts among differing views of the system, as in the case of configuration management tools both preventing conflicting viewpoints from being realized as incompatible code changes, and providing a process for handling conflicts when they occur (merge tools). Tools for representing design and architecture diagrams also help to mediate conflicts by making internal mental models explicit, thereby allowing other actors to identify points of departure from their own views of the system.

Since software is so abstract and malleable, and is created via a process of negotiating multiple viewpoints on the system, it is inevitable that software will have errors. *Consequently, software engineering collaboration also involves the joint identification and removal of error*. This can be seen in software inspections, where multiple engineers bring their unique perspectives to the task of finding latent errors. It is also visible in test teams, where many engineers work together to write system test suites, and use bug tracking software to co-ordinate bug fixing effort.

People have a hard time working together effectively. To work well together, engineers need to understand near-term and long-term goals, be clustered into teams, and understand their personal responsibilities. Engineers also need to be motivated, and receive appropriate reward for their work. Hence, *software engineering collaboration is about creating the organizational structures, reward structures, and work breakdown structures that afford effective work towards goal*. As a consequence, software engineering management and leadership is an integral part of software engineering collaboration.

1.3 Historical Trends in Collaborative Software Engineering

Software engineers have developed a wide range of model-oriented technologies to support collaborative work on their projects. These technologies span the entire lifecycle, including collaborative requirements tools [5, 39], collaborative UML diagram creation, software configuration management systems and bug tracking systems [11]. Process modeling and enactment systems have been created to help manage the entire lifecycle, supporting managers and developers in assignment of work, monitoring current progress, and improving processes [7, 57]. In the commercial sphere, there are many examples of project management software, including Microsoft Project [69] and Rational Method Composer [42]. Several efforts have created standard interfaces or repositories for software project artifacts, including WebDAV/DeltaV [24, 98] and PCTE [96]. Web-based integrated development environments serve to integrate a range of model-based (SCM, bug tracking systems) and unstructured (discussion list, web pages) collaboration technologies.

Tool support developed specifically to support collaboration in software engineering falls into four broad categories. *Model-based* collaboration tools allow engineers to collaborate in the context of a specific representation of the software, such as a UML diagram. *Process support* tools represent all or part of a software development process. Systems using explicit process representations permit software process modelling and enactment. In contrast, tools using an implicit representation of software process embed a specific tool-centric work process, such as the checkout, edit, checking process of most SCM tools. *Awareness tools* do not support a specific task, and instead aim to inform developers about the ongoing work of others, in part to avoid conflicts. *Collaboration infrastructure* has been developed to improve interoperability among collaboration tools, and focuses primarily on their data and control integration. Below, we give a brief overview of previous work in these areas, to provide context for our recommendations for future areas of research on software collaboration technologies.

1.3.1 Model-Based Collaboration Tools

Software engineering involves the creation of multiple artifacts. These artifacts include the end product, code, but also incorporate requirements specifications, architecture description, design models, testing plans, and so on. Each type of artifact has its own semantics, ranging from free form natural language, to the semi-formal semantics of UML, or the formal semantics of a programming language. Hence, the creation of these artifacts is the creation of models.

Creating each of these artifacts is an inherently collaborative activity. Multiple software engineers contribute to each of these artifacts, working to understand what each other has done, eliminate errors, and add their contributions. Especially with requirements and testing, engineers work with customers to ensure the artifacts accurately reflect their needs. Hence, the collaborative work to create software artifacts is the collaborative work to create models of the software system. Systems designed to support the collaborative creation and editing of specific artifacts are really supporting the creation of specific models, and hence support model-based collaboration. Collaboration tools exist to support the creation of every kind of model found in typical software engineering practice.

Figure 1.1 provides an overview of model-oriented collaboration across a software project lifecycle. In the figure, rows represent different types of actors or models, while columns represent different phases in the development of a software system. Overlaps between bubbles for types of people represent collaboration. So, for example, the overlap of stakeholders and requirements engineers in the requirements column represents their collaboration to create the requirements documentation for the system to be built. Project management cuts across all project phases and impacts all types of software engineer, hence it is represented as a horizontal bar. Remote collaboration occurs when the set of people within a bubble is distributed across multiple sites, or when each bubble in a collaboration is at a different site.

Overlap between model type bubbles indicates dependencies between the models. For example, determining a system's software architecture often requires negotiation with the customer over the implications of requirements, and may require an understanding of the fine-grained design of certain system functions. For simplicity, the figure is drawn using a waterfall-type process model. Other process models modify this picture. Spiral development would involve additional negotiation around the importance of various types of risk, and what constitutes acceptable levels of risk. An evolutionary prototyping model would add collaboration between stakeholders and developers in the coding phase, representing the negotiation that takes place after a demonstration of the evolving system prototype to the customer.

In the sections below, we provide an overview of the collaboration that takes place during each project phase, and active areas of research within these phases.

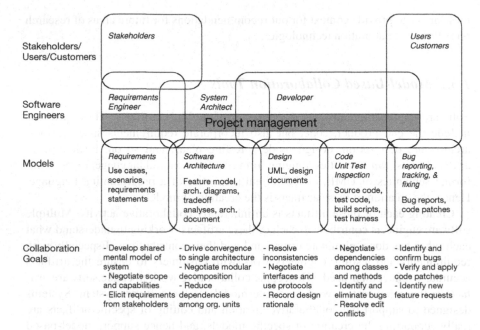

Stakeholders/ Users/Customers	Stakeholders				Users Customers
Software Engineers	Requirements Engineer	System Architect	Developer		
	Project management				
Models	Requirements Use cases, scenarios, requirements statements	Software Architecture Feature model, arch. diagrams, tradeoff analyses, arch. document	Design UML, design documents	Code Unit Test Inspection Source code, test code, build scripts, test harness	Bug reporting, tracking, & fixing Bug reports, code patches
Collaboration Goals	- Develop shared mental model of system - Negotiate scope and capabilities - Elicit requirements from stakeholders	- Drive convergence to single architecture - Negotiate modular decomposition - Reduce dependencies among org. units	- Resolve inconsistencies - Negotiate interfaces and use protocols - Record design rationale	- Negotiate dependencies among classes and methods - Identify and eliminate bugs - Resolve edit conflicts	- Identify and confirm bugs - Verify and apply code patches - Identify new feature requests

Fig. 1.1 Overview of model driven collaboration

1.3.1.1 Requirement Centered Collaboration

In the requirements phase, there are many existing commercial tools that support collaborative development of requirements, including Rational's RequisitePro [43] and DOORS [41] products, and Borland's CaliberRM [8] (a more exhaustive list can be found at [60]). These tools allow multiple engineers to describe project use cases and requirements using natural language text, record dependencies among and between requirements and use cases, and perform change impact analyses. Integration with design and testing tools permits dependencies between requirements, UML models, and test cases to be explicitly represented.

Collaboration features vary across tools. Within RequisitePro, requirements are stored in a per-project requirements database, and can be edited via a Web-based interface by editing a Word document that interacts with the database via a plugin, or by direct entry using the RequisitePro user interface. Multiple engineers can edit the requirements simultaneously via these interfaces. While cross-organization interaction is possible via the Web-based interface, the tool is primarily designed for within-organization use. RAVEN [79] supports collaboration via a built-in checkout/checkin process on individual requirements. While most requirements tools are desktop applications, Gatherspace [29] and eRequirements [29] are web-based collaborative requirements tools, with capabilities only accessible via a Web browser.

Research on collaborative requirements tools has focused on supporting negotiation among stakeholders, use of new requirements engineering processes, and exploration of new media and platforms. Win-Win was designed to support a requirements engineering process that made negotiation processes explicit in the interface of the tool, with an underlying structure that encouraged resolution of conflicts, creating "win–win" conditions for involved stakeholders [5]. ART-SCENE supports a requirements elicitation approach in which a potentially distributed team writes use cases using a series of structured templates accessible via a Web-based interface. These are then used to automatically generate scenarios that describe normal and alternative situations, which can then be evaluated by requirements analysts [63]. Follow-on work has examined the use of a mobile, PDA-based interface for ART-SCENE, taking advantage of the mobility of the interface to show use cases to customer stakeholder in-situ [64]. The Software Cinema project examined the use of video for recording dialog between engineers and stakeholders, allowing these conversations to be recorded and analyzed in depth [17].

1.3.1.2 Architecture Centered Collaboration

Though the creation of final software architecture for a project is a collaborative and political activity, much of this collaboration takes place outside architecture-focused tools. Rational Software Architect is an UML modelling tool focused on software architecture. Engineers can browse an existing component library and work collaboratively on diagrams with other engineers, with collaboration mediated via the configuration management system. Research systems, such as ArchStudio [18, 95] and ACMEStudio [53] typically support collaborative authoring by versioning architecture description files, allowing a turn-taking authoring model. The MolhadoArch system is more tightly integrated with an underlying fine-grain version control system, and hence affords collaboration at the level of individual model elements [73]. Supporting an explicitly web-based style of collaboration, Maheshwari and Teoh [62], describes a web-based tool that supports the ATAM architecture evaluation methodology.

1.3.1.3 Design Centered Collaboration

Today, due to the strong adoption of the Unified Modelling Language (UML), mainstream software design tools are synonymous with UML editors, and include Rational Rose [44], ArgoUML [78], Borland Together [9], and Altova UModel [2] (a more complete list is at [102]). Collaboration features of UML authoring tools mostly depend on the capabilities of the underlying software configuration management system. For example, ArgoUML provides no built-in collaboration features, instead relying on the user to subdivide their UML models into multiple files, which are then individually managed by the SCM system. The Rosetta UML editor [32] was the first to explore Web-based collaborative editing of UML diagrams, using a Java applet diagram editor. Recently, Gliffy [30] and iDungu [45] have web-based diagram editors that support UML diagrams. Gliffy uses linear versioning to record document changes, and can inform other collaborators via email when a diagram has changed. SUMLOW supports same-time, same-place collaborative UML diagram creation via a shared electronic whiteboard [16].

1.3.1.4 Collaboration Around Testing and Inspections

Like requirements, testing often involves substantial collaboration between an engineering team and customers. Testing interactions vary substantially across projects and organizations. Application software developers often make use of public beta tests in which potential users gain advance access to software, and report bugs back to the development team. As well, best practices for usability testing involves multiple people performing specific tasks under observation, another form of testing based collaboration. Adversarial interactions are also possible, as is the case with a formal acceptance test, where the customer is actively looking for lack of conformance to a requirements specification.

Within an engineering organization, testing typically involves collaboration between a testing group and a development team. The key collaborative tool used to manage the interface between testers (including public beta testers) and developers is the bug tracking (or issue management) tool [90]. Long a staple of software development projects, bug tracking tools permit the recording of an initial error report, prioritization, addition of follow-on comments and error data, linking together similar reports, and assignment to a developer who will repair the software. Once a bug has been fixed, this can be recorded in the bug tracking system. Search facilities permit a wide range of error reporting. A comparison of multiple issue tracking and bug tracking systems can be found at [101].

Software inspections involve multiple engineers reviewing a specific software artifact. As a result, software inspection tools have a long history of being collaborative. Hedberg [34] divides this history into early tools, distributed tools, asynchronous tools, and web-based tools. Early tools (circa 1990) were designed to support engineers holding a face-to-face meeting, while distributed tools (1992–1993) permitted remote engineers to participate in an inspection meeting. Asynchronous tools (1994–1997) relaxed the requirement for the inspection participants to all meet at the same time, and Web-based tools supported inspection processes on the Web (1997–onwards). MacDonald and Miller [61] also survey software inspection support systems as of 1999. More recently, Meyer describes a distributed software inspection process using only off-the-shelf communication technologies, including voice over IP, Google Docs (web-based collaborative document authoring), and Wiki. These technologies were found to be sufficient to conduct effective reviews; no specialized review software was necessary [68].

1.3.1.5 Traceability and Consistency

While ensuring traceability from requirements to code and tests is not inherently a collaborative activity, once a project has multiple engineers, creating traceability links and ensuring their consistency is a major task. XLinkit performs automated consistency checks across a project [71], while [65] describes an approach for automatically inferring documentation to source code links using information retrieval techniques. Inconsistencies identified by these approaches can then form the starting point for examining whether there are mismatches between the artifacts created by different collaborators.

1.3.2 Process Centered Collaboration

Engineers working together to develop a large software project can benefit from having a predefined structure for the sequence of steps to be performed, the roles engineers must fulfill, and the artifacts that must be created. This predefined structure takes the form of a software process model, and serves to reduce the amount of co-ordination required to initiate a project. By having the typical sequence of steps, roles, and artifacts defined, engineers can more quickly tackle the project at hand, rather than renegotiating the entire project structure. Over time, engineers within an organization develop experience with a specific process structure. The net effect is to reduce the amount of co-ordination work required within a project by regularizing points of collaboration, as well as to increase predictability of future activity.

To the extent that software processes are predictable, software environments can mediate the collaborative work within a project. Process centered software development environments have facilities for writing software process models in a process modelling language (see [74] for a retrospective on this literature), then executing these models in the context of the environment. While a process model lies at the core of process centered environments, this process guides the collaborative activity of engineers working on other artifacts, and is not itself the focus of their collaboration. Hence, for example, the environment can manage the assignment of tasks to engineers, monitor their completion, and automatically invoke appropriate tools. A far-from-exhaustive list of such systems includes Arcadia [49], Oz [3], Marvel [4], Conversation Builder [51], and Endeavors [7]. One challenge faced by such systems is the need to handle exceptions to an ongoing process, an issue addressed by [50].

1.3.3 Collaboration Awareness

Software configuration management systems are the primary technology co-ordinating file-based collaboration among software engineers. The primary collaborative mechanism supported by SCM systems is the workspace. Typically each developer has their own workspace, and uses a checkout, edit, checkin cycle to modify a project artifact. Workspaces provide isolation from the work of other developers, and hence while an artifact is checked out, no other engineer can see its current state. Many SCM systems permit parallel work on artifacts, in which multiple engineers edit the same artifact at the same time, using merge tools to resolve inconsistencies [67]. Workspaces allow engineers to work more efficiently by reducing the co-ordination burden among engineers, and avoiding turn-taking for editing artifacts. They raise several issues, however, including the inability to know which developers are working on a specific artifact. Palantir addresses this problem by providing engineers with workspace awareness, information about the current activities of other engineers [85]. By increasing awareness of the activities of other engineers, they are able to perform co-ordination activities sooner, and potentially avoid conflicts. Augur is another example of an awareness tool [28]. It provides a visualization of several aspects of the development history of a project, extracted from an SCM repository, thereby allowing members of a distributed project to be more aware of ongoing and historical activity.

1.3.4 Collaboration Infrastructure

Various infrastructure technologies make it possible for engineers to work collaboratively. Software tool integration technologies make it possible for software tools (and the engineers operating them) to co-ordinate their work. Major forms of tool integration include data integration, ensuring that tools can exchange data, and control integration, ensuring that tools are aware of the activities of other tools, and can take action based on that knowledge. For example, in the Marvel environment, once an engineer finished editing their source code, it was stored in a central repository (data integration), and then a compiler was automatically called by Marvel (control integration) [4].

The Portable Common Tool Environment (PCTE) was developed from 1983 to 1989 to create a broad range of interoperability standards for tool integration spanning data, control, and user interface integration [96]. Its greatest success was in defining a data model and interface for data integration. The WebDAV effort (1996–2006) aimed to give the Web open interfaces for writing content, thereby affording data integration among software engineering tools, as well as a range of other content authoring tools [24, 98]. Today, the data integration needs of software environments are predominantly met by SCM systems managing files via isolated workspaces. However, the world of data integration standards and SCM meet in tools like Subversion [75] that use WebDAV as the data integration technology in their implementation.

For control integration there are two main approaches, direct tool invocation, and event notification services. In direct tool integration, a primary tool in an environment (e.g., an integrated development environment, like Eclipse) directly calls another tool to perform some work. When multiple tools need to be coordinated, a message passing approach works better. In this case, tools exchange event notification messages via some form of event transport. The Field environment introduced the notion of a message bus (an event notification middleware service) in development environments [81], with the Sienna system exemplifying more recent work in this space [13].

Ahmadi et al. suggest that future collaboration support for software projects should build upon a foundation of technologies that can be used to create social networking web sites, what they term Social Network Services [1].

1.3.5 Project Management

Software project management is intimately concerned with collaboration, since it structures the effort of the project via the creation of teams, subdivision of work to teams, schedules, and budget. These organizational, task, and cost structures drive the co-ordination and collaboration needs of a project.

Software project management is a subdiscipline of project management, and emerged as a separate concern within software engineering in the 1970s. During this decade, organizations made increasing use of computer-based information technology, leading to a demand for more, and larger software systems. The most influential early project management book is Brook's *Mythical Man Month* (1975) [10]. In 1981 Boehm defined the entire field of software economics in his landmark book of the same name [6] introducing COCOMO, the Constructive Cost Model for software. A January, 1984 edition of IEEE Trans. on Software Engineering [93] portrayed the state of the practice in software project management, and looked into its future. The year 1987 saw the release of DeMarco and Lister's *Peopleware: Productive Projects and Teams*, which emphasizes the importance of team collaboration [19]. A recent book in a similar vein was written in 1997 by McConnell, who proposed a list of Ten Essentials for software projects, based on "hard-won experience" [66].

The past 20 years have seen multiple efforts to capture and codify the knowledge and key practices required to perform effective project management. Watts Humphrey wrote *Managing the Software Process* in 1989, which first introduced the capability maturity model (fully completed in 1993) [38]. This model is significant for providing a multi-stage evolutionary roadmap by which an organization can improve its ability to manage and construct software systems. The IEEE Software Engineering Standards [47] capture many of the fundamental "best practices" of the software engineering project management. The Project Management Book of Knowledge (PMBOK), (1987, with four revisions since) documents and standardizes well-known project management knowledge and practices across a wide range of project types, including software projects [76]. The second edition of Thayer's *Software Engineering Project Management* [92] provides a framework for project management activities based on the planning, organizing, staffing, directing, and controlling model. The ISO 10006 "Quality management – Guidelines to quality to project management" [48], claims to provide "guidance on quality system elements, concepts and practices for which the implementation is important to, and has an impact on, the achievement of quality in project management".

In 2005 Pyster and Thayer decided to revisit software project management and assemble a set of articles that reflect how it has advanced over the past 20 years [77].

1.4 Global and Multi-Site Collaboration

In today's global economy, increasing numbers of software engineers are expected to work in a distributed environment. For many organizations, globally-distributed projects are rapidly becoming the norm [35]. Organizations construct global teams so as to leverage highly skilled engineers and site-specific expertise, better address the needs of users and other stakeholders, spread project knowledge throughout the organization, exploit advantages of specific labor markets, accommodate workers who wish to telecommute, and reduce costs. Mergers and alliances among organizations also create the need for distributed projects. While providing many advantages, global distribution also makes it harder for project members to collaborate effectively.

Global teams find it much harder to develop shared understanding around the evolving software artifact, as the distribution involved makes every aspect of communication more difficult. Team members at different sites lose the ability to have ad-hoc, informal communication due to spontaneous face-to-face interactions. Different sites often involve different national and organizational cultures, creating what Holmstrom et al. call socio-cultural distance [36]. As this distance increases, there is an increase in the challenge of interpreting the meaning of project communication. Engineers spread across many time zones reduce communication windows [33]. In reaction to these challenges, a core set of developers tends to emerge that acts as the key liaisons, or gatekeepers, between teams in different geographical locations. This team not only performs key co-ordination activities, but also contains the most technically productive team members [14].

Research on globally distributed software projects tends to focus on either characterizing their behavior (e.g. [33, 36]), or developing tools and techniques to mitigate the negative aspects of global distribution, so as to leverage its benefits. An example of the latter is the *global software development handbook*, which documents a wide range of issues and techniques for managing a global software project [82]. Lanubile provides a recent overview of tools for communication and co-ordination in distributed software projects [56]. In a hopeful sign that advanced tool support can overcome some of the drawbacks of global distribution, Wolf et al. report on a study of the development of the IBM's Jazz project [103]. This study shows that the Jazz team did not experience a significant decrease in project communication due to the distance between project sites.

Herbsleb presents a thorough survey of research on distributed software engineering in [35], along with thoughts on future research challenges. Herbsleb views the main challenge of distributed software engineering as the management of dependencies (that is, co-ordination) over a distance. We share this view, though this chapter also emphasizes the challenges inherent in creating shared meaning around (and identifying defects in) the many model-oriented artifacts in a software project.

1.5 Social Considerations

1.5.1 Software Teams

All engineering domains have a mix of technical and social aspects. For software engineering, such technical aspects include: software processes used to organise the life-cycle of software development; project management to co-ordinate teams working on software projects; requirements engineering, to capture key user needs of software systems and to specify – formally and/or informally – these needs; design, to identify the approaches via which the software systems will be realised; implementation, constructing executable systems; quality assurance, ensuring developed systems meet user requirements to acceptable thresholds; and deployment, making and keeping software systems available In addition, software very often must be modified over time and "maintained".

All of these technical activities must be carried out – in almost all cases – by a team of software engineers and related personnel. Such a "software team" is responsible for all of these technical aspects of engineering the software system and must be formed, organized, managed, evolved and ultimately disbanded. Team formation may be top-down or bottom-up [12, 99]. Recently team formation has had to take into account a trend to global software engineering including outsourcing, open sourcing and virtual teams [82].

1.5.2 Team Organization

Teams may be organised in a variety of ways [99]. "Tayloristic" teams have specialists filling specific roles, such as a requirements team, design team, testing team, coding team etc. These tend to be specialized, role-specific, task-focused and top-down directed units. "Agile" teams adopt a very different approach [88]. In these teams members tend to be generalists, the team people-focused rather than task-focused, and management bottom-up. Each of these teams brings very different social interaction protocols to bear on software development. Traditional, Tayloristic teams tend to be hierarchical and more centralized which suits some development projects and personalities. Agile teams tend to be more customer-driven, democratic and flexible. While this suits some developer personalities and problem domains it can be problematic. Each style of team organizationteam organization tends to utilize different collaboration approaches, project management strategies and sometimes tool support.

More recent trends have seen the rise of virtual software teams, outsourced software and open source communities. From a social perspective virtual teams need to overcome the challenges of distance, cultural and language differences and often different time zones [12]. Language barriers can mean it is difficult for team members to exchange information, co-ordinate work and communicate without mediation.

Cultural barriers can impact team dynamics in terms of co-ordination strategies, timeliness of work, and task allocation and monitoring. Different time zones delay communication sometimes leading to incorrect actions or incorrect assumptions about software artefacts and processes.

Outsourcing usually requires strong contractual relationships between teams [22]. Two common approaches are to divide an overall team into units of specialisation e.g. requirements, code, test etc., or to divide up the team vertically according to software function, e.g., the payments team, the on-line transaction processing team, the integration team. Collaboration challenges arise on the team boundaries, within teams as per other co-located models as well as for overall project management.

A very interesting set of social dynamics occur in the open source/voluntary software arena [21]. Often effort is either donated or contributed out of a sense of community belonging or mutual interest, in contrast to most other software development endeavours. This can lead to issues of ownership, or lack thereof, co-ordination challenges when available time of "team members" is unknown or opaque, and usually voluntary team membership for most or all members. Opt-in and opt-out to particular parts of a development project or software can often occur.

1.5.3 Team Composition

Team composition has a strong bearing on the social dynamics of both a single team and others its members may need to interact with. Some teams may be composed of a set of specialists while others mainly generalists. Traditional approaches to software team organisation often assume teams of specialists [99] and many outsourcing and virtual team models have also adopted this approach [12, 22]. Specialisation has advantages of clearer division of responsibility among members and ability to leverage particular skill bases. However it has major disadvantages when particular skills are rare or become unavailable for a time; and can lead to team conflict around divisions of work. Generalist teams are often favoured in agile projects [88] and are often a characteristic of many open source "teams" [21] by virtue of opt-in/opt-out driven by particular areas of interest or need.

Some teams include end users, or "customers", of the software product as a matter of course [88] whereas others isolate many team members from these customers [99]. Each has advantages and disadvantages in terms of collaboration support and project co-ordination from a social perspective. Customers generally have a very different perspective on the software project to developers and co-location greatly enhances communication and collaboration. However customers are often driven by self-interest and localised perspectives which may result in limited communication in particular areas.

Team membership can be whole-of-project, short-lived, or periodic. Some teams are created for the lifetime of a project in order to ensure available skill base and to enable deep understanding not only of the project but other team member's skills, abilities and awareness of work. Outsourced projects will typically leverage a remote team for the lifetime of the outsourced activity. Traditional teams may be sensitive to particular skill loss and agile teams try to mitigate this by a stronger emphasis on generalists [88].

Many teams are shared across projects. This is particularly common in virtual and out-sourced domains where specialised teams may be working on several projects at once. This greatly complicates inter-team communication and collaboration. Open source projects are often characterised by some team members participating for the whole duration of a project; some leaving early or joining later; and some participating on and off as their interest and time allows. Sometimes a team or members of a team may be contributing simultaneously to software development in different organisations. Again, virtual teams and particularly open source and outsourced projects may show this characteristic. These situations make building up a "corporate memory" around software a real challenge.

1.5.4 Knowledge Sharing

Knowledge sharing in software development has always been a challenge. The trend to global software engineering – common in virtual teams, outsourcing projects and open source projects – exacerbates this. Working in different time zones means that co-ordination of activities will typically be coarser-grained than possible with co-located teams.

Information may be written in different languages or from very different perspectives. Different emphases may be put on information depending on the cultural background of team members. Approaches to managerial aspects of teams, task division and reporting may need to take careful account and respect of cultural differences to ensure team harmony and effectiveness [55]. Language difference is probably the most obvious – and most challenging – issue when sharing knowledge across teams. However, cultural differences and the impact of different time zones and lack of face-to-face collaboration and co-ordination can also be significant issues [35, 55].

It is common to encounter significant differences in work culture, habits, approach to management and self-organization in cross-cultural teams. Again, open source projects, outsourcing projects and distributed software teams commonly exhibit the need to manage software engineering knowledge in cross-cultural, cross-language and cross-time zone environments.

1.6 Managerial Considerations

Software project management (SPM) includes the knowledge, techniques, and tools necessary to manage the development of software products. In more detail, SPM includes the inception, estimation, and planning of software projects along with tracking, controlling, and co-ordinating the execution of the software project. The goal of SPM is to tackle an optimal balance between planning and execution.

1.6.1 Software Project Management

The Project Management Institute defines project management as "the application of knowledge, skills, tools, and techniques to project activities in order to meet or exceed stakeholder's needs and expectations from a project" [76].

The intent of project management is to drive a project forward through a series of periods, phases and stages tailored to the specific project and its particular development and implementation strategy. These time intervals should be reflective of the product and its environment. Driving a project forward means steering it through these intervals separated by "gates" as a means of ensuring control and continued support by all of the partners involved [100].

Software engineering management can be defined as application of management activities – planning, co-ordinating, measuring, monitoring, controlling, and reporting – to ensure that the development and *maintenance* of software is systematic, disciplined, and quantified [46].

The key issue in Software Project Management (SPM) is decision making. Many of the decisions that drive software engineering are about how the software engineering process should take place, not just what software supposed to do or how it will do it, i.e., the project management has to be viewed in relation with product development and engineering processes.

1.6.2 SPM for Collaborative Software Engineering

There are four management areas that are particularly important in collaborative software engineering: (1) supporting communications in the project; (2) reconciling different stakeholder's viewpoints; (3) improving the process; (4) rapidly constructing the knowledge [25].

1.6.2.1 Supporting Communications in the Project

It is known that large organizations are associated with large communication overhead [6, 10, 54, 86]. For example, it is typical for an engineer in mid to large organizations to spend between half and three quarters of their time on communication, leaving only a fraction of their time for engineering work [86].

While the cost of communication has been noted for a long time, it is becoming increasingly worse. Communication overhead has a broad number of causes: *number of counterparts; differences in backgrounds, notations, and conventions; effectiveness of communication tools; distribution of organizations*. In general, the worse the communication overhead associated with the transmission of information, the less effective and responsive an organization becomes.

1.6.2.2 To Reconcile Conflicting Success Criteria in the Project

One of the problems in software development is to elicit and satisfy the success criteria of multiple stakeholders. Users, clients, developers, and maintainers are involved in different aspects of the development and operating of the software system, and have different and conflicting views on the system [26]. The role of the project manager is to elicit, negotiate, satisfy, and trade-off multiple criteria originating from the key stakeholders so that each stakeholder "wins" to ensure the success and sustainability of the product.

Often, the issue of dealing with conflicting success criteria is not only to reconcile conflicting views, but to identify the key stakeholders of the system and to clarify their success criteria. Once these criteria are known to all, it is much easier to identify conflicts and to resolve them by negotiating compromise alternatives.

To address these issues, there is a need for negotiation techniques and support early in system development, while changes in requirements and technology are possible and cost effective.

1.6.2.3 Improving the Process in the Project

Software engineering literature has provided many models, called life cycle models, of how software development occurs. In practice, software engineering tends to follow a more complex pattern, similar to problem solving in other human activities, which creative, opportunistic, involving, incremental building is followed by radical reorganizations sparked by sudden insights [72]. Moreover, the occurrence and frequency of the radical reorganization depend on the organization and the project context.

The field of software process improvements has gained ground in recent years, in supporting managers and organization in modelling and measuring software development processes. While software process improvement practices lead to more repeatable and more predictable processes, they usually do not deal with creative processes such as requirements engineering and do not support managers in dealing with radical reorganizations.

1.6.2.4 Rapidly Construct the Knowledge in the Project

A knowledge management approach should focus on the informal communication helping navigate and update digital repositories and digital repositories helping to identify key experts and stakeholders. Such a knowledge management approach would also enable stakeholders to create, organize, and capture informal or formal knowledge, in real time. This approach is called rapid knowledge construction [89].

Rapid knowledge construction is often needed when common knowledge needs to be elicited and merged from a number of groups, possibly distributed in the organization. Rapid knowledge construction includes the following challenges: *adaptable to context; real-time capture; enable reuse.*

Knowledge management and rapid knowledge construction are not management activities in the traditional sense (organizing work and resources). However, knowledge management is essentially cross-functional, and hence, requires the participation and facilitation of many levels, including project and program management.

1.7 Future Trends

As our understanding of software engineering collaboration deepens and the range of easily adoptable collaboration technologies expands, opportunities are created for improving collaborative project work. This section outlines several future trends in software collaboration research.

1.7.1 IDEs Shift to the Web

One clear trend in collaboration tools is the existence of web-based tools in every phase of software development. This mirrors the broader trend of many applications moving to the web, afforded by the greater interactivity of AJAX (asynchronous JavaScript and XML), more uniformity in JavaScript capabilities across browsers, and increasing processing power in the browser. Web-based applications have the benefit of centralized tool administration, and straightforward deployment of new system capabilities. They also make it possible to collect highly detailed usage metrics, allowing rapid identification and repair of observed problems. Web application variants can also be evaluated quickly by giving a small percentage of the users a slightly modified version, then comparing results with the baseline. The advantages of web-based applications are compelling, and create substantial motivation to move capability off of desktops and into the web.

Traditionally, the most significant drawback to web-based applications has been the lack of user interface interactivity, and so graphics or editing intensive applications were traditionally not viewed as being suitable for the web. In the realm of software engineering, this meant that UML diagram editing and source code editing were relegated to desktop only applications. Google Maps smashed the low interactivity stereotype in early 2005, and is now viewed as the vanguard of the loosely defined "Web 2.0" movement that began in 2004. Web 2.0 applications tend to have desktop-like user interface interactivity within a web browser, as well as facilities for other sites to integrate their data into the application, or integrate the site's data into another application.

The pathway is now clear for the creation of a completely web-based integrated development environment. The Bespin code editor supports highly interactive, feature-rich source code editing within a browser [70], with direct back-end integration with source code management systems. Due to the high degree of interactivity required, source code editing is the most thorny problem of moving to a totally web-based environment. Bespin demonstrates that completely web-based code editing is possible. With the source code editor in place, editors for other models in the software engineering lifecycle can be integrated. For example, the Gliffy drawing tool supports browser-based UML diagram editing [30]. Web-based requirements and bug tracking tools can also be tied in, along with web-based word processing and spreadsheets, such as Google Docs [31], Zoho Writer [104], and the Glide suite [94]. Web-based project build technologies such as Hudson [37] make it possible to remotely build and unit test software, removing the last threads that bind software development to the desktop.

The technical hurdle of bolting together multiple existing web-based tools into a single environment should be straightforward to overcome. What comes next are the fundamental research questions. To achieve close integration among tools, some form of data integration will be necessary. This then leads to the hard problem of developing data interchange standards among pluggable tools in various parts of the development lifecycle.

The ability to gather finely detailed information about the work practices of software engineers can allow rapid tuning and improvement of web-based environments. It also opens the possibility of a flowering of research in empirical software engineering, as large amounts of software project activity data are gathered across many open source software projects. This, in turn, raises the issue of just what degree of project monitoring is acceptable to developers, and who should have access to collected data.

A web-based environment opens the possibility for integration with other web-based collaboration technologies, such as social networking sites. This leads to our next future direction.

1.7.2 Social Networking

Social networking sites such as MySpace, Facebook, and LinkedIn have, in the space of a few short years, emerged as major hubs of social interaction. By providing awareness of the actions of friends and the ability to build closer social ties, these sites act as a kind of social glue, knitting together communities. These sites are also becoming major software development platforms, leading to the rapid rise of social gaming companies such as Zynga and Playdom.

It is an open question how best to integrate social networking sites into software development teams. The simplest approach is to have all team members use a single social networking site, and use it for non-project oriented socializing. Sites like Advogato [58] and Github [59] provide developer profiles. Advogato provides the ability for developers to rate each others' technical proficiency, creating a trust network. Each user also has a weblog. Github provides automated status update messages shown on a developer's profile page based on activity in Github managed software projects, and project-specific news feeds.

At present, sites like Advogato and Github only have affordances for the identity of each participant as a software engineer. This can be contrasted with sites like Facebook and MySpace, where a broader range of tools make possible the integration and presentation of multiple identities for each participant, though with a bias towards non-work identities. LinkedIn is another choice, clearly focused on business networking and job seeking. Clearly there is a potential for tight integration of software development activities with social networking sites. But how? One possibility is integration with Facebook. However, it seems a bit counter to the site's focus to have successful build and code checkin messages appearing in someone's wall. On the other hand, since sites like Github and Advogato have fewer social affordances, they feel less interesting than Facebook. Even for the most hardcore developers, there is more to life than code alone.

1.7.3 Broader Participation in Design

Many forms of software have high costs for acquiring and learning the software, leading to lock-in for its users. This is especially true for enterprise software applications, where there can be substantial customization of the software for each location. This leads to customer organizations having a need to deeply understand product architecture and design, and to have some influence over specific aspects of software evolution to accommodate their evolving needs. In current practice, customers are consulted about requirements needs, which are then integrated into a final set of requirements that drive the development of the next version of the software. Customers are also usually participants in the testing process via the preliminary use and examination of various beta releases. In the current model, customers are engaged during requirements elicitation, but then become disengaged for the requirements analysis, design, and coding phases, only to reconnect again for the final phase of testing. This can be seen in Fig. 1.1 (earlier in this chapter), where the stakeholders/users/customers row has engagement in requirements, and then again in test.

Broadened participation by customers in the requirements, design, coding and early testing phases would keep customers engaged during these middle stages, allowing them to more actively ensure their direct needs are met. While open source software development can be viewed as an extreme of what is being suggested here, in many contexts broadening participation need not mean going all the way to open source. Development organizations can have proprietary closed-source models in which they still have substantial fine-grain engagement with customers in which customers are directly engaged in the requirements, design, coding, and testing process. Additionally, broadening participation does not necessarily mean that customers would be given access to all source code, or input on all decisions. Nevertheless, by increasing the participation of the direct end users of software in its development, software engineers can reduce the risk that the final software does not meet the needs of customer organizations. As in open source software, a more broadly participative model can allow customers to fix those bugs that mostly directly affect them, even if, from a global perspective, they are of low priority, and hence unlikely to be fixed in traditional development. A participatory development model could also permits customers to add new features, thereby better tailoring the software to their needs.

A completely web-based software development environment would make it easier to broaden participation. In such an environment, it would be possible to give outsiders direct access to limited parts of the source code (and other project artifacts). With direct web-based access, external sites would not need to take source code off-site in order to build and test it, reducing the risk of proprietary information release.

1.7.4 Capturing Rationale Argumentation

An important part of a software project's documentation is a record of the rationale behind major decisions concerning its architecture and design. As new team members join a project over its multi-year evolution, an understanding of project rationale makes it less likely that design assumptions and choices will be accidentally violated. This, in turn, should result in less code decay. A recent study [91] shows that engineers recognize the utility of documenting design rationale, but that better tool support is needed to capture design choices and the reasons for making them.

Technical design choices are often portrayed as being the outcome of a rational decision making process in which an engineer carefully teases out the variables of interest, gathers information, and then makes a reasoned tradeoff. What this model does not reflect is the potential for disagreement among many experienced software engineers on how to assess the importance of factors affecting a given design. One of the strongest design criteria used in software engineering is design for change, which inherently involves making predictions about the future. Clearly we do not yet have a perfect crystal ball for peering into the future, and hence experienced engineers naturally have differing opinions on which changes are likely to occur, and how to accommodate them. As well, architectural choices often involve decisions concerning which technical platform to choose (e.g., J2EE, Ruby on Rails, PHP, etc.), requiring assessments about their present and future qualities. As a result, the design process is not just an engineer making rational decisions from a set of facts, but instead is a predictive process in which multiple engineers argue over current facts and future potentials. Architecture and design are *argumentative* processes in which engineers resolve differences of prediction and interpretation to develop models of the software system's structure. Since only one vision of a system's structure will prevail, the process of architecture and design is simultaneously cooperative and competitive.

Effective recording of a project's rationale requires capturing the argumentation structure used by engineers in their debates concerning the final system structure. Outside of software engineering, there is growing interest in visual languages and software systems that model the structure of arguments [52]. While models vary, argumentation support systems generally record the question or point that is being contested (argued about), statements that support or contest the main point, as well as evidence that substantiates a particular statement. Argumentation structures are generally hierarchical, permitting pro and con arguments to be made about individual supporting statements under the main point. For example, a "con" argument concerning the use of solar panels as the energy source for a project might state that solar electric power is currently not competitive with existing coal-fired power plants. A counter to that argument might state that while this is true of wholesale costs, solar energy is competitive with peak retail electric costs in many markets.

Providing collaborative tools to support software engineers in the recording and visualization of architecture and design argumentation structures would do a better job of capturing the nuances and tradeoffs involved in creating large systems. They would also better convey the assumptions that went into a particular decision, making it easier for succeeding engineers to know when they can safely change a system's design. A persistent challenge in rationale management in software engineering is keeping arguments consistently linked with the artifacts the affect (a form of traceability management). A completely web-based development environment, by providing centralized control over development artifacts, can ease this problem by making it possible to reliably perform link fix-up actions when an argument, or linked artifact, are changed.

1.7.5 Using 3D Virtual Worlds

Software engineers have a long track record of integrating new communication technologies into their development processes. Email, instant messaging, and web-based applications are very commonly used in today's projects to coordinate work and be aware of whether other developers are currently active (present). As a result, engineers would be expected to adopt emerging communication and presence technologies if they offer advantages over current tools.

Networked collaborative 3D game worlds are one such emerging technology. The past few years have witnessed the emergence of massively-multiplayer online (MMO) games, the most popular being World of Warcraft (WoW). These games support thousands of simultaneous players who interact in a shared virtual world. Each player controls an avatar, a graphic representation of the player in the world. Communication features supported by games include instant messaging, voice chat, email-like message services, and presence information (seeing another active player's avatar).

Steve Dossick's PhD dissertation [23] describes early work on the use of 3D game environments to create a "Software Immersion Environment" in which project artifacts are arranged in a physical 3D space, a form of virtual memory palace. Only recently have MMOs like Second Life emerged that are not explicitly role-playing game worlds, and hence are framed in a way that makes them potentially usable for professional work. While Second Life's focus on leisure activities makes it unpalatable for all but the most adventurous of early adopters, these environments still hint at their potential for engineering collaboration. IBM's Bluegrass project [40] is a 3D virtual world explicitly designed to support software project work. Goals of the work include improved awareness of the current status and ongoing work of a project, and project brainstorming. The work exposes many research issues in use of 3D virtual worlds for software project collaboration. Representation of software artifacts in the 3D world is a thorny problem, as there is no canonical way of spatially representing software. One possibility is to have the virtual space represent the organization of the various software project artifacts including requirements, designs, code, test cases, and so on. Alternately, the virtual space could be a form of idealized work environment, where everyone has a nice, large office with window. Combinations of the two are also possible, given the lack of real-world constraints. Virtual worlds typically have avatars that walk about in the world, a slower way of navigating project artifacts than a traditional directory hierarchy. The explicit representation of a developer avatar raises issues of appropriate representation of identity in the virtual space, an issue not nearly so prevalent in email, instant messaging, and other text-based communication technologies.

The utility of adopting a 3D virtual world needs careful examination, as the benefits of the technology need to clearly exceed the costs. It is currently unclear whether this is true.

1.8 Fundamental Tensions

Underneath many of the situations present and advances made in collaborative software engineering lie fundamental tensions that must be acknowledged. Optimizing towards one aspect of collaboration support often involves tradeoffs with respect to other aspects [84]. It is currently an open question as to where the theoretically optimal level of support lies for a given situation, a state some have labeled congruence [15]. Below, we identify some of the key tensions that exist.

What is good for the group may not be good for the individual. For an organization to effectively operate, certain individuals may be required to perform work that is not optimal from their personal perspective. Ultimately, of course, collaborative work must be optimized from an organization's perspective. However, if such optimization goes at the expense of the individuals, it is unlikely that a productive process is achieved. Some kind of balance must be found in which individuals' satisfaction with their work is respected, yet at the same time organizational needs are met. An example of when both can be achieved in parallel lies in the use of awareness technologies with configuration management workspaces [20, 83], where individuals are spared the merge problem, and organizations benefit from a higher quality code base.

What is good in the long term may not be good right now. Ultimately, the goal is to optimize the collaborative process as it plays out over time. This means that, at times, work performed right now is suboptimal in the short term, but crucial to later efficiencies. For instance, it is well-known that it is important to leave sufficient information along with the artifacts produced for later re-interpretation and re-consideration. However, such documentation is not always produced because it is seen as superfluous work, and even when it is produced, keeping it in sync with an ever-evolving code base is a tedious and arduous job.

Co-ordination needs are highly dynamic, but processes and tools in use tend to be largely static. Because of the ever changing nature of software and its underlying requirements, exactly what co-ordination needs exist that give rise to actual collaborations fluctuate [15]. But the processes and tools in use tend to be static in nature, chosen once at the beginning of the project and rarely adjusted after. Some tools have recognized this and provide different modes of collaboration e.g. [87], but in general serious mismatches can emerge between co-ordination needs and affordances.

Tools can, and should, only automate or support so much of collaborative practice. Ultimately, tools formalize and standardize work. Developers rely on tools every day, but it has been observed that they also establish informal practices surrounding the formally supported processes [80]. These informal practices are a crucial part of any effective development project. The tension, then, is how much to automate of the "standard" practices and how much to leave in the developers hands to enable them to own part of the process and flexibly be able to perform their work.

Sharing is good, but too much sharing is not. Much work must be performed in isolated workspaces of sorts to protect ongoing efforts from other ongoing efforts. The canonical example is each developer making their own changes in their own workspace, so they can test their changes in isolation and without interference by changes from other developers that may still be partial in nature. To overcome the issue of insulation becoming isolation, information about work must be shared with others. Such sharing can be beneficial, but must be carefully weighted with the fact that too much sharing leads to information overload, causing developers to ignore the information brought to them. Once again, a balance must be struck.

Record keeping is good, but it could be misused. The canonical example is the manager judging performance via lines of code contributed to a code base; this is a fundamentally flawed metric. With a broad set of new collaborative tools relying on and visualizing key data regarding individuals' practices, choices, and results, misuse of such data could lead to serious problems.

The above represents some of the key considerations that must be kept in mind when one attempts to interpret collaborative software engineering or provide novel solutions. In this book, we will see these tensions come back repeatedly, sometimes explicitly recognized as such, at other times providing implicit motivations and design constraints. These tensions will persist for the time and ages, and always govern how we approach collaboration.

1.9 Conclusions

After 35 years of research and tool making to foster collaboration in software engineering, we now have useful collections of tools, work practises, and understandings to guide multi-person software development activity. Indeed, internet-based collaboration tools and practices directly led to the creation of a globally distributed, open source software ecosystem over the past 20 years, accelerating in the last 10. Clearly, progress has been made in supporting collaborative software development.

Despite this progress, our understanding of collaboration in software engineering is still imperfect, and there is room for improvement in many arenas. A fundamental stumbling block is the lack of established metrics for quantitatively assessing collaboration in software projects. This, in turn, makes it challenging to know when a new collaboration tool has made an improvement, or when a new tool will make a difference. For example, it was only in hindsight that SourceForge (and similar web-based "forge" systems) was viewed as a major advance in software collaboration infrastructure, and not simply the integration of several pre-existing tools.

There are many current challenges in collaborative software engineering research. These include:

- *Understanding how to adapt new communications media for collaboration.* The computer is a rich nursery for new types of media. Social networking sites and 3D virtual worlds are two kinds of computational media that show potential for improving software project collaboration.
- *Reducing the effects of distance on remote collaboration.* Adding distance between people makes it harder to collaborate – is it possible to remove the negative effects of distance with superior tool support?
- *Improve shared understanding of artifacts.* Much work in software projects surrounds the removal of ambiguity in natural language and semi-formal artifacts. Improved collaboration support could assist this process of identifying ambiguity and developing shared understanding. Additionally, there is still room for improvement in the ways developers become aware of the work being performed by others.
- *Improved techniques for leveraging the expertise of others.* A persistent challenge in software engineering collaboration is identifying people within an organization that have expertise relevant to a current problem or task [27].
- *Improved ways of finding and removing errors.* Improving the collaboration between and among users and developers in identifying and fixing errors could help reduce software bugs, and improve the experience of using software.
- *Better understanding of how to motivate people to work together effectively.* As is mentioned in the previous section, there is a tension between individual and group goals. Providing sufficient rewards to encourage project collaboration is important, and not well understood.
- *Improve and integrate software project management, software product development, and software engineering processes.* This goal is often hampered by a great variety of methods and tools in the individual disciplines and limited integration methodologies between project management, product development, and engineering processes. An effective collaborative environment must inject basic elements of project management, including activity awareness, task allocation, and risk management, directly into the software engineering process.

The chapters in this volume address these issues, and more. In so doing, they deepen our understanding of collaboration in software engineering, and highlight the potential for new tools, and new ways of working together to create software projects, large and small.

References

1. Ahmadi N, Jazayeri M, Lelli F, Nesic S (2008) A survey on social software engineering. First International Workshop on Social Software Engineering and Applications (ASE 2008 Workshops), L'Aquila, Italy.
2. Altova (2009) Altova UModel – UML Tool for Software Modeling and Application Development.

3. Ben-Shaul IZ (1994) Oz: A decentralized process centered environment. PhD Thesis, Department of Computer Science, Columbia University.
4. Ben-Shaul IZ, Kaiser GE, Heineman GT (1992) An architecture for multi-user software development environments. ACM SIGSOFT'92: 5th Symposium on Software Development Environments, Tyson's Corner, VA, USA, pp. 149–158.
5. Boehm B, Egyed A (1998) Software requirements neogotiation: Some lessons learned. International Conference on Software Engineering (ICSE'98), Kyoto, Japan, pp. 503–507.
6. Boehm BW (1981) Software Engineering Economics. Englewood Cliffs, NJ: Prentice-Hall.
7. Bolcer GA, Taylor RN (1996) Endeavors: A process system integration architecture. 4th International Conference on the Software Process (ICSP'96), Brighton, UK, pp. 76–89.
8. Borland (2009) CaliberRM – Enterprise Software Requirements Management System. http://www.borland.com/us/products/caliber/index.html.
9. Borland Software Corp. (2009) Borland Together.
10. Brooks FP Jr. (1975) The Mythical Man-Month: Essays on Software Engineering. Reading, MA: Addison-Wesley.
11. Bugzilla Team (2009) The Bugzilla Guide – 3.5 Development Release. http://www.bugzilla. org/docs/tip/en/html/.
12. Carmel E (1999) Global Software Teams. Upper Saddle River, NJ: Prentice-Hall.
13. Carzaniga A, Rosenblum DS, Wolf AL (2001) Design and evaluation of a wide-area event notification service. ACM Transactions on Computer Systems 19(3): 332–383.
14. Cataldo M, Herbsleb JD (2008) Communication networks in geographically distributed software development. CSCW'08, San Diego, CA, USA.
15. Cataldo M, Wagstrom P, Herbsleb JD, Carley KM (2006) Identification of coordination requirements: Implications for the design of collaboration and awareness tools. CSCW 2006, Banff, Alberta, Canada, November, pp. 353–362.
16. Chen Q, Grundy J, Hosking J (2003) An e-whiteboard application to support early design-stage sketching of UML diagrams. IEEE Symposium on Human Centric Computing Languages and Environments, Auckland, New Zealand, pp. 219–226.
17. Creighton O, Ott M, Bruegge B (2006) Software cinema-video-based requirements engineering. 14th International Requirements Engineering Conference (RE'06), pp. 106–115.
18. Dashofy EM (2007) Supporting stakeholder-driven, multi-view software architecture modeling. PhD, Department of Informatics, School of Information and Computer Science, University of California, Irvine.
19. Demarco T, Lister T (1987) Peopleware: Productive Projects and Teams. New York: Dorset House Publishing.
20. Dewan P, Hegde R (2007) Semi-synchronous conflict detection and resolution in asynchronous software development. European Computer Supported Cooperative Work (ECSCW'07), pp. 159–178.
21. DiBona C, Ockman S (1999) Open Sources: Voices from the Open Source Revolution. Sebastopol, CA: O'Reilly.
22. Dominguez L (2006) The Manager's Step-by-Step Guide to Outsourcing. New Delhi: McGraw-Hill.
23. Dossick SE (2000) A virtual environment framework for software engineering. PhD, Department of Computer Science, Columbia University.
24. Dusseault L (2003) WebDAV: Next Generation Collaborative Web Authoring. Indianapolis, IN: Prentice Hall PTR.
25. Dutoit AH, McCall R, Mistrík I, Paech B (2006) Rationale management in software engineering: Concepts and techniques. In: Dutoit AH, McCall R, Mistrík I, Paech B (Eds.) Rationale Management in Software Engineering. Heidelberg: Springer-Verlag, 1–48.
26. Dutoit AH, Paech B (2001) Rationale management in software engineering. In: Chang SK (Ed.) Handbook of Software Engineering and Knowledge Engineering, Vol. 1. Singapore: World Scientific.

27. Ehrlich K, Shami NS (2008) Searching for Expertise. CHI 2008, pp. 1093–1096.
28. Froehlich J, Dourish P (2004) Unifying artifacts and activities in a visual tool for distributed software development teams. 26th International Conference on Software Engineering (ICSE'04), Edinburgh, Scotland, UK, pp. 387–396.
29. Gatherspace (2009) Agile Project Management, Requirements Management – Gatherspace. com. http://www.gatherspace.com/.
30. Gliffy Inc. (2009) Gliffy. http://www.gliffy.com/.
31. Google (2009) Google Docs: Create and Share Your Work Online. http://docs.google.com/.
32. Graham TCN, Ryman AG, Rasouli R (1999) A world-wide-web architecture for collaborative software design. Software Technology and Engineering Practice (STEP'99), Pittsburgh, PA, pp. 22–29.
33. Grinter RE, Herbsleb JD, Perry DE (1999) The geography of co-ordination: Dealing with distance in R&D work. GROUP 1999, Phoenix, AZ, USA, pp. 306–315.
34. Hedberg H (2004) Introducing the next generation of software inspection tools. Product Focused Software Process Improvement (LNCS 3009), pp. 234–247.
35. Herbsleb JD (2007) Global software engineering: The future of socio-technical co-ordination. Future of Software Engineering (FOSE'07), Minneapolis, MN, USA.
36. Holmstrom H, Conchúir EO, Ågerfalk PJ, Fitzgerald B (2006) Global software development challenges: A case study on temporal, geographical and socio-cultural distance. IEEE International Conference on Global Software Engineering (ICGSE'06), Princeton, NJ, USA, August.
37. Hudson Team (2009) Hudson: An Extensible Continuous Integration Engine. https://hudson.dev.java.net/.
38. Humphrey W (1989) Managing the Software Process. Reading, MA: Addison-Wesley.
39. IBM (2009) Getting Started with Rational DOORS. http://publib.boulder.ibm.com/infoceter/rsdp/v1r0m0/topic/com.ibm.help.download.doors.doc/pdf92/doors_getting_started.pdf.
40. IBM (2009) Project Bluegrass: Virtual Worlds for Business. http://domino.watson.ibm.com/cambridge/research.nsf/99751d8eb5a20c1f852568db004efc90/1b1ea54cac0c8af1852573d1005dbd0c?OpenDocument.
41. IBM Rational (2009) Rational DOORS. http://www.ibm.com/software/awdtools/doors/.
42. IBM Rational (2009) Rational Method Composer. http://www.ibm.com/software/awdtools/rmc/.
43. IBM Rational (2009) Rational RequisitePro. http://www.ibm.com/software/awdtools/reqpro/.
44. IBM Rational (2009) Rational Rose. http://www.ibm.com/software/awdtools/developer/rose/.
45. iDungu.com (2009) iDungu.com – Enterprise Architect Web-Based. http://www.idungu.com/.
46. IEEE (1990). IEEE Std. 610.12-1990 (R2002), IEEE Standard Glossary of Software Engineering Terminology.
47. IEEE (1998). IEEE Std 1058–1998, IEEE Standard for Software Project Management Plans.
48. International Standards Organization (ISO) (2003). Quality Management Systems: Guidelines for Quality Management in Projects (ISO Std. 10006).
49. Kadia R (1992) Issues encountered in building a flexible software development environment. ACM SIGSOFT'92: 5th Symposium on Software Development Environments, Tyson's Corner, VA, USA, pp. 169–180.
50. Kammer PJ, Bolcer GA, Taylor RN, Hitomi AS, Bergman M (2000) Techniques for supporting dynamic and adaptive workflow. Computer Supported Cooperative Work (CSCW) 9(3/4): 269–292.
51. Kaplan SM, Tolone WJ, Carroll AM, Bogia DP, Bignoli C (1992) Supporting collaborative software development with conversation builder. ACM SIGSOFT'92: 5th Symposium on Software Development Environments, Tyson's Corner, VA, USA, pp. 11–20.
52. Kirschner PA, Buckingham-Shum S, Carr CS (2003) Visualizing Argumentation: Software Tools for Collaborative and Educational Sense-Making. London: Springer-Verlag.

53. Kompanek A (1998) Modeling a System with ACME. http://www.cs.cmu.edu/~acme/html/WORKING%20Modeling%20a%20System%20with%20Acme.html.
54. Kraut RE, Streeter LA (1995) Coordination in software development. Communications of the ACM 38(3): 69–81.
55. Krishna S, Sahay S, Walsham G (2004) Managing cross-cultural issues in global software outsourcing. Communications of the ACM 47(4): 62–66.
56. Lanubile F (2009) Collaboration in distributed software development. Software Engineering: International Summer Schools, ISSSE 2006–2008 (LNCS 5413), Salerno, Italy.
57. Lerner BS, Osterweil LJ, Sutton SM Jr., Wise A (1998) Programming process coordination in little-JIL toward the harmonious functioning of parts for effective results. European Workshop on Software Process Technology.
58. Levien R (2009) Advogato. http://www.advogato.org/.
59. Logical Awesome (2009) Secure Source Code Hosting and Collaborative Development – GitHub. http://github.com/.
60. Ludwig Consulting Services (2009) Requirements Management Tools. http://www.jiludwig.com/Requirements_Management_Tools.html.
61. Macdonald F, Miller J (1999) A comparison of computer support systems for software inspection. Automated Software Engineering 6(3): 291–313.
62. Maheshwari P, Teoh A (2005) Supporting ATAM with a collaborative web-based software architecture evaluation tool. Science of Computer Programming 57(1): 109–128.
63. Maiden N (2004) Discovering requirements with scenarios: The ART-SCENE solution. ERCIM News 58, July 2004.
64. Maiden N, Seyff N, Grunbacher P, Otojare O, Mitteregger K (2006) Making mobile requirements engineering tools usable and useful. 14th International Requirements Engineering Conference (RE'06), pp. 26–35.
65. Marcus A, Maletic JI (2003) recovering documentation-to-source-code traceability links using latent semantic indexing. 25th International Conference on Software Engineering (ICSE'03), Portland, OR, USA, pp. 125–135.
66. McConnell S (1997) Software Project Survival Guide. Redmond, WA: Microsoft Press.
67. Mens T (2002) A state-of-the-art survey on software merging. IEEE Transactions on Software Engineering 28(5): 449–462.
68. Meyer B (2008) Design and code reviews in the age of the internet. Communications of the ACM 51(9): 67–71.
69. Microsoft Corporation (2009) Project Home Page – Microsoft Office Online. http://office.microsoft.com/en-us/project/default.aspx.
70. Mozilla Labs (2009) Bespin: Code in the Cloud. https://bespin.mozilla.com/.
71. Nentwich C, Capra L, Emmerich W, Finkelstein A (2002) xlinkit: A consistency checking and smart link generation service. ACM Transactions on Internet Technology (TOIT) 2(2): 151–185.
72. Nguyen L, Swatman PA (2001) Managing the requirements engineering process. 7th International Workshop on Requirements Engineering: Foundation for Software Quality, Interlaken, Switzerland.
73. Nguyen TN, Munson EV (2005) Object-oriented configuration management technology can improve software architectural traceability. 3rd ACIS International Conference on Software Engineering Research, Management and Applications (SERA'05), Mount Pleasant, MI, USA, pp. 86–93.
74. Osterweil L (1987) Software Processes are Software Too. International Conference on Software Engineering, Monterey, CA, USA, pp. 2–13.
75. Pilato CM, Collins-Sussman B, Fitzpatrick BW (2008) Version Control with Subversion (2nd Ed). Sebastopol, CA: O'Reilly.
76. Project Management Institute Standards Committee (2003). A guide to the project management body of knowledge (IEEE Std 1490–2003).
77. Pyster AB, Thayer RH (2005) software engineering project management 20 years later. IEEE Software 22(5): 18–21.

78. Ramirez A, Vanpeperstraete P, Rueckert A, Odutola K, Bennett J, Tolke L, Wulp M (2009) ArgoUML User Manual – A tutorial and reference description http://argouml-stats. tigris.org/documentation/manual-0.28/.
79. Ravenflow (2009) RAVEN for Rapid Requirements Elicitation and Definition. http://www. ravenflow.com/products/index.php.
80. Redmiles D, Hoek A, Al-Ani B (2007) Continuous coordination: A new paradigm to support globally distributed software development projects. Wirtschaftsinformatik 49: S28–S38.
81. Reiss SP (1995) The Field Programming Environment: A Friendly Integrated Environment for Learning and Development. Norwell, MA: Kluwer.
82. Sangwan R, Bass M, Mullick N, Paulish D, Kazmeier J (2006) Global Software Development Handbook. Boca Raton, FL: Auerbach Publications.
83. Sarma A, Bortis G, Hoek A (2007) Towards supporting awareness of indirect conflicts across software configuration management workspaces. 22nd IEEE/ACM International Conference on Automated Software Engineering (ASE'07), pp. 94–103.
84. Sarma A, Herbsleb J, Hoek A (2008). Challenges in measuring, understanding, and achieving social-technical congruence. Technical Report CMU-ISR-08-106, Carnegie Mellon University, Institute for Software Research International, Pittsburgh, PA, USA.
85. Sarma A, Noroozi Z, Hoek A (2003) Palantír: Raising awareness among configuration management workspaces. 25th International Conference on Software Engineering, Portland, OR, USA, May, pp. 444–454.
86. Scacchi W (1984) Managing software engineering projects: A social analysis. IEEE Transactions on Software Engineering 10(1): 49–59.
87. Schümmer T, Haake JM (2001) Supporting distributed software development by modes of collaboration. 7th European Computer Supported Cooperative Work (ECSCW'01), pp. 79–98.
88. Schwaber K (2004) Agile Project Management with Scrum. Redmond, WA: Microsoft Press.
89. Selvin A, Buckingham-Shum SJ (2000) Rapid knowledge construction: A case study in corporate contingency planning using collaborative hypermedia. KMAC 2000: Knowledge Management Beyond the Hype, Birmingham, UK, July.
90. Shukla SV, Redmiles DF (1996) Collaborative learning in a software bug-tracking scenario. Workshop on Approaches for Distributed Learning through Computer Supported Collaborative Learning, Boston, MA.
91. Tang A, Babar MA, Gorton I, Han J (2005) A survey of the use and documentation of architecture design rationale. 5th Working IEEE/IFIP Conference on Software Architecture (WICSA'05), Pittsburgh, PA.
92. Thayer RH (2001) Software Engineering Project Management, 2nd edn. Los Alamitos, CA: Wiley-IEEE Computer Society Press.
93. Thayer RH, Pyster AB (1984) Editorial: Software engineering project management. IEEE Transactions on Software Engineering 10(1): 2–3.
94. Transmedia Corp. (2009) Glide OS 3.0 – The First Complete Online Operating System. http://www.glidedigital.com/.
95. UCI Software Architecture Research Group (2009) ArchStudio 4 – Software and Systems Architecture Development Environment. http://www.isr.uci.edu/projects/archstudio/.
96. Wakeman L, Jowett J (1993) PCTE: The Standard for Open Repositories. Englewood Cliffs, NJ: Prentice-Hall.
97. Whitehead J (2007) Collaboration in software engineering: A roadmap. Future of Software Engineering (FOSE 2007), Minneapolis, MN, USA.
98. Whitehead EJ Jr., Goland YY (1999) WebDAV: A Network Protocol for Remote Collaborative Authoring on the Web. 6th European Conference on Computer Supported Cooperative Work (ECSCW'99), Copenhagen, Denmark, pp. 291–310.
99. Whitehead R (2001) Leading Software Development Teams. London: Addison-Wesley.
100. Wideman RM (2009) Wideman Comparative Glossary of Project Management Terms (v. 5.0).

101. Wikimedia Foundation (2009) Wikipedia – Comparison of issue tracking systems. http://en.wikipedia.org/wiki/Comparison_of_issue_tracking_systems.
102. Wikimedia Foundation (2009) Wikipedia – List of UML Tools. http://en.wikipedia.org/wiki/List_of_UML_tools.
103. Wolf T, Nguyen T, Damien D (2008) Does distance still matter? Software Process Improvement and Practice 13: 493–510.
104. Zoho Corp. (2009) Online Word Processor – Zoho Writer. http://writer.zoho.com/.

Part I
Characterizing Collaborative Software Engineering

Ivan Mistrík

Effective collaboration in software engineering is very important and yet increasingly complicated by trends that increase complexity of dependencies between software development teams and organizations [2]. These trends include the globalization of software engineering, leveraging the relationships between requirements and people, the adoption of software product lines, practices in agile software development, and applications of ontologies.

Software engineering collaboration has multiple goals and means spanning the entire lifecycle of development [7]:

Establish the scope and capabilities of a project. Engineers must work with the users and funding sources (stakeholders) of a software project to describe what it should do at both a high level, and at the level of detailed requirements. The form of this collaboration can have profound impact on a project, ranging from the up-front negotiation of the waterfall model, to the iterative style of evolutionary prototyping [5].

Drive convergence towards a final architecture and design. System architects and designers must negotiate, create alliances, and engage domain experts to ensure convergence on single system architecture and design [3].

Manage dependencies among activities, artifacts, and organizations [4]. This encompasses a wide range of collaborative activities, including typical management tasks of subdividing work into tasks, ordering them, then monitoring, assessing, and controlling the plan of activities. Modularization decisions also affect dependencies.

Reduce dependencies among engineers. An important mechanism for managing dependencies is to reduce them where possible, thereby reducing the need for collaboration. Modularization decisions frequently follow organizational boundaries [6] a mechanism for reducing cross-organization co-ordination. Software configuration management systems permit developers to work in per-developer workspaces, thereby isolating their changes from others, and reducing the number of change dependencies among developers. With workspaces, developers no longer need to wait for all developers to finish their current changes before compiling.

Identify, record and resolve errors. Errors and ambiguities are possible in all software artifacts, and many approaches have been developed to find and record their existence. Among the collaborative techniques are inspections and reviews, where many people are brought together so that their multiple perspectives can identify errors, and their questions can surface ambiguities. Testing, where one group creates tests to uncover errors in software developed by others is another collaborative error finding technique. Users of software also collaborate in the identification of errors, whether in explicit beta testing programs, or through normal use, when they submit bug reports. Bug tracking (issue management) systems permit engineers to record problems, as well as manage the process of resolving them.

Record organizational memory. In any long running collaborative project, people may join and leave. Part of the work of collaboration is recording what people know, so that project participants can learn this knowledge now, and in the future [1]. SCM change logs are one form of organizational memory in software projects, as are project repositories of documentation. Process models also record organizational memory, describing best practices for how to develop software.

Chapters in this part of the book are reporting on advances on some issues mentioned above.

Chapter 2 "Global Software Engineering: A Software Process Approach" by Ita Richardson, Valentine Casey, John Burton and Fergal McCaffery thesis is that global software engineering factors should be included in software process models to ensure their continued usefulness in global organizations. They have developed a software process, Global Teaming, which includes specific practices and sub-practices. The purpose is to ensure that requirements for successful global software engineering are stipulated so that organizations can ensure successful implementation of global software engineering.

Chapter 3 "Requirements-Driven Collaboration: Leveraging the Invisible Relationships between Requirements and People" by Daniela Damian, Irwin Kwan and Sabrina Marczak discusses an approach to study requirements-driven collaboration, which is the collaboration during the development and management of requirements. The approach uses the construct of a requirement-centric social network to represent the membership and relationships among members working on a requirement and its associated downstream artifacts and a number of social network analysis techniques to study collaboration aspects such as communication, awareness, and the alignment of technical dependencies driven by development of requirements and social interactions. To demonstrate their approach, the authors describe insights from a case study that examines requirements-driven collaboration within an industrial, globally-distributed software team.

Chapter 4 "Softwares Product Lines, Global Development and Ecosystems: Collaboration in Software Engineering" by Jan Bosch and Petra Bosch-Sijtsema discusses problems of ineffective collaboration and success-factors of five approaches to collaboration in large-scale software engineering. The approaches, i.e., integration-oriented software engineering, release groupings, release trains, independent deployment and open ecosystems, increasingly facilitate compositionality of the system parts.

Chapter 5 "Collaboration, Communication and Co-ordination in Agile Software Development Practice" by Hugh Robinson and Helen Sharp explores in detail, the nature of collaboration, communication and co-ordination involved in agile software development. It focuses specifically on the collaborative activities of pairing and customer collaboration, and the co-ordinating role of two key physical artifacts: the story card and the Wall. The research explicates how this social activity is related to and embodied in the associated technical practice of developing working code.

Chapter 6 "Applications of Ontologies in Collaborative Software Development" by Hans-Jörg Happel, Walid Maalej and Stefan Seedorf discusses the application of ontologies to CSD. Ontologies, which are models that capture a shared understanding of a specific domain, provide key benefits which address several CSD issues. The chapter contains a comprehensive set of application scenarios for ontologies in CSD. In addition, the authors describe Semantic Wikis, Semantic Integrated Development Environments (IDEs) and a Software Engineering Semantic Web as technological backbones.

References

1. Ackerman MS, McDonald DW (2000) Collaborative support for informal information in collective memory systems. Information Systems Frontiers 2(3/4): 333–347.
2. Bosch J, Bosch-Sijtsema P (2009) Softwares product lines, global development and ecosystems: Collaboration in software engineering. In: Mistrík I, Grundy J, Hoek Avd, Whitehead J, Finkelstein A (Eds.) Collaborative Software Engineering. New York: Springer.
3. Grinter R (1999) Systems architecture: Product designing and social engineering. ACM Conference on Work Activities Co-ordination and Collaboration (WACC'99), pp. 11–18.
4. Malone TW, Crowston K (1994) The interdisciplinary study of co-ordination. ACM Computing Surveys 26(1): 87–119.
5. McConnell (1996) Lifecycle planning. In: Rapid Development: Taming Wild Software Schedules. Redmond, WA: Microsoft Press.
6. Sommerville I (2007) Software Engineering, 8th edn. Harlow: Pearson Education Limited.
7. Whitehead EJ (2007) Collaboration in software engineering: A roadmap. Future of Software Engineering (FOSE 2007), 20–26 May 2007, Minneapolis, MN.

Chapter 2
Global Software Engineering: A Software Process Approach

Ita Richardson, Valentine Casey, John Burton, and Fergal McCaffery

Abstract Our research has shown that many companies are struggling with the successful implementation of global software engineering, due to temporal, cultural and geographical distance, which causes a range of factors to come into play. For example, cultural, project management and communication difficulties continually cause problems for software engineers and project managers. While the implementation of efficient software processes can be used to improve the quality of the software product, published software process models do not cater explicitly for the recent growth in global software engineering. Our thesis is that global software engineering factors should be included in software process models to ensure their continued usefulness in global organisations. Based on extensive global software engineering research, we have developed a software process, Global Teaming, which includes specific practices and sub-practices. The purpose is to ensure that requirements for successful global software engineering are stipulated so that organisations can ensure successful implementation of global software engineering.

2.1 Introduction

In today's global economy, increasing numbers of software engineers are expected to operate in a distributed environment [32]. In this environment, geographical distance introduces physical separation between team members and management [6], temporal distance hinders and limits opportunities for direct contact and cooperation [1], and cultural distance negatively impacts on the level of understanding and appreciation of the activities and efforts of remote

I. Richardson (✉)
Department of Computer Science & Information Systems, Lero – the Irish Software Engineering,
Research Centre, University of Limerick, Ireland
e-mail: ita.richardson@ul.ie

I. Mistrík et al. (eds.), *Collaborative Software Engineering*,
DOI 10.1007/978-3-642-10294-3_2, © Springer-Verlag Berlin Heidelberg 2010

colleagues and teams [52]. Therefore, Global Software Engineering (GSE)[1] has complexities over and above those experienced in local software development [7, 22, 31]. While process models such as Capability Maturity Model Integration (CMMI®) [19] and IEC/ISO15504 (International Standards [45] operate successfully in local environments, they do not explicitly provide for the impact of these complexities.

In this chapter, we discuss our research into virtual teams. This has demonstrated that project management must change in the global development environment. Therefore, we developed a project management process area, Global Teaming (GT), which details specific practices for use when organisations are implementing GSE.

2.2 Software Process

Humphrey [34] defines a software process as "the set of tools, methods and practices we use to produce a software product". Paulk et al. [48] expand this definition to "a set of activities, methods, practices and transformations that people use to develop and maintain software and the associated products". Organisations improve their software processes to improve the quality of their product. While there have been arguments that implementing planned processes decrease rather than increase the efficiency of the software development process [26, 37, 39] there is also evidence that there have been increases in productivity and efficiency due to the implementation of planned processes [3, 5, 27, 35, 56]. While we recognise that there are many valid reasons for not implementing planned process models such as CMMI® and ISO/IEC 15504, we also recognise that there are efficiencies to be gained in doing so, and, in particular, there are markets which require planned processes to be in place. For example, in industries such as the Medical Device industry, who are regulated by the Food and Drugs Administration (FDA), and the Automotive industry, who follow Automotive SPICE, planned processes are still required.

2.3 Research Project

The authors completed a study which identified 25 factors to be taken into account when setting up virtual teams in a global environment. Based on this outcome, we developed a software process area, Global Teaming, similar to the structure of CMMI. This can be used as a supporting mechanism for the implementation of GSE.

---

[1]A variety of terms exist: Distributed Software Development, (DSD), Global Software Development (GSD), or Global Software Engineering (GSE). We will use the term GSE this chapter.

2.3.1   Case Studies into GSE

Three case studies were undertaken over a 9 year period in the area into GSE. The first case study was carried out in an Irish company who implemented a strategy to expand their organization's market share by the establishment of local offsite virtual software development teams (Irish Computing Solutions[2]). Prior to implementing this policy the company operated collocated teams based in the capital (Dublin) who worked exclusively on the development of financial and telecommunications software. The organization also had a software development centre located 150 miles from Dublin, which was involved in general application development and maintenance and had lower labour costs. The objective was to leverage staff at both locations and capitalize on the cost advantage offered. A group of twelve offsite engineers were selected and were provided with basic training in the required technology and process. Two virtual teams were established and consisted of two sets of six offsite engineers who were partnered with three experienced onsite engineers based in Dublin. Considerable effort was put into providing the communication infrastructure, process and support for both virtual teams. A key objective of this approach was that the onsite engineers would mentor the inexperienced offsite staff and provide effective knowledge transfer [17].

The second case focused on offshore/nearshore software development [28], where we studied a partnership between a large U.S. based financial organization, Stock Exchange Trading Inc., and an Irish division of a U.S. multinational company Software Future Technologies. While the U.S. and Irish based sites were geographically distant, they were considered linguistically and culturally nearshore [28, 53]. The companies established virtual teams to develop and maintain bespoke financial software. Stock Exchange Trading Inc. was the senior partner in this relationship and had an on-going requirement for development and maintenance. An unanticipated and urgent requirement arose for the development of new software during the initial stage of establishing the virtual teams. To address this need 70% of the Irish team members moved to the U.S., for a period of 1 year to work on collocated teams with their Stock Exchange Trading colleagues. This proved to be a very effective strategy and both groups operated very successfully while collocated within what were to eventually become their virtual teams. It was only when the Irish team members returned to Ireland and the virtual teams were established that serious problems arose. [10, 11, 17].

The third case study centred on offshore virtual team software testing and was undertaken in the Irish division of a large U.S. multinational, Computing World International, who had been operating in Ireland for over 20 years. This division had been very successful and had expanded considerably in that time, during which a large percentage of the projects undertaken had been offshored from their U.S. parent. Therefore, the Irish staff and management were very experienced in having

---

[2] Company names are all pseudonyms.

projects offshored to them. Two years prior to undertaking this case study the organization's corporate strategy changed and they initiated a policy of establishing virtual testing teams. The objective of this policy was to leverage the technical ability of their Irish staff with the competitive salary levels of their Malaysian test engineers. When this research commenced four virtual testing teams were in operation between the Irish and Malaysian divisions. Some teams were established for over a year and a half while others had only been in operation for a number of months. This case study focused on two embedded units of analysis. One was a virtual testing team with members located in Ireland and Malaysia which had been in operation for a period of eighteen months. The second was a virtual team with a similar makeup, but had been established for just over six months [11–13, 18].

2.3.2 Research Methodology

The research methodology employed in the first and second case studies was the action research five-phase cyclical process based approach [2, 58]. Action research entails the analysis of the direct intervention of the researcher. This methodology was selected as the most appropriate for both case studies as one of the authors held a management role in the respective organizations. This approach allowed us to leverage the research opportunities while maintaining the required level of objectivity. For the third case study, the authors had the opportunity to undertake extensive on site research. We selected and implemented a Yin-based embedded case study [60] which incorporated a Strauss and Corbin grounded theory [57] approach to data gathering and analysis. The GSE research which we carried out resulted in the definition of 25 factors which affect the effective implementation of GSE (see Section 2.4.2).

2.3.3 Development of the Global Teaming Software Process Area

Following the definition of these 25 factors, we studied existing software process models to understand how they have implemented GSE, and observe that they do not explicitly focus on its implementation. Given the substantial growth of GSE, we considered this a weakness, and have recognised the importance of presenting explicitly defined processes to support GSE implementation. Through a gap analysis between CMMI® and the findings from our case studies outlined in Section 2.3.1, we observed that the definition of a GSE process to support the implementation of virtual teams is missing. Therefore we have identified a specific process area, Global Teaming (GT), establishing specific goals and sub-practices. While we have structured these to be similar to the CMMI® model, the implementation of the Global Teaming process area does not require CMMI® implementation. Rather it can be used as a process which organisations can implement when establishing global software teams.

2.4 Global Software Engineering

The growth of GSE in recent years requires that many software engineers must collaborate over geographical, temporal and/or cultural distance, collectively termed as "global distance"[3] [6, 50]. The advent of this strategy has been facilitated by factors which include the development of the Internet, increased use of e-mail and low cost international telecommunication infrastructure [44]. In addition, the availability of highly skilled software engineers in low cost locations such as Eastern Europe, Latin America and the Far East [20], coupled with the desire to cut costs and avail of the benefits of establishing operations close to emerging markets, have all contributed to the selection of this strategy. In some cases, application development and maintenance have been outsourced to remote third party organisations. In others, organisations have set up subsidiaries in low cost economies and offshored part or all of their software development to these locations [8, 59]

2.4.1 Virtual Teams

Our initial research focus was on that of the operation of virtual teams. The virtual team has been described as the core building block of the virtual organisation [23, 36, 42]. A traditional team is defined as a social group of individuals who are collocated and interdependent in their tasks. The group undertakes and coordinates their activities to achieve common goals and share responsibility for outcomes [49]. Virtual teams have the same goals and objectives as traditional teams and interact through interdependent tasks, but operate across time, geographical location and organisational boundaries linked by communication technologies [40]. They normally operate in a multicultural and multilingual environment which may cross organisational boundaries [24]. Communication between virtual team members is normally electronic and asynchronous with limited opportunities for synchronous contact [40]. The team may function on a permanent or temporary basis which is contingent on the demands of the business environment in which it is operating. Their overall objective is to function as a single team, with the same goals as if they were in a collocated situation.

However, GSE is not without its inherent business related risks [38]. This has particular relevance when organisational boundaries are crossed. There can be aspects of a software application that provides competitive advantage to the organisation that are having it developed [38]. In this case, they may not wish to grant access to such information to an outside organisation, even where they are temporally partnered with them. To prevent this, the implementation of a virtual team strategy can be employed to allow the partitioning of development across sites. The activities

---

[3]We use the term 'global distance' when we discuss geographical, temporal and cultural distance collectively.

that need to remain confidential are undertaken by the organisation's own virtual team members, whereas related activities are undertaken by external remote team colleagues.

The implementation of a virtual team strategy can simply be a cost based decision. This can be achieved by combining the technical skills and experience of staff located in a high-cost centre with engineers in a low-cost location. If the goal is a short-term strategy, then it may be used simply as a knowledge transfer exercise. If, on the other hand, it is a long-term objective, sustained support will be required for team members at all locations.

While the term "distributed team" simply states the geographical location of the team members in the same organisation, the important difference between a virtual team and a distributed team can be considered as the interdependence of tasks. In this context, all virtual teams are distributed, but not all distributed teams are virtual. It is possible to have a team which is geographically distributed, but where the work has been partitioned in such a manner that there is no interdependence of tasks between team members. In these circumstances this team is distributed, but not virtual. We are proposing a global teaming process for global teams where there is clear interdependence of tasks between team members at both locations i.e. virtual teams.

2.4.2 Project Management Challenges

Within such virtual teams, organisations still face the regular collocated project management challenges of co-ordination, communication and cooperation [30, 43].

Global distance introduces its own barriers and complexities which negatively impacts these project management challenges [7, 22, 31, 46]. Our research has demonstrated that there are 25 factors which come into play during the implementation of global projects [10, 11, 18]. These need to be explicitly considered when implementing a GSE strategy. The factors are listed in Table 2.1.

In addition, these factors often have a compounding effect on each other, further increasing the possibility of negative impact. For example, skills management is complicated when there are language difficulties across global distance. In addition, not only should the factors we identified by considered, but the collaboration models used need to be considered. Research by Smite [55] has shown that, in

Table 2.1 Global software development factors

Communication	Skills management	Language	Tools	Fear
Communication tools	Knowledge transfer	Motivation	Culture	Trust
Temporal issues	Defined roles and responsibilities	Technical support	Teamness	True cost
Effective partitioning	Team selection	Coordination	Visibility	Reporting
Project management	Risk management	Cooperation	Information	Process

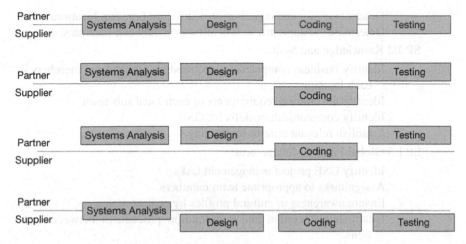

Fig. 2.1 GSE distribution of life-cycle stages in 4 cases [55]

practice, the variety of collaboration models used where parts of the life-cycle are shared between groups [6, 29], is indeed quite substantial. She developed 19 models, four of which are shown in Fig. 2.1. For example, systems analysis, design and testing may be undertaken in one country while coding is undertaken in another. Smite's work focused on four stages of the life-cycle in two-site projects, and it is inevitable that examining more stages in multiple-site projects would have many more models associated with them. Consequently, collaboration by software engineering teams across global distance must be managed correctly to ensure successful development and implementation of software projects [13, 38], and Global Teaming will support this.

2.4.3 Global Teaming – A GSE Process Area

GSE requires cognisance to be taken of the cultural, social, geographical and temporal differences which are experienced and can cause difficulties when implementing a GSE strategy [6, 38] Our research has demonstrated that there are 25 factors which should be taken into account when teams operate in a global environment [18], many of which have been corroborated by other researchers [6, 22, 25, 30]. However, despite the increase in GSE internationally, software process models do not explicitly discuss GSE and factors that affect it. The Global Teaming process area has been developed as an initial step to fill this gap.

Global Teaming has two specific goals (SG), each of which has specific practices (SP) and sub-practices. These are as follows:

- SG1: Define Global Project Management
    SP1.1 Global Task Management:

Determine team and organisational structure between locations.
Determine the approach to task allocation between locations.

SP 1.2 Knowledge and Skills:

Identify business competencies required by global team members in each location.
Identify the cultural requirements of each local sub-team.
Identify communication skills for GSE.
Establish relevant criteria for training.

SP 1.3 Global Project Management:

Identify GSE project management tasks.
Assign tasks to appropriate team members.
Ensure awareness of cultural profiles by project managers.
Establish cooperation and coordination procedures between locations.
Establish reporting procedures between locations.
Establish a risk management risk management strategy.

- SG2: Define Management between Locations

SP 2.1 Operating procedures:

Define how conflicts and differences of opinion between locations are addressed and resolved.
Implement a communication strategy for the team.
Establish communication interface points between the team members.
Implement strategy for conducting meetings between locations.

SP 2.2 Collaboration between locations:

Identify common goals, objectives and rewards
Collaboratively establish and maintain the work product ownership boundaries among interfacing locations within the project or organisation.
Collaboratively establish and maintain interfaces and processes among interfacing locations for the exchange of inputs, outputs, or work products.
Collaboratively develop, communicate and distribute among interfacing teams the commitment lists and work plans that are related to the work product or team interfaces.

2.5 Global Teaming Process Area

In the following sections we list the sub-practices included in the Global Teaming Process Area. We then discuss our rationale for including each sub-practice, which is based on our research to date within GSE and on the research of others (referenced).

2.5.1 Global Teaming Specific Goal 1: Define Global Project Management

Within the Global Teaming process area, specific goal 1 recognises that global project management, while including tasks that would be expected within collocated project management, must also encompass tasks that exist because of the existence of their virtual software engineering team.

2.5.1.1 SP 1.1 Global Task Management (1): Determine Team and Organisational Structure Between Locations

In the software industry, the overall objective of a team structure is to facilitate the successful management, coordination and operation of the team so that they produce specific software artifacts. Implementing such a structure is an important factor for the success of a GSE strategy [38]. To do this, the organisation should create roles, relationships and rules which can facilitate coordination and control over geographical, temporal and cultural distance.

In general, global teams are larger than collocated teams. Overall team size can directly impact on the effective operation of the virtual team [4], as does the number of members situated at specific geographical locations. A concern is that team members may feel that if larger groups are located in one or more remote geographical sites all the work may be centralized in these locations. This can lead to feelings of alienation and fear for the future of their jobs, particularly for team members based at the location from which the work has been outsourced [13]. Furthermore, management at one location may have responsibility for both their local and remote locations. In this case, a danger is that the manager may give undue priority to their divisional or organisational needs, rather than the requirements of the full global team and the specific project on which they are working. The global team should be structured and their operation monitored in such a way that minimises this risk.

The team structure should also cater for the possibility of dual reporting to management at more than one location, particularly where there the team structure is cross divisional or multi-organisational. To address these issues, the organizational and team structure must ensure that the supervision, support and information needs of all team members are met regardless of location. Documenting this structure and providing access to this information is important as this allows staff to clearly understand everyone's roles and responsibilities within the project [38].

2.5.1.2 SP 1.1 Global Task Management (2): Determine the Approach to task Allocation Between Locations

The objective of this sub-practice is to distribute work so that the advantages of GSE are leveraged and the negative factors which are inherent to its operation are minimised. Effective allocation should be based on the organisation's requirements. For example, if proximity to market is the reason that a development team is located in a particular country, then customer-related tasks should be allocated to that team. Tasks which require frequent communication between groups should be retained within collocated teams. However, GSE teams are often subdivided into work modules, so that different locations undertake different development stages of the life-cycle. As illustrated in Fig. 2.1, this subdivision can vary widely. What is important is that management clearly define which stages are carried out within each local sub-team, and that the core competencies for those development stages are identified.

2.5.1.3 SP 1.2 Knowledge and Skills (1): Identify Business Competencies Required by Global Team Members in Each Location

There can be a variety of reasons for businesses implementing GSE strategies. Probably the most commonly quoted is the cost advantage – where companies often integrate lower cost labour with higher cost labour. However, there are other business reasons for implementing GSE, including that a team in another country allows access to a larger customer base in that country. Because of this, the global team needs to have an understanding of that customer base and consequently, the business functions within that country. An example would be where the local team is required to know about the fiscal policy within their home country.

2.5.1.4 SP 1.2 Knowledge and Skills (2): Identify the Cultural Requirements of Each Local Sub-team

There have been many difficulties experienced by GSE teams due to lack of understanding of the socio-cultural requirements of the sub-teams. Culture normally remains below everyday consciousness and only becomes obvious when it is contrasted with different cultural norms, values and assumptions as in GSE teams. Within software development teams, cultural differences can give rise to misunderstandings [25, 30]. To address the issues related to cultural diversity, team members must have a basic understanding of each others' national culture. Important factors which seem to have most effect are [38]:

1. Some cultures do not promote individual responsibility and accountability.
2. Some cultures accept most suggestions without much discussion.

We have identified that training in culture is important, so that each sub-team can understand each other. Furthermore, face-to-face meetings are very useful when and where possible. Having individuals visit locations for extended periods can also be a successful strategy and should be fully leveraged at every possible opportunity.

2.5.1.5 SP 1.2 Knowledge and Skills (3): Identify Communication Skills for GSE

Individual team members are now required to be able to communicate and work with people who they do not know and whose cultures they may not understand. They are expected to use communication tools such as instant messaging, audio conferencing and video conferencing for which they need to develop a new etiquette. Policies should be put in place to support these new requirements. They may also be required to work across different time zones, and impositions on their personal time may also occur. Furthermore, a common practice which should be avoided is that those at an outsourcing or offshoring location schedule all conference calls to suit their local teams' times. This results in permanently inconveniencing remote staff and this adds further to their level of dissatisfaction [7]. This also increases the probability that overworked, trained and competent staff will seek positions elsewhere and leave the organisation.

2.5.1.6 SP 1.2 Knowledge and Skills (4): Establish Relevant Criteria for Training Teams

GSE cannot succeed without effective knowledge transfer and training [30]. While remote team members usually have the required academic background to undertake their respective roles and responsibilities, they may lack domain specific knowledge and experience. To be effective, an evaluation of training needs should be carried out, and cultural and linguistic issues considered. Those implementing training should be aware that training practices which have been successfully implemented in a collocated situation may not be successful in a global environment. The most effective method for the provision of global team training is onsite and face-to-face training [38, 41]. This ensures that the training needs of the team members can be directly assessed and provision made to address their specific requirements.

2.5.1.7 SP 1.3 Global Project Management (1): Identify GSE Project Management Tasks

Global project managers are required to do the tasks that are expected of a local project manager, but they must also plan, facilitate, implement and monitor global communication and coordination related activities with effective policies and procedures. In the ideal situation, the project manager will have been actively involved in the recruitment and selection of team members. In the absence of this, they should be supported by the provision of as much information as possible on the technical and professional experience of potential and existing team members. When teams are in place, they may need to request additional information about individuals, and also, when project details are reported, spend more time understanding how individuals contributed to that project. As they will often be based remotely from their team members, they may not have the opportunity to see their contribution first-hand. The project manager needs to build up their knowledge about each team member.

We have seen, in our research, that in some cases, competent people in the distributed location, often agree to undertake unrealistic amounts of additional work [13]. This can be attributed to their revering of hierarchy and their reluctance for cultural reasons to say no to requests from a superior [6, 33]. This can have serious implications for the individuals involved and is only sustainable in the short term given the level of effort required. Therefore, it is important that the global project manager is aware of this situation and tries to prevent it from happening.

2.5.1.8 SP 1.3 Global Project Management (2): Assign Tasks to Appropriate Team Members

The effective partitioning and allocation of work across the GSE team must be addressed. The objective should be to distribute work so that the advantages of GSE are leveraged and the negative factors which are inherent to its operation are minimised. This can be achieved by implementing one or more of three different approaches to task allocation [6]:

- Modularisation
- Phased-based approach
- Integrated approach

Modularisation, which entails partitioning of work, is a key concept which supports effective organisation and management in globally distributed development and virtual team operation. Modularisation is based on the work of Parnas (1972) who defined it as: "In this context 'module' is considered to be a responsibility rather than a subprogram" [47]. In the GSE team environment, this can be achieved by the effective partitioning of work into modules which have a well defined functional whole [6]. If done successfully, independent or semi-independent units of the project can be undertaken entirely at specific geographical locations, limiting the need for communication and cooperation between team members.

With a *phase-based approach* discrete phases in the development cycle can be undertaken at different locations. This approach can be implemented if phases are relatively independent. It is also required that those who carry out the work understand what is required at each specific stage. The phase-based approach can reduce dependence between locations.

The *integrated*, or "follow the sun" approach endeavours to leverage the temporal difference between global team members' geographical locations. Unfinished work is passed between different locations to fully utilise staff and tools [6], facilitating 24 h a day development and achieving development and testing cycle times which are not possible when implementing a collocated team based strategy [51]. This approach requires high dependence between locations.

2.5.1.9 SP 1.3 Global Project Management (3): Ensure Awareness of Cultural Profiles by Project Managers

In both co-located and GSE teams, team members should have the knowledge and skills to carry out the projects which have been assigned. However, in the case of global teams, it is also important that project managers understand that culture and its understanding (or lack of) can play a major part in the success of a project. This includes religion, gender and power distance [14].

Some organisations consider that their corporate socializing process is adequate to address the cultural issues which arise when managing a GSE team. The reality is that, in a situation where there are major differences between corporate and national cultural norms, this is generally not the case, and often, national cultural differences should be identified and communicated to the management and team members [17]. This can be achieved by providing specific cultural training which gives all team members an opportunity to learn and understand about each other's culture. Training should address national, religious and relevant ethnic issues which have the potential of negatively impacting on the operation of the virtual team and, ultimately, all team members should understand acceptable and unacceptable forms of behaviour. Cultural training should be tailored to team member's specific needs and location [13].

There are often gender issues which need to be dealt with. In some Eastern cultures the female role is seen as subservient to that of the male. In such cultures, attitudes to gender, not normally acceptable in Western countries, are still prevalent and accepted as the norm. This attitude to women is reinforced by religious belief and in some countries, by the legal system. These attitudes to gender have specific implications for managing virtual teams. Males from these cultures may have problems reporting to female team leaders or managers. In one case during our primary research, a male project manager from the Far East would not work with a female project manager from Ireland, on religious grounds, and he was subsequently removed from the project [18]. This illustrates that project managers, while ensuring that employee's legal rights are upheld, should also ensure that cultural profiles for teams are also established. Remote female team members may need to be addressed in a particular way. Furthermore, there is a need for management and staff to show respect for the gender-related cultural values of all colleagues so that they do not negatively impact on the operation of the team.

2.5.1.10 SP 1.3 Global Project Management (4): Establish Cooperation and Coordination Procedures Between Locations

Teamwork is a cooperative activity, and global distance negatively impacts the level of cooperation that takes place between global team colleagues [13, 32]. The project manager must support the establishment and development of effective cooperation within the virtual team. They can implement tools, processes and technology to support cooperation but must also ensure that team members are motivated to use these tools. Furthermore, project managers must be aware of, and take specific measures to address potential problems before they arise. When specific problems are identified, the project manager should implement informed and appropriate measures to address them.

Coordination is another key activity which is negatively impacted by global distance [8, 32]. Effective coordination ensures that adequate planning is carried out and the required resources are provided to undertake GSE, including suitable infrastructure, processes and management procedures. Achievable milestones should be planned and agreed. In addition, projects should be monitored with reference to costs, time, productivity, quality and risk.

2.5.1.11 SP 1.3 Global Project Management (5): Establish Reporting Procedures Between Locations

The project manager needs to be aware of how the project is progressing and therefore needs to establish regular reporting. In the collocated situation, informal reporting can keep management up-to-date with progress, but in the global team, there is rarely the opportunity for those informal updates. Implementing formal reporting for what often should be an "informal" situation can make structures and interactions between management and team members more rigid than would be preferred. However, without implementing such reporting structures, there is a danger that the remote team, given their cultural background, may not report correctly.

Furthermore, when coming from a Western background, in some Far Eastern cultures requests and instructions are accepted without comment or discussion. To disagree is considered impolite and the objective is to avoid conflict at all costs [38]. In these societies, organisational hierarchy is also an important issue and is adhered to strictly. Often, there is no discussion as to whether a request is reasonable or not, and global team members may take on tasks which they are unprepared for technically. Requests must come from the correct authority figure and are then carried out without question or comment.

2.5.1.12 SP 1.3 Global Project Management (6): Establish a Risk Management Strategy

Risk management should be incorporated into all well planned software projects. All software projects have pervasive risks which include issues such as misunderstanding requirements, feature volatility, unrealistic schedules, budgetary over runs and personnel associated problems [38]. Globally distributed virtual team projects carry additional high risk exposure as the risks associated with managing a culturally diverse virtual team are often not understood, underestimated, or in some cases, not even considered [30] as discussed in previous sections.

Another culture-related risk to virtual team project management is that there is often a lack of information among local team members about the culture of remote staff. This has been highlighted by some Far Eastern cultures revering of hierarchy [6, 38]. This manifests itself in a number of ways, often resulting in them not expressing a negative opinion and constantly agreeing to undertake additional work. Rather then saying they are unable to cope with these additional activities they work excessive hours and eventually leave the organization [13]. This can have serious implications for the success of the project as a whole. In addition, risk associated with outsourcing activities to politically unstable locations needs to be identified.

2.5.2 Global Teaming Specific Goal 2: Define Management Between Locations

Specific goal 2 focuses on global project management between locations. This is done through two specific practices. The first ensures that operating procedures are set up correctly. The second focuses on collaboration between locations.

2.5.2.1 SP 2.1 Operating Procedures (1): Define How Conflicts and Differences of Opinion Between Locations are Addressed and Resolved

For successful GSE, an effective and defined conflict management strategy should be implemented [6]. In the collocated situation, staff have the opportunity for regular face-to-face contact and, on that basis, can often work their problems out, and therefore, a less formal approach is needed. This is not the case with remote colleagues. In this setting, as stated by Karolak (1999): "There must be some mechanism for handling conflict resolution and someone who decides that resolution".

When defining the global strategy for dealing with conflict, different types of conflict have to be taken into account. Some are open and easy to recognize. However, in global teams where trust has not been established, and particularly where fear of jobs being outsourced to remote locations exists, conflict can manifest itself. This includes the development of a "them and us" culture which can lead to uncooperative and obstructive behaviour which needs to be addressed in the strategy.

2.5.2.2 SP 2.1 Operating Procedures (2): Implement a Communication Strategy for the Team

Effective communication is a key factor for the successful operation of global teams [6, 38] and we consider it very important that within the operating procedures of GT, a communication strategy is implemented. The objective of good communication is to facilitate the dissemination of relevant information, but the communication process is hampered by global distance. The loss of face-to-face contact and the need to rely on asynchronous tools impact on communication levels. This then impacts on the amount of information that is transmitted between global team members [32]. Good communication must be planned, facilitated, encouraged and monitored. It is useful to provide training on how best to communicate with remote colleagues, including the effective operation of communication tools and procedures and the linguistic and cultural implications which are inherent when communicating remotely.

2.5.2.3 SP 2.1 Operating Procedures (3): Establish Communication Interface Points Between the Team Members

In the GSE environment, individuals across teams do not communicate with each other "on the corridor". Therefore, it is important to put interfaces and processes in place which encourage both formal and informal reporting. Such reporting should ensure that all relevant team members are aware of how and when they will receive inputs to, distribute outputs from and complete work products. Teams should also be aware of other implications such as legal restrictions, or the effect holidays can have on the project timetable in countries within which they are developing the product.

To be effective, global teams require that information about basic issues such as local time and public holidays in each location is available. Information about each team member should be easily accessible by colleagues. Apart from indicating an individual's role within the team and their specific areas of responsibility, this should also include a photograph, their first name, surname, friendly name (if appropriate) and their preferred form of address. The availability of such information is taken for granted in a collocated environment, but it is not always clear when dealing with remote colleagues. Intranets and wikis are invaluable for this purpose.

2.5.2.4 SP 2.1 Operating Procedures (4): Implement Strategy for Conducting Meetings Between Locations

In a collocated situation, meetings are usually easier to organise than in the situation where team members are geographically and temporally distant as in the latter situation it is unlikely that all team members can meet face-to-face. Therefore, alternative means of communication may need to be used. It must be remembered that not all employees will be comfortable participating in meetings held via audio or video, particularly if they have not had the opportunity to meet their global colleagues face-to-face. Project managers may need to change how they conduct shared meetings. In addition, many GSE companies now implement a policy whereby they host the meeting, and then circulate minutes to all attendees, clearly articulating what has been agreed at the meeting. This adds an extra overhead, but it is very useful when following up on work agreed to be done. It is important to ensure that no delay occurs between the meeting and the circulation of minutes as people may be waiting for the minutes before implementing the actions.

2.5.2.5 SP 2.2 Collaboration Between Locations (1): Identify Common Goals, Objectives and Rewards for the Global Team

Global teams require goals and objectives to be agreed and understood by all the team members, regardless of location. Then, team members can focus on the achievement of these goals and success should be measured by their accomplishment [30]. Success can never be measured by the achievements of members at one geographical location. To actively foster this approach, the global team must be seen as an entity in its own right, regardless of the location of its team members and therefore, its performance should be judged and rewarded accordingly.

With regard to acknowledging success, what may be considered a reward in one culture can be seen as insulting to someone from another culture. The idea that "money talks" in every culture is far too simplistic an approach [54]. Cultures place different values on different types of rewards such as money, status and group achievement. Project Managers need to understand the cultural motivation of the different team members and to identify and apply appropriate rewards in each situation when and where relevant. As well as cultural diversity, the economic situation and the income tax laws at each location need to be considered when determining the form of reward provided. The objective is the development of a motivated and focused team who share a common purpose and objectives.

2.5.2.6 SP 2.2 Collaboration Between Locations (2): Collaboratively Establish and Maintain the Work Product Ownership Boundaries Among Interfacing Locations Within the Project or Organisation

Work product ownership boundaries can be defined through the effective partitioning and allocation of work across GSE teams. And it is likely that different stages of product development will occur in different sites (Fig. 2.1). Therefore, it is important that each location understands their role is in the life cycle of the product, and how modifications to the product unit they are developing can affect the other locations. In our research, we have seen requirements changes distributed to specific locations rather than to all sites, which resulted in product interfacing being unsuccessful.

2.5.2.7 SP 2.2 Collaboration Between Locations (3): Collaboratively Establish and Maintain Interfaces and Processes Among Interfacing Locations for the Exchange of Inputs, Outputs, or Work Products

An important aspect of GSE process is ownership. Good software practice recognizes that process ownership and development are best placed with those who are closest to the process. Often, a collocated process from the parent site is simply exported and implemented in the distributed site. We have studied situations where input was not encouraged or welcomed from distributed team members, and this led directly to the alienation of those team members whose needs were not met by the process and whose suggestions for improvement were ignored [13].

Therefore, common process goals should be established across locations. The input of team members at all locations should be sought, encouraged and valued. Process needs to address the specific challenges associated with GSE should be identified. This will ensure that relevant structures and procedures from all sites are taken into account to achieve this goal.

2.5.2.8 SP 2.2 Collaboration Between Locations (4): Collaboratively Develop, Communicate and Distribute Among Interfacing Teams the Commitment Lists and Work Plans that are Related to the Work Product or Team Interfaces

Effective coordination within a distributed software project necessitates that achievable milestones are planned and agreed. In GSE, there is the additional requirement for effective monitoring to be put in place to oversee ongoing progress with reference to costs, time, productivity, quality and risk. The provision of contingencies to address potential risks also has to be considered and procedures established to coordinate their implementation when and if they are required. The effective use of synchronous and asynchronous communication tools is an essential aspect of GSE communication. Therefore, it is important that within the commitments made, team members explicitly include communication plans.

2.6 Discussion

Much of the research on GSE has focused on understanding why there are difficulties with implementing GSE within organisations. While this provides a needed understanding of GSE, it is also important that we, the GSE researchers, present industry with solutions to their GSE difficulties. The Global Teaming process area presented in this chapter is an important step in this direction. Through its development we provide specific goals, specific practices, sub-practices and guidelines which can be used by industry who are implementing a GSE strategy. With the increasing globalisation of software engineering and the distribution of teams internationally, it is important that industry have access to such information. Our next stage of development is to evaluate the model in industry through action research.

2.7 Conclusion

As many organisations have discovered to their cost, implementing a GSE strategy is a complex and difficult task. Extensive research in this area has identified that this is due to a number of factors which include the nature and impact of geographical, temporal, cultural and linguistic distance [6, 15, 38]. In addition, whether undertaken in a collocated or geographically distributed environment, team based software development is not simply a technical activity. It also has important human, social and cultural implications which need to be specifically addressed. While the technical aspects of software development cannot be underestimated, neither can the importance of establishing and facilitating the effective operation of these teams.

Organisations require support in the implementation of their GSE strategy. Our development of the Global Teaming process area was based on the importance of establishing effective software teams in the globally distributed setting. In addition, when implementing software process improvement there is a requirement for tangible results to be achieved in a reasonable time frame. This is particularly important to sustain the level of effort required for improvement to take place [9, 21]. By implementing the Global Teaming process, prompt and effective results can be successfully achieved as it addresses a key aspect of GSE.

Acknowledgement The research presented in this chapter has been supported, in part, by Science Foundation Ireland through the GSD for SMEs cluster project, grant no. 03/IN3/1408C, within Lero – the Irish Software Engineering Research Centre. This research is partially support by the Software Systems Research Centre, Bournemouth University, Poole, Dorset, UK. This research is partially supported by the Science Foundation Ireland (SFI) Stokes Lectureship Programme, grant number 07/SK/I1299.

Glossary

CMMI Capability Maturity Model Integrated

GSD Global Software Development

GT Global Teaming

Insourcing Allocating work to a subsidiary or internal department of the client organisation.

Nearshoring Software development work is either insourced or outsourced to a team located in a country that is geographically close to the client organisation's country.

Offshoring Software development work is either insourced or outsourced to a team located in a country geographically far from the client organisation.

Onshoring Software development work is either insourced or outsourced to a team located in the same country as the client organisation.

Outsourcing Delegating work to a non-client entity, such as a software vendor.

SPICE ISO/IEC 15504

References

1. Agerfalk PJ, Fitzgerald B (2006) Flexible and distributed software processes: Old petunias in new bowls? Communications of the ACM 49(10): 26–34.
2. Baskerville RL (1997) Distinguishing action research from participative case studies. Journal of Systems and Information Technology, 1(1): 25–45.
3. Bergman B, Klefsjo B (1994) Quality from Customer Neets to Customer Satisfaction. Sweden: Studentlitteratur.
4. Bradner E, Mark G, Hertel TD (2003) Effects of team size on participation, awareness, and technology choice in geographically distributed teams. Proceedings of the 36th Annual Hawaii International Conference on System Sciences.
5. Brodman JG, Johnson DL (1997) A software process improvement approach tailored for small organisations and small projects. 9th International Conference on Software Engineering, Boston, MA, USA.
6. Carmel E, (1999) Global Software Teams: Collaboration Across Borders and Time Zones. Saddle River, NJ: Prentice Hall.
7. Carmel E, Agarwal R (2001) Tactical approaches for alleviating distance in global software development. IEEE Software, 2(1): 22–29.
8. Carmel E, Tjia P (2005) Offshoring Information Technology: Sourcing and Outsourcing to a Global Workforce. Cambridge: Cambridge University Press.
9. Casey V (2009) Software Testing and Global Industry: Future Paradigms. In: Richardson, ITA, O'hAodha, M (Ed.) Newcastle: Cambridge Scholars Publishing.
10. Casey V, Despande S, Richardson I (2008) Outsourcing software development the remote project manager's perspective. Second Information Systems Workshop on Global Sourcing, Services, Knowledge and Innovation, Val d'Isére, France.
11. Casey V, Richardson I (2008) The impact of fear on the operation of virtual teams. International Conference on Global Software Engineering, ICGSE, IEEE, Bangalore, India.

12. Casey V, Richardson I (2004) A practical application of the IDEAL model. Software Process Improvement and Practice, 9(3): 123–132.
13. Casey V, Richardson I (2004) Practical experience of virtual team software development. Euro SPI 2004 European Software Process Improvement, Trondheim, Norway.
14. Casey V, Richardson I (2006) Project management within virtual software teams. International Conference on Global Software Engineering, ICGSE 2006, Florianopolis, Brazil.
15. Casey V, Richardson I (2008) A structured approach to global software development. European Systems and Software Process Improvement and Innovation (EuroSPI) 2008, Dublin, Ireland.
16. Casey V, Richardson I (2006) Uncovering the reality within virtual software teams. First International Workshop on Global Software Development for the Practitioner, ICSE 2006, Shanghai, China.
17. Casey V, Richardson I (2005) Virtual software teams: Overcoming the obstacles. 3rd World Congress for Software Quality, Munich, Germany.
18. Casey V, Richardson I (2008) Virtual teams: Understanding the impact of fear. Special Issue: Global software development: Where are we headed? Software Process: Improvement and Practice 6(13): 51–526.
19. CMMI® Product Team (2006) Capability Maturity Model® Integration for Development, in Technical Report, S.E. Institute, Editor.
20. Crow G, Muthuswamy B (2003) International outsourcing in the information technology industry: Trends and implications. Communications of the International Information Management Association 3(1): 25–34.
21. Curtis B (2000) Software process improvement: Best practices and lesson learned. 22nd International Conference on Software Engineering, ICSE 2000, IEEE, Limerick, Ireland.
22. Damian DE, Zowghi D (2003) An insight into the interplay between culture, conflict and distance in globally distributed requirements negotiations. Proceedings of the 36th International Conference on Systems Sciences (HICSS'03).
23. Davidow WH, Malone MS (1992) The Virtual Corporation, New York: Edward Brulingame Books/Harper Business,.
24. DeSanctis G, Staudenmayer N, Wong SS (1999) Interdependence in virtual organizations. In: Cooper CL, Rousseau DM (Eds.) Trends in Organizational Behaviour, Vol. 6. Chichester: John Wiley & Sons, pp 81–104.
25. Ebert C, De Neve P (2001) Surviving global software development. IEEE Software 18(2): 62–69.
26. Fenton N, Whitty R, Iizuka Y (1995) Software Quality Assurance and Measurement – A Worldwide Perspective. London: International Thomson Computer Press.
27. Galin D, Avrahami M (2006) Are CMMI program investments beneficial? IEEE Software 23(6): 81–87.
28. Hayes IS (2002) Ready or not: global sourcing is in your IT future. Cutter IT Journal 15(11): 5–11.
29. Herbsleb JD (2007) Global software engineering: The future of socio-technical co-ordination. Future of Software Engineering (FOSE'07), Minneapolis, MN, USA.
30. Herbsleb JD, Grinter RE (1999) Architectures, coordination and distance: Conway's law and beyond. IEEE Software 16(5): 63–70.
31. Herbsleb JD, Mockus A (2003) An empirical study of speed and communication in globally distributed software development. IEEE Transactions on Software Engineering 29(6): 481–494.
32. Herbsleb JD, Moitra D (2001) Global software development. IEEE Software 18(2): 16–20.
33. Hofstede G, (2001) Culture's Consequences: Comparing Values, Behaviours, Institutions and Organizations across Nations. Thousand Oaks, CA: Sage Publications.
34. Humphrey WS (1989) Managing the Software Process. Reading, MA: Addison-Wesley.

35. Humphrey WS (1998) Three dimensions of process improvement, Part I: Process maturity. CROSSTALK The Journal of Defense Software Engineering, February 1998, pp. 14–17.
36. Jarvenpaa SL, Ives B (1994) The global network organization of the future: Information management opportunities and challenges. Journal of Management Science and Information Systems 10(4): 25–57.
37. Jones C (1996) Patterns of Software Systems Failure and Success. Boston: International Thompson Computer Press.
38. Karolak DW (1999) Global Software Development: Managing Virtual Teams and Environments. Los Alamitos, CA: IEEE Computer Society Press.
39. Kolind JP, Wastell DG (1997) The SEI's capability maturity model: A critical survey of adoption experiences in a cross-section of typical UK companies. IFIP TC8 WG8.6 International Working Conference on Diffusion. McMaster T, et al. (Eds.) Adoption and Implementation of Information Technology, Ambleside, Cumbria, UK, pp. 305–319.
40. Lipnack J, Stamp J (1997) Virtual Teams: Reaching Across Space, Time and Originating With Technology. New York: John Wiley & Sons.
41. Mockus A, Herbsleb JD (2001) Challenges of global software development. Proceedings Seventh International Software Metrics Symposium 2001, London.
42. Mohrman SA (1999) The context for geographically dispersed teams and networks. In: Cooper CL, Rousseau DM (Eds.) The Virtual Organization (Trends in Organizational Behaviour), Vol. 6. Chichester: John Wiley & Sons, pp. 63–80.
43. Nidiffer KE, Dolan D (2005) Evolving distributed project management. IEEE Software 22(5): 63–72.
44. O'Brien JA (2002) Management Information Systems – Managing Information Technology in the Business Enterprise, 6th edn. New York: Mc Graw Hill Irwin.
45. Organisation I S, ISO/IEC 15504 (2006) Information technology process assessment – Part 5: An exemplar process assessment model, ISO/IEC JTC1/SC7.
46. Paré G, Dubé L (1999) Virtual teams: An exploratory study of key challenges and strategies. 20th International Conference on Information Systems, Association for Information Systems, Charlotte, NC, USA.
47. Parnas D (1972) On the criteria to be used in decomposing systems into modules. Communications of the ACM 15(12): 1053–1058.
48. Paulk MC, Curtis B, Chrissis MB, Weber CV (1993) The Capability Maturity Model for Software, S.E. Institute, Editor.
49. Powell A, Piccoli G, Ives B (2004) Virtual teams: A review of current literature and direction for future research. The DATA BASE for Advances in Information Systems 35(1): 6–36.
50. Prikladnicki R, Audy JLN, Evaristo R (2003) Global software development in practice, lessons learned. Software Process Improvement and Practice 8(4): 267–279.
51. Raffo D, Setamanit S, Wakeland W (2003) Towards a software process simulation model of globally distributed software development projects. Proceedings of the International Workshop on Software Process Simulation and Modelling (ProSim'03), Portland, OR, USA.
52. Rutkowski AF, Vogel DR, Van Genuchten M, Bemelmans TMA, Favier M (2002) E-collaboration: The reality of virtuality. IEEE Transactions on Professional Communication 45(4): 219–230.
53. Sahay S, Nicholson B, Krishna S (2003) Global IT Outsourcing: Software Development across Borders. Cambridge: Cambridge University Press.
54. Schneider SC, Barsoux JL (2002) Managing Across Cultures, 2nd edn. Harlow: Financial Times Prentice Hall.
55. Smite D (2007) PhD Thesis, Riga Information Technology Institute, University of Latvia.
56. Strader LB, Beim MA, Rodgers JA (1995) The motivation and development of the space shuttle onboard software (OBS) project. Software Process Improvement and Practice 1(2): 107–113.
57. Strauss A, Corbin J (1998) Basics of Qualitative Research: Techniques and Procedures for Developing Grounded Theory, 2nd edn. Thousand Oaks, CA: Sage Publications.

58. Susman G, Evered R (1978) An assessment of the scientific merits of action research. The Administrative Science Quarterly 23(4): 582–603.
59. Toaff SS (2005) Don't play with "mouths of fire" and other lessons of global software development. Cutter IT Journal 15(11): 23–28.
60. Yin RK (1994) Case Study Research/Design and Methods, 2nd edn., Applied Social Research Methods, Vol. 5. Thousand Oaks, CA: Sage Publications.

Chapter 3
Requirements-Driven Collaboration: Leveraging the Invisible Relationships between Requirements and People

Daniela Damian, Irwin Kwan, and Sabrina Marczak

Abstract In this chapter we introduce *requirements-driven collaboration*, which is the collaboration of a cross-functional team of business analysts, designers, developers and testers during the development and management of requirements. We describe an approach that (1) constructs a requirement-centric social network which represents the membership and relationships among members working on a requirement and its associated downstream artifacts and (2) outlines a number of social network analysis techniques to study collaboration aspects such as communication, awareness, and the alignment of technical dependencies driven by development of requirements and social interactions. To demonstrate our approach, we discuss a case study that examines requirements-driven collaboration within an industrial, globally-distributed software team. Finally, we discuss implications regarding the use of our requirements-driven collaboration approach for research and practice.

3.1 A Requirements Perspective on Collaboration

Requirements Engineering (RE) is an area filled with challenges of a non-technical nature [15]. RE involves activities such as negotiation, analysis and requirements management. RE requires communication from the elicitation phase [1, 6] down to the analysis, implementation and test phases. As such, it involves collaboration among large, often geographically distributed cross-functional teams comprised of requirements analysts, software architects, developers, and testers. This collaboration is driven by coordination needs in software development and relies on communication and awareness.

D. Damian (✉)
Software Engineering Global interAction Lab, University of Victoria, Victoria, BC, Canada
e-mail: danielad@cs.uvic.ca

I. Mistrík et al. (eds.), *Collaborative Software Engineering*,
DOI 10.1007/978-3-642-10294-3_3, © Springer-Verlag Berlin Heidelberg 2010

Coordination – the act of managing interdependencies between activities [26] – is a critical aspect in every activity related to a requirement's analysis, implementation or testing. Developers allocated to developing requirements coordinate to establish a common understanding about the work to be done. Since requirements are volatile, ongoing coordination is necessary to manage interdependencies with those working on the artifacts related to a changed requirement. Changes in one requirement need to be propagated to those who work on dependent requirements and related downstream artifacts. Neglecting coordination with those who work on dependencies may result in failures [8].

Team members coordinate using two methods [33]: by following a pre-defined process, and through communication. Most teams manage technical dependencies by adopting processes that may be supported by tools, such as requirements management, modeling, source code management, plans, or issue tracking tools [12, 16, 36]. However, coordination by communication is prevalent, especially because documentation becomes obsolete and relevant knowledge may reside only with people. Studies found that large projects have extensive communication and coordination needs [7] and developers spend much of their time communicating with others [20, 28].

The awareness one has of another's work affects coordination processes [9, 12, 13, 16, 21, 31]. When project members coordinate with others, they gain knowledge of the task and team [16]. This knowledge, referred to as *team knowledge*, helps them coordinate implicitly. Team knowledge can be divided into two types: *long-term knowledge*, and short-term knowledge or *awareness* [5]. Long-term knowledge is acquired through training and experience. This information is retained and is useful throughout an entire project. Awareness refers to information that is relevant for a task at hand; once the situation passes, the information is no longer relevant. Awareness includes knowing about what others are doing to synchronize actions, or what information others know within a team.

Effective coordination, knowledge management and information sharing among team members with diverse organizational and functional backgrounds is critical. Team members carry out the implementation of requirements, but coordinating such a wide variety of people is a challenge. Often there are communication and organizational boundaries between each of these roles [1], as well as different expectations with respect to communication processes.

Collaboration across geographical distance (i.e., different time zones) and sociocultural distance (i.e., language and culture) creates additional challenges in project members' communication and awareness in the development project (e.g., [11, 16, 19]). A team communicates less effectively with a remote team than with a collocated team, resulting in a lack of knowledge of remote team activities [16]. This hinders a project manager's ability to keep track of the effects of changes as they propagate across sites, and can lead to misunderstanding requirements, low trust among teams, and reduced team productivity [11]. There is little support for monitoring progress of requirements or identifying specialists [6]. While some collaborative tools aiming at supporting RE in distributed teams [25] rely on teams self-subscribing to communication about a particular requirement, we found that teams that have relevant knowledge and work related to particular requirements have dynamic membership with unpredictable patterns [10].

By taking a requirements perspective on collaboration, we seek to further our understanding of the many aspects surrounding the communication, coordination and awareness of cross-functional teams throughout the project life-cycle, and which face challenges of socio-technical and organizational nature.

3.2 An Approach to Study Requirements-driven Collaboration

Requirements-driven collaboration is collaboration that occurs during the development, implementation and management of requirements. To study requirements-driven collaboration, we describe an approach that uses concepts and techniques from social network analysis [34] to obtain insights about the communication, coordination and awareness patterns of those involved in requirements-driven collaboration. Our approach is based on a structure that focuses on the requirement as the unit of work around which collaboration occurs. We term this structure a requirements-centric team. Our approach then consists of two steps:

1. Define the requirements-centric social network as a representation of members and relationships in a requirements-centric team.
2. Define a number of social networks analysis techniques to study aspects of requirements-driven collaboration.

A *requirements-centric team (RCT)* is a cross-functional group whose members' work activities are related to one or more interrelated requirements, as well as downstream artifacts such as design, code and tests. By "related to" we consider relationships such as "working on", "assigned to", and "communicating about".

The membership of an RCT contains individuals that have a relationship to a requirement or multiple interrelated requirements. Such relationships also include relationships to downstream artifacts that trace to the requirement. Thus, the RCT membership includes individuals who work on *project artifacts* such as requirements, design, code and test cases, as well as individuals who send and receive *communication artifacts* such as E-mail and instant messages. As an example, consider a project team comprised of team members Bob, Eva, Frank, Geoff, Lisa, Ron and Todd, and a number of requirements R_1, R_2 and R_3. The following activities and relationships have been recorded: Lisa, a software designer, is *writing a design specification* implementing R_1, *as well as test cases* for R1. Todd has written code that *implements* R_1. Eva and Todd *exchanged an email message* during their work about R_1. Consequently, the RCT associated with R_1 (R_1CT) contains Lisa, Todd, and Eva. This is illustrated in Fig. 3.1 that shows R_1 on the requirements plane, its associated project and communication artifacts on the artifacts plane, and the R_1CT on the requirements-centric team's plane.

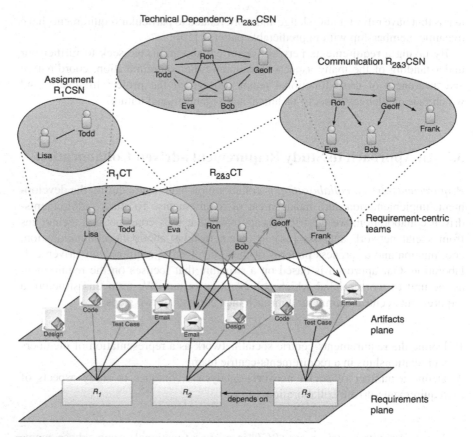

Fig. 3.1 Requirements-centric teams and different RCSNs

Although a requirement-centric team most likely contains people working on a single requirement, it can also provide a view of people who are working on multiple related requirements. If a requirement is related to another through requirement dependencies such as *structural* (e.g., refined-to, changes-to and similar-to dependencies), *constraining* (e.g., requires, and conflict-with dependencies) or *cost/value* (e.g., increases/decreases cost of dependencies) [8], the requirements-centric team associated to the interrelated requirements comprises all project members whose work activities relate to these requirements and their related downstream artifacts. Figure 3.1 also illustrates the RCT associated to R_2&R_3 (R_3 depends on R_2), so the $R_{2\&3}$CT contains Eva, Todd, Ron, Bob, Geoff and Frank.

The RCT also applies to non-functional requirements. As non-functional requirements often have a relationship to functional requirements, and cross-cut many artifacts, an RCT can identify people who should collaborate because their work on non-functional requirements influence those working on functional requirements.

3.2.1 Defining Requirements-Centric Social Networks

To analyze the collaboration within requirements-centric teams, we define a *requirements-centric social network* (RCSN). The RCSN is a social network [34] that represents the members (also called actors) and relationships (also called ties) in a RCT. The actors in an RCSN are among the members of the RCT, and the ties in the network are representations of different relationships during these members' collaboration. For example, a tie can represent project members' requirements-related *communication*, *assignment to* work on the same requirements, *contributions to the development* of requirement, or *awareness* of another's requirements-related work.

Representations such as social networks allow us to capture information about the real world relationships that form among people whose work is related to a requirement, and investigate questions such as Who has worked on artifacts related to particular requirements? How does this compare to the project plan? Who communicated or coordinated about these artifacts? Who are central people in the requirements-based communication and thus are key people in processes of expertise seeking?

Given specific research interests, one can define what relationships to represent in an RCSN, and collect appropriate data with to generate RCSNs containing different relationships. Examples of RCSNs that represent relationships include but are not limited to the following (Fig. 3.1 is used for illustration):

- *Technical dependency RCSN*. A technical dependency RCSN contains members that should coordinate because there are technical dependencies among the artifacts they work on, e.g., those that contribute to the requirement and related downstream artifacts up to the current moment in time. This network is fully connected. In Fig. 3.1, there is a technical dependency between R2 and R3. Because Eva, Todd, Ron, and Bob are assigned to work on R2, and Geoff on R3, the technical dependency network contains all five team members. Such a network can be constructed using repository mining that identifies relationships between artifacts, such as call graphs and trace links.

  This network is useful for identifying how many project members have been involved in modifying the requirement or associated downstream artifacts. The information captured in this network can be used to propagate change information to members working on the requirement, and, more significantly, members working on dependent requirements. If one's work is affected by a dependent requirement, one has to receive information of changes about the related artifacts. Other uses for this network include *expertise seeking* to find members who recently worked on an artifact related to the requirement, and *monitoring the amount of activity* in the development, to identify requirements that may require additional resources.

- *Communication RCSN*. A communication RCSN contains members from the RCT that have communicated about the requirements or its associated downstream artifact. A tie is drawn if one person communicates about the requirement with another person. To construct a communication network, data can be extracted from communication repositories such as mailing lists, online forum systems, instant messenger logs, and comments on bug-tracking systems.

This network is useful for identifying communication activity generated around a requirement, and an indication of behaviors such as asking for clarifications on requirements and communication of changes. This network can be quite larger than the technical dependency network in that it may include members who *emerge* as relevant to the coordination driven by the particular requirement – for instance, by having provided technical expertise – but who do not belong to the technical network because they have not modified any technical artifact. Frank is, for example, an emergent person in the $R_{2\&3}$CSN in Fig. 3.1. Similarly, fewer members than those in a technical dependency relationship may be communicating during the project, indicating a possible lack of coordination in the development of the requirement. Figure. 3.1 shows Bob and Eva as not having communicated in a technical dependency relationship. Because there may be different reasons for communication, such as communication of changes [9, 10], coordinating activities [28], and requesting clarification [29], one can construct and analyze networks that capture only the particular reason for communication.

- *Assignment RCSN.* An assignment RCSN contains members from the RCT that have been assigned to work on the requirement or on its associated downstream artifacts. The network is fully connected because it reflects technical dependencies because the members of this network should coordinate with each other. For example, in Fig. 3.1, Lisa is assigned to work on the design for R1, and Todd is assigned to coding the modules related to R1. Consequently, Todd and Lisa appear in the assignment-R_1CSN. Such a network can be built by extracting data from project planning or bug-tracking systems that contain information about work assignment.

  This network is useful for identifying the expected scope of involvement and coordination in the development of a requirement. When constructed over a period of time, this network can show changes on allocation of members in a certain requirement and this information can be used by senior project management to restructure functional allocation of members in a department or in the company.

- *Awareness RCSN.* An awareness RCSN contains members from the RCT that have been identified to have awareness about other members and their work in the RCT. Awareness is the knowledge that one has about others and their working activities. Examples include knowledge of what is going on in a task in areas that affect that member's work [9, 36]; knowledge of which team members are around, where and when, as relevant for the task [16]; knowledge of how other members can help one in his work [13]; or knowledge of changes made on a project documentation artifact such as requirements specification. In the RCSN a tie is drawn if one person has awareness about the other, using the different types of awareness. To construct an awareness-based network, data can be collected through interviews or questionnaires. A question of the form, "Are you aware of this project member's current tasks?" or "Are you aware of how can these project members can help you in your work on requirement R?" can be asked of individuals in a project team.

This network is useful for identifying who in the organization is knowledgeable about activities that surround one's work. Since coordination activities are a critical component of collaboration in requirements-centric teams, and awareness plays an important role in facilitating coordination, information about the extent to which members in an RCSN have awareness of each other's work is useful in diagnosing the "coordination ability" of members in RCSNs. This network can be different than the communication network because people may become aware through other means than communication. For example, members developing code related to a requirement may stay aware of progress by subscribing to the code repository notification feature. On the other hand, a project manager may stay up-to-date about what is going on in the project by reading status report of member's activities.

3.2.2 Using Requirements-Centric Social Networks to Study Requirements-Driven Collaboration

Having defined requirements-centric social networks, our approach defines a number of techniques from social network analysis as mechanisms to explore collaboration aspects of requirements-driven collaboration. We describe research questions and aspects of collaboration that each of these techniques or analysis can answer.

3.2.2.1 Analysis to Characterize the Networks

The measurements of network properties we present can answer questions such as: What types of requirements require communication-based coordination? Which requirements are problematic because of unclear description? and Which requirements have undergone many changes?

Network size. Network size is the number of members in each RCSN and helps convey the amount of coordination required for each requirement. The proportion of team members involved in a particular requirement out of the total team members in the project may also indicate the relative size and scope of a requirement.

Network density. Network density is the proportion of ties that exist in the network out of the total possible ties. In requirements-driven collaboration, it is a measurement of how tightly-coupled the requirements-centric team is, and reflects

the ability of the team to distribute knowledge [31] about the changes in requirements or clarifications about requirements. For example, a communication RCSN
with high density would suggest that the team members communicate a lot with
each other person working on the requirement. If seeking clarifications is the topic
of discussion in the highly dense communication RCSN then one may conclude
that the requirement is very ambiguous and problematic because it necessitates a
lot of information exchange to clarify it. Similarly, a communication RCSN drawn
from messages about requirements change that has high density is indicative of a
requirement that is highly volatile. In the literature, density has been studied in relationship to coordination ease in distributed teams [22], coordination capacity [23],
and enhanced group identification [30].

3.2.2.2 Analysis of Network Actors

Characteristics of the actors, such as the person's *role* in an organization, *level
of experience* and *geographical location*, may influence relationships observed
in a network. These characteristics are called *actor attributes*. By analyzing the
attributes of network actors one can partition the network into smaller and more
specific groups. By studying how information flows within and across groups
one can study, for example, how frequently project members communicate with
those outside their functional group, or how frequently they communicate across
distance.

We can view the requirements-centric social network as consisting of different
functional groups located at different geographical locations, or as groups of experts
and novices. The actor attributes thus provides a useful dimension of analysis of
"distance" between people in the network [35]. The geographical distance is an
obvious one, but here we present other types of distance such as functional distance
or level of experience. If two people are close in one dimension, they may consider
themselves quite distant in other dimensions and make decisions about information
sharing behavior. For example, an engineer may exchange communication more
frequently with geographically-distant colleagues in his same product area than with
the another engineer in the same office. Thus, one can study relationships between
attributes such as distance, functional role and others on patterns of information flow
in RCSNs.

3.2.2.3 Analysis of Network Structure

Network structure – the observed set of ties linking the actors in the network – is
important in the study of requirements-driven collaboration because it allows us
to examine patterns of behaviour of those in positions to send information about
requirements, or of the entire network making decisions about requirements. We
regard a requirements-centric social network as a conduit for propagation of information or the exertion of influence. Each project member's place in the overall
pattern of relationships, largely determined by actor attributes such as location,
experience and role, determines what information that person has access to, and
who that person is in a position to influence. Thus, patterns of information flow

affect the individual's capabilities in the project and as such there is an important relationship between individual actors' attributes, capabilities and the network structure.

3.2.2.4 Analysis of Collaboration Behavior Within the Same Network

Each type of network defined in our approach lends itself to the analysis of key actors in the networks. Using the following techniques, one can identify mediators of information flow in communication networks, or members who are most aware of what others are doing in the requirements-driven collaboration.

Centrality. Centrality is an indicator of who is at the core of a network. For instance, in a communication RCSN, someone who is central sends and receives messages to a large number of people in the network. Centrality can be computed for each actor, to gain a relative understanding of this actor's position in the network, and a centrality index can be computed for an entire network that quantifies its centrality as a whole. Centrality is important because it has been shown that central network configurations lead to more efficient completion of simple tasks [17]. Specific measures for such as degree centrality and betweenness centrality are useful in the study of requirements-driven collaboration.

The *degree centrality* indicates the number of connection of an actor and is indicative of activity [17]. Similarly, the *betweenness centrality* measure indicates when an actor is in between other actors and thus may be in a position to control interactions between those other actors [17]. While other studies found that betweenness is a predictor for coordination behavior in software development [23], in requirements collaboration the presence of actors with high betweenness centrality may indicate that the information flow has intermediaries, a typical source for misunderstanding in requirements.

Brokerage. As work progresses in an organization, people are naturally divided into subgroups such as teams or geographical locations. Brokerage is the case where one person, called a broker, is a bridge between two subgroups. The broker is in a sensitive position because the person is able to control the flow of information into or out of the subgroup.

Studies of brokers in global software development have identified that brokers effectively disseminate information between distributed sites when maintaining direct relationships is not practical [22]. They are usually the most knowledgeable members of a team regardless of geographical distance [14, 27]. In requirements-driven collaboration, brokers may be essential for enabling effective flow of information between teams. However, this may be problematic if a broker is introducing misunderstandings or limiting information transmitted.

3.2.2.5 Analysis of Collaboration Behavior Across Different Types of Networks

Because requirements-centric social networks capture communication and work relationships, one can compare different types of networks to learn the effects of one type of relationship on another.

Alignment of networks. The alignment between social interactions and technical dependencies has been studied in software engineering with a measure called *socio-technical congruence* (STC) [32]. To compute STC one calculates the ratio of actual social interactions over the expected coordination needs from the technical dependencies in the project. Research suggests that a high congruence of technical dependencies and social interactions improves task completion speed [3]. If a social interaction is missing where a coordination need exists, it is considered a "gap" in socio-technical coordination [14].

In our requirements perspective on collaboration, the assignment and technical RCSNs reflect coordination needs. Similarly, the communication and awareness RCSNs constructed from data on social interaction reflect actual coordination behavior and ability respectively. A STC index can be computed by dividing the number of relationships in the coordination needs network (either assignment or technical RCSN) by the social interaction network (communication or awareness RCSN). In requirements-driven collaboration, a low STC index may by a symptom of a larger problem: for example, not coordinating a requirements change with others who work on interrelated requirements.

Correlation between two network structures. The existence of a relationship in one type of network may have a correlation to the existence of a relationship in another type of network. For example, there may be a correlation between patterns of communication and awareness in requirements-driven collaboration. One can use a social network analysis technique called Quadratic Assessment Procedure (QAP) to investigate correlations [24]. Previous research used QAP correlation in studies of software developer's social networks and found that higher frequency of communication was associated with higher familiarity and awareness of other's work [13].

3.3 A Study of Requirements-Driven Collaboration in an Industrial Project

As an example application of our approach to study requirements-driven collaboration, we describe the insights from a field investigation of a global commercial software project in a large international organization. Our goal was to explore how cross-functional teams related by the work on the same requirement or dependent requirements coordinate through communication and team knowledge. We thus sought to identify, for each requirement in the project, properties of communication in the development of a requirement, as well as of information flow in the development of dependent requirements. We first describe the project and the data available. After describing the social networks we analyzed, we discuss our findings in relation to a set of specific research questions.

We discovered that a RCSN tends to involve more people than initially assigned to work on the requirement. We also determined that, despite low socio-technical congruence in some of the RCSNs, project team members were still able to coordinate their work effectively and deliver the project on time. Finally, the existence of brokers may have been able to help mitigate the effect of large geographical distances on project communication.

3.3.1 Construction of the Requirements-Centric Social Networks

The project involved 12 members distributed over two sites, the USA and Brazil, as follows: 3 in the USA (2 developers, and 1 technical leader) and 9 in Brazil (5 developers, 1 technical leader, 2 testers, and 1 test leader). They had in average 8 years of work experience and were involved with the project since its inception.

A number of data sources were available in the project and allowed us to collect information about project members' activities on requirements and associated downstream artifacts.

From the requirements document we identified a total of 13 functional technical requirements. In this project the requirements represented requests for updates to software components that integrate the application with other software products. For example, one of the requirements referred to upgrading a component in order to avoid issues on the application after rebooting the machines. The requirements were described in a high level since the project team had previous knowledge about the product architecture.

To identify dependencies among the project requirements, we examined the requirements-traceability document and conducted interviews with team members. We identified five pairs of dependent requirements in this project. Of the five pairs, two are structural dependencies and three are constraining dependencies.

To analyze the collaboration around the development of project requirements, we constructed the following social networks:

1. For each of the 13 requirements, we constructed the *assignment RCSN*, reflecting assignment to work to each requirement; the communication RCSN, reflecting actual communication on a particular requirement *during* the project; and the *awareness RCSN*, reflecting awareness of requirements-related activities *during* the project.
2. For each of the 5 pairs of dependent requirements, we constructed the *communication RCSN*.

We were not able to inspect the change management repository and thus were not able to construct the *technical dependency* RCSN.

We constructed each network as follows.

1. To build the *assignment* RCSN for each requirement, we inspected the requirements document and project plan and identified all team members who were allocated to work on the requirement or the associated downstream artifacts. These members were included as actors in the network. We then fully connect the network.

To construct the *communication* and *awareness* RCSNs, we collected data through questionnaires and interviews at the two-thirds point in the project. For each requirement network, we included all members identified in the *assignment* RCSN as well as those who became involved in the coordination associated to the particular requirement but were not included in the project plan. We asked the respondents to indicate any additional members with whom they communicated about a requirement and if they were aware of they were doing that is related to their work respectively. We also captured the reason for communication by asking respondents to indicate whether the communication related any of the following: communication of changes, coordination activities, requirements clarification, requirements negotiation, and synchronization of code. Figure 3.2 exemplifies membership in the assignment and communication RCSNs for a requirement that had John, Kyle, Kim and Jim assigned to its development. The communication RCSN also indicates reasons for communication for each tie in the network.

2. To construct the *communication* RCSN for each pair of dependent requirements (Fig. 3.3), we identified the list of team members who were allocated to work in every task related to the particular set of dependent requirements by inspecting the project plan. If the team member indicated communication with another person about any one of the dependent requirements in the set, then we connected the two people in the communication RCSN for dependent requirements. The data on the reason for communication allowed us to construct a *communication* RCSN for each of the five reasons. We thus constructed a total of 25 networks. Figure 3.3 shows one of the 5 networks constructed for the two dependent requirements R_1 and R_2.

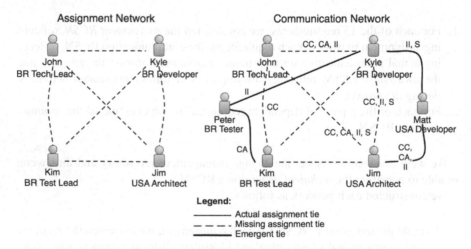

Fig. 3.2 Assignment communication network for requirement 1

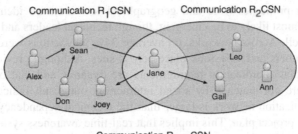

Communication R_1CSN   Communication R_2CSN

Communication $R_{1\&2}$CSN

Fig. 3.3   Construction of $R_{1\&2}$CSN

3.3.2 Communication in Requirements-Driven Coordination

To answer questions about communication in requirements-driven collaboration, we calculated network measurements for the networks we constructed. We analyzed the size, actor attributes and ties for each of the networks associated for each of the 13 requirements in the project as well as the 5 dependent requirements.

How many people are typically working on/communicating about a requirement? In the project of 12, we found that all assignment and communication RCSN involved about 5 and 7 people respectively, from both geographical locations. The mean size of the assignment RCSNs was 5 people (standard deviation of 1) where an average of 3.2 people were in Brazil and 1.7 were in the USA. The mean size of the communication RCSNs was 7.8 people (standard deviation of 1.4) where an average of 5.5 people were in Brazil and 2.3 were in the USA.

Are there more people communicating about a requirement than those assigned to work on the requirement? In terms of amount of communication in each network, we observe that the networks did not exhibit full connectedness though a fair level of interaction. The average number of interactions between members in the network was 38.4, and the average network *density* was about half of a fully connected network: 0.43 (standard deviation 0.16). The project team completed the requirements despite not communicating with every other person in the network, suggesting that the team members were able to coordinate using methods other than communicating.

We then compared the assignment and the communication networks to determine if coordination involved only those individuals assigned to the requirement. We found that communication *during* the development of a requirement, as reflected in the communication network, typically involved more project members than those allocated to work on the requirements through the project plan. These *emergent people* were identified as providing expertise to those who were assigned to the requirement. This expansion of the assignment network indicates a dynamic evolution of membership and interaction in a requirement-centric team.

Using actor properties (role and geographical location), we identified that a developer was most likely to be emergent, though technical leaders and testers were emergent as well. Across networks, on average 34% interactions were with emergent team members and 43% took place across-sites. Although previous research [3] identified that coordination requirements are dynamic and that often coordination needs are not matched by social interaction, our result indicates that the actual communication network is larger than the technical dependency network as reflected in the project plan. This implies that real-time awareness systems that aim at improving coordination should consider providing up-to-date information about those coordinating about a requirement to complement the information available in project plans.

What information do members exchange in an RCSN? To obtain details about the communication around requirements, we asked the participants to indicate the reason for communication that they exchanged with each other member in each of the communication RCSNs (communication of changes, coordination of activities, requirement clarification, requirement negotiation, and implementation issues) and constructed specific communication RCSN for each requirement and each reason for communication.

By counting the ties in each of these topic-specific communication RCSNs we identified that *communication of changes* and *coordination of activities* were the two most frequent reasons for communication, followed by implementation issues. The top type of communication with emergent members was *coordination of activities*, followed by *implementation of issues*. Across sites, no single type of communication stood out. These findings align with our earlier finding that the emergent members are indeed involved in requirements-driven coordination [10]. The fact that the second most-frequent topic for discussion with emergent members was implementation issues corroborates with our finding that most frequent emergent members were developers.

Are people with coordination needs coordinating in practice? To identify whether project members who need to coordinate their work on a common requirement do indeed engage in coordination, we computed the socio-technical congruence between the assignment RCSN (reflecting coordination requirements in the project) and communication RCSN (reflecting actual social interactions) following the description in Section 3.3.

We identified that in average (mean) the 13 RCSNs are 0.73 congruent. For the 13 requirements, there is perfect alignment between the technical dependency and social interactions for 4 requirements, indicating that coordination among team members happened according to the allocation planned by the project manager. For the other 9 requirements however, the STC index is around 0.6 indicating that about 40% of links from the project plan are not realized by communication among project members.

Following this analysis, we observed that the project was able to deliver each of its requirements on time despite the fact that the communication networks were not fully congruent with the assignment networks. Previous studies of socio-technical congruence regarded the presence of gaps as detrimental to project success [14]. Our results call into question the necessity that each person in the network needs to fill communication gaps according to the coordination needs. Cost-benefit considerations include the fact that some communication gaps are too expensive to fill especially in geographically-distributed teams, or may put undue burden on team members to be practical to fill. The participants' role – an *actor attribute* in the network – may also enable us to further examine the gaps in the communication-based network. By bringing socio-technical congruence to the requirements level one can study the communication between different roles other than developers: testers, business analysts, and project leaders can be incorporated into the networks. One may find that some gaps are not necessarily detrimental to project's success. Interesting research questions include "Does always a requirements engineer need to *directly* communicate with coders?" Understanding which gaps must be closed by direct communication or which gaps can be covered by others, such as those in a broker configuration, is important to further the study of requirements-driven collaboration.

Does distance correlate with communication in a RCSN? To analyze the relationship between distance and communication in this project we analyzed the actor attributes (member's geographical location) and the structure of the communication RCSNs. We found a correlation between the geographic distance and the frequency of communication ($r^2=0.426$ and $p<0.02$), indicating that the co-located members tended to communicate more frequently than with those at a distance site. This finding provides implications for knowledge sharing in global teams. Decisions made when members meet informally in the coffee room should be captured and shared with the remote members in order to keep the entire team up-to-date with project information.

Are there key members who mediate the flow of information about requirements? Which are these members' characteristics? Having identified the reasons for communication in requirements-driven collaboration, we decided to identify patterns in how the information was mediated in these networks. We analyzed information flow in the communication networks of the five pairs of dependent requirements (recall there were 25 networks in total). The case of dependent requirements in this project provided us with the example of a communication network that was larger than the one of a single requirement. For an idealized communication between members working on a set of dependent requirements, information from each member in one requirement network should be transferrable to all members in the dependent requirement network. The longer the path used to transfer information, the higher the chance for misinterpretation and loss of information. Therefore, short paths of information-travel are of special interest in requirements management processes. Here we investigated the presence of mediators of information exchange between the two groups of project members working on two dependent requirements by searching for brokers of information flow along paths of length two. A broker is a member who mediates communication between a pair of members that would otherwise be disconnected [18].

Our analysis identified brokers in each of the 25 networks of the five pairs of requirements. We discuss three findings on brokerage.

First, brokerage was predominant in certain types of communication. We found most brokers in the communication of changes, communication about requirements clarifications and communication during coordination activities and almost no brokers in negotiations and communication to synchronize code. This is not a surprising finding since the activities of requirements negotiations or synchronization of code may be less frequent during requirements-driven collaboration and also only involve certain people.

Second, and perhaps one of the most interesting findings on brokers in our study is that the most frequently identified broker in almost all pairs of requirements, was located in the US (referred to as Jane). One would not be surprised that Jane mostly communicated across distances given that the majority of project members are in Brazil (9 out of 12), and because she played a key role in the project, as a development leader. Given that geographical distribution introduces significant communication problems [21], and that maintaining relationships across distances known to be difficult [13, 16], one would expect that for more efficient communication she would have appointed or collaborated with a Brazil-based project member or leader. Surprisingly, that was not our finding. Jane did not only communicate frequently with the distanced members but was a broker for all communication types among Brazilians. We would have expected to see this pattern with a Brazilian-based project member. This can be explained by the familiarity of project members with Jane given her role, and corroborates with evidence that familiarity has influence on communication [10, 13].

Third, we found that knowledge and experience act as determinants for brokerage. Additional contextual project information in our study revealed other factors that relate to brokerage. Jane was part of four of the five pairs of dependent requirements. We believe that her knowledge and experience is a strong determinant for her broker role in most networks. Jane has been a development leader in the company for more than 7 years, and she acquired extensive knowledge of the project in her role as coordinator of negotiation activities with the business partners. Her profile fits what has been referred to as a specialist role and leads her to become a broker in the team's communication. This finding implies that organizations planning to establish a remote team with requirements-driven technical dependencies should consider including experienced team members at the remote team as a mechanism to mitigate the effect of distance on cross-site information flow.

Is there any relationship between frequency of communication and awareness in requirements-driven collaboration? The relationship between communication and awareness is important to study because one would expect that those who communicate more frequently are also aware of relevant working context. The average density of the awareness RCSNs was slightly lower than the average density of the communication networks – 0.43 (standard deviation 0.16) – suggesting that in this project communication may not necessarily ensured awareness of who else was working on the same requirements. We also conducted a QAP correlation test [24] to compare the behavior of the communication and awareness RCSNs for each requirement in the project. We used the data on frequency of communication and awareness of what others are doing that is related to one's work. We found a correlation index of 0.302 (p<0.05), which indicates that those who communicated more were also more aware. When this is analyzed in light of findings that project members keep aware of each other through regular meetings, or unplanned interactions, the considerable reliance on verbal communication or local experts leads to research questions for future work such as: What type of local or verbal interaction facilitates the maintenance of this awareness? How can an awareness system replicate it in the distributed interaction? More investigation is also needed into the impact of other factors such as process or ethnic culture on awareness. While we only sought to correlate awareness with communication in this study, it is also possible that awareness was also maintained as a result of certain procedures for knowledge dissemination in project meetings or may have been hindered due to different communication styles across sites.

3.4 Implications

In this chapter we described a requirements perspective on collaboration in software development and a structured approach to investigate coordination in requirements-centric teams. A researcher using this approach can define network relationships and actor attributes that apply to a specific case of interest. In our case study we chose to investigate the alignment of those assigned to work on a requirement, and their communication, as well as the effects of distance on communication and awareness.

Insights that we obtained about collaborative processes in software development relate to the effect of distance on communication, the effect of awareness on communication, properties of brokers in cross-functional teams and the effects of roles on brokerage.

3.4.1 Research Implications: Future Applications of the Approach

To extend the study of requirements-driven collaboration, the approach described in this chapter should be applied to examine different types of cases of requirements-driven collaboration. In our study, we studied a small project with sets of two dependent requirements. The approach can be applied to larger projects that contain multiple dependent requirements. This will provide insight into the nature of coordination over complex technical dependencies.

The study of requirements-driven collaboration can also include the analysis of digital artifacts, as well as qualitative observations. These artifacts may include email data, requirement databases, and source code that are related to a requirement. An analysis using quantitative data would allow more accurate results regarding the characterization of requirements-driven collaboration.

The effect of roles on network characteristics can also be studied in more detail. Our study explored interactions between developers and testers, but our approach allows one to study interactions that include project managers and requirements analysts as well.

3.4.2 Practice Implications: Designing of Collaboration Tools to Support Coordination of Cross-Functional Teams

The paradigm of a requirements-centric team can be used to develop tools to support cross-functional teams coordinate effectively. Collaborative tools can also assist managers who wish to monitor and improve coordination processes within their organization.

A tool that can generate an RCSN automatically, perhaps using data-mining techniques [2, 37] and automated requirement-traceability tools [4] can identify who works on which artifacts, and trace these artifacts to requirements. Such a tool may be able to extract data from issue-tracking repositories, requirement repositories, mailing lists, and chat logs. These tools can be embedded into software development and management tools to support:

- *Broker identification.* A tool can identify brokers mediating activity on different requirements to make a project manager aware of who the critical people in a project are. Resources can be provided to these persons so they can better do their job. A backup person can be trained to cover for the broker when he is not available.
- *Expertise seeking.* Generating an RCSN based on assignment and communication networks will indicate who is assigned to working on each requirement. Thus, someone who is seeking help will be able to identify who works and communicates on a particular part of the project and consult with that person accordingly.
- *Diagnosing coordination.* A tool can compute social network properties and provide a manager with information to improve project performance. Measurements include the time to complete a task and the number of changes made to an artifact in a time period. Socio-technical congruence is an example of a technique that can identify gaps in coordination. A manager can take actions to increase the alignment between the social structure of the organization and the technical dependencies among artifacts.

References

1. Al-Rawas A, Easterbrook S (1996) Communication problems in requirements engineering: A field study. Conference on Awareness in Software Engineering, London, pp. 47–60.
2. Bettenburg N, Just S, Schröter A, Weiss C, Premraj R, Zimmermann T (2008) What makes a good bug report? International Symposium on Foundations of Software Engineering, Atlanta, USA, pp. 308–318.
3. Cataldo M, Wagstrom PA, Herbsleb JD, Carley KM (2006) Identification of coordination requirements: Implications for the design of collaboration and awareness tools. Computer Supported Cooperative Work, Banff, Canada, pp. 353–362.
4. Cleland-Huang J, Settimi R, Zou X, Solc P (2006) The detection and classification of non-functional requirements with application to early aspects. International Requirements Engineering Conference, Minneapolis, USA, pp. 36–45.

5. Cooke NJ, Salas E, Cannon-Bowers JA, Stout Re (2000) Measuring team knowledge. Human Factors 42(1): 151–173.
6. Coughlan J, Lycett M, Macredie RD (2003) Communication issues in requirements elicitation: A content analysis of stakeholder experiences. Information and Software Technology 45(8): 525–537.
7. Curtis B, Krasner H, Iscoe N (1988) A field study of the software design process for large systems. Communication of ACM 31(11): 1268–1287.
8. Dahlstedt AG, Persson A (2006) Requirements Interdependencies: State of the Art and Future Challenges. Berlin: Springer.
9. Damian D, Izquierdo L, Singer J, Kwan I (2007) Awareness in the wild: Why communication breakdowns occur. International Conference on Global Software Engineering, Munich, Germany, pp. 81–90.
10. Damian D, Marczak S, Kwan I (2007) Collaboration patterns and the impact of distance on awareness in requirements-centered social networks. International Requirements Engineering Conference, New Delhi, India, pp. 59–68.
11. Damian DE, Zowghi D (2003) Requirements engineering challenges in multi-site software development organizations. Requirements Engineering Journal 8: 149–160.
12. de Souza CRB, Redmiles D (2007) The awareness network: To whom should I display my actions? and, whose actions should I monitor? European Conference on Computer Supported Cooperative Work, Limerick, Ireland, pp. 99–117.
13. Ehrlich K, Chang K (2006) Leveraging expertise in global software teams: Going outside boundaries. International Conference on Global Software Engineering, Florianópolis, Brazil, pp. 149–158.
14. Ehrlich K, Helander M, Valetto G, Davies S, Williams C (2008) An analysis of congruence gaps and their effect on distributed software development. Socio-Technical Congruence Workshop at ICSE 2008, Leipzig, Germany.
15. Emam KE, Madhavji NH (1995) A field study of requirements engineering practices in information systems development. International Symposium on Requirements Engineering, pp. 68–80.
16. Espinosa JA, Slaughter SA, Kraut RE, Herbsleb JD (2007) Team knowledge and coordination in geographically distributed software development. Journal of Management Information Systems 24(1): 135–169.
17. Freeman LC, Roeder D, Mulholland RR (1979/1980) Centrality in social networks: II. Experimental results. Social Networks 2(2): 119–141.
18. Gould RV, Fernandez RM (1989) Structures of mediation: A formal approach to brokerage in transaction networks. sociological methodology 19: 89–126.
19. Herbsleb DJ (2007) Global software engineering: The future of socio-technical coordination. Future of Software Engineering at ICSE 2007, Minneapolis, USA, pp. 188–198.
20. Herbsleb JD, Klein H, Olson GM, Brunner H, Olson JS, Harding J (1995) Object-oriented analysis and design in software project teams. Human-Computer Interaction 10(2/3): 249–293.
21. Herbsleb JD, Mockus A (2003) An empirical study of speed and communication in globally distributed software development. IEEE Transactions on Software Engineering 29(6): 481–494.
22. Hinds P, McGrath C (2006) Structures that work: Social Structure, work structure and coordination ease in geographically distributed teams. Computer Supported Cooperative Work, Banff, Canada, pp. 343–352.
23. Hossain L, Wu A, Chung KKS (2006) Actor centrality correlates to project based coordination. Computer Supported Cooperative Work, Banff, Canada.
24. Krackhardt D (1987) QAP partialling as a test of spuriousness. Social Networks 9: 171–186.
25. Macaulay LA (1996) Requirements Engineering. London: Springer-Verlag.
26. Malone TW, Crowston K (1994) The interdisciplinary study of coordination. ACM Computing Surveys 26(1): 87–119.

27. Marczak S, Damian D, Stege U, Schröter A (2008) Information brokers in requirement-dependent social networks. International Requirements Engineering Conference, Barcelona, Spain, pp. 53–62.
28. Perry DE, Staudenmayer NA, Votta LG (1994) People, organizations, and process improvement. IEEE Software 11(4): 36–45.
29. Potts C, Catledge L (1996) Collaborative conceptual design: A large software project case study. Computer Supported Cooperative Work 5(4): 415–445.
30. Rulke DL, Galaskiewicz J (2000) Distribution of knowledge, group network structure, and group performance. Management Science 46(5): 612–625.
31. Sarma A, van der Hoek A (2006) Toward awareness in the large. International Conference on Global Software Engineering, Florianópolis, Brazil. October, pp. 127–131.
32. Valetto G, Helander M, Ehrlich K, Chulani S, Wegman M, Williams C (2007) Using software repositories to investigate socio-technical congruence in development projects. Mining Software Repositories at ICSE 2007, Minneapolis, USA.
33. Ven AHVD, Delbecq AL, Richard Koenig J (1976) Determinants of coordination modes within organizations. Americal Sociological Review 41(2): 322–338.
34. Wasserman S, Faust K (1994) Social Network Analysis: Methods and Applications. Cambridge: Cambridge University Press.
35. Watts DJ (2003) Six Degrees: The Science of a Connected Age. New York: Norton.
36. Whitehead J (2007) Collaboration in software engineering: A roadmap. Future of Software Engineering. IEEE Computer Society, Washington, DC, USA, pp. 214–225.
37. Wolf T, Schröter A, Damian D, Panjer L, Nguyen T (2009) Mining task-based social networks to explore collaboration in software teams. IEEE Software 26: 58–66.

Chapter 4
Softwares Product Lines, Global Development and Ecosystems: Collaboration in Software Engineering

Jan Bosch and Petra M. Bosch-Sijtsema

Abstract Effective collaboration in software engineering is very important and yet increasingly complicated by trends that increase complexity of dependencies between software development teams and organizations. These trends include the increasing adoption of software product lines, the globalization of software engineering and the increasing use of and reliance on 3rd party developers in the context of software ecosystems. Based on action research, the paper discusses problems of in effective collaboration and success-factors of five approaches to collaboration in large-scale software engineering.

4.1 Introduction

Collaboration is perhaps the most important lever for achieving high quality, efficient and effective software engineering practices and results in virtually any software developing organization.[1] Achieving effective collaboration, however, has proven to be a major challenge in many organizations, resulting in failed or late projects, products or systems not aligned to customer requirements, clashes between the research and development (R and D) organization and the rest of the company, etc. Although significant progress has been made over time, through, among others, CMMI (Capability Maturity Model Integration), agile and iterative processes, explicit software architecture management, and effective collaboration in large-scale software development remain a challenge. For purposes in this paper we consider collaboration effective if it generates minimal overhead for the organization while avoiding the aforementioned problems.

J. Bosch (✉)
Intuit Inc, Mountain View, CA 94043, USA
e-mail: jan@janbosch.com

[1] Collaboration is defined as a recursive process where two or more people or organizations work together toward an intersection of common goals.

I. Mistrík et al. (eds.), *Collaborative Software Engineering*,
DOI 10.1007/978-3-642-10294-3_4, © Springer-Verlag Berlin Heidelberg 2010

One can observe three trends that have surfaced over recent years that cause collaboration in software engineering to become significantly more complicated. The first trend is the increasingly broad adoption of software product lines [1, 2, 6, 21]. Software product lines have proven to be perhaps the most successful approach to improving productivity in software engineering; see, e.g., the product line hall of fame [10]. However, transitioning an organization that has traditionally worked in a product-centric fashion to a product line-centric way of working is a very complicated change process. The primary reason for the difficulty in changing the organization is because the product-line approach causes dependencies to be created between software assets, and between teams responsible for those assets, that did not exist earlier. In other words, an additional level of collaboration between software engineering teams and organizational units is required.

The second trend is the globalization of software development [4, 9, 19]. More and more global companies have either introduced several software development sites or engaged in strategic partnerships with remote companies, especially in India and China, due to several reasons; e.g., reduction of cycle time, reduction of travel cost, use of expertise when needed, entering new markets, and responsiveness to markets and customers [5]. Global development has many advantages but brings along its own set of challenges due to differences in culture, time zone, software engineering maturity and technical skills between teams in different parts of the world. Again, significant additional demands are placed on the collaboration between teams in the organization. When teams need to closely cooperate during iteration planning and have a need to exchange intermediate developer releases between teams during iterations in order to guarantee interoperability, the coordination cost starts to significantly affect the benefits normally associated with global development (cf. [11]).

A third important trend seen is the increasing adoption of ecosystems approaches [15]. We define software ecosystem as follows: a software ecosystem consists of a software platform, a set of internal and external developers and a community of domain experts in service to a community of users that compose relevant solution elements to satisfy their needs. Once a product or family of products has become successful in the market, a significant business opportunity appears in the form of third party developer and customer contributions to the product (family). This requires that the internal product (line) software is converted into a platform that is opened up to developers and development teams external to the organization. In addition, this requires that customers buying a product that is part of the software product line want to extend the functionality of the product with solutions available in the community or developed by 3rd party developers after the product has been deployed at the customer. Again, a significant additional demand is placed on the ability of the organization and the ecosystem as a whole to collaborate effectively as part of the software engineering process.

The trends discussed above have one important aspect in common: all increase the amount of coupling between software assets as well as between organizational unites. Below, we analyze the concept of decoupling in more detail. At the top level, coupling (defined as the absence of decoupling) can be broken into two main categories, i.e., software asset coupling and organizational coupling. The former category is concerned with the dependencies that exist between technology assets, complicating their composition in planned and unplanned configurations. During the 1970s, this was already studied in the context of structured design [23] and during the last decade the research around software architecture has continued that tradition. Organizational coupling is a reflection of the dependencies between software assets in that the ability of teams to work independently is constrained because of dependencies between the software assets that the teams are responsible for.

For both types of coupling, in many contexts the term decoupling is used as the term of choice as it indicates that explicit steps have been taken to decrease dependencies between software assets that naturally are tightly connected. Based on our research, however, we take the position that the amount of coupling between software assets is a consequence of the beliefs of the software architects designing the system. Typically, the perceptions by the architects about what functionality is expected to vary versus which functionality is not, causes certain dependencies to be created without inhibitions whereas in other areas explicit decoupling techniques are applied.

Architects often are a product of the development organization they grew up in and, consequently, tend to assume a certain approach to large-scale software development. This approach assumes certain operating mechanisms to be present between different software development teams in order to govern their collaboration. The challenge, however, is that due to the three trends discussed above, the, often implicitly defined, approach to software development becomes increasingly inefficient.

We address that concern, by explicitly defining five approaches to inter-team collaboration, which are based on action research of several companies. We focus on which different collaborative approaches large-scale software development companies apply, when these approaches are most applicable and discuss some of their challenges we found in the case companies. The different models show how companies organize large-scale software development, ranging from a highly integrated to a fully decoupled, inter-organizational approach, i.e., integration-centric approach, release groupings, release trains, independent deployment and open (eco-) system development.

In the remainder of the paper we discuss these five approaches for collaboration in large-scale software as well as specific problems that arose within these approaches. We conclude the paper with discussing in which context these approaches would be most applicable.

4.2 Architecture, Process, Organization

Collaboration in software engineering is challenging and, as we discussed in the introduction, there are several trends that are complicating collaboration even further. In this section, we discuss the key challenges or problems that we have identified in our research. The problem statement is organized according to three areas: (1) software architecture; (2) engineering processes and (3) the organization (mainly research and development). This is related to Herbsleb et al. [8] who perceives software architecture, plans (in our case organization) and processes as vital coordination mechanisms in software projects in order to have effective communication between software development teams. In the industrial reality, these areas are deeply interconnected, but we use this structure intentionally. Ideally, architecture and technology choices are derived from the business strategy and should drive process and tools choices. These, in turn, should drive the organizational structure of the R and D organization [13, 14]. In industry however, the three areas mentioned above are not always aligned. Often, the current organizational structure defines the processes and through that the architectural structure for the product or platforms and consequently constrains the set of business strategies that the company can aspire to implement. When companies define new growth strategies, the business strategy often collides with the existing organizational structure and consequently the process and architecture choices. The paradox is that the software development department still is responsible for releasing existing products and platforms while at the same time, needs to embark on new business strategy implementation. Typically, the architecture, process and organization approaches allow for too tight coupling and the problems discussed later can almost always be addressed by increasing the decoupling between architecture or organization elements.

Perhaps the key area for enabling effective collaboration in software engineering is software architecture. Collaboration often breaks down due to too many unnecessary dependencies between components and the teams responsible for those components. The dependencies not only need to be individually managed, but the overall system complexity grows exponentially with a growing number of dependencies.

The software architecture has a significant impact on the collaboration in the software development organization responsible for a system or platform. However, software architecture is only an enabler of effective collaboration; it does not define the collaboration itself. The engineering processes, both formal and informal, define the actual collaboration between teams and between individuals.

Next to the software architecture and processes, the organizational context and structure are important for effective collaboration in large-scale software development projects. Several aspects mentioned in literature are globalization [9, 19] co-ordination of interdependencies, knowledge management (transferring tacit knowledge into explicit knowledge for example [17]), and alignment of the architecture, processes and the organization. In the next section, we discuss five approaches found in industry according to the dimensions of architecture, process and organization.

The research and approach presented in this paper is based on an action research methodology applied by the authors in numerous software-intensive system companies as well as in other industries. The action research method seeks to bring together action and reflection, theory and practice, in participation with others, in the pursuit of practical solutions to issues of pressing concern to people, and more generally the flourishing of individual persons and their communities [20, 1].

Table 4.1 Overview of case studies

Cases	Company A	Company B	Company C
Product	Embedded systems	Consumer electronics	Software products
Market	Global	Global	North America, Asia
Type and size of teams	Component teams (between 10–30 team member) Global teams (between 10–30 team member) Platform organization (500+ members)	Division platform team (150+ members) Product platform team (200+ members) Product team (50+ members) Global teams (30+ members)	Product platform team (200+ members) Product team (25+ members)
Method and duration of study	Participant observer, 3 years	Participant observer, 3 years	Participant observer, 2 years
Data collection methods	Interviews, workshops	Interviews	Participant observation

We studied several R and D (Research and Development) units and software development departments in three global companies (Fortune 100 and 500 companies), who developed embedded products and software and service products for different markets (European, US and Asian markets). In Table 4.1 we present an overview of the cases investigated. Data was collected with help of semi-structured and unstructured interviews (which were coded) and participant observatory methods. We applied a two-phase analysis method of first within-case analysis and later on cross-case analysis method.

4.3 Five Collaborative Approaches

From all the units and teams we studied, at least two cases reported one of the five approaches being applied for large-scale software development. These approaches are discussed below. We organize the discussion around three dimensions: architectural, process and organizational aspects of large scale software development and conclude with success factors of the different approaches. In Table 4.2 we present a summary of the five collaborative approaches.

4.3.1 Integration-Centric Development

Description: We found several firms applying an integration-centric approach, in which the organization relies on the integration phase of the software development lifecycle. During the early stages of the lifecycle, there is allocation of requirements to the components. During the development phase, teams associated with each component implement the requirements allocated to the component. When the development of the components making up the system is finalized, the development

Table 4.2 Collaboration models for large global software development

Approach	Integration-centric	Release grouping	Release trains	Independent deployment	Open (eco-)system development
Description	Deep interconnections between the elements of the system.	Loosely coupled subsystems with high internal dependency	System components decoupled, but deployment coordinated	System components decoupled, deployment independent	Platform and 3rd part solutions decoupled and deployed independently
Architecture challenge	Strongly interconnected architecture – Tight interdependency and complexity challenge	High integration within release grouping, high decoupling between groupings – Management challenge of decoupling interfaces	High decoupling between components – Teams develop independently, while maintaining backward compatibility	High decoupling between components – Coordination and execution complicated	Highly decoupled with sand boxes for third party functionality – Security models in platform architecture challenge
Process challenge	Continuous coordination between teams – Lockstep evolution challenge	Continuous coordination within grouping – Variation challenge between and inside release groupings	Short iteration cycles; only coordination at start/end of cycle – Teams independent, but all teams need to release as same point in time	Each team selects length, frequency and time of iteration cycle – Challenge for high degree of automation and coverage of testing	Each team selects length of iteration cycle – Certification process possible
Organization challenge	High interdependency between teams – Mismatch architecture and organization structure	Teams responsible for different release groupings can be distributed – Coordination costs and completion time challenge	Distributed teams within organization – Reduction of coordination costs	Distributed teams within organization – Coordination performed by software architecture	Distributed teams across organizational boundaries – Challenge of misalignment business case of provider and external developers
Success factors	1. Release cycle long. 2. Deep integration of components 3. Co-location of team	1. Geographical distribution of teams aligned with release groupings 2. High integration within application domain	1. Frequent releases beneficial for firm. 2. High level of maturity needed	1. Different iteration cycles for different layers of the stack. 2. High level of maturity needed	1. Market approach 2. Teams highly dispersed. 3. High level of maturity needed

enters the integration phase in which the components are integrated into the overall system and system level testing takes place. During this stage, typically, many integration problems are found that need to be resolved by the component teams.

If the component teams have not tested their components together during the development phase, this phase may also uncover large numbers of problems that require analysis, allocation to component teams, co-ordination between teams and requiring continuous retesting of all functionality as fixing one problem may introduce others.

In response to the challenges discussed above, component teams often resort to sharing versions of their software even though it is under development. Although this offers a means of simplifying the integration phase, the challenge is that the untested nature of the components being shared between component teams causes significant inefficiency that could have been avoided if only more mature software assets would be shared. One approach discussed frequently in this context is continuous integration [12], but in our experience this often addresses the symptoms but not the root causes of decoupling.

Architecture: The architecture of the system or system family is typically not specified and if documentation exists, the documentation is often outdated and plays no role except for introducing new staff to the course grain design of the system. Because of this, the de-facto architecture often contains inappropriate dependencies between the components that increase the coupling in the system and cause unexpected problems during development.

In our cases, we found a typical architectural challenge that seems to be prevalent with this approach: the system architects failed to keep it simple. The key role of the software architect is to take the key software architecture design decisions [3] that decompose the system into consistent parts that can continue to evolve in relative independence. However, as has been studied by several researchers, (e.g., [22]) no architectural decomposition is perfect and each has crosscutting concerns as a consequence. These concerns cause additional dependencies between the components that, as discussed above, need to be managed and add to the complexity of the system. Techniques exist to decrease the "tightness" of dependencies, such as factoring out the crosscutting concerns and assigning them to a separate component or by introducing a level of indirection that allows for run-time management of version incompatibilities. In the initial design of the system, but especially during its evolution, achieving and maintaining the absolutely simplest architecture is frequently not sufficiently prioritized. In addition, although complexity can never be avoided completely for any non-trivial system, it can easily be exacerbated by architects and engineers in response to addressing symptoms rather than root causes, e.g., through overly elaborate version management solutions, heavy processes around interfaces or too effort consuming continuous integration approaches.

Process: Although most organizations employing this approach utilize techniques like continuous integration and inter-team sharing of code that is under development, the process tends to be organized around the integration phase. This often means a significant peak in terms of work hours and overtime during the weeks or sometimes months leading up to the next release of the product.

A challenge we found was lockstep evolution. When the system or platform can only evolve in a lockstep fashion, this is often caused by evolution of one asset having unpredictable effects on other, dependent assets. In the worst case, with the increasing amount of functionality in the assets, the cycle time at which the whole system is able to iterate may easily lengthen to the point where the product or platform turns from a competitive advantage to a liability. The root cause of the problem is the selection of interface techniques that do not sufficiently decouple components from each other. APIs may expose the internal design of the component or be too detailed that many change scenarios require changes to the API as well.

Organization: The development organization has a strong tendency to concentrate all-important work to one location. Even if the organization is distributed, there is often a constant push to concentrate development and the team members in remote locations tend to travel extensively.

One problem we found was a mismatch between architectural and organizational structure. In one of the organizations, we were involved in transitioning the company from a product-centric to a product-line centric approach to software development. This requires a shared platform that is used by all business units. The organization, however, was unwilling to adjust the organizational structure and instead asked each business unit to contribute a part of the platform. Each business unit had to prioritize between its own products and contributing to the shared platform and as a consequence the platform effort suffered greatly. Although the importance of aligning the organization with the architecture has been known for decades [7] in our case studies the organizations violate this principle frequently.

Success factors: Although the integration-oriented approach has its disadvantages, as discussed above, it is the approach of choice when two preconditions are met. First, if conditions exist that require a *very deep integration between the components* of a system or a family of systems, e.g., due to severe resource constraints or challenging quality requirements, the integration-oriented approach is, de-facto, the only viable option. Second, if the *release cycle* of a system or family of systems is *long*, e.g., 12–18 months, the amount of calendar time associated with the integration phase is acceptable.

4.3.2 Release Groupings

Description: In this approach, the development organization aims to break the system into groups of components that are pre-integrated, i.e., a release group, whereas the composition of the release groups is performed using high decoupling techniques such as SOA-style (Service-Oriented-Architecture) interfaces [16]. At the level of a release group, the integration-centric approach is applied; whereas at the inter-release group level coordination of development is achieved using periodic releases of all release groups in the stack.

Architecture: In this approach, the architecture has been decomposed into its top-level components, which are aligned with the release groupings. Often, the organization has run into the limits of the previously discussed approach and has taken the action to decouple the top-level parts of the system.

In the typical scenario, the organization evolves from an integration-centric to a release groupings approach. As the organization has allowed for many dependencies between components, the management of interfaces between release groupings often is insufficient. The definition of the APIs does not sufficiently decouple release groupings from each other. APIs may expose the internal design of the release grouping or are too detailed causing many change scenarios to require changes to the APIs.

Process: Similar to the architecture, the process is now also different between the release groupings, but the same as the previously discussed approach within the release grouping. The decoupling allows the release groupings to be composed, with relatively few issues. This is often achieved by more upfront work to design and publish the interface of each release group before the start of the development cycle.

In several of the cases that we studied, the organization failed to realize that processes needed to vary between and inside release groupings. This lead to several consequences, including features that cross release groupings tend to be underspecified before the start of development and need to be "worked out" during the development by close interaction between the involved teams. This defeats the purpose of release groupings and causes significant inefficiency in development.

Organization: As discussed in the description, the allocation of release groupings often mirrors the geographical location of teams and the definition of release grouping interfaces the level of the geographical boundaries significantly decreases the amount of communication and co-ordination that needs to take place and, consequently, efficiency is improved.

In our cases, we found that working geographically distributed increases the amount of time required to accomplish tasks due to cultural differences, time zone differences and engineers need to spend more time in co-ordinating their work across the globe. Engineers have to allocate more of their time for global coordination, which makes development less efficient. Although the release groupings approach addresses this concern to some extent, we found that the coordination cost still is quite significant.

Success factors: The release grouping approach is particularly useful in situations where teams responsible for different subsets of components are *geographically dispersed* . Aligning release groupings with location is, in that case, an effective approach to decreasing the inefficiencies associated with co-ordination over sites and time zones. A second context is where the architecture covers a number of application domains that require *high integration within the application domain, but much less integration between application domains.* For instance, a system consisting of video processing and video storage functionality may require high integration between the video processing components, but a relatively simple interface between the storage on processing parts of the system. In this case, making each domain a release grouping is a good design decision.

4.3.3 Release Trains

Description: In the third approach, the decoupling is extended from groups of components to every component in the system. All interfaces between components are decoupled to the extent possible and each component team can by and large work independently during each iteration. The key coordination mechanism between the teams is an engineering heartbeat that is common for the whole R and D organization. With each iteration, e.g., every month, a release train leaves with the latest releases of all production-quality components on the train. If a team is not able to finalize development and validation of its component, the release management team does not accept the component. Once the release team has collected all components that passed the component quality gates, the next step is to build all the integrations for the software product line. For those components that did not pass the component quality gates, the last validated version is used. The integration validation phase has two stages. During the first stage, each new release of each component is validated in a configuration consisting of the last verified versions of all other components. Component that do not pass this stage are excluded from the train. During the second stage, the new versions of all components that passed the first stage are integrated with the last verified versions of all other components and integration testing is performed for each of the configurations that are part of the product family. In the case where integration problems are found during this stage, the components at fault are removed from the release train. The release train approach concludes each iteration with a validated configuration of components, even though in the process a subset of the planned features may have been withdrawn due to integration issues between components. The release trains approach provides an excellent mechanism for organizational decoupling by providing a heartbeat to the engineering system that allows teams to synchronize on a frequent basis while working independently during the iterations.

Architecture: The architecture now needs to be fully specified at the component level, including its provided, required and configuration interfaces. No dependencies between components may exist outside the interfaces of the components.

In a web service-centric architecture inside an organization, the teams associated with components develop independently while maintaining backward compatibility for their provided interfaces. This allows each team to release at the end of the development cycle and, after a, typically automated, testing effort the new component versions are released at the same time.

Process: The key process challenges, as discussed above, are the pre-development cycle work around interface specification and content commitment and the process around the acceptance or rejection of components at the end of the cycle. In addition, especially when the organization uses agile development approaches, sequencing the development of new features such that dependent, higher level features are developed in the cycle following the release of lower level features allows for significantly fewer ripple effects when components are rejected.

The release train approach allows team to work independently from each other during the development of the next release, but it still requires all teams to release at the same point in time. The process of testing the new version of components consists of two stages. First, each new version of a component is tested in the context of the released versions of all other components. This verifies backward compatibility. In the second stage, the new versions of all components are brought together to verify the newly released functionality across component boundaries.

Organization: As the need for co-ordination and communication between the teams has been reduced and is much more structured in terms of time and content, the organization can be distributed without many of the negative consequences found in the earlier approaches.

In one of the companies that we studied, this approach reduced the coordination cost quite considerably. Teams co-ordinated around the release of new versions of components to plan for the next release. However, limited centralized planning was necessary. Instead, teams co-ordinated with each other at the interface boundaries.

Success factors: The release train approach is particularly suited for organizations that are required to deliver *a continuous stream of new functionality in their products or platform*; either because new products are released with a high frequency or because existing products are released or upgraded frequently with new functionality. The organization has a business benefit from frequent releases of new functionality. Companies that provide web services provide a typical example of the latter category. Customers expect a continuous introduction of new functionality in their web services and expect a rapid turnaround on requests for new functionality. The release train approach does require a relatively *mature development organization and infrastructure*. For instance, the amount and complexity of validation and testing that is required demands a high degree of test automation. In addition, interface management and requirements allocation processes need to be mature in order to achieve sufficient decoupling, backward compatibility and independent deployment of components.

4.3.4 Independent Deployment

Description: The independent deployment approach assumes an organizational maturity that does not require an engineering heartbeat (a heartbeat in the engineering system allows teams to synchronize on a frequent basis while working independently during iterations) including all the processes surrounding a release train [18]. In this approach, each team is free to release new versions of their component at their own iteration speed. The only requirement is that the component provides backward compatibility for all components dependent on it. In addition, the teams develop and commit to roadmaps and plans. The lack of an organization-wide heartbeat does not free any team from the obligation to keep their promises. However, the validation of a component before being released is more complicated in this model as any component team, at any point in time, may decide to release its latest version.

Architecture: Similar to the release trains approach, the architecture needs to be fully specified at the component level. Architecture refactoring and evolution is becoming more complicated to co-ordinate and execute on.

In one of the cases, the business realities forced some fundamental architectural design decisions to be revoked and replaced with alternative solutions. This required the independent teams to resort to significantly more coordinated ways of working until the architecture had stabilized after several release iterations.

Process: The perception in the organization easily becomes that there no longer is an inter-team process for development as any team can develop and release at their leisure. In practice, this is caused because the process is no longer a straightjacket but more provides guardrails within which development takes place. The cultural aspects of the software development organization, especially commitment culture and never allowing deviations from backward compatibility requirements, needs to be deeply engrained and enforced appropriately.

As the process does not enforce joint releasing of components, any component team can release at their own frequency and time. This requires an even higher degree of automation and coverage of the testing framework in order to guarantee the continued functioning of the overall system.

Organization: Similar to the release trains approach, the organization can take many shapes and forms as long as the development teams associated with a component are not distributed themselves.

As the process and geographic co-location of the development organization is not longer something that one can rely on, the key organization principle is now centered on the software architecture. Co-ordination is no longer process and human-driven, but instead is performed via the software architecture. As a consequence, where as team leads and engineers talk very little to other teams, the architects in the organization typically increase their interaction to guide the evolution of the architecture.

Success factors: The independent deployment approach is particularly useful in cases where *different layers of the stack have very different "natural" iteration frequencies* . Typically, lower layers of the stack that are abstracting external infrastructure iterate at a significantly lower frequency. This is both because the release frequency of the external components typically is low, e.g. one or two releases per year, and because the functionality captured in those lower layers often is quite stable and evolves more slowly. The higher layers of the software stack, including the product-specific software, tend to iterate much more.

The key factor in the successful application of the independent deployment approach is the *maturity of the development organization*. The processes surrounding road mapping, planning, interface management and, especially, verification and validation, need to be mature and well supported by tools in order for the model to be effective.

4.3.5 Open Ecosystem

Description: The final approach discussed is an approach in which inter-organizational collaboration is strived after. Successful software product lines are likely to become platforms for external parties that aim to build their own solutions on top of the platform provided by the organization. Although this can, and should, be considered as a sign of success, the software product line typically has not been designed as a development platform and providing access to external parties without jeopardizing the qualities of the products in the product line is typically less than trivial. Even if the product line architecture has been well prepared for acting as a platform, the problem is that external developers often demand deeper access to the platform than the product line organization feels comfortable to provide.

The typical approach to address this is often twofold. First, external parties that require deep access to the platform are certified before access is given. Second, any software developed by the certified external parties needs to get validated in the context of the current version of the platform before being deployed and made accessible to customers.

Although the aforementioned approach works fine in the traditional model, modern software platforms increasingly rely on their community of users to provide solutions for market niches that the platform organization itself is unable to provide. The traditional certification approach is infeasible in this context, especially as the typical case will contain no financial incentive for the community contributor and the hurdles for offering contributions should be as low as possible. Consequently, a mechanism needs to be put in place that allows software to exist within the platform but to be sandboxed to an extent that minimizes or removes the risk of the community-offered software affecting the core problem to any significant extent.

The open ecosystem development model allows unconstrained releasing of components in the ecosystem not only by the organization owning the platform but by also by certified 3rd parties as well prosumers and other community members providing new functionality. Although few examples of this approach exist it is clear that a successful application of this approach requires run-time, automated solutions for maintaining system integrity for all different configurations in which the ecosystem is used.

Architecture: The main architectural focus when adopting this approach is to provide a platform interface that on the one hand opens up as much useful platform functionality for external developers and on the other hand provides an even higher level of quality and stability as the evolution of interfaces published to the ecosystem is very time and effort consuming as well as constraining. In addition, security precautions have to be embedded in the interface to provide the best defense mechanisms for accidental or intended harm to the customers in the ecosystem.

Especially in the case where external developers can release directly to customers without involvement of the platform company, the architecture has to be developed defensively at its external interfaces. In two of the cases that we studied, this translated into the implementation of an elaborate security model in the platform architecture to control access of external code in the platform.

Process: As the ecosystem participants are independent organizations, no common process approach can be enforced, except for gateways, such as security validation of external applications. However, each limitation put in place causes hurdles for external developers that inhibit success of the ecosystem, so one has to be very careful to rely on such mechanisms.

In one of the cases that we studied, the platform company felt obliged to introduce a certification process for externally developed code as the risk for customers was considered to be too great.

Organization: The organization in this approach is best described as a networked organization, i.e., the platform providing organization has a rather central role, but the external developers provide important parts, often the most differentiating and valuable parts of the functionality.

The key difference that the two of the cases that we studied struggled with is that the business case for the platform organization is not necessarily aligned with the business case of external developers. Although the platform company should strive to achieve this situation, there is a natural tension in terms of monetization: the platform company has to leave sufficient value in the ecosystem for external developers to have an acceptable return on investment.

Success factors: The open ecosystem model is a natural evolution from the release train and independent deployment models when the organization decides to *open up the software product line to external parties*, either in response to demands by these parties or as a strategic direction taken by the company in order to *drive adoption by its customers*.

The key in this model, however, is the ability to provide proper architectural decoupling between the various parts of the ecosystem without losing integrity from a customer perspective. In certain architectures and domains, the demand for deep integration is such that, at this point in the evolution of the domain, achieving sufficient decoupling is impossible, either because quality attributes cannot be met or because the user experience becomes unacceptable in response to dynamic, run-time composition of functionality.

Two areas where this approach is less desirable are concerned with the platform *maturity* and the *business model*. Although the pull to open up any software product line that enjoys its initial success in the market place, the product line architecture typically goes through significant refactoring that can't be hidden from the products in the product line or the external parties developing on top of the platform defined by the architecture. Consequently, any dependents on the product line architecture are going to experience significant binary breaks and changes to the platform interface. Finally, the transition from a product to a platform company easily causes conflicts in the business models associated with both approaches. If the company is not sufficiently financially established or the platform approach not *deeply ingrained in the business strategy*, adopting the open ecosystem approach fail due to internal organizational conflicts and mismatches.

4.4 Conclusion

Collaboration can be viewed as the most important lever for achieving high quality, efficient and effective software engineering practices and results in virtually any software developing organization. Although collaboration has been complicated, several trends increase the complexity of managing dependencies between software development teams and organizations. These trends include the increasing adoption of software product lines, the globalization of software engineering and the increasing use of and reliance on 3rd party developers in the context of software ecosystems. The trends share as a common characteristic that the coupling between the software assets as well as between the organizational units is increased. Consequently, decoupling mechanisms need to be introduced to address the increase in coupling.

In this paper, we have discussed the challenges of decoupling approaches for large-scale software collaboration from an architecture, process and organization perspective. From extensive action research involving several cases, we found five different approaches on a continuum ranging from low to high decoupling. We illustrated the challenges of these approaches in specific instances from the case study examples. Our experience shows that these challenges are caused due to the application of a collaboration model that is not applicable for a specific situation. In most cases that we studied, significant problems were caused by the application of a collaboration approach that did not provide sufficient decoupling and could or were addressed by the introduction of a more decoupled approach to collaboration.

The contribution of the paper is that it presents a clear overview of possible collaboration approaches for large-scale software development and their particular challenges where surprisingly little literature exists in this area. With this paper we give an insight in different decoupling approaches, their specific challenges and their success factors (applicability).

References

1. Bosch J (2000) Design and Use of Software Architectures: Adopting and Evolving a Product Line Approach, Pearson Education. London: Addison-Wesley & ACM Press.
2. Bosch J (2002) Maturity and evolution in software product lines: Approaches, artifacts and organization. Proceedings of the 2nd Software Product Line Conference (SPLC).
3. Bosch J (2004) Software architecture: The next step. Proceedings of the First European Workshop on Software Architecture (EWSA 2004), Springer LNCS.
4. Carmel E, Agarwal R (2001) Tactical approaches for alleviating distance in global software development. IEEE Software 1(2: 22–29.
5. Cascio F, Wayne S, Shurygailo S (2003) E-leadership and virtual teams. Organizational Dynamics 31(4): 362–376.
6. Clements P, Northrop L (2001) Software Product Lines: Practices and Patterns. Reading, MA: Addisson-Wesley.
7. Conway ME (1968) How do committees invent. Datamation 14(5): 28–31.
8. Herbsleb JD, Grinter RE (1999) Architectures, co-ordination and distance: Conway's law and beyond. IEEE Software 16(5): 63–70.
9. Herbsleb JD, Moitra D (2001) Global software development. IEEE Software 18(2): 16–20.

10. HOF http://www.sei.cmu.edu/productlines/plp_hof.html.
11. Kraut R, Steinfield C, Chan AP, Butler B, Hoag A (1999) Co-ordination and virtualization: The role of electronic networks and personal relationships. Organization Science 19(6): 722–740.
12. Larman C (2004) Agile and Iterative Development: A Manager's Guide. Reading, MA: Addison-Wesley.
13. Linden F van der, Bosch J, Kamsties E, Kansala K, Obbink H (2004) Software product family evaluation. Proceedings of the Third Conference Software Product Line Conference (SPLC 2004), Springer Verlag LNCS 3154, pp. 110–129.
14. Linden F van der, Schmid K, Rommes E (2007) Software Product Lines in Action: The Best Industrial Practice in Product Line Engineering. Berlin Heidelberg: Springer Verlag.
15. Messerschmitt DG, Szyperski C (2003) Software Ecosystem: Understanding an Indispensable Technology and Industry. Cambridge, MA: MIT press.
16. Newcomer E, Lomow G (2005) Understanding SOA with Web Services. Upper Saddle River, NJ: Addison Wesley.
17. Nonaka I (1994) The Knowledge Creating Company. How Japanese Companies Create the Dynamics of Innovation. New York: Oxford University Press.
18. Ommering R van (2001) Techniques for independent deployment to build product populations. Proceedings of WICSA 2001, pp. 55–64.
19. Sanwan R, Bass M, Mullick N, Paulish DJ, Kazmeier J (2006) Global Software Development Handbook. Boca Raton, FL: CRC Press.
20. Reason P, Bradbury H (2001) Handbook of Action Research. (Eds.) Thousand Oaks, CA: Sage Publishing.
21. SPLC http://www.splc.net/.
22. Tarr P, Ossher H, Harrison W, Sutton SM Jr (1999) N degrees of separation: Multi-dimensional separation of concerns. Proceedings 21st International Conference Software Engineering (ICSE'1999), IEEE Computer Society Press, pp. 107–119.
23. Yourdon E, Constantine LL (1979) Structured Design. Englewood Cliffs, NJ: Prentice-Hall.

Chapter 5
Collaboration, Communication and Co-ordination in Agile Software Development Practice

Hugh Robinson and Helen Sharp

Abstract This chapter analyses the results of a series of observational studies of agile software development teams, identifying commonalities in collaboration, co-ordination and communication activities. Pairing and customer collaboration are focussed on to illustrate the nature of collaboration and communication, as are two simple physical artefacts that emerged through analysis as being an information-rich focal point for the co-ordination of collaboration and communication activities. The analysis shows that pairing has common characteristics across all teams, while customer collaboration differs between the teams depending on the application and organisational context of development.

5.1 Introduction

Agile software development is a group of software engineering methodologies, e.g., eXtreme programming (XP) [4] Scrum [26] Crystal [11] that became popular in the early 2000s. Agile advocates claim to increase overall software developer productivity, deliver working software on time, and minimise the risk of failure in software projects. Whilst its effectiveness and applicability remain uncertain, (e.g., [1, 19]) it is attracting increasing interest from the software engineering community, (e.g., [6, 24]). A summary of what is involved in agile software development is given in this description by Cockburn [10: 29]:

> It calls for all the developers to sit in one large room, for there to be a usage expert or "customer" on the development staff full time, for the programmers to work in pairs and develop extensive unit tests for their code that can be run automatically at any time, for those tests always to run at 100% of all code that is checked in, and for code to be developed

H. Robinson (✉)
Centre for Research in Computing, The Open University, Milton Keynes, MK7 6AA, UK
e-mail: h.m.robinson@open.ac.uk

I. Mistrík et al. (eds.), *Collaborative Software Engineering*,
DOI 10.1007/978-3-642-10294-3_5, © Springer-Verlag Berlin Heidelberg 2010

in nano-increments, checked in and integrated several times a day. The result is delivered to
real users every 2–4 weeks.[1]

In exchange for all this rigor in the development process, the team is excused from producing any extraneous documentation. The requirements live as an outline on collections of
index cards, and the running project plan is on the whiteboard. The design lives in the oral
tradition among the programmers, in the unit tests, and in the oft-tidied-up code itself.

Agile software development produces working software by *technical* practice
that also creates, and depends upon, intimate *social* activity which emphasises close
collaboration, co-ordination and communication within the development team. This
chapter explores the detailed nature of this social activity and its relationship to
and embodiment in the technical practice. The analysis is based on the results of
empirical studies we have carried out with six co-located mature XP software development teams, covering a range of organisational settings, application domains
and development environments. Our approach to both data collection and analysis is ethnographically-informed [25] which results in a validated account of the
detailed collaboration, co-ordination and communication mechanisms employed
and their relationships to each other and to technical practice. The approach is not
hypothesis-driven, but data-driven.

The analysis is in two parts. First, in section 5.3, we discuss and demonstrate
how the reality of agile technical practice involves *collaborative* and *communicative* social activity. This is illustrated with consideration of two aspects of technical
activity which have key social characteristics: pairing and customer collaboration.
Second, in section 5.4, we analyse the critical work of *co-ordination* of collaborative and communicative activity via the mechanisms associated with key physical
artefacts: story cards and the Wall. As background to this analysis, we introduce XP
as a social activity (section 5.1.1), and describe the fieldwork on which the analysis
is based (section 5.2). Following on from the analysis, we discuss the significance
of our findings in Section 5.5, and end with our conclusions in Section 5.6.

5.1.1 XP as a Social Activity

XP is commonly perceived in terms of technical practice. XP articulates its technical
practice as a set of mutually supportive components – *practices* – that include, for
example, small releases, simple design, testing, refactoring, pair programming and
continuous integration. In [3] 12 practices are listed, which are refined and extended
into 13 primary practices and 11 corollary practices in [4]. Beck states that the practices interact to mutually support one other: "Any one practice doesn't stand well on
its own (with the possible exception of testing). They require the other practices to
keep them in balance." [3: 69]. Consequently, any analysis and evaluation of one of

---

[1] Time-boxed units of development lasting 1–4 weeks are called "iteration's" in XP; time-boxed
units of development around four weeks are called "sprints" in Scrum.

the XP practices has to take into account the manner in which it works in concert with other practices.

As well as being technical practice, XP is also fundamentally a social activity, with explicit values, such as communication and respect, and explicit principles, such as humanity and reflection [4]. Interviewing Beck, Highsmith observes that his "vision is about changing social contracts, changing the way people treat each other and are treated in organizations" and quotes Beck's response to an article that attempted to revise XP: "I was furious that someone would strip out all of the social change and still call it XP." [16: 53]. Beck states that: "Just as values bring purpose to practices, practices bring accountability to values." [4: 14]. Such claims by XP advocates as to the importance of social activity are sustained by several researchers, (e.g., [9, 20, 31]), and practitioners, (e.g., [11, 21]).

The reliance of software engineering practice on purposeful social activity has been recognised elsewhere, (e.g., [14, 30]), and so XP is not unique in this respect. However the detailed nature of this social activity and its relationship to and embodiment in technical practice has not been investigated and analysed. In this chapter we focus specifically on exploring and analysing XP's collaborative, communicative and co-ordinating dimensions. Our account of social activity will meet two important requirements. First, it will be an account that attends to the technical as well as the social. Second, it will be rooted in the reality of what practitioners do – XP in the wild,[2] so to speak – and that demands empirical fieldwork.

5.2 Fieldwork

Our findings represent a synthesis of results from a series of six empirical studies of software practice. Our empirical studies were all fieldwork studies of teams based in industry, engaged in software development, and using XP. Each team was mature at the time of the fieldwork; that is, they had successfully transitioned to XP[3] and had been using all of Beck's original 12 practices [3] for at least a year. Each team consisted of software developers and other team members carrying out various roles providing business, project management and specialist technical skills. The number of developers in the team varied from 23 to 5 and the overall team size varied from 7 to 26 (see Table 5.1).

For example, Team C had two business development staff and a project manager; another – Team E – had a project manager, two business analysts, a database administrator and a technical database user. The business settings of the six teams varied

---

[2] cf. Edwin Hutchins' Cognition in the Wild, MIT Press, Cambridge, MA, 1995.

[3] Transitioning to XP is a process that can take place over a weekend or can require several months, depending on a range of factors such as team size, organizational culture and team member attitude, for example.

Table 5.1 Team composition and business setting

Team	Overall team size	Number of developers	Business setting
A	12	8	Web-based intelligent adverts
B	23	16	Document use in multi-author work environments
C	26	23	Travel information web pages & alerts
D	15	12	Large international bank
E	10	5	Large international bank
F	7	5	Large telecommunications company

(see Table 5.1). Each team was physically co-located, essentially in a large, open room.

Each team was studied for a period of a week (sometimes with additional spells of observation, so that, in effect, iterations of more than a week were accommodated), with further follow-up meetings to discuss findings. An ethnographically-informed approach [25] was taken with the researcher immersing themselves in the day-to-day business of XP development, documenting practice by a variety of means that included contemporaneous field notes, photographs/sketches of the physical layout, copies of various documents and artefacts, and records of meetings, discussions and informal interviews with practitioners. Data was analysed ethnographically and thematically, emphasising validation through the seeking of confirming and disconfirming instances. The thematic, ethnographic analysis of the data was complemented with an analysis from a cognitive dimensions [15] theoretical perspective for some of the data [28]. An analysis informed by a distributed cognition theoretical perspective, based on DiCOT (Distributed Cognition for Teamwork) [5] was also employed for the data collected with three of the teams [27].

5.3 The Social in the Technical: Collaboration and Communication

The Agile Manifesto [2] emphasises collaboration and interactions, and the reality of XP software development offers evidence that this emphasis is borne out in practice. Observing practice makes it clear to the researcher that the work of an XP team visibly and continually involves collaboration and communication – and that collaboration and communication are part of the technical business of creating working software. In this section we explore and analyse this intimate relationship between the social and technical via two key XP practices which illustrate this relationship: *pairing* and *customer collaboration*. We find that pairing has considerable commonalities across the six teams, while the detail of customer collaboration varies, dependent on the team's specific situation.

5.3.1 Pairing

By *pairing* we refer to the social activity of two team members (usually developers[4]) sitting together and working. Pairing work encompasses several of the mutually supportive components of technical practice: pair programming, test-first coding, refactoring, simple design and continuous integration. That is, pairing does not just involve two programmers together writing production code: it also involves test-driven development, the refining of code structure, the removal of complexity as soon as it is discovered, and the integration of new, or changed, code into the existing code base via the 100% passing of automated tests.

The collaborative activity of pairing is dominated by communication: talk between the two programmers, as they discuss, investigate, reason, understand and develop the task at hand. Understanding is shared and affirmed (*"So, are you saying there's an AddAllocation? Yes."*)[5] and action is negotiated and carried out (*"Why don't we do the simplest thing and put in a test... that's easy to test.", "It's the simplest thing and it's compatible with refactoring."*), lack of progress is acknowledged (*"So, detecting everything else wasn't a very good idea"*) and completion signalled (*"I'll commit that!"*). Silence is also an accepted feature of the talk, as code is being run through a series of tests, when an unexpected "red bar" (failing test) is encountered or simply when thought is required.

In our fieldwork, the talks, and the talkers' roles, were fluid depending on the nature of the task, the developers involved and the progress being made. For example, an experienced developer would pair with a less-experienced colleague so that the experienced developer could gain familiarity with portions of the code base that the less-experienced colleague had been working on. Alternatively, experienced developers may pair where the portion of the code base being modified is particularly complex or the required change is tricky. In particular, contrary to claims by XP advocates, (e.g., Beck [3: 58]), there was no evidence of any clear split in roles, with one developer controlling the keyboard and mouse to produce code while the other was thinking more strategically. Rather, both developers would adopt these roles interchangeably as the talk progressed and the possession and use of the keyboard and mouse oriented to the talk (and not the other way around); this is confirmed by others and a more detailed study of this phenomenon is reported in [7]. The talk sometimes involved more than the two developers who were pairing, when someone in another pair would overhear the talk and offer their clarification or understanding (if it were part of the code base in which they had expertise). Indeed, the ability of pairs to peripherally overhear each other was taken for granted as desirable and was exploited to make progress for the team.

As well as involving developers, the talk also actively involved the code and its various manifestations in terms of the windows and panes of the many development

---

[4] We have observed pairings of a developer with a graphic designer, and a developer with a business analyst.

[5] Such italicized, bracketed material, in quotes, is an illustrative extract from our field notes.

tools employed by the developers. The conversational turns of this third partner were orchestrated by the developers as they summoned and dismissed panes, launched tools, etc. The response of the third partner could – and would – shape the talk of the developers, demanding close attention to what the code was expecting of them. The code was a central focus in the talk.

Pairing is intimate and intense at both the social and technical level and this was reflected in the developers' organisation and management of their working environment in terms of time, relationships between individuals and space. The organisation of the working day ensured that pairing did not take up much more than 5–6 hours in the day – more than this was regarded as stressful and not sustainable. Similarly, the period of pairing itself was actively managed, with recognition of the need for breaks. In all our teams, pairs would swap around regularly – anything from half a day to several days may be spent in one pair, depending on the functionality being worked on. However, framed by this organisation and management, pairing was visibly a period where developers both expected and displayed great concentration and focus.

Whilst pairing sessions themselves are intense and intimate, pairing as an ongoing activity – on a daily, week-in, week-out basis – has its own intensity that requires a level of maturity and social management from developers to accommodate inevitable clashes of programming style, attitude and personality. The development teams studied recognised this in a variety of ways. The leader of one team monitored and adjusted pairing to ensure active and effective engagement. Another team likened the individual relationships of pairing to those of marriage and sought to display all the skills of compromise, sensitivity and negotiation that this required. And another team made use of a qualified social worker to help the team understand the overall social health of its relationships. On a daily basis, many of our teams kept a record of pairings, e.g. a pairing ladder that highlighted common and uncommon pairings to make sure that rotation was evenly spread among team members.

The organisation of the space of the working environment oriented to the nature of pairing. This orientation ranged from the reconfiguration of desks for pairing to the separation of space into an area for pairing, as well as areas for activities that did not involve pairing, such as meetings, email and phone use.

Collaboration and communication occurs between pairs as well as within pairs. Apart from the exploitation of peripheral awareness mentioned above, collaboration and communication also occurs between pairs in the "stand up." The stand up is a daily meeting, taking place early in the day, before pairing begins. All developers attend and the meeting is short (no more than 15 min) – and people stand for the duration. The meeting uncovers the collaboration and communication that must take place across the developers in the coming day and initiates its co-ordination. This is achieved by each developer quickly reporting in a three-part fashion: what they've done since the last stand up that others need to know about, what they will be doing next that others need to know about, and what if any obstacles are holding them back (and that others can help with). The stand up emphasises reporting, and prolonged discussion does not take place. As a result of what is reported, various discussions will take place during the day, although rarely in the setting of another meeting.

5.3.2 Customer Collaboration

By "customer collaboration" we refer to the activity associated with the on-site customer component of XP technical practice, where the customer generates requirements, answers developers' queries and provides understanding, sets priorities, and provides feedback on iterations. Beck describes the on-site customer thus: "A real customer must sit with the team, available to answer questions, resolve disputes, and set small-scale priorities. By 'real customer' I mean someone who will really use the system when it is in production." [3: 60]. That is, in the ideal XP world of Beck's advocacy, the people filling the on-site customer role would be co-located with the developers; would "speak with one voice"; would be potential users of the system; and would be collaborative, representative, authorised, committed and knowledgeable. It is an accepted fact of XP practice that this ideal is rarely realised for a variety of reasons: client organisations may be unwilling or unable to spare people to become part of the development team; different customers may have conflicting requirements; potential users of the system may not have the authority to identify and prioritise system features, whereas decision makers may not understand the needs of users; and so on. XP practitioners have recognised this fact and devised approaches and methods to deal with the gaps between the ideal and the reality, (e.g., [22, 23, 29]). These approaches and methods are contingent upon, and are shaped by, the specific context and circumstances of the development team and who is taking the role of the "customer."

To demonstrate the nature of customer collaboration we briefly describe the collaborative and communicative activity of each of our six teams, focussing on interactions between the customer and developers.

The first setting involved a team where the on-site customer role was carried out by marketing personnel who dealt directly with individual paying clients on a regular basis. This direct involvement with the client brought great clarity and authority to the development process. However, the role of marketing personnel demanded that they respond quickly (minutes rather than hours) to requests from clients. Usually, such requests necessitated consultation (and hence considerable interaction) with developers. Much as the developers valued customer collaboration, the frequency of such interruptions proved too distracting given the demands for focus and concentration from the intensity of pairing. The solution explored was that of an "exposed pair": each day a pair of developers was identified who could be interrupted if a client had an urgent request. Such a solution could only work because of the shared understanding and responsibility created by other XP practices including pairing.

In the second of our settings, the on-site customer role was carried out by project managers who worked with marketing but were firmly part of the development team. As such, they understood both the market requirements and positioning of the company's various products and the needs of the software development that would create those products. Project managers organised a considerable amount of the detail of software development, as well as orchestrating and managing requests from marketing. They therefore managed a complex set of interactions between various groups and individuals. It was noticeable that pairing was more "interruptible" here: *ad hoc* discussions involving pairs and a project manager would naturally occur and often would involve individuals from another pair, or testers, or the team coach. Once the particular issue was resolved, pairing would resume and there was no sense that what had occurred was an "interruption." A variation of this occurred with our third setting where the team were the basis of a small software company with a flat organisational structure. Here, the on-site customer role was carried out by the handful of individuals who were management with collaboration and communication activities that were similar to those described above.

Our fourth setting concerns a team working in a large international bank, developing the software that would support the institution's management of operational risk. The management of operational risk was a new regulatory body requirement and hence the details of the institution's methodology were taking time to emerge. The on-site customer role was carried out by two individuals with expertise in the institution's methodology but it was a new area and there were sponsors and stakeholders, senior to the two individuals, who needed to finalise and agree the methodology. As a consequence, requirements were often subject to change. In addition, the on-site customer was not the intended user of the various applications, and the institution had a strong tradition of conventional, plan-driven software development with all its expectations of how sponsors, stakeholders and users interact with software developers. The on-site customer was also not co-located with the developers although relatively close and in the same building. Importantly, the on-site customer had significant responsibility for the overall success of the applications under development. All of these factors made collaboration and communication particularly demanding for both the on-site customer and the developers. Both worked actively to manage the relationship and overcome problems, and reported positively on this aspect at a retrospective. Developers proactively involved the customer at a range of opportunities, including planning meetings, seeking them out after a stand-up, and ensuring their involvement in the team's coffee breaks. Considerable effort was expended in developing a shared understanding of the risk methodology via *adhoc* meetings.

The other team in this same bank (our fifth team) were migrating a range of existing independent databases, each with their own, different schema, to one integrated database, with its own, new schema. For them, the customer role was taken by a technical database user who had many years' experience with the existing databases. He was co-located with the team, but not always available. Communication and collaboration here were complicated by the inclusion of business analysts who were creating the new database schema, and hence needed to communicate with both the customer and the developers. This required three-way communication and co-ordination and a double stand-up meeting each morning – one only for developers and one with developers, customer and business analysts. All of this was overseen by a project manager who was responsible for liaising with the offshore database administrators and the team's immediate line management.

Our final setting concerns that of a team working in a large telecommunications company. The customer (a representative of a large department who were the main stakeholder in the work) was not on-site and was located several hundreds of miles from the developers. Interaction between the customer and the developers routinely took place once a week via a telephone conference, with other calls during the week as and when queries arose. A wiki was also used to share information. Despite the customer and developers rarely meeting each other, developers reported that this arrangement worked effectively because they had worked with the system under development for several years and believed that they had a good understanding of what was likely to be acceptable to the customer and what was not.

In summary, collaboration and communication with the customer is rich and varied but also is highly situated. As such, and unlike pairing, it is difficult to identify recurring collaboration activities and communication patterns. For example, it is highly unlikely that the approach taken in our final setting would work so effectively in the situation of our fourth setting.

5.4 The Social in the Technical: Co-ordination

We now consider how these collaborative and communicative activities in XP practice are co-ordinated. Specifically, we analyse the co-ordinating role of two key physical artefacts identified through our analysis: the Wall and story cards. Figure 5.1 is an example of the Wall and two story cards from our fieldwork. The "Wall" is our term but it is a term, and a role, that practitioners readily recognised and agreed with in feedback sessions with them on our fieldwork. The Wall is an example of the Informative workspace primary practice of Beck & Andres [4]. However, Beck & Andres describe the primary practice simply in terms of "An interested observer should be able to walk into the team space and get a general idea of how the project is going in 15 seconds". They neither explicate nor advocate the key, detailed co-ordinating role of the Wall.

5.4.1 Story Cards

Stories are the key unit of communication between the customer and developers and are small units of functionality for which working code can be developed after a day or maybe two days' effort. Such fine granularity is facilitated by the identification and refinement of "epic stories" and larger chunks of functionality [12, 13]. Jeffries [18] suggests that there are three parts (the three "C"s') to a story: the Card, the Conversation and the Confirmation.

> The Card: Stories are usually written on... index cards. Cards are small, physically independent entities. Their size constrains the amount of information that can be written on it, while

Fig. 5.1 An example of the wall and story cards from one fieldwork site

its independent nature means that it can be annotated and manipulated during meetings or discussions.

The Conversation: Because the card can only hold a limited amount of information, the development team has to talk to others in order to explore the detail of the story and to refine their understanding of it.

The Confirmation: Testable and measurable user acceptance tests are agreed between the customer and the development team, so that everyone concerned understands when a story has been implemented successfully.

Each of these three parts has strong social characteristics that are significant in co-ordination: the card's independent, almost ubiquitous, nature; its role as a summons for shared understanding; and its insistence on an operational definition of completion and closure.

Stories are usually thought of as being customer-initiated and as being about customer-visible functionality. Our fieldwork revealed that stories can also be developer-initiated and be about developer-required technical change such as refactoring. Furthermore, a story is often broken down into smaller units, known as tasks. For example, in Fig. 5.1, the top card is a story card ("Show travel news headlines and details for London") and the bottom card is a task card ("Create WML travel news pages") which is one of the tasks of the story. Figure 5.1 does not show that, in fact, the top story card is green and the bottom task card is white, so that the use of different coloured cards indicates the level of granularity. The use of different coloured cards here is deliberate and a common practice amongst teams. All of the teams we studied made use of stories and all, with one exception, made use of story (index) cards. The exception was a team which had moved from the use of index cards to an electronic, Word document. This Word document permitted considerably more detail about what was required than would have been possible on an index card and also included full details of the acceptance test.

At the start of an iteration, an iteration planning meeting is held to determine which stories will be developed in the coming iteration. The cards that are being considered for the iteration[6] are often physically dealt on to the meeting table. The planning meeting is collaborative with all team members and the on-site customer being involved. Customers are asked to prioritise stories for the coming iteration, and developers ensure that they have estimated how long each story will take and that the cards are annotated with this information (such an estimate appears in the bottom left corner of the (top) story card in Fig. 5.1). Working together, the team determines how many and which stories will be included in the coming iteration. Frequently, the physical space of the meeting table and the independent nature of the cards are used to group and arrange cards to aid this process.

5.4.2 The Wall

Once the stories for the coming iteration have been determined they are taken and arranged on the Wall. The Wall may be a convenient physical wall, as in the case of Fig. 5.1, or it may be whatever is to hand. Examples from our fieldwork include the vertical front surface of a collection of filing cabinets (see Fig. 5.2), a flip chart, and a large (foldable and highly portable) piece of cardboard. That is, it matters to teams that they have a Wall and they will create one in the most difficult of settings. Even the team who held stories electronically had a cut-down version of the Wall.

The exact way in which each team arranged, and manipulated, story cards on the Wall varied and we give here a simplified, but nevertheless, essential description where the team worked in iterations of 3 weeks. The Wall is divided into three main sections, one for each week of the iteration. The section for a week is sub-divided into a "to do" area and a "done" area (see Fig. 5.3). At the start of the iteration, the team considers how the cards need to be distributed across each of the 3 weeks and carefully construct the Wall accordingly. Initially, only the "to do" area within the Wall section for each week has any cards and the "done" area is empty. Within the "to do" areas, cards are arranged so that task cards are with their associated story card.

Following the first stand up of the iteration, some cards are removed from the "to do" area of the first week – each card being taken by a pair of developers. The Wall is annotated to indicate that a card has been moved (e.g., in Fig. 5.3 by the dotted rectangle). In the case of the Wall of Fig. 5.1, a ghost of the moved card would be drawn on the glass so that the card's position on the Wall was preserved. The pair

---

[6] Software is released after a series of iterations, typically every few months. There is a layer of release planning, which helps scope out the functionality of an iteration that we have not touched on here.

Fig. 5.2 Filing cabinets used as the wall

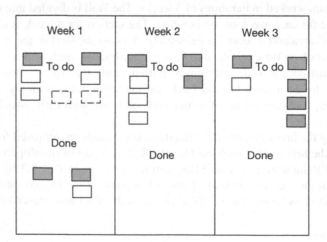

Fig. 5.3 A schematic of the wall shown in Fig. 5.1

takes the card to a workstation, stick the card to the monitor, and engage in pairing. Once they have produced tested, integrated working software, they annotate the card with their initials, the actual time taken, and a large tick to indicate that it has been completed and return the card to the Wall,[7] placing it in the "done" area for the week, erasing the annotation in the "to do" area that indicated the card was being worked on by a pair.

Daily stand ups are conducted around the Wall, with individuals often pointing at the Wall or taking cards from the Wall. By taking a card from the Wall, a developer signals that they want to speak about the card and that they are exercising a form of ownership[8] over the work it represents. During the day, developers often look at the Wall when considering progress, or the work left to be done.

At the start of the next week, the Wall is carefully studied by the team and rearranged appropriately if the team has not completed all the stories initially allocated to the week that has just finished.

This essential account makes it clear that the Wall and its associated cards are not just visible signs of progress for visitors, managers and team members, as the advocacy literature of Beck [3] or Cockburn [11] would suggest. Rather, they are an information-rich focal point for the co-ordination of collaboration and communication. The Wall and its associated story cards work in a complementary manner. The card is annotated in strict ways as it progresses through the development cycle, but the card itself represents too small a chunk of development to stand alone – it is important to see the wider overall picture of progress and activity. The Wall provides this overview, and is designed spatially to carry extra information which complements the detail shown on each card. Much of the mechanics we have described – card annotation, displaying stories on a wall, taking cards to a workstation when implementation has started, etc – are focussed on co-ordination of the team members' efforts. However the way in which this co-ordination is achieved underpins the collaborative and communicative nature of the team's work and makes it possible for such close collaboration and communication to be successful.

5.5 Discussion

In order to make technical progress, code must be implemented, and in order to make that code useful, requirements must be understood through interaction with customers. In XP, pairing supports the creation of code, and customer collaboration supports understanding requirements. These two activities are clearly technical practices, but our accounts also show the key facilitating role played by social activity.

---

[7] All actions that involve a card are carried out with a care that transcends its deceptive simplicity and informality. Indeed, one team studied had an internal wiki entry entitled "The care and feeding of story cards."

[8] Collective ownership is part of the technical practice of XP: "Anybody who sees an opportunity to add value to any portion of the code is required to do so at any time." [3: 59].

A striking difference between pairing and customer collaboration is that pairing involves repeatable patterns of collaborative and communicative activity that transcends teams and their contexts, while interaction with the customer is very rich and highly situated. In order for regular communication to take place between customers and developers, the activity of pairing needs to be interrupted, and different teams handle such interruptions differently. Teams also vary in terms of whether and how often the customer attends the daily stand-up. As others have noted, the role of customer is rarely (in our six teams – never) taken by the ideal individual and the individual circumstances of that person affects the nature of collaboration and communication. For example, how much authority the customer has in making decisions; how much knowledge of the domain the customer has; where the customer is located relative to the developers; and so on. All of these impact the nature of the collaborative and communication activities required to support technical development.

Much of the co-ordination activity supported by the Wall and the cards captures progress information rather than functional information. The Wall, supported by annotations on the story cards, is good at showing an overview of the team's progress, but it is not good at showing an overview of the structure of the code, or the functionality being offered. Instead, the functional attributes and structure of the software is communicated, evolved and kept safe through social activities such as pairing and customer collaboration as described above.

One consequence of this is that project management tools, commonly in use within the software industry, need to link into the Wall and its mechanisms for capturing progress. A tempting solution may be to digitise story cards and the Wall to enable this linkage, but software tools based around the Wall and the cards must support the facilitation, management and visibility of working activity offered by their physical counterparts rather than just produce electronic versions of these artefacts, however sophisticated (see [8] for a compelling example of such an approach to the computerisation of a workflow system in the print industry). Developments such as that of Iterex [17] are promising. The Iterex system supports the creation of story cards in accordance with Jeffries' three "C"s', the breaking down of a story into tasks, the colour coding of stories/tasks and their arrangement and their printing for use "as technology in their own right." Importantly, the system links support for story cards into the other activities of tracking iteration and release progress, visualising project velocity, scope and burn down/up and planning future releases based on past performance.

Another consequence of the Wall's focus on progress and not functionality is that the social activity underpinning the discussion, evolution and agreement of functional development and progress is crucial to effective code development.

5.6 Conclusion

The social activity we have described and analysed – the collaboration and communication of pairing and customer collaboration, and the co-ordination of the Wall and its associated story cards – brings purpose and meaning to the technical practice of XP: to pair programming, test-driven development, refactoring, simple design, continuous integration, and the on-site customer. Similarly, the technical practice makes the activities of collaboration, communication and co-ordination accountable: it is not just any ("warm and fuzzy") collaborative, communicative and co-ordinating activity that is acceptable but the detailed work, intimately connected to the technical that our analysis has revealed. The creation of working software is a socio-technical enterprise.

References

1. Abrahamsson P, Warsta J, Siponen MT, Ronkainen J (2003) New directions on agile methods: A comparative analysis. Proceeding of ICSE'03, ACM, New York, pp. 244–254.
2. Agile Manifesto http://agilemanifesto.org/, accessed 7th October 2008.
3. Beck K (2000) eXtreme Programming Explained: Embrace Change. San Francisco: Addison-Wesley.
4. Beck K, Andres C (2004) eXtreme Programming Explained: Embrace Change. San Francisco: Addison-Wesley.
5. Blandford A, Furniss D (2005) DiCoT: A methodology for applying distributed cognition to the design of team working systems. Proceedings of DSVIS'05, Springer, Berlin, Heidelberg, New York.
6. Boehm B, Turner R (2004) Balancing Agility and Discipline. Boston, MA: Addison-Wesley.
7. Bryant S, Romero P, du Boulay B (2008) Pair programming and the mysterious role of the navigator. IJHCS 66(7): 519–529.
8. Button G (2004) Changing ways of working, seminar given at the IBM Alamaden Institute, presentation available at http://www.almaden.ibm.com/institute/2004/bio/2004/index.shtml?button.
9. Chong J (2005) Social behaviours on XP and non-XP teams: A comparative study. Proceedings of Agile 2005, IEEE, Los Alamitos, pp. 39–48.
10. Cockburn A (2000) Balancing lightness with sufficiency. Cutter IT Journal 13(11): 26–33.
11. Cockburn A (2004) Crystal Clear: A Human-Powered Methodology for Small Teams. San Francisco: Addison Wesley.
12. Cohn M (2004) User Stories Applied. San Francisco: Addison-Wesley.
13. Davies R, Sharp H (2006) Early and often: Elaborating agile requirements. Cutter IT Journal 19(7): 6–11.
14. Good J, Romero P (2008) Collaborative and social aspects of software development. IJHCS 66(7): 481–483.
15. Green TRG, Petre M (1996) Usability analysis of visual programming environments: A 'cognitive dimensions' framework. Journal of Visual Languages and Computing 7: 131–174.
16. Highsmith J (2002) Agile Software Development Ecosystems. San Francisco: Addison-Wesley.
17. Iterex (2008) http://www.planningcards.com/site/, accessed 13th October 2008.
18. Jeffries R (2001) Essential XP: Card, Conversation, Confirmation, accessed 04.11.07 http://www.xprogramming.com/xpmag/EXPCardConversationConfirmation.htm.
19. Kruchten P, Adolph S (2008) Scrutinizing agile practices or shoot-out at the agile corral. Workshop at ICSE 2008, Leipzig, Germany.
20. MacKenzie A, Monk S (2004) From cards to code: How extreme programming re-embodies programming as a collective practice. CSCW 13: 91–117.
21. Mackinnon T (2003) XP – call in the social workers. In: Marchesi M, Succi G, (Eds.) Proceedings of XP2003, Lecture Notes in Computer Science, Vol. 2675. Berlin, Heidelberg, New York: Springer, pp. 288–297.

22. Martin A, Biddle R, Noble J (2004) The XP customer role in practice: Three case studies. Proceedings of the Second Agile Development Conference, Salt Lake City, Utah, June 22–26. IEEE, Los Alamitos.
23. Martin A, Noble J, Biddle R (2003) Being Jane Malkovitch: A look into the world of an XP customer. In: Marchesi M, Succi G (Eds.) Proceedings of XP2003, Lecture Notes in Computer Science, Vol. 2675. Berlin, Heidelberg, New York: Springer, pp. 234–243.
24. Paulk MC (2001) Extreme programming from a CMM perspective. IEEE Software, November/December 2001, pp. 19–26.
25. Robinson HM, Segal J, Sharp H (2007) Ethnographically-informed empirical studies of software practice. Information and Software Technology 49(6): 540–551.
26. Schwaber K, Beedle M (2002) Agile Software Development with SCRUM. Englewood Cliffs, NJ: Prentice Hall.
27. Sharp H, Robinson HM (2008) Collaboration and co-ordination in mature eXtreme programming teams. IJHCS 66: 506–518.
28. Sharp H, Robinson HM, Petre M (2009) The role of physical artefacts in agile software development: Two complementary perspectives. Interacting with Computers 21: 108–116.
29. Sharp H, Robinson HM, Segal J (2004) eXtreme programming and user-centered design: Friend or foe? Proceeding of HCI2004, Leeds.
30. Weinberg G (1998) The Psychology of Computer Programming. New York: Dorset House.
31. Whitworth E, Biddle R (2007) The social nature of Agile teams. Proceedings of Agile 2007, Washington, DC, August, IEEE, Los Alamitos, pp. 13–17.

Chapter 6
Applications of Ontologies in Collaborative Software Development

Hans-Jörg Happel, Walid Maalej, and Stefan Seedorf

Abstract Making distributed teams more efficient is one main goal of Collaborative Software Development (CSD) research. To this end, ontologies, which are models that capture a shared understanding of a specific domain, provide key benefits. Ontologies have formal, machine-interpretable semantics that allow to define semantic mappings for heterogeneous data and to infer implicit knowledge at run-time. Extending development infrastructures and software architectures with ontologies (of problem and solution domains) will address coordination and knowledge sharing challenges in activities such as documentation, requirements specification, component reuse, error handling, and test case management. The purpose of this article is to provide systematic account of how ontologies can be applied in CSD, and to describe benefits of both existing applications such as "semantic wikis" as well as visionary scenarios such as a "Software Engineering Semantic Web".

6.1 Introduction

In software engineering ontologies are playing a minor role until now, although they show similarities to conceptual models, which are broadly used in the software engineering community. An ontology captures a shared understanding of a problem domain and is usually specified in a logical language by describing concepts, relationships and additional logical axioms. Knowledge included in an ontology is designed for both humans and machines. It can be integrated in development infrastructures and in developed software to support various software project activities. One would therefore expect that ontologies are common in software engineering. But for long, ontology engineering and software engineering have been presenting two parallel communities of interest with relatively little overlap. With the

H.-J. Happel (✉)
FZI Research Center for Information Technology, 76131 Karlsruhe, Germany
e-mail: happel@fzi.de

I. Mistrík et al. (eds.), *Collaborative Software Engineering*,
DOI 10.1007/978-3-642-10294-3_6, © Springer-Verlag Berlin Heidelberg 2010

emergence of the semantic web [11], leading standardization organizations such as the World Wide Web Consortium (W3C)[1] and the Object Management Group (OMG)[2] took initiatives to better integrate both areas, by e.g., defining ontology development platforms and investigating best practices for ontology-driven software architectures. Novel applications of ontologies have been proposed, e.g., in Model-Driven Development [24] or in Service-oriented Computing [48]. While some approaches have also applied ontologies in Collaborative Software Development (CSD), a general framework, which systematically describes how ontologies can contribute to CSD does not yet exist.

CSD deals with coordinated software project activities that are characterized by a form of distance (e.g., location, organization, time or culture) between the stakeholders. Distributed development and collaboration in projects has increased in recent years, which have lead to various problems. For example, several studies have proven that distributed teams are less efficient due to lower communication bandwidth, a lack of informal contact, shared context and awareness [33]. Hence, making distributed teams more efficient is one of the main goals of CSD research. To this end, ontologies – both as conceptual and technical artifacts – provide several advantages that make them a primary candidate for addressing key CSD problems.

In the following, we give an introduction to ontologies from a Software Engineering perspective (Section 6.2). We then identify key problem areas in CSD where the application of ontologies promises advantages over traditional approaches (Section 6.3). After that we present existing ontologies and their applications (Section 6.4). In particular, we discuss how CSD can benefit from deploying so-called "semantic wikis", ontology-based development infrastructures as well as the more visionary scenario of a "Software Engineering Semantic Web". While ontology-based approaches show a huge potential for improving some long-standing problems in CSD, their large-scale applicability is partially still an open question. We will discuss effort and process steps to support CSD scenarios in practice (Section 6.5).

6.2 Foundations

The term ontology stems from the Greek nominative ov (on), which means being, and $\lambda o' \gamma o \varsigma$ (logos), which means study or science. In philosophy, ontology concerns the study of being or existence. It seeks to define and describe phenomena, properties and relations in every part of reality. Ontology is considered to be the basic subject matter of metaphysics.

In the last decades, the term ontology has been transferred into the world of computer- and information science and is gaining popularity ever since [47]. One of

---

[1] W3 Consortium, see http://www.w3.org/2001/sw/BestPractices/SE/ODA/

[2] Object Management Group, see http://www.omg.org/ontology/

the most common definitions describes an ontology as *a formal, explicit specification of shared conceptualization* [27]. Ontologies can be understood as *models* that describe sets of objects, their relationships and constraints in a domain of interest. This domain is either a part of reality or an entirely fictitious environment. The universe of objects and relationships is expressed in a declarative, formal vocabulary that collectively constitutes the knowledge about the domain [25].

Models and abstractions are not new to software engineering. Bruegge and Dutoit primarily understand software engineering as a modeling activity, where "engineers deal with complexity through modeling, by focusing at any one time on only the relevant details and ignoring anything else" [14]. Modeling has turned out to be an essential activity in several stages of a software project. For example, requirement engineers extract problem domain concepts based on interviews with customers and problem statements. Experienced developers model well proven technical solutions for particular problems as design patterns. Programmers draft complex algorithms and data structures in pseudo-code or UML models. Models are used for communication (an engineer draws a UML diagram to explain a component), documentation (technical documentation does not include source code but models) and development (Code generation based on models). In the following section we describe the main differences between ontologies, models and meta-models.

6.2.1 Ontologies vs. Models

The main difference between ontologies and models, such as entity-relationship (ER) models or UML models, is *Scope*. Whereas models are usually intended for one particular project, ontologies are targeting a much larger audience, which may bridge across several projects and organizations. In that sense, ontologies represent universally valid or widely accepted truth, i.e. knowledge, about a restricted domain. It encompasses future projects and developments including potential, possibly still unknown users. An ontology provides a domain theory and not the description of plain data structures. For example identifiers in a database are used specifically for a concrete system, while ontology resources are globally identified in the domain. The second main difference that follows from the scope is the *Open World Assumption*. In opposite to the Closed World Assumption used in common models, the absence of a particular statement within the ontology means, that the statement has not been made explicitly yet, irrespectively of whether it would be true or not, and irrespectively of whether we believe (or would believe) that it is (or would be) true or not. Other differences between ontologies and models are:

- *Expressiveness*: Languages for representing ontologies, e.g., OWL, are syntactically and semantically richer than common modeling languages, e.g., UML. [43].
- *Target*: An ontology describes the domain in a semi-structured way. An ontology includes "tagged" text in natural language and can be processed by machines and

read by humans. Common modeling languages either target humans, e.g., UML notations, or machines, e.g., SQL and domain specific languages.

- *Reasoning*: If an ontology is specified in a logical language (e.g., OWL is based on Description Logics), a reasoner can be used to derive implicitly defined knowledge. It is then possible to automatically derive a hierarchy of concepts and determine inconsistencies. This poses a significant advantage compared to standard modeling languages lacking expressiveness and formal semantics required for automated reasoning.
- *Integration and Interoperability*: Ontologies are well suited to define semantic mappings for heterogeneous data.

Meta-models are considered to be more related to ontologies [46]. However, their characteristics and goals are different [43]. Meta-models aim to improve the rigor of syntactically similar but semantically different models, while ontologies do the same for semantically similar models. In addition, without an ontology, different knowledge representations of the same domain can be incompatible even when using the same implementation meta-model . Finally, while an ontology is descriptive and primarily concerns a particular problem domain, a meta-model is generally considered to be more prescriptive and primarily concerns a solution domain.

Software engineering has always been a complex endeavour – in terms of mastering the problem domain as well as the software process itself. Not only modeling is considered as an important activity but also providing meta-information which describes the semantics of terms, data and functions. To this end, conceptual models, meta-models, and ontologies promote knowledge sharing and reuse in a human- as well as a machine-understandable manner. However, ontologies offer distinct advantages over conceptual models and meta-models [43, 23, 50]. Ontologies:

- Enable a new and effective way to reuse knowledge.
- Support a better understanding of a knowledge area.
- Separate problem domain knowledge from solution domain knowledge.
- Support an analysis of the structure of knowledge.
- Can be easily extended.
- Help in reaching a consensus on the understanding of a knowledge area.
- Share common information structure among people and systems.
- Enable a machine to use the knowledge in an application.

With respect to software engineering several advantages of ontologies can be identified. First, ontologies can be used to represent a commonly agreed vocabulary of concepts from the software engineering domain. For example, a top-level ontology for software engineering could be based on SWEBOK [7]. Keeping in mind that terms and expressions used to describe the software engineering domain are often confusing and ambiguous for both humans and machines [50], the terminology provided by an ontology adds clarity and facilitates a shared understanding. Unlike conceptual modeling languages, ontology languages allow for defining precise logical statements that describe what these concepts are, how they are related, and can be related to each other.

Ontologies do not only contribute to resolving conceptual ambiguities and creating a shared understanding among several participants. If knowledge is codified in an ontology language it becomes machine-interpretable. Thus, a reasoner can be used to infer new knowledge on both terminology and instances. In the software process, for example, ontologies enable the exchange of information between different software tools. Moreover, they could be an integral part of a software development environment, e.g., to support knowledge management. Alternatively, ontologies can also be employed in a software solution as the central part of the application logic. A thorough classification of the various applications of ontologies in software engineering can be found in [31].

6.2.2 Ontology Representation Languages

Popular ontology representation languages are RDF,[3] RDF Schema and *OWL*.[4] OWL (Web Ontology Language) is a recommendation by the World Wide Web Consortium. This specification includes the definition of three variants with different expressivity levels:

- *OWL Lite* intends to support classification hierarchies and simple constraints.
- *OWL DL* includes all OWL language constructs under some restrictions to preserve decidability.
- *OWL Full* is based on a different semantics from OWL Lite or OWL DL. There are no reasoners that support complete OWL Full reasoning.

OWL DL is often preferred [49], since it provides maximum expressivity, while retaining computational completeness, decidability and the ability of practical reasoning algorithms. All ontology languages share the following main components:

- *Classes* represent concepts, similar to types in object oriented modeling.
- *Properties* represent types of associations between concepts.
- *Axioms* represent formal sentences that are always true [27].
- *Instances* represent elementary elements or phenomena.

In RDF ontologies are represented as a set of statements in the form of subject-predicate-object expressions. The subject denotes the resource, while the predicate denotes traits or aspects of the resource and expresses a relationship between the subject and the object. For example the notion "John has the role of project

---

[3] Resource Description Framework, cf. http://www.w3.org/RDF/
[4] Web Ontology Language, cf. http://www.w3.org/2004/OWL/

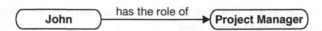

Fig. 6.1 Subject-predicate-object expression

manager" is represented as a triple with the subject "John", the predicate "has the role of" and the object "Project Manager" (Fig. 6.1).

Ontology engineering is supported by a wide range of different tools, covering aspects such as ontology editing, mapping, learning or reasoning [26]. Many of these tools – such as the well-known ontology editor Protégé[5] – are geared towards the creation and maintenance of so-called *heavyweight* ontologies, which are used to model complex domains such as medicine or biology. On the other hand, many web-based applications are based on so-called *lightweight* ontologies which can be created or maintained by end-users in a collaborative fashion.

6.2.3 Semantic Web

With the emergence of the *Semantic Web* vision in 2001 [11] ontologies have been attracting much more visibility both in academia and industry. According to W3C the Semantic Web is about two things: It is about common formats for integration and combination of data drawn from diverse sources, while the original Web mainly concentrated on the interchange of documents. It is also about a language for recording how the data relates to real world objects. That allows a person, or a machine, to start off in one database, and then move through a continuous set of databases which are connected not by wires but by being about the same thing. The Semantic Web effort provides standards and technologies for the definition and exchange of metadata and ontologies. Available standard proposals provide ways to define the syntax (RDF) and semantics of metadata based on ontologies (OWL). There is an ongoing research covering privacy and security issues.

6.3 Uses of Ontologies in CSD

The software engineering community has dealt with various aspects of collaboration. In the earlier days, when programs became more complex, issues of manpower and project coordination have been raised and discussed in order to meet quality, resource and time contracts in large projects. Later researchers studied formal and informal communication mechanisms in software projects to understand how development teams work [35]. Recent years have further stressed these issues, driven by an increasing *distribution* of software development endeavors.

---

[5] Protégé: http://protege.stanford.edu/

According to Merriam-Webster, *collaboration* means to work jointly together with others. In software projects collaboration may have different dimensions:

- Collaboration takes place among various *roles*, e.g., users, developers or testers.
- Collaboration *nature* ranges from tightly interwoven to loosely coupled.
- Collaboration *time* may be asynchronous (as in teams spanning time-zones) or highly synchronous (as in pair programming).
- Collaboration *purpose* might be required, optional, anticipated or unforeseen.

There are two main functions of collaborative work: *coordination* and *knowledge sharing*. Both rely on *communication* as a fundamental building block. Coordination describes the most crucial and fundamental functions of collaborative work. The need for coordination typically stems from dependencies among tasks, which require different persons to coordinate towards a common goal or a product [42]. A typical coordination problem in software development is the limited awareness of other's work [44]. Knowledge sharing denotes the dual problem of searching for (looking for and identifying) and transferring (moving and incorporating) knowledge across organization subunits [28]. Knowledge sharing needs are usually not explicit, but defined by the gap between the background of individual developers. Personalization and codification are the core strategies for knowledge sharing [19]. The personalization strategy primarily relies on personal communication to share tacit knowledge, which only exists in the "heads" of individuals [19]. In turn, the codification strategy targets explicit knowledge, which is captured in documents. In the following we give a systematic overview on uses of ontologies in CSD. We discuss advantages of ontologies for supporting coordination and knowledge sharing. Then we describe several *to-be* scenarios from the daily development work.

6.3.1 Coordination

Awareness Creation: Finding the right balance between information overload and a lack of awareness is a challenge in today's software projects. Ontologies can enable a more precise and efficient collaboration by including semantic annotations in both system (e.g., test-case) as well as collaboration (e.g., email) artifacts. Interest groups can be dynamically built by linking semantically annotated content to ontology-based stake-holder profiles. Information is then shared precisely to stakeholders (in a pull or push mode) depending on their interests. This will increase the effectivity and efficiency of awareness creation measures and decrease the overwhelming amount of communication and information overload, e.g., by sending every information to a large static mailing-list [40].

Tool-Integration: Different project stakeholders use different tools, they are familiar with. These tools use proprietary standards and models for managing information. The same information object can be, e.g., called "issue", "bug", "bug report", or "change request" in different tools. Ontologies facilitate the integration of heterogeneous information and tools, in a syntactic (unified referencing, unified property mapping) and semantic (synonyms, composites, specialization) manner.

Agility Support: A major challenge of today's software projects is to increase teams' flexibility to deal with frequent changes in requirements and design, while coping with coordination issues resulting from increased size and distribution of projects. Due to their extensibility and support of the open world assumption, ontologies supports project stakeholders to deal with change, if they are used to manage project information. Ontologies also support advanced querying mechanism, which enables the generation of check lists – a popular tool in agile teams. In a project with frequent changes and releases, development-, test- and integration-checklists, release notes as well as management reports (all inherently dependent of different participants) can be automatically extracted if the corresponding information is semantically rich. Participants can publish and register for information they require, like RSS feeds. A query like "list manual tests that need to be conducted for the next release" can be supplied by selecting fixed issues, affected components and requirements and then retrieving related tests [40].

6.3.2 Knowledge Sharing

Research indicates that the absence of awareness about the existence of certain knowledge (information access) and the low level of experience sharing (information provision) are major blockers for knowledge sharing, especially in distributed settings [20]. Given the existence of large amounts of reusable artifacts like specifications, source code or binaries – in both corporate repositories and the Internet – there is a large potential to improve the software development efficiency.

Information Access: The creation of large-scale information reposi-tories, such as the Internet or corporate intranets has brought a large amount of information for developers. However, due to constraints in time and mental capacity, it is hard for humans to find information suitable for solving a given task. Thus, information systems, which provide an intelligent information retrieval are desirable in CSD [17]. Ontologies can facilitate information access for software developers due to inclusion of semantics, reasoning ability as well as support for powerful querying constraints, as Witte et al. illustrate for the case of software maintenance [51].

Information Provision: Even if large repositories are a good starting point for supplying developers' information need, information provision plays a major role in increasing the effectivity and efficiency in CSD. Developers often avoid documentation effort or do not address differences in background knowledge – especially when providing information to distant team members. Examples are the rationale behind certain decisions or experience sharing, such as the steps followed to fix a particular bug. Ontologies can help to explicitly capture contextual information (such as the system configuration when a bug occurred) and give developers a more precise, unambiguous vocabulary to express certain information. Furthermore, certain contextual clues can be automatically derived from software artifacts by using information extraction methods [13].

6.3.3 Development

The use of ontologies brings several benefits to the various activities and roles involved in a software project.

Requirements Specification: Since software engineers are often no domain experts, they need to learn about the problem domain from the customers. A different understanding of the domain may lead to an incorrect and incomplete implementation. Gaining a shared understanding of the problem domain is particularly challenging in multi-site development, where informal communication between the participants is much harder to achieve [45]. To this end, ontologies can be used for the formal and unambiguous specification of requirements [37, 52]. Particularly concepts, relations and business rules of the domain model can be expressed in ontologies with varying degrees of formalization and precision.

Artifact Tracing: Project stakeholders consume and produce different artifact types, using different vocabularies and languages. However, the information in these artifacts is highly interlinked. On the one hand, technical concepts are referenced in user manuals and managerial reports. On the other hand, domain concepts are traced in design documents and source code documentation. Collaborating on creating and maintaining project documentation is a non-trivial task due to the various backgrounds of participants. A key problem is that traceability between artifacts is usually not sufficiently maintained. This becomes even more complex when project participants are distributed, and the content creation context is not shared. Ontologies can serve as a shared foundation for referencing, reusing and localizing information in projects with a high degree of collaboration. They are well suited for describing the semantic relationships between heterogeneous information resources, including text documentation, email, notes, models and code. Ontologies can furthermore be used for representing automatically recovered traceability information during maintenance [55].

Component Reuse: Component documentation, if it exists, is insufficient to describe all ways to reuse a component. Correct component integration, effective work with powerful frameworks or successful usage of design patterns requires significant background knowledge and experience about concerned components. Such knowledge is scattered across different sources such as emails, forums, specifications or bug reports, especially in open source development. Ontologies can be applied to addressing the component retrieval as well as the integration issues. First, they enable to join information which normally resides isolated in separate information sources. For example, format mappings can be defined to automatically create a knowledge base from component descriptions, which minimizes the extra modeling effort [29]. Second, ontologies may provide additional background knowledge (e.g., about the properties of a certain software license) that enables non-experts to query from their point of view (ask for a license that allows to modify source code).

Error Handling: Error handling is a highly collaborative endeavor. It is difficult to define the exact scope and detail of an issue when it is reported for the first time. In the case of semantically rich errors such as unexpected system behaviors or runtime errors, the state of the practice is to 'google' for error message excerpts or keywords describing the context, in order to find relevant hints how to handle that error. It is, e.g., useful to find out where other developers looked for help while having similar problems. Thereby a main issue arises from the different contexts between the developer who seeks for help, and the developer who provides knowledge about the error situation. Typically these situations are never identical, resulting in a "context gap". Ontologies can mediate between the different contexts of developers handling errors, since typically these situations are never completely identical.

Test Specification: Software tests represent an essential quality assurance measure. However, writing test cases is expensive and does no directly yield business value. The derivation of a "suitable" test case demands both problem and solution domain knowledge, which can be included in ontologies in a machine processable format. Basic test cases can therefore be generated. A simple example for this would be regarding cardinality constraints. Since those constraints define restrictions on the association of certain classes, they can be used to derive equivalence classes for testing. Formalisms like OCL that are specialized for such tasks already exist. However, ontologies decrease the ambiguity of different used vocabularies and can link to other project and domain-related information. Thus, testers – who are usually not as involved in the problem domain as the developers – can more easily understand initial business requirements and derive suitable test cases.

6.4 Ontology-Based Tools in CSD

We introduce existing ontologies and discuss three ontology-based infrastructures for collaboration tasks: "semantic" wikis, semantic development environments and the more visionary scenario of a "Software Engineering Semantic Web".

6.4.1 Ontologies

Ontologies have recently been applied for various Software Engineering tasks [31]. In this section, we describe selected ontologies which target collaborative software development and tightly related issues.

6.4.1.1 Collaboration Ontologies

We briefly introduce a number of standard ontologies, which describe human agents and their interactions. These describe general collaboration entities and form "building blocks" for reuse by other ontologies.

FOAF: The "mother" of all Semantic Web ontologies is the "Friend-of-a-friend" vocabulary ("FOAF") [1, 21, 2]. FOAF was created as one of the first application examples of the Semantic Web and has been heavily reused by other ontologies. In essence, the FOAF vocabulary allows to resemble social networks in a decentralized manner. Therefore, every user creates his or her own FOAF profile, which specifies basic personal information (such as address or employer) and allows to draw "knows" relations to other persons. Once joined, all these little pieces of semantic data allow to form a network of relationships among the individual persons. As simple as the initial idea, the FOAF specification [2] is small, defining only basic concepts such as Person, Group or Organization as well as various properties of these entities such as name, knows, workplaceHomepage. The following listing shows a snippet of FOAF data.

```
<rdf:RDF
  xmlns:rdf="http://www.w3.org/1999/02/22-rdf-syntax-ns#"
  xmlns:rdfs="http://www.w3.org/2000/01/rdf-schema#"
  xmlns:foaf="http://xmlns.com/foaf/0.1/">
<foaf:PersonalProfileDocument rdf:about="">
  <foaf:maker rdf:resource="#me"/>
  <foaf:primaryTopic rdf:resource="#me"/>
  <admin:generatorAgent rdf:resource="http://www.ldodds.com/foaf/foaf-a-matic"/>
</foaf:PersonalProfileDocument>
<foaf:Person rdf:ID="me">
  <foaf:name>Hans-Joerg Happel</foaf:name>
  <foaf:depiction rdf:resource="http://www.hjhappel.de/images/site/hj.jpg"/>
  <foaf:phone rdf:resource="tel:+49-(0)-721-9654-814"/>
  <foaf:workplaceHomepage
  rdf:resource="http://www.fzi.de/ipe/eng/mitarbeiter.php?id=418"/>
  <foaf:knows>
    <foaf:Person>
      <foaf:name>Walid Maalej</foaf:name>
      <foaf:mbox
      rdf:resource="mailto:maalejw@in.tum.de"/></foaf:Person></foaf:knows>
  <foaf:knows>
    <foaf:Person>
      <foaf:name>Stefan Seedorf</foaf:name>
      <foaf:mbox rdf:resource="mailto:seedorf@uni-mannheim.de"/>
    </foaf:Person></foaf:knows>
</foaf:Person>
</rdf:RDF>
```

SIOC: While FOAF has its merits as a pioneering work and a ground vocabulary for persons and organizations, it lacks more sophisticated concepts such as roles and concepts for further interactions and specific domains. One particular extension of this kind is the vocabulary for "Semantically-Interlinked Online Communities" (SIOC) [3, 6, 5]. SIOC extends FOAF and adds concepts and properties to describe interactions and content in online communities such as message boards, wikis and weblogs. Figure. 6.2 depicts example concepts such as Forum, Item, Role, Space and Thread. The vocabulary allows site owners and tool providers to semantically annotate their content and thus exchange and join data across different sites.

6.4.1.2 Software Development Ontologies

While maintaining software and handling errors, several kinds of related information exist without an explicit connection. This is problematic since a unified

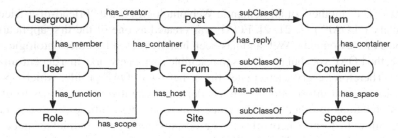

Fig. 6.2 General overview of SIOC [5]

view could avoid redundant work and speed up problem solving. A bug resolution process for example usually involves the discovery and reporting of a bug (often into a bug tracking system), subsequent discussion inside a developer group, and finally changes in the code that resolve the bug. While the discussion on the mailing list and the code changes are clearly triggered by the bug report, their relation is not explicit and often kept separately. Since it is difficult to manage larger amounts of bugs without all existing context information, the lack of tool support lead to delays in bug fixing and duplicate work or discussions.

Dhruv: Dhruv [8, 9] is a semantic-web enabled tool which aims to assist the software maintenance/bug resolution process, by recommending relevant information during bug inspection. Therefore, Dhruv is integrated in a web-based bug tracking system and displays recommendations in a special sidebar. Recommendations may involve source code files, mailinglist discussions or similar bug reports (c.f. Fig. 6.3). Dhruv does not operate on a special user profile. The context for recommendation is always the bug report for which related information is retrieved. This information is included automatically when creating the report page.

DOAP: The "Description of a Project" ontology (DOAP [22]) extends the FOAF ontology to describe software projects. Core concept is the software project with various properties such as category, license and bug tracking URL. Making this information available in a standardized way provides several benefits. Dameron

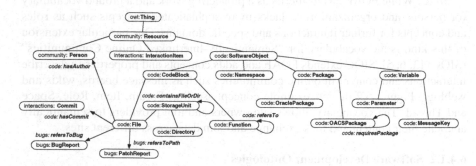

Fig. 6.3 Basic concepts of the Dhruv ontology [8]

describes how to automatically update the Protégé ontology editor and its plug-ins [18]. The author uses an extension of the DOAP ontology and a python script that retrieves the most recent version number and a download URL by calling a web service that does reasoning. The basic advantage of an RDF-based solution in contrast to e.g., describing the download information in XML is exten-sibility. Using an XML schema, all plug-in providers must provide their data in the specified format. In order to stay compatible to the update script, changes would have to be done centrally and distributed to all plugin providers. Using an RDF ontology, every provider is free to add or subclass concepts from the initial version without being at risk to become incompatible.

6.4.2 Semantic Wikis

Wikis are easy to use, web-based tools for collaborative knowledge acquisition and sharing. The first wiki, initiated by Ward Cunningham in 1995, served as a distributed knowledge repository for design patterns. Since then, software engineering remains an important application domain for wikis [38]. Wikis are used by Open Source communities and by enterprises such as SAP, Novell, and Yahoo for purposes as diverse as knowledge transfer, technical documentation, quality and process management, release planning, and error tracing [10, 41, 4].

However, for specific, well-structured content, traditional wikis often reach their limits with their core functionality. While the content of a wiki page might provide structure and meaning to a human reader, it does not possess any machine-interpretable semantics. These limits are best described by an example: In a software project, one wiki page is mantained for every entity, e.g., a stakeholder, a use case, or a software component. The hyperlinks between pages then describe relationships between entities. For example, a component will realize one or more use cases. However, the meaning of the hyperlink remains implicit and can only be interpreted by humans, but not by the wiki engine itself. Also, the type an entity (or page) is not specified in a traditional wiki. Thus the set of all *use cases* and all *components* cannot be automatically derived.

The lack of structure in traditional wikis is tackled by a completely new class – so-called *Semantic Wikis*. They allow to impose a knowledge model (i.e., ontology) onto previously unstructured page content. In a semantic wiki, the embodied knowledge can be structured by annotating pages and hyperlinks with types. In our example, all pages describing a use case are of the type *Use Case* which is also an ontology concept (see Fig. 6.4). Similarly the hyperlinks between the pages will carry a semantic meaning in many cases. The link between *Component X* and *Use Case 1* describes the relation *realizes*. Likewise the links between *Stakeholder S* and *Use Case 1* and *Use Case 2* describe the relation *participatesIn*.

Semantic wikis provide various advantages for software projects. First, they enable an incremental formalization of underlying knowledge across various software engineering activities. Unlike a development or a collaboration infrastructure with a fixed scheme (e.g., a bug repository), semantic wikis support both the

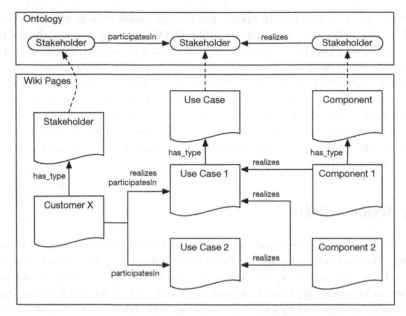

Fig. 6.4 Pages and hyperlinks in a semantic wiki correspond to ontology concepts and properties

evolution of content and schema. Furthermore, by adding semantic meaning to pages and grounding it in the ontology, the wiki content becomes machine-interpretable and can be enriched with further background knowledge. For example, the question *Which stakeholders use component X?* can be now formulated as a semantic query and automatically answered by the wiki engine. Thus, semantic linking capabilities enable a better traceability between different software engineering entities [40].

Prototypes of semantic wikis have been realized in a number of projects, either by implementing a completely new wiki engine or by extending an existing one. Although the core idea of all semantic wikis is to provide a machine-processable knowledge model described in the wiki pages, they vastly differ in terms of required user experience and knowledge representation languages. For example, the Semantic MediaWiki project adds some extra syntax for the semantic annotations to the wiki markup language [36]. It therefore realizes an open approach where a user can optionally add semantic markup. In other approaches, every page is interpreted as an entity so that the wiki's semantics are defined in a more rigorous style [32].

6.4.3 Semantic Development Environments

Integrated development environments (IDEs) have become powerful tool suites to support developers work. However, several authors have noted, that state-of-the-art IDEs – while well supporting individual developers' tasks – neglect the collaborative nature of software development [16]. A number of recent tools and scientific prototypes has addressed this issue. The IBM Jazz toolsuite [16] addresses the collaboration needs by integrating communication and awareness functionalities into the development environment. Integrating collaboration brings the payoff of reduced friction in the development process, a greater sense of context, and immediate traceability between collaboration artifacts and system artifacts. A similar approach presented by Bruegge et al. is focussing on the modeling activities of software engineering [15]. The Mylyn Eclipse plugin [34] addresses the problem of information overload faced by developers in a single development environment. The core idea is, that not all classes in large software projects are relevant for working on a given task. Thus, mylyn identifies and hides or blurs classes which are less relevant. Mylyn assumes that developers are sequentially working on fine-grained tasks (e.g., fixing a bug), which affect only a subset of source code files. It maintains a simple model, assigning each source code file a "degree-of-interest" value in a given task context which is calculated from the previous modifications of a particular code elements. Mylyn allows developers to share their task context, which helps to reproduce the working context.

However, these approaches lack a deeper understanding of developer's actual activities. Jazz for instance offers several collaboration services, but maintains no internal model about actual collaboration needs and opportunities. Similarly, mylyn has no deep understanding of the semantics of developer's interactions, but aggregates all interactions into a single "degree-of-interest" value.

Thus, while already useful, these approaches only partially ease the mental burden of developers. As Zeller lined out [54], IDEs bear large potential for automated support in tasks which machines can do better than human developers. Examples for such tasks are the creation of developers' work logs, awareness about other developers' activities in distributed development, management of dependent libraries or navigating information in complex projects [30].

Two major building blocks are required to support such scenarios. First, IDEs need a more precise understanding of developers' activities (e.g., developing vs. debugging), semantics of a code change (e.g., changing an interface vs. changing its implementation), interdependencies between different software artifacts and the organizational structure of a development team. Parts of these issues are already addressed by ontologies mentioned in Section 6.4.

The actual interpretation and data creation has to be carried out by developer observation frameworks, which record the actions of a developer and infer higher level activities. While mylyn can be seen as a low-level developer observation component that allows to derive a very particular piece of information (artifacts related to a task), the TeamWeaver project[6] realizes a more generic and extensible framework with an implementation for the Eclipse IDE [39].

With these two building blocks, IDEs can become not just "collaboration-aware", but even "context-aware". A concrete example is context-aware recommendation, which proactively provides developers with pieces of information (e.g., about the

---

[6] http://www.teamweaver.org

new version of a component or a bug fix) when they need it. In existing software engineering recommendation systems such as CodeBroker [53] or Hipkat [17] recommendations have to be triggered by the user and are thus *not proactive*, since these approaches are based on a simplified model of developers' actions.

Ontologies can contribute to the realization of intelligent, context-aware development environments by providing a backbone model for describing meaningful entities and activities from the development domain. Filled by observation tools, this semantic information can be applied to support developers in tasks, which machines can do better than human developers.

6.4.4 Software Engineering Semantic Web

The idea of a "Software Engineering Semantic Web" takes several concepts from semantic development environments further into a web-scale environment. One core premise of CSD is the fact, that major systems can not be built "from scratch" by a single organizational entity. Systems of reasonable size and complexity build upon powerful platforms, reuse existing libraries and have to interact with the "outside world". Accordingly, developing and maintaining these systems implies coordination activities with various actors. Coordination tasks can span the awareness of other developers' activities, the observation of new releases and problems in used libraries or the negotiation of system requirements. While such activities can not be totally avoided in a complex development ecosystem, we argue that the coordination activities as such can be supported in a much better and deeper way. For example, a developer monitoring the release status of an external library needs to find out the exact name and version of the library used, locate information about the release status (e.g., on a project webpage) and then monitor the status of this library (e.g., by reading a mailing list). Thus, developers are forced to carry out a lot of tedious "micro-level" activities which serve towards fulfilling an actual development goal.

The vision of the "plain" Semantic Web (Section 6.2.3) is driven by a very similar observation. As in our developer's example, people have to deal with lots of information in their daily life. Scheduling a doctors appointment involves drawing information from various sources, selecting a suitable doctor (e.g., based on geographical and/or administrative preferences) and finally negotiating a suitable date from both parties' calendar [11]. Again, people are burdened with a number of little nasty tasks to carry out a rather simple activity. The Semantic Web assumes that in many of such situations, electronic information already exists, which could be the basis for computer-based support. However, this information is typically created and stored by different actors in a decentralized way – and thus heterogeneous and often not machine-readable. The Semantic Web provides means (including standards and according tools) to allows these actors to formally annotate their data, such that agents can interpret it to carry out certain tasks. An important aspect is, that the formal ontology languages for the Semantic Web do not enforce homogeneity, but instead provide means for data mapping and integration. A Software Engineering Semantic Web is a Web, in which agents fulfill useful development tasks based on semantically enriched data. We argue that software engineering is an adequate domain for this vision, since knowledge in software projects is typically scattered across various people, systems, formats and spaces. Especially in large projects, development information is distributed and heterogeneous. This is, a.o. due to reusing libraries and frameworks, which are provided by other organizations.

The Software Engineering Semantic Web has not yet been realized. In the following we sketch a possible realization based on various roles and actors involved and reference initial building blocks.

We start with *components providers*, whose libraries and frameworks are used for building larger applications. These actors typically offer additional services to the actual software, such as notifications about updates, security issues or code examples. This project data is often available in a structured or semi-structured format. Projects hosted at large Open Source development portals such as SourceForge offer various kinds of information, e.g., about software releases or bugs. Commercial vendors also have same information in their "hidden web" of intranets and company networks. This structured data can be easily exposed in a semantic way [12], and already several platforms have adopted this practice.[7] Open Source projects would profit from this practice since the availability of "clean" project information is an important criterion for trust in a project and its success. For commercial providers, offering structured, machine-interpretable data streams could be an additional service which generates additional revenue.

Second, information provision and collaboration aspects have long been neglected [16] from *tool developers*. One reason is the heterogenity of such data, which makes it hard to integrate it into tool workflows. However, extending tools to consume and produce semantic data (c.f. Section 6.4.3) can give them a competetive advantage. First, the easy integration of relevant external information helps to make developers more productive and causes less interruptions. Second, semantic interoperability improves the tool-spanning workflow of developing artifacts and thus eases the integration of the overall development landscape.

Finally, *application developers* will benefit from improvements in their development environment. Time-consuming tasks will be simplified and novel, advanced development scenarios will possible to support (c.f. Section 6.3). Semantically-empowered IDE's can blend relevant external information into the current context of a developer. This includes data from the project's own development sever, status notifications of remote co-workers or new versions of depending libraries. Developers can thus get a much more precise and complete overview of information related to their current task. Developers can also benefit from additional features such as an easy sharing and access to others' development experiences or consistency checks – e.g., concerning license compatibility, bugs or security issues.

---

[7] see e.g. http://doapspace.org/

While some of these applications are promising, the realization of a Software Engineering Semantic Web depends on three major factors: the existence of semantic metadata, the existence of suitable ontologies and finally the existence of powerful tools for leveraging this data to provide new services. Formal metadata is already widely available due to the large amount of structured and semi-structured data in software development. Publishing this data in a semantically meaningful way thus primarily requires suitable ontologies and mappings between the different sources.

Creating these ontologies does not have to be difficult. In many cases it is sufficient to transform existing metadata schemas in a suitable ontology representation. Further steps as integrating and mapping heterogeneous schemas can then be adressed by various means. Tool-vendors or interested parties can build and offer baseline ontologies. First examples are already available as described in Section 6.4 or under development such as the Baetle project[8] covering issue tracking data.

It seems as if tools are still the major bottleneck for a Software Engineering Semantic Web. So far, only research prototypes embrace semantic metadata in a large way, while state-of-the-art development tools are not yet adopting it. However, the increasing maturity of the Semantic Web tool landscape and the huge potential of easily available metadata in the software engineering domain make us confident that tool vendors will integrate according features in their programs.

The Software Engineering Semantic Web enables scenarios described in Section 6.3, which cannot be realized simply by a semantic wiki or a semantic development environment. A Software Engineering Semantic Web is nothing more than an interconnection of distributed semantic development infrastructures and tools. These tools are clients for consuming semantic data and realizing appropriate assistance functionality, but they also support developers in sharing information into a Software Engineering Semantic Web. While it may take time to let this vision appear in a large scale, we believe that an increasing number of actors in software development ecosystems will embrace semantic metadata.

6.5 Conclusion

In this chapter, we provided an introduction into knowledge representation with ontologies and existing as well as visionary applications in CSD. Since CSD is much about managing implicit and explicit dependencies among developers and development artifacts, the semantic expressivity of ontologies adds key benefits to existing work practices.

Although ontologies have been around for many years, several factors promote their increasing adoption. First, with a number of W3C standards such as RDF and OWL issued in recent times, tools and methodologies for creating and managing ontologies have matured. Second, the success of the Web enables developers

---

[8] http://code.google.com/projects/baetle

to collaborate in a richer and more dynamic way, instead of working in de facto isolation.

Both factors contribute to a slow but growing number of semantic approaches addressing CSD issues. However, we have to keep in mind that the creation and maintenance of ontologies is a challenge of its own, which needs to be justified by efficiency gains. Proving such efficiency gains is sort of "a chicken/egg problem", since the success of several visionary scenarios depends on their adoption. What is clear, is that there will not be a single "CSD-ontology" satisfying all needs. Applications of ontologies in software development can be manifold and so the resulting ontologies will differ in expressivity, scope and purpose.

References

1. The friend of a friend (foaf) project (2007) URL http://www.foaf-project.org/.
2. Foaf vocabulary specification (2007) URL http://xmlns.com/foaf/spec/.
3. Semantically-interlinked online communities (sioc) ontology submission request to w3c (2007) URL http://www.w3.org/Submission/2007/02/.
4. Twiki success stories (2007) URL http://twiki.org/cgi-bin/view/Main/TWikiSuccessStories.
5. Sioc core ontology specification (2008) URL http://rdfs.org/sioc/spec/.
6. The sioc project (2008) URL http://sioc-project.org/.
7. Abran A, Moore J, Bourque P, DuPuis R, Tripp L (2004) Guide to the software engineering body of knowledge-2004. IEEE-CS-Professional Practices Committee.
8. Ankolekar A (2005) Towards a semantic web of community, content and interations. Ph.D. thesis, School of Computer Science, Carnegie Mellon University.
9. Ankolekar A, Sycara K, Herbsleb J, Kraut R, Welty C (2006) Supporting online problem solving communities with the semantic web. WWW'06. ACM, NY, USA.
10. Bachmann F, Merson P (2005) Experience using the web-based tool wiki for architecture documentation. Technical Note CMU.
11. Berners-Lee T, Hendler J, Lassila O (2001) The semantic web. Scientific American, May, pp. 35–43.
12. Bizer C, Cyganiak R (2006) D2r server-publishing relational databases on the semantic web (poster). International Semantic Web Conference.
13. Bontcheva K, Sabou M (2006) Learning ontologies from software artifacts: Exploring and combining multiple sources. Workshop on Semantic Web Enabled Software Engineering, GA, USA.
14. Bruegge B, Dutoit AH (2003) Object-Oriented Software Engineering: Using UML, Patterns and Java, 2nd edn. Englewood Cliffs, NJ: Prentice Hall.
15. Bruegge B, Dutoit AH, Wolf T (2006) Sysiphus: Enabling informal collaboration in global software development. International Conference on Global Software Engineering. IEEE CS, Washington, DC, USA.
16. Cheng LT, De Souza CR, Hupfer S, Patterson J, Ross S (2004) Building collaboration into ides. Queue 1(9): 40–50.
17. Cubranic D, Murphy GC, Singer J, Booth KS (2005) Hipikat: A project memory for software development. IEEE Transactions on Software Engineering 31(6): 446–465.
18. Dameron O (2005) Keeping modular and platform-independent software up-to-date: Benefits from the semantic web. 8th International Protégé Conference, Stanford Medical Informatics, Stanford University, USA.
19. Davenport T, Prusak L (1998) Working Knowledge. Boston, MA: Harvard Business School Press.

20. Desouza KC, Awazu Y, Tiwana A (2006) Four dynamics for bringing use back into software reuse. Communications of the ACM 49(1): 97–100.
21. Dumbill E (2002) Finding friends with xml and rdf. URL http://www.ibm.com/developerworks/xml/library/x-foaf.html.
22. Dumbill E (2004) Describe open source projects with xml. URL http://www128.ibm.com/developerworks/xml/library/x-osproj.html.
23. Noy FN, McGuiness DL (2001) Ontology development 101: A guide to creating your first ontology. Online. URL http://www.ksl.stanford.edu/people/dlm/papers/ontology101/ontology101-noymcguinness.html.
24. Gasevic D, Djuric D, Devedic V (2006) Model Driven Architecture and Ontology Development, 1st edn. Berlin: Springer.
25. Genesereth MR, Nilsson NJ (1987) Logical foundations of artificial intelligence. San Francisco, CA: Morgan Kaufmann Publishers Inc.
26. Gomez-Perez A, Corcho-Garcia O, Fernandez-Lopez M (2003) Ontological Engineering. Secaucus, NJ: Springer-Verlag New York, Inc.
27. Gruber TR (1993) A translation approach to portable ontology specifications. Knowledge Acquisition 5(2): 199–220.
28. Hansen MT (1999) The search-transfer problem: The role of weak ties in sharing knowledge across organization subunits. Administrative Science Quarterly 44: 82–111.
29. Happel HJ, Korthaus A, Seedorf S, Tomczyk P (2006) Kontor: An ontology-enabled approach to software reuse. 18th International Conference on Software Engineering and Knowledge Engineering. San Francisco, CA, USA.
30. Happel HJ, Maalej W (2008) Potentials and challenges of recommendation systems for software development. International Workshop on Recommendation Systems for Software Engineering. ACM.
31. Happel HJ, Seedorf S (2006) Applications of ontologies in software engineering. International Workshop on Semantic Web Enabled Software Engineering. Athens, USA.
32. Happel HJ, Seedorf S (2007) Ontobrowse: A semantic wiki for sharing knowledge about software architectures. 19th International Conference on Software Engineering and Knowledge Engineering, SEKE 2007, Boston, MA, USA, pp 506–512.
33. Herbsleb JD, Mockus A (2003) Formulation and preliminary test of an empirical theory of coordination in software engineering. SIGSOFT Software Engineering Notes 28(5): 138–147.
34. Kersten M, Murphy G (2006) Using task context to improve programmer productivity. 14th International Symposium on Foundations of Software Engineering. ACM, NY, USA.
35. Kraut RE, Streeter LA (1995) Coordination in software development. Communications of the ACM 38(3): 69–81.
36. Krötzsch M, Vrandecic D, Völkel M (2006) Semantic mediawiki. Proceeding on 5th International Semantic Web Conference (ISWC06), pp 935–942.
37. Lin J, Fox MS, Bilgic T (1996) A requirement ontology for engineering design. Concurrent Engineering 4: 279–291.
38. Louridas P (2006) Using wikis in software development. IEEE Software 23: 88–91.
39. Maalej W, Happel HJ (2008) A lightweight approach for knowledge sharing in distributed software teams. 7th International Conference on Practical Aspects of Knowledge Management, Lecture Notes in Computer Science. Springer.
40. Maalej W, Panagiotou D, Happel HJ (2008) Towards effective management of software knowledge exploiting the semantic wiki paradigm. Software Engineering, volume 121 of LNI, pp. 183–197.
41. Majchrzak A, Wagner C, Yates D (2006) Corporate wiki users: results of a survey. ACM, Odense, URL http://portal.acm.org/citation.cfm?id=1149472, pp. 99–104.
42. Malone TW, Crowston K (1994) The interdisciplinary study of coordination. ACM Computing Surveys 26(1): 87–119. DOI http://doi.acm.org/10.1145/174666.174668.
43. Ruiz F, Hilera JR (2007) Ontologies for Software Engineering and Technology. Berlin/Heidelberg: Springer.

44. Sarma A, Noroozi Z, Hoek, Avd (2003) Palantir: raising awareness among configuration management workspaces. 25th International Conference on Software Engineering. IEEE CS, DC, USA.
45. Sengupta B, Chandra S, Sinha V (2006) A research agenda for distributed software development. ACM, Shanghai, China, pp. 731–740.
46. Södestrom E, Andersson B, Johannesson P, Perjons E, Wangler B (2001) Towards a framework for comparing process modelling lan.guages. International Conference on Advanced Information Systems Engineering.
47. Staab S, Studer R (Eds.) (2004) Handbook on Ontologies. Berlin: Springer.
48. Studer R, Grimm S, Abecker A (2007) Semantic Web Services: Concepts, Technologies, and Applications, 1st edn. Heidelberg: Springer-Verlag.
49. Wang TD, Parsia B, Hendler J (2006) A survey of the web ontology landscape. Technical Report, University of Maryland and University of Manchester.
50. Wille C, Abran A, Desharnais J, Dumke R (2003) The quality concepts and subconcepts in swebok: An ontology challenge. Workshop on Software Measurement.
51. Witte R, Zhang Y, Rilling J (2007) Empowering software maintainers with semantic web technologies. 4th European Semantic Web Conference, LNCS. Springer.
52. Wouters B, Deridder D, Paesschen EV (2000) The use of ontologies as a backbone for use case management. Workshop on Objects and Classifications, a Natural Convergence.
53. Ye Y, Fischer G (2005) Supporting reuse by delivering task-relevant and personalized information. Automated Software Engineering 12(2): 199–235.
54. Zeller A (2007) The future of programming environments. Integration, synergy, and assistance. Future of Software Engineering. IEEE CS, Washington, DC, USA.
55. Zhang Y, Witte R, Rilling J, Haarslev V (2008) Ontological approach for the semantic recovery of traceability links between software artifacts. IET Software 2(3): 185–203.

Part II
Tools and Techniques

André van der Hoek

Tools have served a critical role in collaborative software engineering throughout. They are used to automate tasks that otherwise humans would have to do by hand; tasks that tend to be repetitious, labor-intensive, tedious, or difficult to perform. Their use has made it possible to scale the size of software development teams and the projects in which they engage. The kinds of extremely large projects undertaken today just would not be possible without, for instance, the concurrency management facilities provided by SCM systems. Collaborative software engineering tools have also afforded new ways of working. The open source movement in its current scale is only possible due to the internet, CVS, mailing lists, and online project management sites such as Source Forge.

In the early days of software engineering, tools focused strongly on the management of the artifacts that were produced. Version control systems are the chief example, automating tracking of changes to (code) artifacts in order to maintain a historical record as well as to enable concurrent access to the same code base by multiple developers at the same time [6]. Shared editors emerged relatively early as well, built on the paradigm of instant sharing of edits instead of following the lock-edit-merge cycle promoted by version control systems (e.g., MMM [3]). A wealth of policies has emerged since that attempt to codify and support various intermediate levels of concurrent access and sharing among groups of developers [4]. Primarily, these policies target changes to code or textual artifacts; artifacts that are stored in binary represent a challenge since they require turn-key diff and merge algorithms to be inserted into the generic collaborative work infrastructure.

Another class of tools has focused on supporting the overall process of collaborative software engineering. Early incarnations of these tools aimed to address two issues: (1) planning, by assisting project managers in creating GANTT charts and other such schedules of work, and (2) workflow, by controlling the flow of documents across tasks and people throughout an organization. A host of specialized workflow and process management tools emerged, including high-end environments that supported reflective processes and even multiple versions of the same process to be active at the same time [1]. More recently, we have witnesses a reversal from specialized process environments upon which the remainder of the development tools rest to environments in which pre-determined, or at least highly constrained, processes are built in. IBM's Jazz, for instance, is an extension to Eclipse that provides an editor-centric environment that revolves around a limited, more agile process [7]. This trend has also allowed tools to start presenting task-centric advice to developers; for instance, Mylyn reduces the set of visible entities in the development environment to those that pertain to the current task and/or change at hand [8].

Another category of tools focuses on communication among collaborating parties. A number of these communication tools are general, as developers rapidly adopted e-mail, newsgroups, and instant messaging for their purposes. More specific communication tools were also developed. One of the most important such tools have been bug trackers (also called issue trackers). These tools provide a central location where all bugs and feature requests are collected and from where they can be assigned to individuals to address them in the code base. Recently, a host of awareness tools have emerged, aiming to inform developers of important issues needing their attention. Palantír [11] CollabVS [5] and FastDash [2] are examples of such tools, all aiming to keep developers abreast of the efforts of their colleagues and especially of those efforts that may lead to potential merge issues later on. At the same time, some communication tools focus on the question of who to talk to pertaining to certain issues. In particular, expertise finding tools assist developers in identifying those developers who have expertise over a certain portion of the code base [9, 10].

Today's tools face several key challenges. First and foremost is the fact that software increasingly is being developed in a distributed and even decentralized fashion, with multiple organizations responsible for different parts of the software system or different tasks with respect to the development process. Collaboration support, thus, must extend across separately-developed components, geographical boundaries, and independent teams. This brings with it entirely new concerns in terms of privacy and intellectual property issues, as well as the need to respect different work practices that are being bridged. Second is the issue of cross-life-cycle support. Most collaboration tools still focus on a single phase of the life cycle, often just programming, ignoring other phases. Much still is to be gained with advanced tool support in this regard. Third is the issue of control, particularly when it comes to process tools. For many years, the tools placed the organization in control, enforcing its processes and practices on the individuals. Recent tools, recognizing that individuals are resourceful and effective in dealing with unforeseen problems, place some of that control back in the hands of the individuals. Permeating all three issues is a key emerging consideration underlying most of today's work in the collaborative software engineering tools arena: tool solutions must be developed keeping in mind that the ultimate solution is one of "tool plus person", that is, tools in and of themselves do not lead to changed practices, it is in how individuals work with and leverage tools that new practices arise. It is this social-technical interplay that ultimately decides upon a tool's success in improving collaboration practices.

The next five chapters provide a sampling of today's research into collaborative software engineering tools, ranging from theoretical expositions, to new tools, to concerns regarding how to evaluate collaborative software engineering tools, to overviews of the present state of the art. Together, the papers provide a mere glimpse of the depth and breadth of research activities taking place at this moment in time with respect to tools, as it is a very active and engaged community.

Chapter 7 by Dewan provides an overview of a broad variety of collaborative software engineering tools (over 50), grouped into two categories. The first category of tools distinguishes itself by aiming "towards being there", that is, these tools overcome geographical and other boundaries by providing technological solutions that mimic co-located collaboration as closely as possible. The second category of tools aims "beyond being there", introducing functionality that is generally not available in co-located collaboration yet useful in supporting the collaborative effort. Through a historical and incremental analysis of how new tools fix deficiencies with previous tools, a holistic perspective emerges.

Chapter 8 by Sarma, Al-Ani, and co-authors introduces a host of collaborative software development tools that were developed under the continuous co-ordination paradigm, blending formal and informal co-ordination techniques to enable effective and spontaneous co-ordination actions to take place. The paper also highlights the difficulties involved in evaluating collaborative software engineering tools. Short of real-world use, compromises must be made. Using the DESMET evaluation framework, each of the tools in the continuous co-ordination suite is evaluated according to its objectives.

Chapter 9 by Murta, Werner, and Estublier examines the state-of-the-practice in software configuration management and places it in the context of five critical collaboration needs: communication, awareness, co-ordination, shared memory, and shared space. For each of these, the paper first discusses how the need is supported by the current generation of (commercial) software configuration management tools, and then presents key ongoing research towards improving how each need is supported. The paper concludes with an outlook at future trends, including challenges introduced by such advances as model-driven engineering and cloud computing.

Chapter 10 by Lago, Farenhorst, and co-authors addresses a different artifact than source code, choosing to focus on architectural knowledge management through the GRIFFIN Collaborative Virtual Community. The paper introduces a set of collaboration scenarios among architects as they are located at different locations and exhibit different backgrounds and roles, and uses the scenarios to define a conceptual model for a virtual community of architects. Key is that the scenarios and community support both formal and informal interactions, a necessity to provide broad and effective support.

Chapter 11 by Nakakoji, Ye, and Yamamoto examines the topic of expertise communication and its role in collaboration. Through a carefully thought out theoretical perspective, it particularly identifies expertise communication as a different form of communication from co-ordination communication, with its own challenges, demands, and needs. It then provides a set of nine key design principles to be followed when designing and implementing expertise communication functionality in developer-centered collaborative software development environments.

References

1. Bandinelli SC, Fuggetta A, Ghezzi C (1993) Software Process Model Evolution in the SPADE Environment. IEEE Transactions on Software Engineering 19 (12): 1128–1144.
2. Biehl J et al. (2007) FASTDash: A visual dashboard for fostering awareness in software teams. SIGCHI Conference on Human Factors in Computing Systems, pp. 1313–1322.
3. Bier EA, Freeman S (1991) MMM: A user interface architecture for shared editors on a single screen. Proceedings of the ACM Symposium on User Interface Software and Technology, pp. 79–86.
4. Conradi R, Westfechtel B (1998) Version models for software configuration management. ACM Computing Surveys 30(2): 232–282.
5. Dewan P, Hegde R (2007) Semi-synchronous conflict detection and resolution in asynchronous software development. European Computer Supported Co-operative Work, pp. 159–178.
6. Estublier J, Leblang D, Clemm G, Conradi R, Hoek Avd, Tichy W, Wiborg-Weber D (2005) Impact of the Research Community on the Field of Software Configuration Management. ACM Transactions on Software Engineering and Methodology 14(4): 1–48.
7. IBM Jazz, http://www.jazz.net, accessed 04 July 2009.
8. Kersten M, Murphy GC (2006) Using task context to improve programmer productivity. Proceedings of the 14th ACM SIGSOFT International Symposium on Foundations of Software Engineering, Portland, OR, USA. (05–11 November 2006) SIGSOFT'06/FSE-14, ACM, New York, pp. 1–11.
9. Mockus A, Herbsleb JD (2002) Expertise browser: A quantitative approach to identifying expertise. Proceedings of the 24th International Conference on Software Engineering (Orlando, FL, 19–25 May 2002) ICSE'02, ACM, New York, pp. 503–512.
10. Nakakoji K, Ye Y, Yamamoto Y (2009) Supporting expertise communication in developer-centered collaborative software development environments, In: Mistrík I, Grundy J, Whitehead J, van der Hoek A, Finkelstein A (Eds.) Collaborative Software Engineering. New York: Springer.
11. Sarma A, Noroozi Z, Hoek Avd (2003) Palantír: Raising awareness among configuration management workspaces. Twenty-fifth International Conference on Software Engineering, pp. 444–453.

Chapter 7
Towards and Beyond Being There in Collaborative Software Development

Prasun Dewan

Abstract Research has shown that the productivity of the members of a software team depends on the degree to which they are co-located. In this chapter, we present distributed tools that both (a) try to virtually support these forms of collaboration, and (b) go beyond co-located software development by automatically offering modes of collaboration not directly supported by it.

7.1 Introduction

A variety of novel tools have been created to allow software developers to collaborate with each other. This chapter classifies them based on whether they try to (a) make software developers feel they are co-located, or (b) provide features not found in co-located collaboration. The result is an overview that relates concepts not linked together earlier, which include not only research tools but also studies that motivate/evaluate them. Each of the surveyed works is described by showing how it builds on or overcomes problems of other research addressed in this chapter. By focusing only on the differences among these works, the chapter covers a large variety of concepts, from over fifty papers. It is targeted mainly at the practitioner familiar with the state of the art, rather than the researcher working on improving current practices. Nonetheless, the interrelationships among the referenced works should be of interest to everyone. In particular, a new researcher in this area should be able to find holes in existing designs and evaluations.

Naturally, not all aspects of all research in collaborative software development are covered, or all viewpoints taken. By focusing on the "being there" and beyond themes, this discussion concentrates on the nature of the collaboration rather than the form of software engineering such as design and inspection. It addresses tools

P. Dewan (✉)
Department of Computer Science CB 3175, University of North Carolina, Chapel Hill, NC 27599-3175, USA
e-mail: dewan@cs.unc.edu

I. Mistrík et al. (eds.), *Collaborative Software Engineering*,
DOI 10.1007/978-3-642-10294-3_7, © Springer-Verlag Berlin Heidelberg 2010

and related studies, rather than collaboration theories, cultural issues, organizational structures, studies that have not yet informed tool design, and other aspects of collaborative software development. Finally, it is intended to be a broad overview of the area, identifying relationships among diverse classes of research, rather than among different approaches within a particular class such as expert finders.

It begins by identifying the various degrees of physical co-location that have had an impact on software productivity. It then presents virtual channels that allow distributed developers to simulate these forms of co-location, and go beyond.

7.2 Productivity vs. Co-Location Degrees

Complex software must be developed collaboratively. However, Brooks [4] observed that adding more people to a software team can result in disproportionate increase in coordination cost, thereby reducing the productivity of the individual programmer. Surveys have found that, on an average, 50–80% of software developers' time is taken by communication [2, 44] and they are interrupted every three minutes [24].

These results seem unintuitive for two reasons. First, modular decomposition of software products should isolate software developers. Second, documentation should reduce the need for direct communication. However, studies have found that the approaches of documenting and partitioning are far from a panacea. Curtis et al. [10] found documentation is problematic for several reasons. Requirements, designs and other collaborative information keep changing, making it hard to keep their documentation consistent. After finishing an activity, software developers often choose to proceed to the next task rather than document the results of what they have done. People may deliberately hide information for career advancement. Sometimes there is conflicting information from different stakeholders that needs to be resolved through meetings. For example, for a defense project, the following stakeholders may provide different requirements: the champions responsible for getting the project approved the procurement office responsible for setting and monitoring the goals, the commanders, and the actual operators of the software to be created by the project.

Perry et al. [43] found that modularizing a project into multiple files does not isolate programmers. They studied Lucent's 5ESS system and found a high level of concurrency in the project – for example, they found hundreds of files that were manipulated concurrently by more than twenty programmers in a single day. Often the programmers edited adjacent or same lines in a file. They found that the more a file is accessed concurrently, the more the numbers of defects in it, despite the fact that state-of-the-practice versions control tools were used. There are many possible reasons for this correlation. After checking-in a file, a programmer may remember that some necessary change was not made, and to correct this mistake, may change the file in-place without creating a new version [26]. Programmers concurrently working on different private spaces (created from the same base) often race to finish first to avoid having to (a) deal with merging problems [26] and/or (b) re-run test suites on the merges [13, 14]. Programmers may not look at the documentation of previous versions to understand the code they are modifying [27]. Indirect conflicts on related files are not caught by differencing or file-based locking. Few people have a sense of the overall picture or the broad architecture [10, 27] which is required to reduce indirect conflicts.

All of the studies above assumed that team members are co-located in a single building and work from separate cubicles. If coordination/communication is really an issue, as these studies indicate, then distributing the team should further aggravate this problem and radically co-locating it, that is, requiring all team members to work in a single war-room, should reduce it. Two independent studies have found that this is indeed the case – the productivity of distributed teams was lower than that of co-located teams [32] and the productivity of radically co-located teams was higher than that of co-located ones [53].

The study comparing co-location and distribution [32] found that in distributed team development, it was harder to find people, get work-related information through casual conversation, get access to information shared with co-located co-workers, get timely information about plan changes, have clearly formed plans, agree about plans, be clear about assigned tasks, and have co-workers assist with heavy workloads, beyond what they are required to do. Interestingly most people thought that they gave help equally to local and remote collaborators but received more help from local collaborators. The study found that the perception of received help was the only factor that correlated with productivity.

The study on radical co-location [53] found two main factors that made it work better. First, there was continuous face-to-face communication among team members. Second, they were able to overhear and see each other's activity, which allowed them to solve their problems and interject commentary, clarifications and corrections. On the other hand, the study found that people sometimes wanted private spaces, and there was concern about distraction and getting individual recognition for work.

In radical co-location, even though the members of the team work in one room, they use different workstations. Higher physical coupling is achieved in pair programming, wherein two programmers sit next to each other, sharing a workstation and working on a single task, with only one programmer providing input to the workstation at one time. One study comparing pair and individual programming produced several interesting findings. It found that in the pair programming case (a) 80% of programmers felt higher satisfaction, (b) more alternatives were explored and fewer lines written, and (c) there was more team building as programmers were involved with each other and enjoyed celebrating project-completion together. Even more interesting, it found that pair programming took more person hours but resulted in fewer bugs [55]. Assuming certain times for fixing and detecting bugs, the study established that pair programming actually increases the productivity of an individual programmer. This result seems to contradict Brooks's law [4] which says that adding more programmers to a late project makes it later. The two results are not, in fact, contradictory, because Brooks assumed programmers were co-located but in separate cubicles. Thus, he did not consider radical co-location or pair programming.

The above studies, together, show that (a) communication and coordination are problems in team software development, (b) the more the physical coupling between members of a team, the less the severity of these problems. The moral, then, seems to be to increase the co-location degree among team members to the maximum degree possible.

Other work has shown that this conclusion is not necessarily correct. Nawrocki and Wojciehowski [39] found pair programming often took about twice as many person hours, though the pair-programming times showed less variance. Ratcliffe and Robertson [45] found that programmers with high (self-reported) skills did not like being paired with those with low skills.

More interesting, recent work has proposed a variation of pair programming, called side-by-side programming, wherein two programmers, sitting next to each other and using different workstations, work together on the same task [7]. A study showed that, in comparison to pair programming, side-by-side programming offers significantly lower completion times [40] while slightly reducing the understanding developers have of code written by their partners. It also found that developers who liked working together on a single task preferred side-by-side programming to pair programming.

The more complicated argument, then, seems to be that there are both benefits and drawbacks of tight physical coupling. Its strength is that multiple programmers can communicate with each other about a problem and possibly discuss it. Its weakness is that it reduces concurrency even when communication/discussion would be useless. More important, tight coupling may not always be preferred or even possible. For team members who are geographically dispersed, a closer physical coupling is not an option. Even when a team is co-located, because of lack of war-rooms in the workplace and the concerns mentioned above regarding radical co-location, team members may work in different rooms/cubicles. Pair programming is not widely practiced currently, and not always the most preferred or productive coupling, and even if it were, different pairs would have looser physical couplings. Thus, the communication/coordination problems of these couplings remain.

One way to address these problems is to provide virtual channels that simulate a variety of physical couplings, making the team members feel that they are together in a single building or room, or sitting in adjacent seats, or sharing a single workstation. This is consistent with the idea of taking steps towards virtually "being there." A complementary solution is to support virtual channels that reduce collaboration problems existing in all forms of co-location. This is consistent with the idea of virtually going "beyond being there" [34].

Examples of both kinds of channels exist in traditional – that is, state-of-the-practice – tools. For example, IM systems provide the "towards being there" functionality of synchronously chatting, and version control systems provide the "beyond being there" functionality of asynchronous merging. The fact that, despite the pervasiveness of these tools, communication/coordination is still a major issue in team software development seems to indicate that there are opportunities to significantly improve existing collaboration channels. Several research efforts have explored such opportunities. The remainder of this chapter surveys some of the concepts identified by these research efforts, and experience with these concepts.

7.3 Towards Being There

7.3.1 Virtual Co-location and Radical Co-location

Co-location, especially radical co-location, allows developers to easily communicate to the whole team events of shared interest. When the team is distributed, several approaches have been devised and used for conveying this information. A version control system provides a way for distributed programmers to formally communicate some of this information through check-in comments. Grudin and Poltrock [28] advocate the use of project Blogs to informally communicate with co-developers. Gutwin et al. [29] found that email can be a practical alternative for announcing important, infrequent events such as the starting and termination of tasks.

For supporting continuous "stream of consciousness babbling" [31] of the kind that can be expected in radical co-location, lighter weight tools have been developed. Elvin [22] is an example of such a tool. Messages posted by a team continuously scroll in a ticker tape. A tool with similar goals is RVM (Rear View Mirror) [31] so named because it is intended as an unobtrusive background "rear view mirror" for the members of the team as they performed their tasks. User studies yielded several counter-intuitive results about desired features. Originally, the tool showed users only the last few hours of those messages that were exchanged when they were logged on. Based on user feedback it was changed to support all of the conversation. Also previously, an explicit permission had to be given to each person viewing presence information. Based on user feedback, the system was changed to allow each member of a team to see the presence information of all the other members. Presence information was liked more than chat. In fact, managers exchanged only two chat messages during the study!

A potential problem with the tools above is that a developer interacting with a programming environment must switch to a separate tool to see the presence information of and interact with co-developers. Jazz [6] and CollabVS [30] provide these facilities, in-place, within the programming environment. A study of CollabVS found that programmers preferred in-place presence and communication [30].

7.3.2 Distributed Pair Programming

The channels above simulate physical channels in radical and regular co-location. Let us next consider concepts supporting the higher physical coupling provided by pair programming.

The easiest way to support such coupling is to use a generic desktop-sharing system, which traps window level input events and window or frame-buffer level screen updates, and transmits them to a remote collaborator. An alternative is to couples the edit buffers and other components of the semantic state of the programming environment of the developers [20, Schummer #1092]. The former is slower and requires use of a special, potentially unfamiliar system for sharing. On the other hand, the latter requires the developers to manually synchronize their views. A hybrid approach, taken in Jazz [6] and CollabVS [30] is to add commands to the user-interface of a programming environment to invoke a desktop sharing system [6, 30].

A study comparing distributed and co-located serial pair programming found that physical distance does not matter [1]. This is an interesting result because, as mentioned above, studies of individual programming have found that distance reduces productivity [32].

7.3.3 Distributed Side-by-Side Programming

As mentioned above, a variation of pair programming is side-by-side programming, wherein two programmers sit next to each other working on the same task. It offers (potentially) looser coupling than pair programming, as the developers can work concurrently on different aspects of the task; and tighter coupling than radical co-location, as they are required to work on a single task that has not been decomposed for them; and more important, are able to see all actions of their partners.

Dewan et al. [17] have devised a distributed analog of this idea. Each developer in the pair interacts with two computers – one primary computer to act as the driver of his subtask, and an awareness computer to act as the navigator for the partner's subtask. In other words, each programmer interacts with the windows displayed on his primary computer, and each awareness computer shows the screen of the partner's primary computer. The developers use the phone to talk to each other. No video channel is established between them in this set-up.

A desktop sharing system is used to ensure that each awareness computer shows the screen of the partner's desktop. In addition a model-sharing system such as a file system or a Web server is used to synchronously share edits to code made concurrently on the two primary computers. Thus, the same input is shared at multiple levels of abstraction – at the window level by the desktop sharing system and at the semantic level by the model sharing system.

In this architecture, local response is not affected by the network delays, as is the case in single-computer (desktop-sharing based) distributed pair-programming implementations. Thus, the two-computer solution offers good response times for even pure pair programming.

A study of distributed side-by-side programming showed that developers used its ability to dynamically switch between pair programming, independent programming, and several other intermediate synchronous programming modes such as concurrent searching/programming [17].

7.3.4 Distributed Synchronous Design and Inspection

Distributed pair programming is only one form of distributed synchronous software engineering. It is particularly interesting because, traditionally, programmers collaborate asynchronously on different parts of a project rather than synchronously on every line of code. On the other hand, activities that precede and succeed the coding phase – design and inspection – are typically carried out in synchronous, face-to-face meetings. Therefore, tools have been built and effectively used for distributed synchronous design [41] and inspection [38]. A study of distributed synchronous inspection has shown that it is as effective as face to face inspection in terms of faults found, but developers preferred face-to-face inspection [38].

7.3.5 Other "Towards Being There" Mechanisms

There are a variety of other kinds of distributed tools such as connected kitchens [35] video walls [25] and media spaces [37] which provide elements of being there in the same building or room. However, as there have been no studies of their use in team software development, we ignore them in this chapter. See [15] for a survey of these and other tools that have not been targeted at software development.

7.4 Beyond Being There

Software tools that go beyond being there automate various aspects of collaboration, and are thus useful for both (radically) co-located and distributed teams.

7.4.1 File System Events

Traditional version control systems provide an important form of collaboration automation. When users check-out or check-in files from a version control repository, interested users are automatically notified about these events. O'Reilly et al. [42] point out that it is also useful to monitor operations at the file-system level, for several reasons. Sometimes users manually change the permissions of files to make them writeable instead of checking them out from the repository. A new project file is not known to the repository until it is checked in. A repository tracks events at the user level – sometime a user takes multiple personas, creating multiple different private workspaces from the same base. While working on one of these workspaces, it is not possible for him to be notified about actions he took in another workspace.

Therefore they extend the repository events above with the following additional events: (a) Added/removed: A file known to the repository has been added to/removed from project working directory pending commit. (b) Updated: A file in the repository has been updated in the working directory. (c) Needs checkout: A file in the working directory has been updated in the repository. (d) Needs merge: A file has been updated both in the working directory and the repository. (e) Unknown added/removed/updated: A file in the working directory not known to the repository has been added/removed/updated.

7.4.2 Persistent Awareness vs. Notifications

An alternate to notifying interested developers about operations of their collaborators on files is to update a persistent view of the file status in the user-interface of a programming environment or a separate tool. For example, the Jazz [6] and CollabVS [30] programming environments continuously indicate to developers which files have been checked-out or are being edited by their team members. In FASTDash [3] a separate tool provides this facility. Thus, programmers interested in knowing, for example, if a file is being currently edited by a collaborator need only look at the persistent view rather than mine through the event history to determine this information. On the other hand, changes to the awareness information may go unnoticed. For example, if two developers start editing the same file, neither of them may notice the change to the view of the file status. Thus, both persistent awareness of and notifications about collaborators' operations on files/versions are useful.

7.4.3 Programming Environment Events

Operations on objects maintained by a programming environment that are not known to the file or version control system may also be of interest to collaborators. These include starting/stopping of the editing of a particular program construct such as method or class [19, 50, 51] and concurrent editing of the same or dependent program constructs [19, 46, 50]. Awareness of this information can be provided through notifications or updates of persistent status views. For example, in CollabVS, concurrent editing of dependent program constructs results in both notifications and updates of awareness views [19].

Three studies have shown the usefulness of providing awareness of programming environment events. A study of Tukan found that when programmers found themselves editing the same program construct, they transformed their individual coding sessions into a joint pair programming session [51]. Two studies, of CollabVS and Palantír, respectively, have found that programmers used information about concurrent editing of dependent constructs to prevent direct and indirect conflicts [19, 48]. The comments from the CollabVS study [19] also showed that programmers liked having information about programming environment events even when these events had no apparent benefit such as conflict prevention. Hegde and Dewan [30] give several scenarios in which awareness of programming environment events may be useful. For example, if Alice sees Bob taking an undue amount of time editing a method, she can offer to help him with the task.

7.4.4 Shared Version with Multiple Views

Suppose Alice does wish to help Bob finish his task. One approach to do so is to use distributed pair or side-by-side programming. As mentioned above, distributed pair programming requires her to work lock step with Bob, not allowing concurrent work on the task. The scheme for distributed side-by-side programming described above addresses this issue, but suffers from two related drawbacks in its attempt to faithfully mimic co-located side-by-side programming. First, it requires each programmer to view a separate display to observe his partner's incremental updates. Second, to receive these edits, the developer must manually pull them from the file system or web server. These updates are not automatically pushed to him.

Some software development systems have addressed these two problems using a variation of distributed side-by-side programming. In these systems, as in side-by-side pair programming, the developers work on the same version of the code-base. The difference is that they can edit it concurrently using different views of it that are updated automatically or manually. This is a special case of the general idea of editing the same model using multiple views [18]. Changes to the model can be pulled and pushed at various time and space granularities depending on the coupling between the views [18].

An early system supporting this approach was Flecse [20] which provided tools that allow programmers to do synchronous concurrent editing, debugging, testing and inspection. As motivation for such tools, the paper on Flecse [20] provides the following hypothetical scenario. Three users have finished creating different procedures of a matrix multiplication program. One of them finds an error in the output. Two of them use the Flecse collaborative debugger to jointly work with another to find the bug. The two users find that the bug can be fixed by changing the semantics of one, of two procedures and cannot agree on which, one of these should be changed. They use the Flecse multi-user inspection tool to hold a more formal code-review meeting involving all three users to make the decision. The tool allows them to make their annotations privately before discussing them in public. The code review session suggests changing both procedures to eliminate other related errors.

A follow-up to this work was CAIS [38] an inspection tool supporting both asynchronous and synchronous inspection. User studies with this tool [38] found that people preferred to perform software inspection asynchronously, until the discussion became controversial, when they switched to synchronous discussion.

Several other tools have been built based on these ideas. CollabVS [30] allows developers to asynchronously share the contents of their edit buffers before checking them to the version control system. SubEthaEdit and Sun's JSE 7 allow synchronous editing of the same file in different views. JSE 7 also supports synchronous collaborative inspection by allowing code to be sent through the chat tool, which correctly formats it. Users can independently scroll the shared code and user comments about it in the chat window, thereby seeing different views of the inspection data.

Unlike the scheme for distributed side-by-side programming, none of these systems require a special awareness screen. In these systems, when developers edit the

same model using different views, they can lose track of the activities of their collaborators. As a separate screen for showing these activities is not guaranteed, more
space efficient and thus higher level mechanisms are needed for allowing the team
members to be aware of each others' views. These mechanisms are different from
those we saw above that allow developers to be aware of the semantic or model
changes of their collaborators. For example, a multi-user scrollbar in SubEthaEdit,
which shows the scrollbars of the collaborators, provides view awareness, while
awareness about the methods being edited by collaborators, provided by CollabVS
[30] provides model awareness.

Few studies have been performed in which software developers concurrently
interact with different views of a shared version without special awareness screens.
Two exceptions are [30] and [8] which were targeted mainly at determining if such
a mechanism could reduce conflicts, and found that this is indeed the case.

7.4.5 Searching and Mining

Allowing developers to easily search for project-related information is another form
of automation that can be supported by a beyond being there tool. Microsoft's Team
Visual Studio allows developers to easily track information related to work items.
It associates a work item with status information indicating whether it is active,
pending, resolved, or closed. A check-in can be linked to the work item implemented
by it. In addition, if the work item is a bug correction request, it can be linked to the
build and test suites that identified the bug. These links allow the system to search
for various kinds of project information – in particular the status of work items, the
users assigned to a work item, and duplicate work items.

Hipikat [9] extends the above concept by linking additional kinds of information,
deriving some of these links automatically based on similarity of documents, and
providing sorted recommendations in response to requests for similar documents.
These queries are made from the programming environment by asking the system to
provide documents similar to the one that is selected. The user can then recursively
look for documents similar to the recommendations.

To determine how well these features worked, two user studies were performed,
involving an "easy" and "difficult" task. In the easy task, programmers were asked to
extend Eclipse's hover capability. Given the task description, Hipikat automatically
found a very similar past task as the highest recommendation. As a result, novice
programmers who used Hipikat were as successful as expert programmers who did
not. In the hard task, programmers were asked to extend Eclipse's version system
integration. Expert programmers who did not use Hipikat missed some subtle issues
while some novice programmers who used Hipikat addressed them because the system provided a recommendation that identified these issues. On the other hand, some
of the Hipikat users also missed these issues as the relevant recommendation was
not the highest ranked one. Studying each recommendation was a difficult heavy-
weight task – hence when users found a relevant recommendation, they did not look

for lower ranked recommendations that provided additional information. Thus, the recommendations were used shallowly to understand how to start a task, rather than deeply to understand the system architecture.

The general idea of mining the software artifacts created by groups of software developers has several other useful manifestations. Document similarity can be used to trace different versions of some software artifact, and thereby gain a better understanding of the project [36]. SpotWeb [54] finds reuses of the classes of a framework, and classifies the reused classes as hotspots (coldspots) if there are several (few) reuses of the classes. Hotspots (coldspots) can be expected to more (less) tested and hence reliable than the average classes. More important, from the point of team software development, new developers in a team can, instead of consulting older members, look at hotspots and associated reuses to understand how to use the framework. Zou and Godfrey [57] mine interaction histories to automatically separate newcomers and experts – the latter tend to focus on a smaller set of artifacts. This information can be used to find experts, and also to pair developers in pair programming.

Cataldo et al. [5] have found that mining the version-control logs provides a method for finding useful dependencies, which complements the static analysis used in CollabVS and Palantír. For example, files that are committed together have been found to be closely related to each other. They classify communication among developers as "good" or "bad" based on whether or not the programmers are modifying dependent artifacts. Xiang et al. [56] build on this idea by automatically recommending communication among developers working on dependent files. Schroter et al. [49] support a variation of this idea on in which the communication is recommended only on failed builds.

7.4.6 Visualization

Visualization is an alternative to query-based searches. Instead of specifying a query to find some aspect of data, users locate it in a visualization of the data. Tools have been developed to provide visualization (a) in-the-large of the entire software engineering project, (b) in-the-medium of sets of files, and (c) in the small of components of a file.

Doppke et al. [21] visualize and enforce the software process by mapping it into MUD abstractions [11]. Each task is mapped to a MUD virtual room containing representations of the artifacts manipulated to perform the task. For example the testing activity is mapped to a room containing the executable being tested, the inputs fed to it, and the output produced by it. A human enters a room with artifacts to perform the associated activity, and cannot leave until the activity is finished. On leaving, the human is directed to the next activity in the workflow.

Doppke et al. found that software processes could not be mapped completely too traditional MUD spaces, for several reasons. (a) In a traditional MUD environment, a person can be in a single room at a time, while in a software process, a human can be in multiple activities simultaneously. Therefore, they defined the abstraction of a persona, which is a person's activity thread. A persona is always at a particular stage in the activity. When a person enters a room taking on the role of the persona in the room, he carries on work from that stage onwards. A persona rather than person is mapped to a room. They defined several typical software engineering personas such as generic developer and programmer. (b) A software process is associated with constraints – therefore they extended MUDs to support programmer-defined constraints for entering and leaving a room. (c) A software task can have several subtasks, which in turn can have their own subtasks. This was modeled by creating sub-buildings within rooms.

Instead of or in addition to displaying the current state of the formal process associated with a project, it is also possible to visualize the informal collaboration describing its state. Jazz [6] creates such a visualization, called "Team Jam," which is a persistent virtual place that includes a discussion board, links to transcripts of chats, and notifications of the kind of events we saw earlier such as check-in and check-out of code.

Instead of seeing the complete communication regarding a project, as in Team Jam, it may be useful to understand the impact various aspects of the communication has on a project. Sarma et al. [47] have recently developed a browser/visualize, called Tesseract, that allows programmers to relate artifact dependencies, communication patterns, and features/bug fixes. For instance, given a bug-fix, a user can see a visualization of all files and developers involved with the bug, and which of these developers communicated with each other. Similarly, it visualizes the relationship between the amount of communication among developers working on related artifacts and the number of bugs.

Tesseract, Team Jam, and the MUD-like process visualization address visualization in the large of the entire project. Let us consider next techniques for visualizing in the medium and small.

Palantír [48] provides visualization of concurrent accesses to hierarchic objects checked-in by a user to a private workspace. Each object checked out by the user is associated with a stack of tiled boxes. Different tiles in the stack correspond to parallel checked out versions. Each tile can contain sub-stacks corresponding to sub-objects. The stacks are sorted by severity of divergence among the tiles in the stack. Palantír allows the application to calculate the severity, and proposes some simple measures including changed vs. not changed, lines changed/total lines, and number of interface changes. Thus, Palantír provides visualization in the medium of sets of files as sorted, nested collections of file stacks.

Several examples of visualization in the small exist. One of them is based on the notion of physical wear, which is a useful concept in the physical world – by following worn paths, we can find our way in an unknown terrain; and by looking for worn pages in a recipe book, we can find the popular recipes. Hill and Hollan [33] create a virtual concept out of physical wear. They associate a line of text with edit and read wear. Edit wear counts the number of edits made to the line. Edits can be differentiated based, for instance, on time and author, to create different categories of wear. Read wear measures how long the line was viewed before it was scrolled out or the viewing user became inactive. Edit/read wear can be used to determine, for instance, which sections are currently changing the most or of most interest.

In the visualization provided by Hill and Hollan [33] collaboration-related information about a file is shown in-place by widths of lines in the scrollbar of a window displaying the file. Froehlich and Dourish [23] provide an alternative approach wherein collaboration information is displayed by coloring a miniature of the file displayed in a separate tool. Each line of text in a program is represented by a graphical line consisting of three parts. The first two parts are of fixed length, while the length of the third part is proportional to the length of the associated text line. All three parts are colored to indicate collaboration attributes of the text, which include author, age (time of last edit), and structure (method, comment, import, variable declaration).

Froehlich and Dourish deployed this system and found that people liked the fact that they could see project growth over time. Users reported discovering notable aspects of the team development such as finding (a) from the drastic changes to a file one day that re-factoring happened that day, (b) up to 15 authors for some files, (c) files with unusual growth patterns, (d) different indentation and import styles, (e) changes made by others to files they thought were owned by them, (f) heavily indented files that were candidates for re-factoring, (g) structures of large functions without scrolling.

7.4.7 Context-Based Automatic Filtering

In both searching and visualization, a software developer must explicitly find information of interest. An alternative is to automatically show information relevant to the current task of the developer that is based on the activities of the whole team. An example of this approach is supported by Team Tracks [12]. It allows developers to identify those classes of the current project that are often visited by the team. (These are different from hotspots which are classes that are often reused but not necessarily often visited). In addition, if the developer is currently viewing some program construct, Team Tracks shows a list of related items that are often visited before or after the construct by the team.

A lab study of Team Tracks showed that the participants used and liked these features and were able to use them to better understand code. A field study shows ways in which it could be improved. Code that was often visited to fix bugs in it was not of interest to people not responsible for fixing these bugs. Moreover, programmers also wanted to explicitly filter related items by person and time.

7.4.8 Tagging

TagSEA [52] shows how the above limitations of Team Tracks can be addressed. Like Team Tracks, it can be used by a developer to identify important locations in a route through the program, which may be a "maintenance pattern" [52] so that other developers can easily take the same route. Thus, instead of trying to automatically deduce interesting routes, it requires developers to manually specify them. Developers can tag any construct using a shared structured tag name and description, which essentially identifies the route. TagSEA supports both the search and visualization approaches to finding tagged constructs. A developer can ask the system to show all constructs matching a tag/route. In addition, when a file is opened for editing, all tagged constructs are highlighted.

The general lesson to be learnt from TagSEA is that developers interested in finding some information can be helped not only by tools but also other developers. It would be useful to integrate the Team Tracks and TagSEA approaches by supporting semi-automatic identification of routes. For instance, a system could automatically tag constructs that are visited before or after a construct with the same name, and allow developers to later edit these tags.

7.5 Summary

We have taken above a tour of several novel collaborative software development concepts. The tour provides a high-level overview of the rationale and nature of these concepts. More important, it classifies these concepts based on several criteria, thereby providing an efficient taxonomy for describing the large range of research tools in which these concepts are implemented.

The "towards being there" virtual channels simulate physical channels available in face-to-face collaboration. These include light-weight communication channels such as ticker-tape, which support distributed "stream of consciousness babbling"; desktop sharing and multi-user programming environments, which supports distributed pair programming; and multi-user inspection/design tools, which support distributed synchronous inspection and design.

The "beyond being there" features offer automation that is useful even in face-to-face collaboration. Some of these make collaborators aware of events that would otherwise have to be communicated manually. Others allow them to share a single version using multiple flexibly coupled views. The last form of computer automation discussed here consists of helping developers locate some information of interest.

This taxonomy is a relatively superficial/high-level classification of collaborate software development concepts. It is possible to provider more detailed taxonomies such as the one given in [16] for conflict management. It would be useful to create detailed taxonomies for other features presented here such as view and model awareness and information visualization.

This chapter provides a basis for creating some of these more detailed taxonomies.

Acknowledgements This work was funded in part by NSF grants IIS 0312328, IIS 0712794, and IIS-0810861, and DARPA/RDECOM Contract N61339-04-C-0043. The comments of the reviewers improved the chapter.

References

1. Baheti P, Gehringer EF, Stotts PD (2002) Exploring the efficacy of distributed pair programming. Proceedings of the Second XP Universe and First Agile Universe Conference on Extreme Programming and Agile Methods – XP/Agile Universe 2002 Springer-Verlag, pp. 208–220.
2. Barstow D (1987) Artificial intelligence and software engineering. Proceedings of the 9th International Conference on Software Engineering.
3. Biehl JT, Czerwinski M, Smith G, Robertson GG (2007) FASTDash: A visual dashboard for fostering awareness in software teams. Proceedings of the SIGCHI Conference on Human Factors in Computing Systems.
4. Brooks F (1974) The mythical man-month. Datamation 20(12): 44–52.
5. Cataldo M, Wagstrom PA, Herbsleb JD, Carley KM (2006) Identification of co-ordination requirements: Implications for the Design of collaboration and awareness tools. Proceedings of the 2006 20th Anniversary Conference on Computer Supported Cooperative Work ACM. Banff, Alberta, Canada, pp. 353–362.
6. Cheng LT, Hupfer S, Ross S, Patterson J (2003) Jazzing up eclipse with collaborative tools. Proceedings of the 2003 OOPSLA Workshop on Eclipse Technology Exchange.
7. Cockburn A (2005) Crystal Clear: A Human-Powered Methodology for Small Teams. Boston, MA: Addison-Wesley.
8. Cook C, Irwin W, Churcher N (2005) A user evaluation of synchronous collaborative software engineering tools. Proceedings of the 12th Asia–Pacific Software Engineering Conference (APSEC'05), pp. 705–710.
9. Cubranic D, Murphy GC, Singer J, Booth KS (2004) Learning from project history: A case study for software development. Proceedings of the 2004 ACM Conference on Computer Supported Co-operative Work.
10. Curtis B, Krasner H, Iscoe N (1988) A field study of the software design process for large systems. Communications of the ACM 31(11): 1268–1287.
11. Curtis P (1992) Mudding: Social Phenomena in Text-Based Virtual Reality. Palo Alto, CA: Xerox Palo Alto Research Center.
12. DeLine R, Czerwinsky M, Robertson G (2005) Easing program comprehension by sharing navigation data. IEEE Symposium on Visual Languages and Human-Centric Computing.
13. de Souza, CRB, Redmiles D, Dourish P (2003) "Breaking the code," moving between private and public work in collaborative software development. Proceedings of the 2003 International ACM SIGGROUP Conference on Supporting Group Work, Sanibel Island, FL, USA.
14. de Souza, CRB, Redmiles D, Mark G, Penix J, Sierhuis M (2003) Management of inter-dependencies in collaborative software development. International Symposium on Empirical Software Engineering, ISESE'03.
15. Dewan P (2004) Collaborative applications. In: Singh M (Ed.) The Practical Handbook of Internet Computing, Vol. 5. London: Chapman & Hall, pp. 1–26.
16. Dewan P (2008) Dimensions of tools for detecting software conflicts. Proceedings of the 2008 International Workshop on Recommendation Systems for Software Engineering ACM. Atlanta, Georgia, pp. 21–25.
17. Dewan P, Agarwal P, Shroff G, Hegde R (2009) Distributed side-by-side programming. ICSE Workshop on Co-operative and Human Aspects of Software Engineering (CHASE), IEEE, Vancouver.
18. Dewan P, Choudhary R (1995) Coupling the user interfaces of a multiuser program. ACM Transactions on Computer Human Interaction 2(1): 1–39.
19. Dewan P, Hegde R (2007) Semi-synchronous conflict detection and resolution in asynchronous software development. Proceedings of the 2007 Tenth European Conference on Computer-Supported Co-operative Work.
20. Dewan P, Riedl J (1993) Toward computer-supported concurrent software engineering. IEEE Computer 26(1): 17–27.

21. Doppke J, Heimbigner CD, Wolf AL (1998) Software process modeling and execution within virtual environments. ACM Transactions on Software Engineering and Methodology 7(1): 1–40.
22. Fitzpatrick G, Mansfield T, Kaplan S, Arnold D, Phelps T, Segall B (1999) Instrumenting and augmenting the workaday world with a generic notification service called Elvin. Proceedings of the Sixth European Conference on Computer Supported Co-operative Work.
23. Froehlich J, Dourish P (2004) Unifying artifacts and activities in a visual tool for distributed software development teams. International Conference on Software Engineering.
24. Gonzalez VM, Mark G (2004) "Constant, constant, multi-tasking craziness": Managing multiple working spheres. Proceedings of the SIGCHI Conference on Human Factors in Computing Systems.
25. Goodman GO, Abel MJ (1987) Communication and collaboration: Facilitating co-operative work through communication. Information Technology & People 3(2): 129–145.
26. Grinter RE (1995) Using a Configuration Management Tool to Co-ordinate Software Development. Proceedings of Conference on Organizational Computing Systems (COOCS'95).
27. Grinter RE (1998) Recomposition: Putting it all back together again. Proceedings of ACM Conference on Computer Supported Cooperative Work (CSCW'98).
28. Grudin J, Poltrock S (2005) Enterprise knowledge management and emerging technologies. Unpublished.
29. Gutwin AC, Penner R, Schneider K (2004) Group awareness in distributed software development. Proceedings of the 2004 ACM Conference on Computer Supported Co-operative Work.
30. Hegde R, Dewan P (2008) Connecting Programming Environments to Support Ad-Hoc Collaboration. Proceedings of the 23rd ACM/IEEE Conference on Automated Software Engineering.
31. Herbsleb JD, Atkins DL, Boyer DG, Handel M, Finholt TA (2002) Introducing instant messaging and chat in the workplace. Proceedings of the SIGCHI conference on Human factors in computing systems.
32. Herbsleb JD, Mockus A, Finholt TA, Grinter RE (2000) Distance, dependencies, and delay in a global collaboration. Proceedings of the ACM Conference on Computer Supported Cooperative Workshop.
33. Hill WC, Hollan JD (1992) Edit wear and read wear. Proceedings of the SIGCHI Conference on Human Factors in Computing Systems.
34. Hollan J, Stornetta S (1992) Beyond being there. Proceedings of ACM CHI'92 Conference on Human Factors in Computing Systems.
35. Jancke G, Venolia GD, Grudin J, Cadiz J, Gupta A (2001) Linking public spaces: Technical and social issues. Proceedings of the SIGCHI Conference on Human Factors in Computing Systems.
36. Lucia AD, Oliveto R, Tortora G (2008) IR-based traceability recovery processes: An empirical comparison of "one-shot" and incremental processes. Proceedings of 23rd IEEE/ACM Conference on Automated Software Engineering (ASE).
37. Mantei M, Backer RM, Sellen AJ, Buxton WAS, Milligan T, Wellman B (1991) Experiences in the use of a media space. Proceedings of CHI'91.
38. Mashayekhi V, Feulner C, Riedl J (1994) CAIS: Collaborative Software Inspection of Software. Proceedings of the ACM SIGSOFT Symposium on the Foundations of Software Engineering.
39. Nawrocki J, Wojciehowski A (2001) Experimental evaluation of pair programming. European Software Control and Metrics, London.
40. Nawrocki JR, Jasinski M, Olek L, Lange B (2005) Pair programming vs. side-by-side programming. Software Process Improvement, Springer, Berlin/Heidelberg, pp. 28–38.

41. Olson JS, Olson GM, Storrosten M, Carter M (1992) How a group editor changes the character of a design meeting as well as its outcome. Proceedings of the ACM Conference on Computer Supported Co-operative Work.
42. O'Reilly C, Morrow P, Bustard D (2003) Improving conflict detection in optimistic concurrency control models. 11th International Workshop on Software Configuration Management.
43. Perry DE, Siy HP, Votta LG (2001) Parallel changes in large-scale software development: An observational case study. ACM TOSEM 10(3): 308–337.
44. Perry DE, Staudenmayer N, Votta LG (1994) People, organization, and process improvement. IEEE Software 11(4): 36–45.
45. Ratcliffe TL, Robertson A (2003) Code warriors and code-a-phobes: A study in attitude and pair programming. Proceedings of the SIGCSE Technical Symposium on Computer Science Education.
46. Sarma A, Bortis G, Hoek Avd (2007) Towards supporting awareness of indirect conflicts across software configuration management workspaces. Twenty-second IEEE/ACM International Conference on Automated Software Engineering (ASE), Atlanta, Georgia.
47. Sarma A, Maccherone L, Wagstrom P, Herbsleb J (2009) Tesseract: Interactive visual exploration of socio-technical relationships in software development. ICSE 09, Vancouver.
48. Sarma A, Noroozi Z, Hoek Avd (2003) Palantír: Raising awareness among configuration management workspaces. Proceedings of the 25th International Conference on Software Engineering.
49. Schroter A, Kwan I, Panjer LD, Damian D (2008) Chat to succeed. Proceedings of the 2008 International Workshop on Recommendation Systems for Software Engineering, ACM. Atlanta, Georgia, pp. 43–44.
50. Schummer T (2001) Lost and found in software space. Proceedings of the 34th Annual Hawaii International Conference on System Sciences, Hawaii.
51. Schummer T, Haake JM (2001) Supporting distributed software development by modes of collaboration. Proceedings of the Seventh European Conference on Computer Supported Co-operative Work.
52. Storey MA, Cheng LT, Bull I, Rigby P (2006) Shared waypoints and social tagging to support collaboration in software development. Proceedings of the 2006 20th Anniversary Conference on Computer Supported Co-operative Work ACM. Banff, Alberta, Canada, pp. 195–198.
53. Teasley S, Covi L, Krishnan MS, Olson JS (2000) How does radical collocation help a team succeed? Proceedings of ACM Conference on Computer Supported Cooperative Work.
54. Thummalapenta S, Xie T (2008) SpotWeb: Detecting framework hotspots and coldspots via mining open source code on the web. Proceedings of 23rd IEEE/ACM Conference on Automated Software Engineering (ASE).
55. Williams L, McDowell C, Nagappan N, Fernald J, Werner L (2003) Building pair programming knowledge through a family of experiment. Proceedings of the International Symposium on Empirical Software Engineering, p. 143.
56. Xiang PF, Ying ATT, Cheng P, Dang YB, Ehrlich K, Helander ME, Matchen PM, Empere A, Tarr PL, Williams C, Yang SX (2008) Ensemble: A recommendation tool for promoting communication in software teams. Proceedings of the 2008 International Workshop on Recommendation Systems for Software Engineering ACM. Atlanta, Georgia, pp. 1–1.
57. Zou L, Godfrey MW (2008) Understanding interaction differences between newcomer and expert programmers. Proceedings of the 2008 International Workshop on Recommendation Systems for Software Engineering ACM. Atlanta, Georgia, pp. 26–29.

Chapter 8
Continuous Coordination Tools and their Evaluation

Anita Sarma, Ban Al-Ani, Erik Trainer, Roberto S. Silva Filho, Isabella A. da Silva, David Redmiles, and André van der Hoek

Abstract This chapter discusses a set of co-ordination tools (the Continuous Co-ordination (CC) tool suite that includes Ariadne, Workspace Activity Viewer (WAV), Lighthouse, Palantír, and YANCEES) and details of our evaluation framework for these tools. Specifically, we discuss how we assessed the usefulness and the usability of these tools within the context of a predefined evaluation framework called DESMET. For example, for visualization tools we evaluated the suitability of the level of abstraction and the mode of displaying information of each tool. Whereas for an infrastructure tool we evaluate the effort required to implement co-ordination tools based on the given tool. We conclude with pointers on factors to consider when evaluating co-ordination tools in general.

8.1 Introduction

Co-ordination has been studied in different domains and within different contexts, as any kind of group work entails co-ordination [1, 32]. For our purposes, we focus on co-ordination efforts that are required to understand interdependencies among artifacts and developers in a software project, and to take appropriate steps to produce results with minimal conflicts. We recognize that co-ordination is not a static process, but one that needs continuous adjustments. This means that concerned individuals have to have the ability to respond to ongoing changes in the project and the effects of these changes on their work. Furthermore, co-ordination efforts occur at multiple levels: among developers, between managers and their teams, among multiple teams working together, and so on. The information required by an individual strongly correlates with their role in the team and their perspective of the project. Therefore, tool support for co-ordination needs to ensure that the right information

A. Sarma (✉)
Department of Computer Science & Engineering, University of Nebraska, Lincoln, NE 68588-0115, USA
e-mail: asarma@cse.unl.edu

I. Mistrík et al. (eds.), *Collaborative Software Engineering*,
DOI 10.1007/978-3-642-10294-3_8, © Springer-Verlag Berlin Heidelberg 2010

is presented to the right individual at the right time using appropriate presentation techniques. To achieve this goal, we created a suite of co-ordination tools that meets the different needs of different kinds of software development activities.

Evaluation of co-ordination tools is both critical and challenging [29]. In this chapter, we discuss the strategies we used to evaluate our co-ordination tool suite as well as results from the evaluation. In particular, we discuss our goals when evaluating the tools with respect to their usefulness and usability. Generally, the usefulness and functionality of our tool set has been largely motivated by our own ethnographical studies of multiple software development teams [11, 15].

This chapter discusses our approach to evaluate the usability, as well as, in some cases, the usefulness of each tool based on DESMET, Kitchenham et al.'s framework for evaluating software engineering tools [29]. The evaluation of each tool followed a subset of the nine evaluation types listed by DESMET, which was based on the nature/features of the tools as well as their maturity level. We found that evaluation should be iterative in nature as has been recommended for prototyping in software development [27].

The rest of the chapter is organized as follows. The next section provides a brief introduction to our approach. Section 8.1.2 provides a review of related work in which we discuss interdependencies and the need for co-ordination in addition to evaluation methodologies. This background section is followed by a description of the DESMET framework and our extension of this framework. We then present an outline of the Continuous Coordination (CC) principles, the origin of the CC tools, the evaluation approaches adopted for each, and the lessons learned as a result. The chapter concludes with a discussion of threats to the validity of our work and conclusions regarding the evaluation of the usefulness and usability of the CC tools.

8.2 Research Context

In software development the need for co-ordination among developers generally arises because of the underlying technical dependencies among work artifacts; as well as the structure of the development process [13, 7, 8]. Researchers in the software engineering as well as Computer-Supported Co-operative Work (CSCW) communities have recognized this problem and created a host of tools to improve team co-ordination. However, evaluating the usability and usefulness of such tools has proven to be extremely difficult. Here we focus on different evaluation approaches that are applicable for co-ordination tools.

There exists a diverse range of approaches to evaluating collaborative tools, e.g., [41, 4, 35, 56, 18, 31, 50]. Adopting a combination of empirical evaluation approaches is perceived as means to meet the challenges typically encountered [49]. The diversity of existing tools and evaluation approaches reflect the many challenges of facilitating co-ordination in teams [24].

Further, several evaluation frameworks have been proposed to support software tool evaluation, e.g., [29, 10, 30], among others. We base our evaluations of the

CC tool suite based on the DESMET framework [29]. We chose DESMET because it provides the desired level of abstraction that readily lends itself to adoption and matches our research objectives. This framework has also been successfully adopted by other researchers to evaluate software tools, e.g., [34, 36, 25].

8.3 The CC Evaluation Framework

The DESMET evaluation methodology separates evaluation approaches into two broad classes: (1) quantitative evaluations aimed at establishing measurable effects of using a tool, and (2) qualitative evaluations aimed at establishing method tool appropriateness, i.e., how well a tool fits the needs and cultures of an organization. These two methods are further subdivided into experiments, case studies, surveys, feature analyses, and screening to form nine distinct evaluation approaches. We used six of the evaluation approaches listed by Kitchenham et al. Note, we did not use all the approaches for each tool; rather a different combination of approaches was used based on the particular features, level of maturity, and the goal of the tool, i.e., usefulness or usability factors. Some of the factors that we considered when evaluating usefulness or usability were the effort that users' expended to utilize and/or understand a CC tool together with the perceived benefits. Moreover, we considered issues relating to the appropriateness of information that a tool shares with the development team (e.g., level of abstraction and mode of display).

We used the DESMET framework to determine which evaluation methodology to use per tool. Here, we present an overview of the evaluation approaches that we adopted, within the context of the framework as defined by Kitchenham et al.:

1. *Qualitative screening* is defined as a feature-based evaluation done by a single individual (or cohesive group) that not only determines the features to be assessed and their rating scale, but also performs the assessment. In the initial screening, the evaluations are usually based on literature describing the software method/tools rather than actual use of the methods/tools. We conducted such a screening by surveying existing tools and their features as reported in literature. Consequently, we surveyed related work for each one of our tools.
2. *Hybrid method 1*: Qualitative effects analysis is defined as a subjective assessment of the quantitative effect of methods and tools, based on expert opinion. We have used this analysis approach repeatedly at different phases of tool development. All our tools followed iterative prototyping and at the end of each prototyping cycle, we demonstrated our tools to industry experts as well as researchers to get their feedback on both usability and usefulness.
3. *Qualitative experiment* is defined as a feature-based evaluation done by a group of potential users who are expected to try out the tools on typical tasks before evaluating them. The tasks are performed by staffs that have used the tool on a real project. We requested that participants also "think out loud" during the experiment to get an idea of which features are difficult to understand in addition

to gaining insights into the reasoning behind their actions [19]. Another subcategory in this approach is the "feature analysis" experiment which is typically adopted when a tool's impact is not directly measurable on one project and is thus evaluated across multiple projects. We conducted such experiments with mature tools.

4. *Quantitative case study* is defined as an investigation of the quantitative impact of tools organized as a case study. This mode of evaluation can be used to understand the usefulness of a tool when applied to a real project as well as the scalability of the tool. We utilized data made available in open-source software projects repositories as case study data. This data was collected from a real and ongoing large scale project.

5. *Hybrid method 2*: Benchmarking is defined as a process of running a number of standard tests usually comparing one tool to alternative tools and assessing the relative performance of the tools against those tests. We selected a set of open source infrastructures to be compared with our tool as a benchmark in this instance of evaluation.

6. *Quantitative experiment* is defined as an investigation of the quantitative impact of tools organized as a formal experiment. We used a large enough sample size in our experiments to overcome the anticipated effects of individual and team differences. We typically adopted this methodology to evaluate mature tools because of the extensive effort and time required.

A detailed description of each tool is presented in the following section together with details of the evaluation approaches adopted. Appendix presents a summary of the tools and the evaluation approaches we utilized within the context of DESMET.

8.4 Continuous Coordination (CC) Tools: Their Origin and Evaluation

Co-ordination occurs at different levels and involves different stakeholders (e.g., developers, managers, testers, clients), who may have differing co-ordination requirements. Our suite of co-ordination tools attempts to meet different requirements among different stakeholders.

The CC tool suite was designed while keeping four critical questions in mind [42]. The first involves identifying *when* the tool should provide information. Providing a constant stream of information can overwhelm users, whereas infrequent sharing of information may lead to some users lacking information critical to completing their tasks. The information provided to the user depends on their role within the team. "*What* kind of information does the user need?" is the second question that guides our work. For example, a manager would typically need to be aware of team structure and work products to co-ordinate a project. A programmer, however, would generally need to be aware of changes to the design. These considerations lead us to ask, "*Who* should information be provided to?" For example, should information be provided to all programmers, to managers, or to a sub-set of these? Finally, *how* information is presented should also be considered. In general, our tools visualize graphical representations of co-ordination information because it can be more efficient and easier to understand information presented graphically than textually [52, 5].

In the following sections, we discuss a subset of the CC tool suite we subjected to more than one type of evaluation approach and the lessons we learned.

8.4.1 Ariadne

Ariadne is a visual tool that infers dependencies between people based on the modules they author. Our field studies led us to conclude that the management of dependencies becomes a daunting task as a project evolves and grows in the number of artifacts and contributors [14, 16]. These studies gave us insight into several types of communication and co-ordination problems, which helped us develop several representative scenarios that revealed the different types of dependency relationships managers and developers need to understand [14]. We call these relationships "socio-technical" because they involve both artifacts and the people who work on them.

Ariadne visualizations allow developers and managers to identify relevant socio-technical relationships central to their co-ordination needs. First, Ariadne creates a call-graph representing dependencies between source-code modules. Second, the tool annotates this graph with authorship information by connecting to a project's configuration management repository. Finally, Ariadne calculates a sociogram [54] representing dependencies between developers through the modules with which they work. The visualization is designed to take advantage of available screen real estate and thus occupies the entire screen.

Ariadne visualizations were designed to make the most of available screen real estate (shown in Fig. 8.1). Ariadne lays out called code units on the horizontal axis and developers on the vertical axis. It draws connections from a dependent author to the code unit they are dependent upon and back to the author responsible for that code unit and repeats this for each code unit in the project. Further details on its visualization and its advantages have been reported elsewhere [51].

8.4.1.1 Objective of Evaluation Process and Steps Taken

Ariadne visualizes socio-technical relationships using highly abstract representations of dependency information, such as shapes, colors, and axes. As such, effort is required to learn how to use the tool to accomplish specific tasks. We thus decided upon an evaluation strategy that would allow us to evaluate this effort in early stages of the tool's design.

A survey, or qualitative screening, of literature and existing socio-technical tools revealed the general need to support awareness of dependencies and identifying

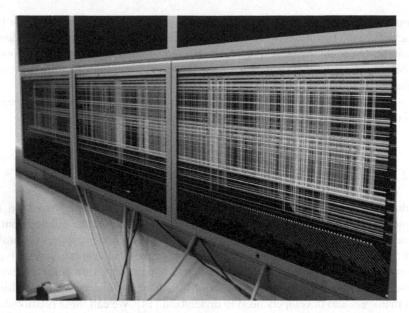

Fig. 8.1 An overview and zoomed in view of a project's socio-technical dependencies using Ariadne

developers of interest via visual interpretation. Literature in the information visualization field identified usability as one important barrier to tool adoption by end-users [2, 3, 40]. Moreover, evaluating tools in real settings and with real users (in our case, developers and managers) is expensive in terms of the effort required, especially in the early stages of design. In an effort to get usability feedback "cheaply", we applied multiple inspection usability inspection methods: Nielsen's Heuristic Evaluation [37] Lewis and Polson's Cognitive Walkthrough [55] and Thomas Green's Cognitive Dimensions of Notations [22]. In addition, we applied Edward Tufte's general principles of information presentation [52, 53]. We performed each inspection method with a team comprised of four colleagues. They had no experience using the new visualization. This unfamiliarity helped us to identify problematic design assumptions about new users' expectations and assumptions about interacting with and drawing conclusions from the visualization. Further information of our evaluations is detailed elsewhere [51].

After this qualitative inspection, we performed a case study where we selected several open-source projects from Sourceforge.net to visualize. These projects had been active for several years, and were active at the time of our evaluation. Thus they represented a test-bed from which to confirm the scalability of the visualization to real-world projects. In parallel to the previous study, with the help of industry partners and open-source developers, we assessed the usefulness of current features and incorporated suggested feedback into the tool. These activities, in combination with the application of usability inspection methods, constituted a qualitative effects analysis in terms of DESMET.

8.4.1.2 Lessons Learned with Respect to the Tool

We were able to tease out commonly occurring problems with respect to usability through the combined application of evaluation approaches. For example, the use of color to indicate individual developers and the directionality of dependencies proved to be more difficult than we originally thought, especially as we visualized larger projects. The Cognitive Walkthrough, Tufte's principles, and the Cognitive Dimensions analyses highlighted this issue. The Heuristic Evaluation and Cognitive Dimensions revealed the potential need to allow users to undo certain filtering actions in order to trace back their steps, as well as the option to view different configurations of developers, e.g., aggregating them into teams. All three methods suggested the need to improve feedback (e.g., to indicate that specific dependencies have not been created instead of displaying no search results).

Ariadne allows users to identify patterns in the way developers call different parts of code in the system that form a general overview of a project's socio-technical dependencies. Throughout the course of applying the usability inspection methods discussed above, we realized that these patterns would heavily depend on the way the different axes were ordered. For example, a pattern generated from a temporal ordering of the code units (arranged by date last modified) might not show up if the code units were arranged in alphabetical order instead. Thus, the ordering makes a difference in the patterns that users will see, identify, and flag for future identification.

8.4.1.3 Lessons Learned with Respect to Evaluation

The usability inspection methods we applied to Ariadne thus far have allowed us to make certain corrections to Ariadne's visualization before deploying the tool to real users in real settings. However, evaluations of this sort cannot account for organizational issues relating to adoption. This is one limitation of our evaluation strategy. Publicly exposing sensitive information normally stored in software repositories may have effects on the way developers work or even Ariadne's results. In one instance, we showed some of our early visualizations to several open source developers who commented that they would avoid "touching" certain classes to avoid breaking dependent code. To an extent, Ariadne can be used by managers and supervisors to gauge developer's progress, or lack thereof. Further, as speculated by our interviewees, individuals may "game" the tool to show an increase in their contributions, especially if they feel that a lack of activity may be used against them.

Some researchers claim that new evaluation approaches for visualizations are needed because current approaches test the wrong users and unconventional user interface components hurt user performance [2, 3]. We have described the impracticality of deploying Ariadne to our intended end-users in early design. To address the second point, the results from our evaluation indicate that usability inspection methods can be usefully applied to abstract visualizations instead of traditional interface components such as methods and drop-down menus. Moreover, despite the fact that Tufte's principles of information are general rather than domain-specific; our work serves as one of the few examples of the application of these rules-of-thumb to novel, interactive socio-technical visualizations for software engineering. Thus, traditional evaluation approaches are still useful for incremental prototyping and iterative design of our research tools. As we continue to develop and refine Ariadne, visualization-specific evaluation heuristics like those suggested by other researchers [57] will become more useful. We expect the aforementioned evaluation to be used as a point-of-comparison for researchers evaluating socio-technical visual interfaces in early design.

8.4.2 Workspace Activity Viewer

Workspace Activity Viewer (WAV) provides a highly scalable view of all ongoing parallel development activities in a software project [43]. WAV visualizes information in 3D to illustrate changes to a software project over time, the types and sizes of the changes, and provides various filters to examine aspects of workspace activities in more detail. WAV reveals social evolution via a movie-like playback of the state of the project, showing what developers are active when, and to which types of artifacts they contribute (Fig. 8.2). As such, WAV can benefit both developers and managers, and provides two different views: artifact-centric and developer-centric, accordingly. Both views use a cylinder metaphor to represent workspace changes, where the width of the cylinder represents the size of a change. In the artifact-centric view, cylinders represent artifacts, with each segment of a cylinder denoting a developer who has made changes to that artifact. In the developer-centric view, cylinders represent developers, with each segment of a cylinder denoting an artifact that developer has touched. As stacks (artifacts or developers) become dormant, the associated stack of cylinders slowly moves to the back of the display. A more detailed account of the tool is reported elsewhere [43].

8.4.2.1 Objective of Evaluation Process and Steps Taken

The objective of our evaluation of WAV was to confirm the accuracy of the tool's playback of the activities occurring in real software development projects and to test the visualization's capacity to scale to large software projects [43]. In terms of display technique, we wanted to see if all relevant workspace events could be clearly visualized using the screen real-estate WAV requires. As we have seen in the case of Ariadne, deploying tools in real settings is a difficult challenge, especially in early prototyping. Thus, we decided to evaluate WAV through a case study and report results to project managers and developers.

We applied WAV to five open-source projects: ArgoUML, GAIM, Freemind, jEdit, and Scarab. In addition, we analyzed project data from a local company that collaborates with our research group. Since we used archived data for our case study, we did not gather information of real-time workspace edits. To overcome this problem, we simulated workspace data based on CVS change metadata (e.g., who checked the file in, when they did it, and how much changed). This metadata

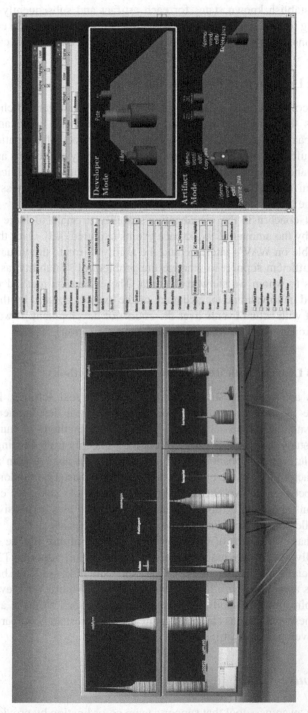

Fig. 8.2 Developer-centric mode on six monitors (*left*) and artifact-centric mode with user-definable filters on the (*right*)

allowed us to establish known states for each artifact and subsequently generate events correlating to workspace activity before the commit occurred. The evaluation we performed constitutes a qualitative-effects analysis and a quantitative case study.

8.4.2.2 Lessons Learned with Respect to the Tool

Visualizing the collective activity in a project can allow managers to choose and identify patterns that may lead to co-ordination breakdowns. For example, the movie-like playback feature of WAV allows one to see periods of stagnation which may indicate insufficient progress. Whereas spurts of activity as artifacts and developers' piles expand upward and move to the front may indicate conflicts. These patterns can then be used as potential "red flags" to indicate the possibility of problems over the lifecycle of a project.

An important concern is the visualization's ability to scale to large software projects caused by the amount of workspace events captured [43]. Over this range, the filters available on WAV's interface and the ability to rotate the visualization's axes provided sufficient support to manage the problem of scalability, as reported by the managers to whom we showed the data. The evaluation method we chose for WAV allowed us to validate the accuracy of the events captured by the tool by correlating them with actual events over the course of development. It was further validated by a project manager who confirmed our observations.

8.4.2.3 Lessons Learned with Respect to Evaluation Methods

Our evaluations are not a substitute for assessment in real settings. However, they come close by looking at real project data from real development teams. Unlike costly evaluation approaches such as talk-aloud methods or human subjects tests, case-study data can be collected relatively cheaply from existing, (often) publicly available project repositories. While we were not able to gain access to real workspace activities, we were able to simulate them based on randomizations of the patterns between known check-ins and check-outs. As such, we could still make observations about the evolution of the projects. The most expensive part of the process is reflecting findings back to the original participants.

One aspect that evaluations of this type leave out is usability for the end-user, which is typically one of the main barriers to visualization adoption [2, 3, 40]. Usability is especially important in the context of the work discussed here because of the upfront costs associated with human subjects testing. Future WAV evaluations involves the application of usability inspection methods such as those applied to Ariadne [51]. These evaluations can reveal patterns of interest and compare activity between both developers and artifacts.

8.4.3 Lighthouse

Lighthouse is an awareness tool that supports team co-ordination by providing each developer with information of ongoing activities in the project [9]. The goal of the

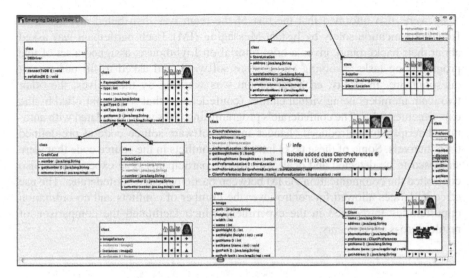

Fig. 8.3 Lighthouse emerging design

tool is to improve a developer's understanding about others' activities and how one's own activities affect the others. The tool builds an Emerging Design diagram, an always up-to-date abstraction of the source code components, dependencies, authorship and current changes. The diagram consists of a UML-like class representation of the code as it exists on the developers' workspaces (Fig. 8.3). All information about changes made to the code is collected automatically by Lighthouse from the IDE and the SCM system and is propagated immediately to all project members.

Lighthouse visualization supports early detection of design decay by allowing users to identify unintended design changes. Problems like conflicting changes in shared artifacts and duplicate work can also be spotted as soon as they surface. A detailed account of the tool's features and the nature of the support it provides is reported elsewhere [9].

8.4.3.1 Objective of Evaluation Process and Steps Taken

Lighthouse has been evaluated both via qualitative effects analysis and qualitative experiments. We demonstrated Lighthouse to various industry experts and academic researchers, obtained and incorporated their feedbacks. Later we evaluated Lighthouse via a qualitative observational study to investigate its usefulness in warning participants of emerging conflicts, as well as the effort required by an individual to investigate and resolve conflicts.

This study recruited four graduate student volunteers who had sufficient knowledge about the Java programming language, the Eclipse IDE, and the software configuration management (SCM) tool (preferably Subversion). These volunteers used the prototype to execute small programming tasks on a simulated software development team. More specifically, participants were told that they would be joining a pre-existing team, substituting a developer who recently left the project.

They were also informed that the rest of the team was distributed and available for communication solely by Instant Messaging (IM). Each participant was asked about their background, given a brief tutorial on Lighthouse, assigned a set of five programming tasks involving online store software, and asked to fill out an exit questionnaire. In reality, each participant was working by themselves; the other two team members being virtual entities (confederates) that were controlled by the experimenters [44]. The confederate's programming tasks were simulated with automated scripts that introduced changes in the software source code at pre-defined time intervals. Some of these tasks introduced conflicts in the source code that were supposed to be detected and dealt with by the participants. The experimenter also controlled the communication via IM between participant and confederates. The use of confederates allowed for control over the number of conflicts and co-ordination opportunities introduced in the experiment which facilitated the comparison of results across experiments.

8.4.3.2 Lessons Learned with Respect to the Tool

For the experiment, we introduced two direct conflicts (concurrent changes to the same artifact) and two indirect conflicts (conflicting changes to dependent artifacts). We observed that the timing of conflict introduction was a decisive factor on detecting direct conflicts; developers who had already started coding a task before the confederate created the duplicated effort did not detect the conflict. We also observed that changes made by confederates were either noticed as soon as they surfaced or not until the end of the task, when participants faced merge problems because of the SCM system. All changes detected on time, though, were quickly and appropriately addressed. When indirect conflicts were introduced during the experiment, only half of the participants recognized the conflict in one task and none could complete the other task in the given time.

We designed the experiment to understand the role of "emerging design" is helping participant's co-ordinate their work. At the end of the study participants reported that they found that the emerging design served as a reference for understanding the software structure, which were corroborated by our observations on how participants explored the diagram during the study. We also found that participants by using filters that highlighted recent changes to the emerging diagram were able to use the diagram as a way of identifying ongoing changes in the project. Finally, in many cases the emerging design stimulated communication in a team. For example, when trying to contact a confederate to resolve a conflict, participants always first looked for the author of conflicting changes using the emerging design diagram. In all cases, participants contacted the most adequate confederate to address the issue. Further, changes that were unrelated to the tasks being performed were correctly ignored, thereby showing that Lighthouse streamlines communications in a project. However, we observed that participants were sometimes confused regarding which changes were local and which remote. Consequently, this usability problem might hinder users from responding to remote emerging conflicts. Our future work will provide means to differentiate between local and remote changes, which will help overcome this problem.

8.4.3.3 Lessons Learned with Respect to the Evaluation of Tool

Our study suffered from threats to validity common for user experiments. The total time of 1 h was insufficient for subjects to complete all the tasks and a simple walk-through of Lighthouse's features was insufficient for them to appropriately learn all the tool features. We found that the complexity of Lighthouse's different interactive features meant participants required more time to learn how to use them. Further, to understand how the software code was evolving and its effect on the given tasks required a much longer experiment involving a more complicated code base. Such an experiment would allow independent changes made in different parts of the code to interact and create more intricate conflicts. Finally, the pressure of having to complete all the tasks within a limited period of time might have made participants spend less time observing and understanding the emerging design. We plan to follow this study with a more detailed in situ study of real developers working on their projects.

8.4.4 Palantír

Palantír is a workspace awareness tool that automatically and unobtrusively intercepts local edits as well as all CM operations in a workspace and transmits these events across relevant workspaces to inform developers of ongoing changes in the project [46]. Each workspace summarizes the events it receives and communicates these to a developer via subtle awareness cues.

The purpose of these cues is to unobtrusively draw the user's attention to emerging conflicts, both direct and indirect, without undue distractions or overwhelming the user with too much information (Fig. 8.4). Palantír currently detects indirect conflicts that arise because of changes to public methods and variables [45]. Palantír was integrated into the Eclipse development environment such that annotations in the package explorer view inform developers of activities in other workspaces (top inset in Fig. 8.4) and a new Eclipse view, the conflict view, allows users to obtain further details of changes causing conflicts (bottom inset in Fig. 8.4). The goal is for the textual annotations to warn developers of impending conflicts and when the users need further information, they can investigate the conflict via the Palantír conflict view, where various kinds of icons provide additional information about the state of a conflict.

8.4.4.1 Objective of Evaluation Process and Steps Taken

Palantír is one of the more mature prototypes in the CC tool suite. Therefore it has iteratively undergone several evaluation approaches. Qualitative screening by surveying other tools via literature survey and iterative qualitative effects analysis, to get feedback from experts, helped us determine its specific awareness and display

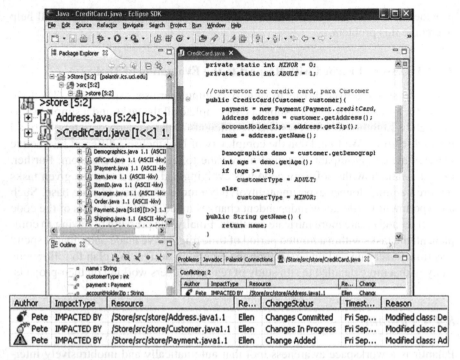

Fig. 8.4 Palantír workspace awareness

features early on in the project. We then validated the feasibility of our approach
via feature analysis experiments, where we integrated Palantír with three SCM
systems – CVS, RCS, and Subversion. We subsequently performed initial qualitative experiments to validate and obtain feedback on our experimental setup before
performing our quantitative user experiments. These experiments were designed to
test the usefulness of Palantír in enabling participants discover potential conflicts
and test its ease of use and the effort required by participants to notice, investigate,
and resolve conflicts in their tasks.

The experiments were specifically designed to observe a participant making edits
in a group setting with (and without) using Palantír to co-ordinate their changes.
Particular individual differences that concern our experiment are differences in how
a team member interacts in the group and a programmer's technical skills. We
controlled for differences in group interaction by using confederate based design,
similar to Lighthouse evaluations, where a participant could interact with the two
other team members via IM.

We controlled individual differences that stem from technical skills by conducting stratified random assignment. Further, we benchmarked the non-programming
tasks evaluations with our results from an analogous experiment with programming
tasks. In "textual" experiment, we chose a sample text that was neither too complex
nor too interesting to overwhelm or distract the participants. The text reflected some
key properties of software, primarily modularity and dependency. Modularity was

attained by using text which was comprised of separate files (chapters). Whereas, dependency was simulated by text containing references that linked text across modules and which had to be kept consistent. The textual experiment was followed by a "Java" experiment to evaluate Palantír in the programming domain. This experiment sought to confirm results from the first experiment. However, here we sought to take into account the limitation of the programmer's individual differences becoming visible, especially in the time it takes for them to complete change tasks.

8.4.4.2 Lessons Learned with Respect to the Tool

The evaluation of Palantír sought answers to three principle questions regarding the tool's usefulness and usability. First, *does workspace awareness help users in their ability to identify and resolve a larger number of conflicts?* We found with statistical significance that participants in the Experiment group detected and resolved a larger number of conflicts for both conflict types (direct and indirect). We found that participants typically noticed information provided by Palantír before embarking on their task or right after finishing it. Second, *does workspace awareness affect the time-to-completion for tasks with conflicts?* An obvious effect of workspace awareness tools is the fact that they incur some extra overhead as developers must spend time and effort to monitor the information that is provided to them. Further, if they suspect a conflict then they spend time and effort to investigate and resolve it. We examine this overhead by comparing the average time, which includes the time to detect, investigate, co-ordinate, and resolve a conflict that participants in each of the treatment groups took to complete tasks. We found that on average participants using Palantír detected a larger number of conflicts without significant overheads. Finally, *does workspace awareness promote co-ordination?* We observed that on detecting a conflict participants generally took one of the following actions: synchronize, update, chat, skip the particular task, or implement the task by using a placeholder. In general, we saw a comparable number of co-ordination actions for direct conflicts between the control and experiment groups, but a sharp increase in the number of co-ordination actions for indirect conflicts for the experiment group.

8.4.4.3 Lessons Learned with Respect to the Evaluation of Tool

Our experiments led us to conclude that evaluating co-ordination tools that require a group of people to understand and use the information provided to co-ordinate with each other is extremely complex. While we took great care to control individual differences between participants we still found large enough variances in the time to completion of tasks. Another way of controlling individual differences would have been to perform a between subject test, i.e., test the same participant in both the control and experiment conditions using two very similar projects. Additionally, in our experiment we seeded the same type of conflicts in the same order. It is possible that participants may learn from past conflicts and change their behavior with how they react to new conflicts; therefore, changing the order in which we introduced the direct and indirect conflicts may produce different results. Finally, in the Java experiment, participants were not required to integrate their changes and build the entire project. Therefore, nearly all participants in the control group and some in the experiment group did not detect the conflicts remaining in the code base. This fact combined with the fact that we did not penalize the task with unresolved conflicts precluded us from quantifying the benefits of workspace awareness with respect to the time and effort saved in co-ordination. While this experiment design decision was disadvantageous, finding the perfect balance between the amounts of time required for participants to learn about the tool, complete tasks, and the complexity of the project is not trivial.

8.4.5 YANCEES

Notification servers (or publish/subscribe infrastructures) support the continuous co-ordination requirements of disseminating information from distributed information producers to different information consumers in a timely fashion [39]. They provide mechanisms for publishing, routing, filtering and disseminating information in the form of events. As such, publish/subscribe infrastructures have been used in support of different event-driven applications [12, 17, 26, 46]. Whenever a new event-driven application is conceived, developers face two alternatives: build a publish/subscribe infrastructure from scratch, or reuse one of many existing research and industrial systems. A qualitative screening of existing publish/subscribe infrastructures revealed different architectural patterns adopted by industrial and research publish/subscribe infrastructures in the support of the evolving and heterogeneous requirements of different application domains [48]. For example: minimal core, one-size-fits-all, co-ordination languages and compositional models. Most of these patterns are neither extensible nor configurable in the set of features they provide, making their adaptation and reuse a difficult endeavor. This observation motivated the development of YANCEES, which is an extensible and configurable publish/subscribe infrastructure based on plug-ins [47]. As such, our goal in the development of YANCEES was twofold. First, from the infrastructure developers' perspective, we sought the reduction of the development effort. Second, from the point of view of infrastructure consumers, we sought an infrastructure that can reduce the development effort of event-driven applications. In order to evaluate these goals, we designed the following evaluation.

8.4.5.1 Objective of Evaluation Process and Steps Taken

Our evaluation had three major objectives. First, we sought to assess the usefulness of YANCEES i.e., its ability to support the performance and application-specific requirements of different application domains. Second, we sought to evaluate its usability, which is measured as the development effort of both infrastructure developers and consumers. Finally, our evaluation compares these measures with existing approach in both the literature and industry. We took the following steps to achieve these goals:

1. We performed qualitative screening of industrial and research infrastructures with the goal of identifying major architectural patterns adopted by these tools in the support of different application domains requirements. The screening revealed four new alternatives which included: (a) employing generalization in the construction of minimal APIs; (b) supporting extensibility through the use of co-ordination languages; (c) employing variation in the construction of one-size-fits-all infrastructures; (d) or supporting flexibility by the use of component frameworks as is the case with YANCEES.
2. We selected a set of open source infrastructures, one for each category to be compared in a benchmark. These included Siena [6] representing generalized minimal APIs; Sun JavaSpaces [20] representing co-ordination languages; CORBA Notification Service (or CORBA-NS) [38] representing one-size-fits-all infrastructures, and YANCEES [47] representing flexible compositional infrastructures.
3. We selected three feature-rich event-driven application domains as the source of requirements for our study. These were usability monitoring represented by EDEM, awareness represented by CASSIUS and collaborative environments represented by Impromptu [17, 28]. These infrastructures were selected first for their diversity of requirements, and second, for the previous experience of the authors in their development, which provides both access to the source code, and expertise in their set of requirements.
4. The requirements of each application were then abstracted into a set of reference APIs representing ideal features that a publish/subscribe infrastructure must support in each domain. We implemented each one of these tree reference APIs using the four selected infrastructures. We also implemented each API from scratch, as a control implementation.
5. Finally, we performed a quantitative evaluation of the resulting implementations, measuring their average responsiveness and the total development effort of each. The development effort is calculated as the product of the number of lines of code (LOC) and the McCabe Cyclomatic Complexity (or McCabeCC) of the code required to adapt each infrastructure in the implemnetatoin of each API [33]. The goal of the performance benchmark in our study is to determine the usefulness of the infrastructure, in serving its purpose within the requirements of each application domain.

8.4.5.2 Lessons Learned with Respect to the Tool

In our performance benchmarks, we compared responsiveness of an infrastructure implemented with YANCEES with the same infrastructure implemented reusing the other infrastructures. The results of one of the three benchmarks are shown in Fig. 8.5 (left). The results show that YANCEES performance is comparable to that

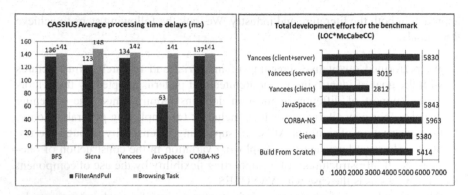

Fig. 8.5 YANCEES performance benchmark (*left*) and comparative development effort (*right*)

obtained by reusing existing infrastructures or even to the cases where the APIs are built from scratch.

This demonstrates YANCEES ability to support the requirements of different application domains and its usefulness in supporting the development of application-specific infrastructures, with no significant performance penalty.

We also compared the total development effort (measures at the product of LOC and McCabeCC) to determine the usability of YANCEES when the other infrastructures are used to support the three application domains Fig. 8.5 (right). It is important to note that infrastructures (e.g., Siena, CORBA-NS, etc.,) are reused as black-boxes. They are extended "from the outside", by building the required functionality around their provided APIs. YANCEES, on the other hand, is configurable and extensible "from the inside", allowing the modification of the set of features its supports. This fundamental difference is reflected in the graphs of (Fig. 8.5) where both client and server side development efforts are shown, together with combined effort (client + sever) in a separate bar.

Figure 8.5 (right) demonstrates that while the total cost of reuse of YANCEES in all the three scenarios (client + server) is comparable with existing approaches, its ability to separate client and server-side development has two important advantages. First, it allows the separation between publish/subscribe infrastructures producers and consumers, dividing the development effort (the two bars: YANCEES client and YANCEES server in Fig. 8.5). Second, it reduces the application development effort, since the infrastructure can be configured and extended to support the exact application-specific set of features required by the application domain. This is made evident by the lower YANCEES client effort (Fig. 8.5). Contrary to our expectations, the total (server + client) side development effort when using YANCEES was not significantly lower than the other approaches. This can be the consequence of the additional effort devoted to configuration and extension of the infrastructure.

8.4.5.3 Lessons Learned with Respect to the Evaluation

When comparing different software infrastructures, developed with different original goals, it is important to strive for a fair evaluation process. Different strategies were adopted in the design of our benchmark to increase equitable comparison between the different approaches. First, we chose to implement the benchmark ourselves to eliminate the variance that may come by the use of different developers at different levels of expertise. Second, we adopted best of breed design practices in all implementations [21] and modularized common features into components that were reused throughout the different implementations. We also adopted the same algorithms used by the original applications (EDEM, CASSIUS, Impromptu) we emulated. Finally, we aligned the different implementations to follow the same task structure. This facilitates our data collection and analysis. These strategies collectively increase the likelihood that code style, algorithms and overall software architecture were similar throughout our experiments. Finally, the benchmark tests were conducted in the same set of machines (one client and one server), connected via a 100 Mbps local Ethernet, thus providing a constant environment.

While the overall comparison of different infrastructures reusability based on the number of LOC and McCabeCC allows the comparison of the total development effort of these infrastructures, they do not reveal important details about the individual concerns and costs involved in each approach. For example, the costs of adaptation, extension and configuration. In order to investigate these costs in more details, we are currently conducting a finer-grained analysis of the code uses in our benchmark.

8.5 Discussion

Our goal was to evaluate the usability and usefulness of different co-ordination tools constituting our CC tool suite. Our tools were motivated by findings from a set of ethnographic studies on co-ordination in software teams [14, 16] and a qualitative screening of existing co-ordination tools. While these studies formed the basis on which we determined the usefulness of the tool features, each tool's usefulness and usability was further evaluated using the DESMET evaluation framework. The particular approach used for a particular tool was determined based on its functionality, the specific aspect that was being evaluated (usefulness or usability), and the maturity level of the tool.

The majority of our tools strive to provide appropriate information of ongoing project activities to the user, therefore, a primary goal of our evaluations was to study the usefulness of the tools based on whether a tool achieved an appropriate level of abstraction. Depending on the desired functionality of a co-ordination tool and the target audience, different levels of data abstraction are required, which can then be visualized via text, tables, charts, or other visualization metaphors. Most of our CC tools have a visualization component. These components vary, from being completely unobtrusive and subtle, such as information display as extensions to the development editor, or more intensive displays requiring separate stand alone visualizations that work best in auxiliary display units (second monitor or ambient devices) or as large scale visualization that acts as a command control center. Thus, a key evaluation criterion was to assess the usefulness of a tool's display technique. In particular, we investigated the tradeoff between the amounts of information that was displayed and the obtrusiveness of the display. Towards this goal, we observed that *qualitative effects* analysis and *usability inspections* served as a good first level of analysis to obtain user feedback. Further, most software projects are large, which requires that our tools can scale well to large data sets. Towards assessing the scalability of our tools, we used *quantitative case studies*, namely, using our tools to visualize large scale open source projects and then interviewing developers or managers from those projects to obtain their feedback.

The next important criterion for our evaluation was to test the usability of our tools. We primarily evaluated the usability of a tool by investigating the trade-offs between the efforts users are willing to expend in operating and/or learning a tool, versus the estimated benefits gained. Moreover, since many visualization tools rely on novel metaphors to help users interpret and navigate the vast information space generated by software, it is important to evaluate the time and effort it takes users to understand visualizations. Therefore, we also evaluated the effort expended by individuals to understand the information provided by a tool via user experiments (both qualitative and quantitative).

We found that two challenges are typically encountered when evaluating co-ordination tools: (1) differences in outcome because of differences in the technical aptitude of participants and (2) differences in how a group reacts to tasks and conflicts. Through our experiments, we sought to control for both these differences. We controlled for differences in technical aptitude by stratifying our participants based on their background and then randomly selecting participants from each stratum. Further, we benchmarked our results first by using non-programming tasks and then confirming these results in a programming domain. We controlled for differences in group interactions by using confederate based design, which ensured consistency in the kind and timing of conflicts, as well as group interactions via IM.

While we took special care to control external factors to be able to test specifically the usability of our tools, our study suffers from the common external threats to research validity that arise in user experiments. For example, selecting students as participants in several of our evaluation threatens the ability to generalize from our results. We sought to recruit different participants each time with varying levels of expertise (i.e., graduate and post-graduate students) to limit this threat. We used confederates to achieve consistency in our experiments. As such, we realize that results can differ if events are introduced closer to the completion of the task or at random intervals, as may happen in practice. Thus, the controlled introduction of an event at a specific time can also threaten the generality of our results.

We note that the evaluation of a co-ordination infrastructure tool such as YANCEES, require different evaluation methods than other front end co-ordination tools. Therefore, its evaluations follow a slightly different format, although they still fall within the DESMET evaluation framework. We tested the usefulness of YANCEES mainly through qualitative screening; and the usability and robustness of YANCEES by implementing three feature rich applications using YANCEES and three other competing event notification services. A quantitative evaluation of the resulting implementations was performed that assessed the average responsiveness and total development effort required per implementation.

Finally, we encountered internal threats in the form of bias that may have been introduced during our qualitative screening evaluations. The potential for bias also exists in the feedback participants provided because tool developers typically conducted the experiments and were direct recipients of the feedback. We strove to minimize the impact of these threats by conducting a combination of different evaluation approaches for each tool.

8.6 Conclusions

In this paper, we described a set of co-ordination tools as known the CC tool suite. The focus of this chapter was to describe in detail the different evaluation methodologies that we followed for assessing the usefulness and usability of our tools. In conclusion, we maintain there is no one evaluation method for a tool; rather, tools should be iteratively evaluated using multiple evaluation methods to obtain well rounded evaluation results. We found that a different evaluation methodology is often needed to assess usefulness or usability aspects of a tool. Finally, the experience acquired while researching continuous co-ordination has led us to conclude that we need to consider the co-ordination information in terms of *what, how, when,* and *who* shares it, which means that the evaluation of these tools would benefit from evaluating whether these aspects of the tools address developers' needs.

Future plans for each tool were specified in their respective sections. However, we have specific tasks ahead of us that hold true for most of the CC tools at both the individual and organizational level. For example, at the individual level we need to evaluate the impact that the order of events has on the outcome of our evaluations and the possible co-ordination patterns that can emerge. CC tools typically share potentially sensitive information, thus it would be beneficial to investigate the issues relating to individual privacy and data confidentiality. Both are important issues that need to be carefully assessed to design usable co-ordination tools. Co-ordination tools can fail if individuals perceive that the tool is used as a managerial performance metric or used by their competitors [23]. We also need to evaluate the use of CC tools within an organizational context. A tool that requires changes to the typical workflow in an organization will generally encounter more resistance because potential users do not readily change their work processes to adopt a new tool.

Acknowledgements This research was supported by the U.S. National Science Foundation under grants 0534775, 0326105, 0093489, and 0205724, by the Intel Corporation, by two IBM Eclipse Technology Exchange grants, and an IBM Technology Fellowship.

Appendix

Table 8.1 Summary of evaluation approaches for each CC tool

Tool	Purpose of tool	Purpose of evaluation	DESMET	Evaluation approach
Ariadne	Allows developers to explore and analyze socio-technical dependency information.	Identify usability issues with Ariadne's visual interface.	Qualitative screening; Qualitative-effects analysis; Quantitative case-study.	Usability inspection methods: Heuristic evaluation Cognitive walkthrough Cognitive dimensions of notations Tufte's principles of information presentation.
WAV	Provides a 3D view of all parallel workspace activities and supports playback over time.	Demonstrate accuracy of data collected and to test scalability of the visualization.	Qualitative screening; Qualitative-effects analysis; Quantitative case-study.	Post-mortem analysis (e.g. case study) of existing open-source projects and validation of results with project members.
Lighthouse	Creates the emerging design, an always up-to-date abstraction of the software code.	Observe the usefulness of lighthouse in helping users understand ongoing project activities, detect emerging conflicts, and communicate with team members.	Qualitative screening; Qualitative-effects analysis; Qualitative experiments.	Informal user experiment involving Observation by experimenters Think aloud techniques Exit survey.
Palantír	Promote workspace awareness by transmitting information of ongoing project activities to detect emerging direct and indirect conflicts at real time.	Statistically determine the usefulness of Palantír in detecting emerging conflicts and promoting coordination to resolve conflicts.	Qualitative screening; Qualitative-effects analysis; Qualitative experiments (user experiment; interoperability); Quantitative experiment; Benchmarking of experiment results.	Formal sser experiment (Benchmark: use text data to control for individual difference arising due to difference in technical skills; Confederate design: control the type, number, and timing of conflicts to overcome variances in group interaction) Observation by experimenters Think aloud techniques Exit survey.

Table 8.1 (continued)

Tool	Purpose of tool	Purpose of evaluation	DESMET	Evaluation approach
YANCEES	Improve the support for heterogeneous set of requirements of continuous coordination tools.	Assess the reusability and performance of YANCEES, comparing the results with existing approaches.	Qualitative screening to determine existing approaches. Quantitative experiment: reusability Benchmarking: performance.	Implement three APIs based on selected infrastructures, measuring the development effort. Benchmark: evaluate the performance of the resulting implementations.

References

1. Amrit C (2005) Co-ordination in software development: the problem of task allocation. Proceedings of the 2005 Workshop on Human and Social Factors of Software Engineering (ACM), St. Louis, Missouri, pp. 1–7.
2. Andrews K (2006) Evaluating Information Visualizations. AVI Workshop on Beyond Time and Errors: Novel Evaluation Methods for Information Visualization (ACM), Venice, Italy, pp. 1–5.
3. Ardito C, Buono P, Costabile MF, Lanzilotti R (2006) Systematic inspection of information visualization systems. AVI Workshop on Beyond Time and Errors: Novel Evaluation Methods for Information Visualization (ACM), Venice, Italy.
4. Barkhuus L, Rode JA (2007) From Mice to Men – 24 Years of Evaluation in CHI. CHI 2007 http://www.viktoria.se/altchi/.
5. Card SK, Mackinlay JD, Shneiderman B (1999) Readings in Information Visualization: Using Vision to Think. San Francisco, CA: Morgan Kaufmann.
6. Carzaniga A, Rosenblum DS, Wolf AL (2001) Design and evaluation of a wide-area event notification service. ACM Transactions on Computer Systems 19(3): 332–383.
7. Cataldo M, Wagstrom PA, Herbsleb JD, Carley KM (2006) Identification of co-ordination requirements: Implications for the design of collaboration and awareness tools. Computer Supported Co-operative Work, Banff, Alberta, Canada, pp. 353–362.
8. Crowston K (1997) A co-ordination theory approach to organizational process design. Organization Science 8(2): 157–175.
9. da Silva I, Chen P, Van der Westhuizen C, Ripley R, Hoek Avd (2006) Lighthouse: Co-ordination through emerging design. OOPSLA Workshop on Eclipse Technology eXchange, Portland, Oregon, pp. 11–15.
10. Damianos L, Hirschman L, Kozierok R, Kurtz J, Greenberg A, Walls K, Laskowski S, Scholtz J (1999) Evaluation for collaborative systems. ACM Computing Surveys 31(2es), Article No. 15.
11. de Souza CRB (2005) On the relationship between software dependencies and co-ordination: Field studies and tool support. Ph.D. dissertation, Donald Bren School of Information and Computer Sciences, UC, Irvine, CA.
12. de Souza CRB, Basaveswara SD, Redmiles D (2002) Lessons learned using notification servers to support application awareness. Meeting of the Human Computer Interaction Consortium, Frasier, CO.

13. de Souza CRB, Froehlich J, Dourish P (2005) Seeking the source: Software source code as a social and technical artifact. ACM SIGGROUP Conference On Supporting Group Work, Sanibel Island, FL, USA, 06–09 November 2005, pp. 197–206.
14. de Souza CRB, Quirk S, Trainer E, Redmiles DF (2007) Supporting collaborative software development through the visualization of socio-technical dependencies. 2007 International ACM Conference on Supporting Group Work (ACM), Sanibel Island, FL, USA, pp. 147–156.
15. de Souza CRB, Redmiles D, Cheng LT, Millen D, Patterson J (2004) How a good software practice thwarts collaboration – The multiple roles of APIs in software development. Foundations of Software Engineering, ACM Press, Newport Beach, CA, 31 October–5 November 2004, pp. 221–230.
16. de Souza CRB, Redmiles D, Dourish P (2003) "Breaking the code", moving between private and public work in collaborative software development. ACM SIGGROUP Conference on Supporting Group Work (ACM), Sanibel Island, FL, USA, November 9–12 2003, pp. 105–114.
17. DePaula R, Ding X, Dourish P, Nies K, Pillet B, Redmiles D, Ren J, Rode J, Silva Filho RS (2005) In the eye of the beholder: A visualization-based approach to information system security. International Journal of Human-Computer Studies – Special Issue on HCI Research in Privacy and Security 63(1–2): 5–24.
18. Ellis JB, Wahid S, Danis C, Kellogg WA (2007) Task and social visualization in software development: Evaluation of a prototype. SIGCHI Conference on Human Factors in Computing Systems, San Jose, CA, 28 April–03 May 2007, pp. 577–586.
19. Ericsson KA, Simon HA (1993) Protocol Analysis – Rev'd Edition: Verbal Reports as Data. Cambridge, MA: MIT Press, p. 496.
20. Freeman E, Hupfer S, Arnold K (1999) Java Spaces Principles, Patterns, and Practice. The Jini Technology Series. Portland, OR: Book News, Inc.
21. Gamma E, Helm R, Johnson R, Vlissides J (1995) Design Patterns: Elements of Reusable Object-Oriented Software. Addison Wesley Professional Computing Series. New York: Addison-Wesley Publishing Company.
22. Green TRG (1989) Cognitive dimensions of notations. Fifth Conference of the British Computer Society, Human-Computer Interaction Specialist Group on People and Computers, Cambridge University Press, University of Nottingham, pp. 433–460.
23. Grudin J (1988) Why CSCW applications fail: Problems in the design and evaluation of organization of organizational interfaces. Computer Supported Co-operative Work, Portland, OR, pp. 85–93.
24. Grudin J (1994) Groupware and social dynamics: Eight challenges for developers. Communications of ACM 37(1): 92–105.
25. Hedberg H, Lappalainen J (2005) A preliminary evaluation of software inspection tools, with the DESMET method. International Conference on Quality Software (IEEE Computer Society) 19–20 September 2005, pp. 45–54.
26. Hilbert D, Redmiles D (1998) An approach to large-scale collection of application usage data over the internet. 20th International Conference on Software Engineering (ICSE'98), IEEE Computer Society Press, Kyoto, Japan. 19–25 April 1998, pp. 136–145.
27. Huang EM, Mynatt ED, Russell DM, Sue AE (2006) Secrets to success and fatal flaws: The design of large-display groupware. IEEE Computer Graphics and Applications 26(1): 37–45.
28. Kantor M, Redmiles D (2001) Creating an infrastructure for ubiquitous awareness. Eighth IFIP TC 13 Conference on Human-Computer Interaction (INTERACT 2001), Tokyo, Japan, pp. 431–438.
29. Kitchenham BA (1996) Evaluating software engineering methods and tool – Part 1: The evaluation context and evaluation methods. SIGSOFT Software Engineering Notes 21(1): 11–14.
30. Lethbridge TC, Sim SE, Singer J (2005) Studying software engineers: Data collection techniques for software field studies. Empirical Software Engineering 10(3): 311–341.

31. Lungu M, Lanza M, Girba T, Heeck R (2007) Reverse engineering super-repositories. Proceedings of the 14th Working Conference on Reverse Engineering (IEEE Computer Society), pp. 120–129.
32. Malone TW, Crowston K (1994) The interdisciplinary study of co-ordination. ACM Computing Surveys 26(1): 87–119.
33. McCabe TJ (1976) A complexity measure. IEEE Transactions on Software Engineering, December 1976, pp. 308–320.
34. Mealy E, Strooper P (2006) Evaluating software refactoring tool support. Proceedings of the Australian Software Engineering Conference (IEEE Computer Society), pp. 331–340.
35. Michelis GD, Loregian M, Martini P (2006) Directional interaction with large displays using mobile phones. Proceedings of the 4th Annual IEEE International Conference on Pervasive Computing and Communications Workshops (IEEE Computer Society), 13–17 March 2006, p. 5.
36. Morera D (2002) COTS evaluation using DESMET methodology & analytic hierarchy process (AHP). 4th International Conference on Product Focused Software Process Improvement (Springer-Verlag), pp. 485–493.
37. Nielsen JK (1994) Heuristic Evaluation. New York: Wiley.
38. OMG (2004) CORBAcos notification service version 1.1 formal/04-10-13, (Object Management Group), p. 229.
39. Patterson JF, Day M, Kucan J (1996) Notification servers for synchronous groupware. ACM Conference on Computer Supported Co-Operative Work (CSCW'96), Boston, MA, pp. 122–129.
40. Plaisant C (2004) The challenge of information visualization evaluation. Working Conference on Advanced Visual Interfaces (ACM), Gallipoli, Italy, pp. 109–116.
41. Ramage M (1999) The learning way: Evaluating co-operative systems, PhD Dissertation, Department of Computer Science, Lancaster, UK, p. 142.
42. Redmiles D, Hoek Avd, Al-Ani B, Hildenbrand T, Quirk S, Sarma A, Silva Filho R, de Souza CRB, Trainer E (2007) Continuous co-ordination: A new paradigm to support globally distributed software development projects. Wirtschaftsinformatik 49: 28–38.
43. Ripley R, Sarma A, Hoek Avd (2007) A visualization for software project awareness and evolution. Workshop on Visualizing Software for Understanding and Analysis, Alberta, Canada, pp. 137–144.
44. Russell J, Roberts C (2001) Angles on Psychological Research. Cheltenham: Nelson Thornes Ltd., p. 256.
45. Sarma A, Bortis G, Hoek Avd (2007) Towards supporting awareness of indirect conflicts across software configuration management workspaces. Conference on Automated Software Engineering, Atlanta, USA, pp. 94–103.
46. Sarma A, Noroozi Z, Hoek Avd (2003) Palantír: Raising awareness among configuration management workspaces. Twenty-fifth International Conference on Software Engineering, Portland, OR, USA, pp. 444–454.
47. Silva Filho RS, Redmiles D (2005) Striving for versatility in publish/subscribe infrastructures. 5th International Workshop on Software Engineering and Middleware (SEM'05), ACM Press, Lisbon, Portugal, 5–6 September 2005, pp. 17–24.
48. Silva Filho RS, Redmiles DF (2005) A survey on versatility for publish/subscribe infrastructures. Technical Report UCI-ISR-05-8, (Institute for Software Research), Irvine, CA, pp. 1–77.
49. Sjoberg DIK, Dyba T, Jorgensen M (2007) The future of empirical methods in software engineering research. Future of Software Engineering, 2007, pp. 358–378.
50. Storey MA, Cheng LT, Bull I, Rigby P (2006) Shared waypoints and social tagging to support collaboration in software development. Proceedings of the 2006 20th Anniversary Conference on Computer Supported Co-operative Work (ACM), Banff, Alberta, Canada, pp. 195–198.

51. Trainer E, Quirk S, de Souza CRB, Redmiles DF (2008) Analyzing a socio-technical visualization tool using usability inspection methods. IEEE Symposium on Visual Languages and Human Centric Computing, Washington, DC, pp. 78–81.
52. Tufte E (1990) Envisioning Information. Cheshire, CT: Graphics Press, p. 126.
53. Tufte E (2006) Beautiful Evidence. Cheshire, CT: Graphics Press, p. 213.
54. Wasserman S, Faust K (1994) Social Network Analysis: Methods and Applications. Cambridge: Cambridge University Press.
55. Wharton C, Rieman J, Lewis C, Polson P (1994) The cognitive walkthrough method: A practitioner's guide. In Nielsen J, Mack RL (Eds.) Usability Inspection Methods. New York: Wiley, pp. 105–140.
56. Xiaojun B, Yuanchun S, Xiaojie C (2006) uPen: A smart pen-liked device for facilitating interaction on large displays. First IEEE International Workshop on Horizontal Interactive Human-Computer Systems, Adelaide, South Australia, 5–7 January 2006.
57. Zuk T, Schlesier L, Neumann P, Hancock MS, Carpendale S (2006) Heuristics for information visualization evaluation. AVI Workshop on Beyond Time and Errors: Novel Evaluation Methods for Information Visualization (ACM), Venice, Italy.

Chapter 9
The Configuration Management Role in Collaborative Software Engineering

Leonardo Gresta P. Murta, Claudia Maria L. Werner, and Jacky Estublier

Abstract This chapter discusses the impact of configuration management on collaborative software engineering, analyzing both the state-of-the-practice and the state-of-the-art. It starts with a brief introduction of the configuration management field and presents how this field has been supporting collaborative software engineering. It also analyzes the current researches on configuration management that will potentially help on establishing a better support to collaborative software engineering in the future. Finally, it presents a summary that details how each configuration management function and system relates to each collaboration aspect of software engineering.

9.1 Introduction

Configuration Management is a discipline responsible for controlling the evolution of products [12]. It dates from the 1950s, but has only been applied to software since the late 1960s [8]. Since then, configuration management is considered to be one of the core supporting process to software development [7] and a research field of software engineering [20].

According to IEEE [26] the five main functions of configuration management are: configuration *identification*, configuration *control*, configuration *status accounting*, configuration *evaluations and reviews*, and *release management* and delivery. However, these five functions are traditionally supported by three main subsystems: issue tracking system, version control system, and build management system.

Because the primary focus of configuration management is keeping the consistency of products, it is concerned with how people interact to develop and maintain

L.G.P. Murta (✉)
Instituto de Computação, Universidade Federal Fluminense, Niterói,
RJ 24210-240, Brazil
e-mail: leomurta@ic.uff.br

I. Mistrík et al. (eds.), *Collaborative Software Engineering*,
DOI 10.1007/978-3-642-10294-3_9, © Springer-Verlag Berlin Heidelberg 2010

these products. The complexity of software products led to the need of geographically distributed teams composed of a large number of developers with different background. These teams collaborate during software engineering activities, and configuration management can be considered as an enabling technology to allow this collaboration.

Collaboration in the context of software engineering encloses different aspects, such as [1, 14, 27] implicit and explicit *communication* among developers, *awareness* regarding other developers' actions, *co-ordination* of development tasks to avoid rework and to achieve the project goals, keeping a *shared memory* with previous development actions history, and providing a *shared space* where the work made by a developer is available to other developers.

This chapter analyzes how configuration management is providing support to boost up collaboration in software engineering. This analysis is performed via an investigation on how each configuration management function (e.g., identification, control, etc.,) and system (e.g., issue tracking, version control, etc.,) influences the collaboration aspects (e.g., communication, awareness, etc.,) of software engineering. Moreover, this chapter also discusses how present and future researches in the field of configuration management can leverage the state-of-the-practice collaboration support in software engineering.

It is organized into four sections besides this introduction. Section 9.2 presents the area of configuration management, presenting its main functions and systems. Section 9.3 shows how each configuration management function and system supports aspects of collaboration in software engineering. Section 9.4 discusses how current and future research in configuration management may help improving collaboration in software engineering in the future. Finally, Section 9.5 summarizes the findings and provides a roadmap for further readings.

9.2 Configuration Management

The Configuration Management discipline has arisen in the 1950s as a response to the increasing complexity of documenting aircraft and spacecraft production [20, 24, 28]. In the 1960s and 1970s, Configuration Management started to deal with software artifacts, leading to a derived discipline named Software Configuration Management (we will use configuration management or SCM from now on with the meaning of software configuration management) [8]. Despite its almost 40 years of existence, it was only from the beginning of the 1980s, with the wide availability of tools such as RCS and Make, and the first commercial SCM systems such as DSEE, that SCM became widely used by industry for all kinds of software, and not only for critical software.

IEEE Std 610.12 [25] defines configuration management as "a discipline applying technical and administrative direction and surveillance to: identify and document the functional and physical characteristics of a configuration item, control changes to those characteristics, record and report change processing and implementation status, and verify compliance with specified requirements." According to this definition, configuration management is not intended to establish why or when software artifacts should be changed, but to support the software development process by providing control and guidance through the changes that invariably occur.

One of the key concepts of configuration management is the baseline, defined by IEEE Std 610.12 [25] as "a specification or product that has been formally reviewed and agreed upon, that thereafter serves as the basis for further development, and that can be changed only through formal change control procedures."

The configuration management discipline can be analyzed under different perspectives, depending on the role of the stakeholder in the software development process [3] as shown in Fig. 9.1. In a management perspective, configuration management can be subdivided into five main functions [26] configuration identification, configuration control, configuration status accounting, configuration evaluations and reviews, and release management and delivery.

The *configuration identification function* intends to provide unique, persistent, and immutable identification and content to the items that are subject to configuration management. It is the data model supported by the SCM system; it includes the naming, versioning model, attributes, and relationships between items.

The *configuration control function* intends to track item evolution; its main goal is to support the controlled evolution of a previously specified baseline of the product. It usually defines: (1) the change request, which describes the improvements suggested and problems identified in specific items; (2) change classification, which prioritizes the change request; (3) impact analysis, which establishes the change request impact in terms of risk, effort, schedule, and cost; (4) change evaluation, which decides if the change request will be implemented, deferred, or rejected, according to the impact analysis report; (5) change implementation, which incorporate the change into the product; (6) change verification, which compares the

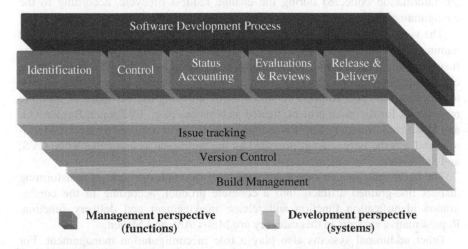

Fig. 9.1 Configuration management perspectives

change request with the actual change; and (7) baseline update, which propagates the change to other stakeholders. This function is usually automated via the combination of issue tracking and version control systems. ClearQuest, Bugzilla, and Trac are examples of configuration control tools.

The *configuration status accounting function* stores fine-grained information produced by the other functions and provides this information to authorized stakeholders, according to their needs. Usually, the information needs are related to measurement of process improvement, future costs estimation, and management reports generation. The issue tracking system is usually customized to collect the necessary information. For instance, tools like JIRA and ClearQuest allow the definition of which information should be collected via forms presented during the execution of the other configuration management functions.

The *configuration evaluations and reviews function* takes place periodically or at least before the baseline release. It usually comprises functional audit, which reviews test plans, test data, test methodology, and test results, aiming at ensuring that the product is correct, according to its requirements. Moreover, it also comprises physical audit, which aims at ensuring that the product is complete according to the contractual clauses.

The *release management and delivery function* intends to support the product building, producing derived items from source items, composing a consistent product baseline, and deploying the product in the production environment. Traditionally, tools such as Make were responsible to automate this function, but currently some recent tools such as Ant and Maven are getting popular.

On the other hand, in the development perspective, configuration management can be subdivided into three main systems: issue tracking system, version control system, and build management system.

The *issue tracking system* (e.g., ClearQuest, JIRA, Bugzilla, and Trac) manages the configuration control function in a systematic way. It also stores and reports the information collected during the change request lifecycle, according to the configuration status accounting function.

The *version control system* allows the identification of items, according to the naming and versioning schema, and their posterior evolution in a concurrent way. It supports the well known *import*, *update*, and *commit* functions (i.e., check-in and check-out) between the repository and a file system. Some system adds support to decentralized (peer-to-peer) version control, allowing the existence of multiple repositories for the same project, treated as branches (e.g., BitKeeper, Bazaar, Git, and Mercurial). Version control is the fundamental layer required by any SCM system; and it is the only support provided by the traditional systems like RCS, CVS, and Subversion.

The *build management system* automatizes the complex process of transforming distinct fine-grained artifacts into a concrete product, according to the configuration identification function and release management and delivery function. Representative systems in this category are Make, Ant, and Maven.

Other additional systems also play a role in configuration management. For example, the *workspace management system*synthesizes and glue together the services provided by the other systems. A workspace is a piece of the file system populated with copies of shared space items, allowing each developer to perform a task in isolation. Most often a workspace is created to perform a well defined task on a well defined piece of the product (e.g., implementing a change request on a baseline). The workspace management system controls the multiple change requests performed in parallel and enforces concurrent engineering policies by combining a high degree of discipline together with agility, making it possible to support distributed teams working on the same product. The workspace management system is above the version control system and uses the services and information provided by the other systems (change control, issue tracking, and build management) to provide high level support.

All advanced system offer, in a way or another, workspace management functionalities. Some system combine issue tracking and version control together like Borland StarTeam and Microsoft Team Foundation Server. Full fledge SCM systems provide a deep integration and synergy between the different functions, including process support (e.g., IBM Rational ClearCase, Telelogic Synergy, and Serena Dimensions).

Finally, each system should be tailored to the specific needs of the functions. For example, different change request lifecycles may be adopted according to the project characteristics, different naming and numbering schemas can be used by specific organizations, and a more rigorous approach for product release in a critical scenario may entail formal verification of marketing viability and product quality level measurement [28]. These procedures are specified via processes that define how configuration management should be applied in a specific context. Mature organizations typically use a two-level process for configuration management: a standard process at organizational level and a defined process at project level. In this case, the defined process is usually derived from the standard process according to specific customization guidelines [7].

9.3 Configuration Management as an Enabling Technology for Collaboration

This section discusses how each configuration management function and system currently helps the execution of collaborative tasks in software engineering. These configuration management functions and systems are analyzed in terms of five collaboration aspects [1, 14, 27] communication, awareness, co-ordination, shared memory, and shared space.

9.3.1 Communication

The communication aspect of collaborative software engineering entails both formal and informal exchange of information among members of software development teams and other stakeholders [14]. In this context, it is possible to identify tacit communication, usually performed in an informal way, or explicit communication, performed in a formal and organized way [33].

This collaborative aspect is supported at least in some degree by all configuration management functions, with a particular emphasis to the configuration control and configuration status accounting functions, which are especially intended for this purpose. Some classical reports are frequently generated to increase the knowledge of the team regarding the development process status. This usually includes [28] change request reports, which describe the status of all change requests filled in the change control process; progress report, which summarizes the status of change tasks under development; item report, which describes all items of the product; and transaction report, which lists all changes performed over a specific item.

Some issue tracking systems such as ClearQuest, JIRA, and StarTeam allow the modeling of the change lifecycle workflow. This workflow establishes how stakeholders should communicate to implement the configuration control function. Moreover, issue tracking systems are usually used as forums over specific issues, where developers can post their opinions and see other opinions regarding the way an issue should be implemented in the system. Trac is an example of an issue tracking system implemented over a wiki system with the main goal of allowing collaborative editing of issues. Version control systems also support explicit communication via commit comments, where developers detail in natural language what they did in the product. When issues tacking and version control are integrated (for example ClearQuest with ClearCase) it is possible to navigate from high level before-the-fact motivation (issue tracking) to low level after-the-fact implementation (version control system).

9.3.2 Awareness

The awareness aspect of collaborative software engineering entails understanding activities performed by other stakeholders in the software development process [15]. This kind of information is vital to contextualize team work, helping to avoid rework and to stimulate collaboration. The shared space can be seen as a (passive) way for stakeholders to be aware of what occurs in the project. In addition, SCM systems can notify stakeholders when relevant event occurs; it is what is called awareness here. From course to fine grain, three different functions provide awareness.

The Configuration status accounting function analyzes the information stored in the repository and propagates this information to the stakeholders, providing an understanding of the current status of every change request being processed.

The configuration control system, having in charge the change lifecycle workflow, has the necessary information for appropriately notifying stakeholders when some actions occurred over specific change requests. For instance, when Bugzilla is used to implement the configuration control function, every change in the status of an issue is automatically notified to all involved stakeholders, including the client, developers, and quality assurance team.

At a fine grain, it is the workspace management system which is responsible for supporting awareness. This is critical awareness information since work under way is performed in the many concurrent, independent, and isolated workspaces. Most current systems only provide after-the-fact information in the form of the version control system logs. Some systems (e.g., CVS) provide a rudimentary awareness support, sending an e-mail to the related developers when some parallel work starts to happen over a specific file. Advanced awareness systems can notify in real time the involved developers each time concurrent changes are performed on the same file, or even on closely related files in two different workspaces. So far this level of awareness is available only in research prototypes [18, 34].

9.3.3 Coordination

The co-ordination aspect of collaborative software engineering entails managing the dependencies of software development activities [29]. This includes understanding how stakeholders collaborate and finding ways to orchestrate such collaboration. Co-ordination usually focuses on improving efficiency of the development process. Lack of co-ordination may lead to rework or suboptimal usage of physical and human resources.

In basic version control tools like CVS and Subversion, co-ordination is not at all addressed. In SCM systems, process support directly addresses the co-ordination aspect; and it is what mostly distinguished low-end to high-end SCM systems. Most SCM systems include change control; the change request lifecycle is a simple process for co-ordinating implementers during development and maintenance, both within a given change, and between concurrent changes. High-end systems, such as ClearQuest, provide more advanced ways to define processes and to embed best practices.

In practice, the issue tracking system is used by many organizations as a task assignment tool, and a usual workday may comprise checking pending activities in the issue tracking system and performing these activities. Systems such as ClearQuest explicitly differs an issue of a task. In this case, different tasks can be derived from the same issue and each task can be assigned to different development teams.

Version control systems traditionally offer two co-ordination policies: pessimistic and optimistic. The pessimistic concurrency policy forces work serialization, while the optimistic policy allows parallel work but demands an additional merge activity [9]. For instance, Subversion allows any combinations of such policies, selected on-the-fly. Team Foundation Server has an interesting support for a more generic definition of the whole project development style, with pre-configured options for Agile or CMMI [7] projects. On the other hand, systems such as CVS and Microsoft Visual SourceSafe only allow a specific policy, respectively, optimistic and pessimistic.

9.3.4 Shared Memory

The shared memory aspect of collaborative software engineering entails storing the history, both in the activity and product dimensions [14]. In other words, this aspect is responsible for registering all actions performed by stakeholders and the effect of these actions on the products.

All the information collected is stored to constitute the project history. This information is available for direct, indirect, and statistical inquiries. An example of direct inquiry is when a stakeholder wants to know the status of a specific change request and who has already worked on this request. This is supported by the issue tracking system. An example of an indirect inquiry is when the manager wants to know how precise the cost was and schedule impact analysis provided by a specific analyst. This indirect metric can be manually computed if data from a project management tool is combined with data from the issue tracking system. Finally, an example of a statistical inquiry is when the manager wants to know if the number of critical corrective requests will grow in the next month according to the behavior of the previous six months. Even simple systems, such as Bugzilla, provide graphical reports based on time series. However, extrapolation may require some additional processing. This shared memory is mostly supported by the issue tacking system and focuses on the activities dimension.

The version control function provides support in the product dimension. It stores each change in the products and the related metadata (why, what, when). This system also allows queries over the project history. For instance, Subversion allows listing all product changes performed by a specific developer or listing all items changed together to implement a specific change request.

Once again, the integration of the issue tracking system together with the version control system is the key to improve the shared memory aspect. This integration allows navigating through the activities and product dimensions. For example, integrated tools like StarTeam or ClearQuest together with ClearCase can compare two moments in time for the same product and check the difference in terms of implemented change requests (from the issue tracking system) or in terms of added and removed product items (from the version control system). They also allow the navigation from a change request to the lines of code that implemented the change request, and vice versa.

9.3.5 Shared Space

The shared space provides a place where stakeholders can access artifacts produced by other stakeholders [27]. Shared spaces distinguish from shared memory because it is concerned with how to allow people interact over a set of artifacts, not with how to store the history of this interaction. On the other hand, shared space distinguishes from co-ordination because co-ordination is concerned with activities dependencies, and shared space is concerned with artifacts sharing.

The main feature of a configuration control system is the management of the artifacts produced during the project life cycle. For that purpose, a configuration control system is organized around two repositories, one containing the metadata (often using a traditional data base), which constitute the shared history; and another repository containing the artifacts (often using the file system), which constitutes the shared space.

The shared space management is strongly related to two configuration management functions: configuration control and workspace management. Configuration control is involved since it establishes who is entitled to make changes, when, to which (shared) artifact and why. Workspace management is involved since it establishes where and how this change is supposed to be performed. Finally, when the change on the shared artifact is done, configuration control is involved again since it defines the conditions under which the changed artifacts can be published (sometimes called *promoted*) in the shared space.

The version control system provides some significant support to this collaborative aspect of software engineering. It is responsible for storing the different versions of shared artifacts and the evolution history of these artifacts. Artifacts are immutable; old versions are never overwritten but new versions are created to store the changes. With this strategy, every historical version is available in the shared history (metadata) and in the shared space (artifacts).

9.4 The Future Role of Configuration Management

The future role of configuration management in the context of collaborative software engineering can be analyzed via two complementary dimensions: the state-of-the-art researches in the configuration management field and the future trends of configuration management to deliver a better support for collaborative software engineering. The following two subsection focus on these dimensions.

9.4.1 On-Going Researches

The current research is analyzed in this section in terms of the five previously discussed aspects.

Regarding *communication* when items are identified, a good practice adopted by some organizations is to establish the dependencies among them [23] together with information regarding teams that are assigned to work on specific items [5]. Some researchers [37] show that this knowledge may indicate which teams should communicate to better develop the product. In [30] the last check-ins are analyzed to recommend experts for specific problems; in [31] the same is achieved using data from issue tracking system. Wiki systems are now used with the goal of leveraging communication. For instance, JIRA uses the Atlassian Confluence wiki system.

In terms of *awareness*, the current support is provided after a check-in is performed to the repository, which may lead to rework. Some researches [18, 34, 36] try to minimize this problem by providing awareness regarding changes performed in concurrent workspaces in "real time." Continuous integration tools, such as

Apache Continuum, CruiseControl, and Atlassian Bamboo, are providing awareness regarding the effects of changes in the product.

The *co-ordination* aspect provided by version control system is limited to the pessimistic and optimistic strategies which sometimes deal with problems during reconciliation. Presently, some researches [19] focus on increasing the co-ordination over parallel work via team decomposition, reference workspaces, visibility levels, and co-ordination policies. Besides the existence of some research in configuration management applied to co-ordination, this is one of the most needed collaborative aspects.

The *shared memory* aspect of collaborative software engineering is responsible for storing information regarding actions performed in the past and artifacts produced by these actions. As discussed before, issue tracking and version control systems provide valuable support to this aspect. However, it is usually difficult to extract valuable information from such systems. Some current researches [11, 16, 38] focus on mining configuration management repositories and providing high level knowledge from them. The International Workshop on Mining Software Repository is a traditional forum that congregates data mining, program comprehension, and configuration management communities to focus on detection and extraction of information from configuration management repositories. For instance, Gall et al. [22] use release data to detect logical coupling between modules. Ball et al. [4] have performed some cluster analysis of C++ classes stored in configuration management repositories. Other works also perform historical analysis over configuration management repositories. Shirabad et al. [35] use inductive learning to find out different concepts of relevance among logically coupled files. Eick et al. [17] argue that code decay is related to the difficulty to perform changes. For this reason, they analyze change history applying decay indexes to identify risk factors. Draheim et al. [16] argue that product quality is dependent of process quality. Due to that, the development process activities are analyzed and some metrics are applied over a version control system. Finally, Zimmermann et al. [38] have evidenced that mining configuration management repositories can be useful for predicting likely further changes, detecting hidden dependencies, and preventing incomplete changes.

When analyzing the *shared space* aspect of collaborative software engineering, one of the key research challenges is to keep interrelated artifacts consistent in response to changes. Currently, some researches focus on detecting and keeping traceability links among these artifacts [2, 6, 13, 32] or triggering the build management system from the version control system to automatically update some artifacts in response to changes in other artifacts [10, 21].

9.4.2 Future Trends

The on-going trends can be analyzed from two perspectives. The deep trends, which can be seen almost from the origin of the disciplines (1970s and 1980s), and those related with the changes in the context in which configuration management is performed.

Data model, System model. Among the traditional trends, we can mention the effort made to improve the underlying data model, also called system model. This is of fundamental importance, since it allows defining more accurately the dependencies between artefacts, at the logical level, and the structure of the artefact, at the physical level. It is easy to relate this trend to the researches mentioned above. A good system model should allow a better description and management of dependencies not only among items but also tasks, business, stakeholders and the organisation. Based on a good and accurate system model, it becomes easy to improve communication and co-ordination since we know the artefacts each team is interested in and the tasks they have to perform.

Co-ordination is improved since the process is known: the tasks under way, the future tasks and their temporal dependencies, the artefacts on which they operate, and the teams involved.

Of course, the shared memory which stores the system model and its evolution, and which maintains the traceability between tasks, teams, and artefact versions, becomes an excellent source of information. This is also true for the shared space.

Slowly, the data model used in commercial systems is improving. The difficulty comes from many reasons, including the unavailability of databases, the interoperability, and the difficulty to get and maintain an accurate model.

Process support. Since the early 1990s, process support is considered to be the most distinctive feature for high end SCM systems; it is the most appreciated, but also the most demanding. In the ideal, a good process support should allow filling the gap between the company business processes, its development process, its change control process and its co-operation process. Having a complete traceability between these levels obviously would help each stakeholder, at each level of responsibility, to better plan its future actions. Clearly, co-ordination would be significantly improved, for all classes of stakeholders.

Currently only some low level operational processes, like issue tracking and change control, are really supported. Most of the other processes are not formalized and supported, and when they are supported, it is through third party tools like workflows and project management.

Awareness. From collaborative engineering point of view, this is an important feature which is almost fully missing today. Intra workspace awareness is a current research topic, which could be considered a special case of process support. However the techniques and concepts needed for awareness support call for a separate research area. Even if some prototypes have shown the feasibility, conceptual, technical and ergonomical issues are still to be solved before seeing such features embedded into commercial products.

Integration vs. Interoperability. As already mentioned, communication and co-ordination call for a deep integration between the different SCM sub-systems. It has also repeatedly shown that all the collaborative aspects are improved when more activities and functions, at different levels in the company, are connected. This calls for extending the functional coverage of the tool. It is the approach that was privileged by high end SCM vendors, and led to the emergence of Application Lifecycle Management (ALM) infrastructures. These infrastructures focus on combining different software engineering tools in an integrated way, usually grounded in configuration management systems. For instance, some commercial initiatives of ALM are IBM/Rational Team Concert, constructed over the Jazz platform, Microsoft Visual Studio Team System, and the Borland solution, combining different tools from requirement, team and configuration management.

This trend toward even more heavy weight and large scope systems increases the functional overlapping between them, their complexity, cost and inflexibility. Many researchers think that the solution is better on composing (making interoperate) simple and specialized independent systems. This is the interoperability trend, followed by open source and low-end systems. Unfortunately, the limitations of today technology make problematic the implementation of the high level features (no common data model, duplication, and inconsistencies). It is not possible today to really integrate a third party workflow or project management system with a SCM system, or to make co-operate SCM and PDM (Product Data Management) systems. Interoperability of independent (and complex) systems, with many overlapping but incompatible features, is acknowledged as a major and difficult research issue.

Model Driven Engineering (MDE). MDE has impact on the SCM systems since the artefacts to manage are no longer programs but models with, in general complex derive chains. From the collaboration point of view only, the potential high number of derivations/transformations in which humans can interfere increases the need for collaboration, co-ordination, and awareness. Transformations, traceability, and reverse engineering are current hot research topics. Most of the SCM aspects like evolution control, diff and merge, co-operative policies; and most collaborative aspects: collaboration, co-ordination, and awareness are not really addressed in the current MDE technology. Clearly, all the engineering topics addressed in "traditional" software engineering including, of course, the collaborative aspects, will have to be revisited in the frame of MDE. We can expect many years of work before getting a similar level of support. Even if a promising approach, in its current state and from collaboration perspective, MDE represents more a step back than a progress.

Cloud computing. With the rising of cloud computing, configuration management starts to ground almost every collaborative work, even if it is not related to software engineering or computer science. This can be seen as ubiquitous configuration management, where people that do not even know what configuration management are, have their lives directly influenced by these systems. For instance, services like Google Docs, Microsoft Office Live Workspace, and Apple MobileMe make intensive use of configuration management algorithms and infrastructures.

9.5 Conclusion

This chapter presented how configuration management has been supporting collaborative software engineering in the last decades. Aiming at providing an overview of this support, we ran a survey among 11 accredited specialists from

Table 9.1 Relationship among configuration management functions and collaboration aspects

Functions x Aspects	Communication	Awareness	Coordination	Shared Memory	Shared Space
Identification	Low $\mu = 1.2$ $\sigma = 0.8$	Low $\mu = 0.8$ $\sigma = 0.9$	Low $\mu = 1.1$ $\sigma = 0.7$	Low $\mu = 1.1$ $\sigma = 0.9$	Low $\mu = 1.3$ $\sigma = 0.9$
Control	High $\mu = 1.9$ $\sigma = 1.0$	High $\mu = 2.1$ $\sigma = 1.0$	Medium $\mu = 2.1$ $\sigma = 0.7$	High $\mu = 2.1$ $\sigma = 0.8$	Low $\mu = 2.0$ $\sigma = 1.0$
Status Accounting	Medium $\mu = 1.8$ $\sigma = 0.9$	Medium $\mu = 1.7$ $\sigma = 0.9$	Low $\mu = 1.7$ $\sigma = 0.8$	Medium $\mu = 1.8$ $\sigma = 0.8$	Medium $\mu = 1.3$ $\sigma = 0.8$
Evaluations and reviews	Low $\mu = 1.3$ $\sigma = 0.9$	Low $\mu = 1.0$ $\sigma = 1.0$	Low $\mu = 1.2$ $\sigma = 1.0$	Low $\mu = 1.3$ $\sigma = 1.0$	Low $\mu = 1.2$ $\sigma = 1.0$
Release management and delivery	Medium $\mu = 1.6$ $\sigma = 0.9$	Medium $\mu = 1.3$ $\sigma = 1.0$	Low $\mu = 1.5$ $\sigma = 0.9$	Low $\mu = 1.3$ $\sigma = 0.6$	Medium $\mu = 1.8$ $\sigma = 0.8$

industry and academia. This survey asked to rank the configuration management functions and systems support to collaborative aspects according to the following Likert interval scale levels: high, medium, low, and none, and mapped respectively to 3, 2, 1, and 0. Table 9.1 summarizes the relationship among the configuration management functions and the collaboration aspects discussed along this chapter. The results presented in this table are: mode (in bold) followed by mean (μ) and standard deviation (σ).

It is possible to notice, after analyzing Table 9.1, that configuration control and configuration status accounting is the functions that provide most support to collaborative software engineering. On the other hand, communication, awareness, and shared memory are the collaborative aspects that take most advantage from the adoption of configuration management functions.

Table 9.2 is similar to Table 9.1, but summarizes the relationship among the configuration management systems and the collaboration aspects discussed along this chapter. It is possible to notice that issue tracking, just followed by version control, is

Table 9.2 Relationship among configuration management systems and collaboration aspects

Systems x Aspects	Communication	Awareness	Coordination	Shared Memory	Shared Space
Issue Tracking System	High $\mu = 2.4$ $\sigma = 0.9$	High $\mu = 2.1$ $\sigma = 1.0$	Medium $\mu = 2.2$ $\sigma = 0.9$	Medium $\mu = 2.4$ $\sigma = 0.5$	Low $\mu = 1.6$ $\sigma = 1.0$
Version Control System	Low $\mu = 1.3$ $\sigma = 0.6$	Medium $\mu = 1.6$ $\sigma = 0.8$	Medium $\mu = 2.0$ $\sigma = 0.8$	Medium $\mu = 2.2$ $\sigma = 0.6$	High $\mu = 2.7$ $\sigma = 0.5$
Build Management System	Low $\mu = 0.7$ $\sigma = 0.5$	Low $\mu = 0.7$ $\sigma = 0.6$	Low $\mu = 0.7$ $\sigma = 0.5$	Low $\mu = 1.0$ $\sigma = 0.6$	Low $\mu = 1.4$ $\sigma = 0.8$

Fig. 9.2 Configuration
management perspectives
supporting collaborative
software engineering aspects

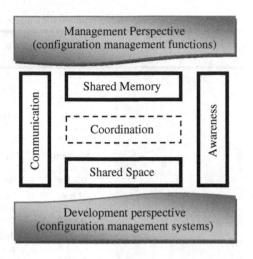

the system that provides most support to collaborative software engineering. On the other hand, we can notice that communication, awareness, and shared space are the collaborative aspects that take most advantage from the adoption of configuration management systems.

Figure 9.2 draws some interesting conclusions regarding the support provided by configuration management over collaborative software engineering aspects. It is possible to notice that the management perspective of configuration management, represented by configuration management functions, provides a higher support for communication, awareness, shared memory, and lower support for co-ordination and shared space. However, the scenario is not the same in the case of the development perspective, where communication, awareness, and shared space receive higher attention. According to this survey, co-ordination is the collaboration aspect that receives less support from configuration management as a whole.

Currently, the configuration management research community has to deal with a delicate challenge: to continue providing scalable procedures and systems, but with an increased support to collaborative tasks. Collaboration without control may lead to rework. However, control without collaboration may lead to inefficient work due to lack of parallelization.

SCM has been understood primarily as a control system which guaranties that past items and configurations can be clearly identified and safely rebuild at any later time. In this view, the immutable repository is emphasized, with little facilities for collaboration (in the 1970s and 1980s). Then the developer and engineering work was emphasized, based on independent and isolated workspaces and change control as a key function (1990s). This allows for scalability, parallel work, and control, but not for awareness and communication. Recent work tends to improve team support, emphasizing co-ordination, through an improvement of the process support function and emphasizing collaboration and awareness through the controlled visibility of the activities occurring in the many concurrent workspaces.

Finding the right degree of control and collaboration for specific projects may be the key to success for collaborative software engineering in the future.

References

1. Altmann J, Pomberger G (1999) Co-operative software development: Concepts, model and tools. Proceedings of the Technology of Object-Oriented Languages and Systems IEEE Computer Society, Santa Barbara, CA, USA, pp. 194–207.
2. Antoniol G, Canfora G, Casazza G, De Lucia A, Merlo E (2002) Recovering traceability links between code and documentation. IEEE Transactions on Software Engineering (TSE) 28(10): 970–983.
3. Asklund U, Bendix L (2002) A study of configuration management in open source software projects. IEE Proceedings – Software 149(1): 40–46.
4. Ball T, Kim J, Porter AA, Siy HP (1997) If your version control system could talk.... Workshop on Process Modeling and Empirical Studies of Software Engineering, May.
5. Bowman IT, Holt RC (1999) Reconstructing ownership architectures to help understand software systems. Proceedings of the 7th International Workshop on Program Comprehension IEEE Computer Society.
6. Briand LC, Labiche Y, O'Sullivan L (2003) Impact analysis and change management of UML models. International Conference on Software Maintenance (ICSM), September, pp. 256–265.
7. Chrissis MB, Konrad M, Shrum S (2003) CMMI: Guidelines for Process Integration and Product Improvement. Boston, MA: Addison-Wesley.
8. Christensen MJ, Thayer RH (2002) The Project Manager's Guide to Software Engineering's Best Practices. Los Alamitos, CA and New York: IEEE Computer Society Press and John Wiley & Sons.
9. Conradi R, Westfechtel B (1998) Version models for software configuration management. ACM Computing Surveys 30(2): 232–282.
10. Corrêa CKF, Murta LGP, Werner CML (2008) Odyssey-MEC: Model evolution control in the context of model-driven architecture. Conference on Software Engineering and Knowledge Engineering (SEKE), pp. 67–72.
11. Dantas CR, Murta LGP, Werner CML (2007) Mining change traces from versioned UML repositories. Brazilian Symposium on Software Engineering (SBES), pp. 236–252.
12. Dart S (1991) Concepts in configuration management systems. International Workshop on Software Configuration Management (SCM), June, pp. 1–18.
13. De Lucia A, Fasano F, Oliveto R, Tortora G (2004) Enhancing an artifact management system with traceability recovery features. International Conference on Software Maintenance (ICSM), September, pp. 306–315.
14. Dias MS, Borges MRS (1999) Development of groupware systems with the COPSE infrastructure. International Workshop on Groupware, pp. 278–285.
15. Dourish P, Bellotti V (1992) Awareness and coordination in shared workspaces. Conference on Computer Supported Cooperative Work, October, pp. 107–114.
16. Draheim D, Pekacki L (2003) Process-centric analytical processing of version control data. International Workshop on Principles of Software Evolution (IWPSE), September, pp. 131–136.
17. Eick SG, Graves TL, Karr AF, Marron JS, Mockus A (2001) Does code decay? Assessing the evidence from change management data. IEEE Transactions on Software Engineering (TSE) 27(1): 1–12.
18. Estublier J, Garcia S (2006) Concurrent engineering support in software engineering. Proceedings of the 21st IEEE/ACM International Conference on Automated Software Engineering IEEE Computer Society.

19. Estublier J, Garcia S (2007) Workflows and cooperative processes. Software Process: Improvement and Practice 12(5): 415–427.
20. Estublier J, Leblang D, Hoek Avd, Conradi R, Clemm G, Tichy W, Wiborg-Weber D (2005) Impact of software engineering research on the practice of software configuration management. ACM Transactions on Software Engineering and Methodology (TOSEM) 14(4): 1–48.
21. Estublier J, Vega G (2007) Reconciling software configuration management and product data management. Proceedings of the 6th Joint Meeting of the European Software Engineering Conference and the ACM SIGSOFT Symposium on the Foundations of Software Engineering ACM, Dubrovnik, Croatia.
22. Gall H, Jazayeri M, Klösch R, Trausmuth G (1997) Software evolution observations based on product release history. International Conference on Software Maintenance (ICSM), October, pp. 160–196.
23. Gulla B, Gorman J (1996) Experiences with the use of a configuration language. International Workshop on Software Configuration Management, Berlin, Germany, pp. 198–219.
24. Hass AMJ (2003) Configuration Management Principles and Practices. Boston, MA: Pearson Education, Inc.
25. IEEE (1990) Std 610.12 – IEEE Standard Glossary of Software Engineering Terminology. Institute of Electrical and Electronics Engineers.
26. IEEE (2005) Std 828 – IEEE Standard for Software Configuration Management Plans. Institute of Electrical and Electronics Engineers.
27. Laurillau Y, Nigay L (2002) Clover architecture for groupware. Proceedings of the 2002 ACM Conference on Computer Supported Co-operative Work ACM, New Orleans, LA, USA.
28. Leon A (2000) A Guide to Software Configuration Management. Norwood, MA: Artech House Publishers.
29. Malone TW, Crowston K (1994) The interdisciplinary study of coordination. ACM Computing Surveys 26(1): 87–119.
30. McDonald DW, Ackerman MS (2000) Expertise recommender: a flexible recommendation system and architecture. Proceedings of the 2000 ACM Conference on Computer Supported Cooperative Work ACM, Philadelphia, PA, USA.
31. Mockus A, Herbsleb JD (2002) Expertise browser: A quantitative approach to identifying expertise. Proceedings of the 24th International Conference on Software Engineering ACM, Orlando, FL.
32. Murta LGP, Hoek Avd, Werner CML (2008) Continuous and automated evolution of architecture-to-implementation traceability links. Automated Software Engineering 15(1): 75–107.
33. Nonaka I, Takeuchi H (1995) The Knowledge-Creating Company: How Japanese Companies Create the Dynamics of Innovation. Oxford: Oxford University Press.
34. Sarma A, Noroozi Z, Hoek Avd (2003) Palantír: Raising awareness among configuration management workspaces. International Conference on Software Engineering (ICSE), May, pp. 444–454.
35. Shirabad JS, Lethbridge T, Matwin S (2001) Supporting software maintenance by mining software update records. International Conference on Software Maintenance (ICSM), November, pp. 22–31.
36. Silva Ida, Chen PH, Westhuizen Cvd, Ripley RM, Hoek Avd (2006) Lighthouse: Coordination through emerging design. Proceedings of the 2006 OOPSLA Workshop on Eclipse Technology Exchange ACM, Portland, OR.
37. Souza CRB de, Redmiles D, Cheng LT, Millen D, Patterson J (2004) How a good software practice thwarts collaboration: The multiple roles of APIs in software development. Proceedings of the 12th ACM SIGSOFT Twelfth International Symposium on Foundations of Software Engineering ACM, Newport Beach, CA, USA.
38. Zimmermann T, Weisgerber P, Diehl S, Zeller A (2004) Mining version histories to guide software changes. International Conference on Software Engineering (ICSE), May, pp. 563–572.

Chapter 10
The GRIFFIN Collaborative Virtual Community for Architectural Knowledge Management

Patricia Lago, Rik Farenhorst, Paris Avgeriou, Remco C. de Boer, Viktor Clerc, Anton Jansen, and Hans van Vliet

Abstract Modern software architecting increasingly often takes place in geographically distributed contexts involving teams of professionals and customers with different backgrounds and roles. So far, attention and effort have been mainly dedicated to individuals sharing already formalized knowledge and less to social, informal collaboration. Furthermore, in Web 2.0 contexts, little to no attention has been given to practitioners carrying out complex, collaborative, and knowledge-intensive tasks in organizational contexts.

This chapter shows how we can effectively support the combination of formal and informal collaboration and build a Virtual Community for architectural knowledge sharing. We present a set of collaboration scenarios that define a conceptual model for such a Virtual Community. A solution in this area would realize the expectations of companies involved in IT and working in distributed settings to effectively exploit their expertise, and turn their professional knowledge into a global IT portfolio.

10.1 Introduction

The notion of software architecture is one of the key technical advances to the field of software engineering over the last decade. The advantages of using explicit software architecture include early interaction with stakeholders, its basis for establishing work breakdown structure and early assessment of quality attributes [2].

The GRIFFIN project develops notations, tools, and associated methods to extract, represent, and use architectural knowledge that currently is not documented or represented in the system. In GRIFFIN, Architectural Knowledge (AK) is defined as the integrated representation of the software architecture of a software-intensive system or a family of systems, the architectural design decisions, and the external context/environment. The project emphasizes sharing architectural knowledge in a

P. Lago (✉)
VU University Amsterdam, 1081 HV Amsterdam, Netherlands
e-mail: patricia@cs.vu.nl

I. Mistrík et al. (eds.), *Collaborative Software Engineering*,
DOI 10.1007/978-3-642-10294-3_10, © Springer-Verlag Berlin Heidelberg 2010

distributed, global context. Some of the results can be found in [6, 7, 8, 9, 10, 11, 12, 13, 16, 17].

GRIFFIN is a joint research project of the VU University Amsterdam and the University of Groningen, both in the Netherlands. The research is carried out in a consortium with various industrial partners, both large and small. These partners provide us with case studies and give feedback. The domains of these case studies range from a family of consumer electronics products to a highly distributed system that collects scientific data from around 15,000 sensors to a service-oriented system in a business domain.

Although considerable progress has been made, we still lack techniques for capturing, representing, and maintaining knowledge about software architectures. While much attention has been given to documenting architectural solutions, the rationale for these solutions often remains implicit and is often exchanged in inter-personal, informal communication. The incomplete representation of the needed AK leads to several problems that are generally recognized in any software engineering project, and that become just worse in distributed and global software development:

- *Lack of first-class representation* [3] architectural solutions, design decisions, and rationale lack a first class representation in the software architecture. Consequently, the knowledge about the "what and how" of the software architecture is quickly lost. Experience shows that this documentation on architecture design decisions is difficult to interpret and use by individuals not involved in the initial design of the system.
- *Architectural knowledge is cross-cutting and intertwined* [3] architectural knowledge addresses technical, business, organizational, and cultural aspects that influence architectural decisions and design solutions. Due to its inter-disciplinary nature, architectural knowledge is cross-cutting, affecting multiple components and connectors, and one piece of architectural knowledge often becomes intimately intertwined with another piece of architectural knowledge.
- *High cost of change* [3] a resulting problem is that a software architecture, once implemented, is prohibitively expensive to change. Moreover, changing or removing existing design decisions is difficult.
- *Design rules, constraints, and rationale violated* [3] during the evolution of software systems, designers and even architects may easily violate the design rules, constraints, and rationale imposed on the architecture during earlier design iterations.
- *Obsolete design decisions not removed* [3] removing obsolete architecture design decisions from an implemented architecture is typically avoided, or performed only partially, because of (1) the effort required, (2) perceived lack of benefit and (3) concerns about the consequences, due to the lack of knowledge about them. The consequence is a rapid erosion of the software system, resulting in high maintenance cost.
- *Architectural knowledge is dispersed and undocumented*: documented or formalized architectural knowledge is usually limited to technical architectural solutions. Non-technical knowledge such as business and cultural aspects remains

tacit and only known to individuals. This architectural knowledge is then lost, and difficult (if not impossible) to trace back and reuse in later developments.

• *Documented architectural knowledge neglects interdisciplinary use*: architectural knowledge documentation should convey the overall architecture to persons with different culture, skills, and responsibilities in different architectural aspects or subsystems. Persons working at the subsystem level easily lose track of relations between their "part" and the overall architecture. This hampers traceability and may lead to changes that conflict with the general architectural decisions, which instead should orchestrate the differences between the involved parties.

When software engineering projects are distributed or global, the problems above are aggravated. Knowledge transfer is a communication process requiring strict interaction and agile information exchange. In local software development, it is already difficult to rationalize the type and amount of knowledge we need to exchange. If in addition exchanges occur remotely and via a technological infrastructure, we have to make this knowledge explicit, and we need to identify agile means to render this process as dynamic and powerful as possible.

In this chapter, we describe the conceptual collaborative scenarios implementing a virtual community aimed at sharing architectural knowledge in a distributed setting. As envisaged by Zhuge [25] "Modern communication facilities like the Internet provide people with unprecedented social opportunities for knowledge generation and sharing". To improve this knowledge generation and sharing, Zhuge designed a knowledge grid that supports social activities in different environmental spaces. In our work we aim at realizing such a knowledge grid for professionals involved in the software architecture processes. To this end, we first highlight some trends in architectural knowledge representation and sharing. Then, we define the collaboration requirements for the GRIFFIN virtual community followed by the scenarios realizing them. We further show how this set of scenarios combine formalized and informal AK sharing; a combination that can be finally mapped on Web 2.0 services.

10.1.1 From a Codification/Personalization to a Hybrid Knowledge Management Strategy

In most literature, e.g. [21], knowledge is classified into tacit, documented, and formalized knowledge. *Tacit knowledge* (e.g., organization strategies or best practices) is implicitly known and used by software architects, but not made explicit. *Documented knowledge* about software architecture (e.g., design decisions or rationale) can be interpreted and used by humans, whereas *formalized knowledge* (e.g., domain-specific ontologies) can be created and used by both humans and software systems.

In software development organizations much knowledge is kept in unstructured forms: FAQs, mailing lists, email repositories, bug reports, lists of open issues, etc. Lightweight tools such as wikis, weblogs, and yellow pages are other examples of relatively unstructured repositories to share information in global projects.

In the knowledge management literature, a distinction is made between a *personalization strategy* and a *codification strategy* [14]. A personalization strategy emphasizes interaction between knowledge workers. The knowledge itself is kept by its creator. One personalization strategy is to record who knows what, as e.g., in yellow pages. Each person then has his/her own way to structure the knowledge. The threshold to participate is usually low, but the effort to find useful information is higher. In a codification strategy, knowledge is codified and stored in a repository. The repository may be unstructured (as in wikis) or structured according to some model. In the latter case, the structure of the repository can be used while querying. An advantage of a structured repository is that the information has the same form. A disadvantage is the extra effort it takes to cast the information in the form required. A *hybrid strategy* may be used to have the best of those different worlds [1, 11].

10.1.2 From Closed to Open Virtual AK Communities

When we speak of knowledge virtual communities we are immediately brought back to the concepts of open source software communities [4] and Internet and web-based communities [23]. Both were born as *open social environments of peers*. As such, access from non-members is allowed and aspects like task assignment and work progress are delegated to the initiative of the individual.

In the early 2000s we observed the shift of the so-called *closed communities* living inside business and governmental organizations toward more open, agile practices. This shift witnessed the creation in large business organizations of hybrid communities, such as inner-source software communities created according to the same principles of OSS development, collaborating (to some extent) with external, open communities but living within the boundaries of the organization. In a similar way, with the advent of Web 2.0, principles such as "radical trust on mass-contributed contents" or "using the web as a knowledge sharing platform" [22] enterprises applied the same principles to let their employees share the organizational know-how. For example, Yakovlev [24] gives an overview of widely known Web 2.0 mechanisms that enable the autonomous creation of virtual communities of peers. Among them we find wikis (used by enterprises to aggregate input from members of various focused groups), RSS feeds (allowing community members to remain up-to-date on selected subjects), social networking (supporting autonomous community building) and folksonomies (supporting users of a social environment in collaboratively creating and managing tags to annotate and categorize content).

In summary, organizations moved from closed to open (but regulated) communities thanks to the acceptation of modern principles and the adoption of enabling technologies. The GRIFFIN virtual community provides one example of such communities. It is meant to support a community of professionals (software architects) to effectively carry out their daily work and further contribute to (and learn from) the community with its own (architectural) knowledge. A combination of strategies for knowledge codification and personalization should provide each individual with the necessary flexibility, to fit in the own working practice and to provide sufficient incentives for successful AK management.

10.2 Requirements for Collaboration in a Distributed Environment of Software Architects

Within the context of architectural knowledge management, four broad topics can be identified:

- *AK sharing* focuses on methods, tools, and techniques for exchanging AK among stakeholders directly (through personalization) or indirectly (through codification).
- *AK discovery* focuses on the methods, tools, and techniques to find, extract, and make accessible the relevant AK dispersed across the documentation that accompanies a software product.
- *AK traceability* focuses on methods, processes, and tools for codifying and interrelating AK.
- *AK compliance* focuses on ensuring that the architectural design decisions are known, understood, and complied with in the resulting system.

The combination of the four topics of AK sharing, discovery, traceability and compliance poses the following requirements for collaboration in distributed environments of software architects:

Manage architectural decisions. Architecting is a decision making process and architects have to consider lots of technical and non-technical requirements, constraints, and concerns. To assist architects in the thought process of balancing these forces, the collaborative virtual community needs to offer support for managing architectural decisions and all associated knowledge. This will allow sharing of the "reasoning behind" architectural designs, because this is what architectural decisions and their rationale represent. It also allows maintaining an explicit backlog of open issues, concerns, and decisions [15]. This requirement for the collaborative virtual community includes providing overviews of architectural decisions taken, plus the relationships between those decisions. Finally, insight in the completeness, correctness, and consistency of a set of architectural decisions helps architects in reflecting on the developed solutions, and in identifying conflicts between decisions taken.

Codify architectural knowledge. The result of the processes of architecting are reported in artifacts like documents and models. Sharing them allows AK transfer. In this way the architects and stakeholders not directly involved in decision making, can participate or acquire after-the-fact information.

Search architectural knowledge. Next to assisting practitioners in producing architectural knowledge, support during consumption of such knowledge (e.g., searching) is equally important. The need for a more balanced view on AK sharing, in which support for both producing and consuming AK is included, has been discussed before [19]. Moreover, one of the main requirements practitioners stated is support in retrieving the *right* architectural knowledge at the *right* time [12]. This can boost reuse of AK (reusable assets are better accessible) and stimulate learning among practitioners (knowledge can be found more easily).

Support community building. Due to the size and complexity of most software systems, it is often infeasible for one architect to be responsible for everything himself. This focus on teamwork is especially true in global software engineering environments where the architect-role is often fulfilled by multiple collaborating architects. Consequently, AK management support should support community building. This may include facilities to hold discussions or chat with colleagues, to organize and plan meetings, workshops or events, to peer-review deliverables of colleagues, to find contact information, expertise and interests of colleagues, and to retrieve information about what colleagues are currently working on.

Provide intelligent support. We argue that architects would welcome intelligent support (advice, guidelines) just after or during activities producing and assessing AK (e.g., writing an architectural description). Intelligent support is more useful if combined with a certain level of pro-activity. For instance, intelligence and pro-activity can be provided using avatars that think along with practitioners and suggest ideas, challenge decisions, play the devil's advocate, etc.

Enrich architectural knowledge. Ideally architectural knowledge should be produced and shared *below the surface* without bothering architects. Automatically distilling patterns out of unstructured data, for example, would lead to production of AK without an architect explicitly doing this. Producing and consuming architectural knowledge should thus not be considered an extra, resource-consuming activity but rather an invisible part of other organizational processes. Enrichment of architectural knowledge means support for intelligence and pro-activity, which would also benefit practitioners in their daily work, is the (semi-) automatic interpretation of content in order to enrich this content. Text mining services could for example be employed to automatically sift and winnow through existing architectural knowledge stored (e.g., in a database) looking for new patterns, defining best practices, or locating trends. Based on the findings additional meta-data could be generated by such a service and eventually presented to the practitioner.

10.3 A Collaborative Virtual Community for AK Management

Within GRIFFIN, we envision a virtual and distributed community of professionals willing to create and share knowledge.

A *virtual community* is defined on Wikipedia as "a group of people that primarily interact via communication media [...] rather than face to face, for social, professional, educational or other purposes". We extend this definition to embrace organizations as well as individuals. Accordingly, we consider a virtual community as a group of *virtual spaces,* where each virtual space can correspond to whole

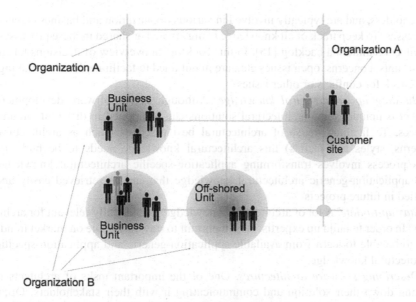

Fig. 10.1 Distributed community of organizational virtual spaces

organizations, teams of people or individuals. As illustrated in Fig. 10.1 organizations can share AK in a grid-like configuration of connected sites (like organization A) and/or departments or business units (like organization B) where employees carry out collaborative activities. Individuals hence work in their virtual space where they can manage their own knowledge and eventually share part of this knowledge with (remote) counterparts in a collaborative social network of professionals.

10.3.1 Support for Collaborative AK Management

For each of the four AK management topics introduced before (AK sharing, AK discovery, AK traceability, and AK compliance) we researched the state-of-the-practice as well as the challenges experienced by the GRIFFIN industrial partners. For each topic, the following illustrates the related virtual spaces that we designed and developed, and the architecture process activities they support.

10.3.1.1 Virtual Spaces for AK Sharing

There are several broad activities within the architecting process that demand for architectural knowledge sharing (AKS). These include:

Decision making. Architecting is inherently a decision making process. Architects need to balance quality criteria, stakeholder concerns and requirements, and take a number of architectural design decisions in which they reuse architectural styles and patterns. Architects guide the architecting process by interacting with stakeholders, and are typically involved in various organization and business related processes. To keep track of all knowledge being created or shared in these processes, architects maintain a backlog [15]. In this backlog an overview of decisions taken, constraints, concerns, open issues etc., are maintained to facilitate decision making, and check for conflicts or other issues.

Building up architectural knowledge. Although every software development project is unique, some architectural solutions can be applied in different circumstances. To facilitate reuse of architectural best practices (such as architectural patterns, styles and tactics) this architectural knowledge needs to be built up. This process involves transforming application-specific architectural knowledge into application-generic architectural knowledge that can be retrieved easily and applied in future projects.

Stay up-to-date. A lot of architectural knowledge is potentially relevant for architects. In order to build up expertise it is important to stay up-to-date on market trends and to be able to learn from available application-generic and application-specific architectural knowledge.

Describing software architectures. One of the important tasks of architects is writing down their solution and communicating it with their stakeholders. Often architecture design is described using a number of architectural views and viewpoints. In creating an architecture description important aspects are both the structure of the document and its completeness and internal consistency. To achieve this, annotation of AK within an architecture description is necessary.

Personalization support in a community. It is important that architects know where to find and how to contact each other when needed, so that the expertise of one architect can assist others. Services such as a chat service or yellow pages service ("who knows what") can be used for this purpose.

To carry out these AK sharing activities, several conceptual scenarios have been designed for the AKS virtual spaces, some of which we show below:

Discuss and negotiate (Scenario $S_{AKS,1}$)

Situation: Architect(s) need to decide for an architectural design. This involves meeting all needs and concerns of the relevant stakeholders.

Problem: Each stakeholder has its own concerns and needs that often conflict with the overall goals of the system to be developed. Architects need to balance all these concerns in a satisfactory way.

Solution: With a decision making component architects are better supported in negotiating or discussing with colleagues or other stakeholders in the architecting process about which decisions to take and why. This component acts as an automated way of managing the backlog. It facilitates architects in dealing with multiple concerns at the same time by visualizing the decision space, indicating which decisions conflict with each other, etc. This also helps in personally analyzing tradeoffs and conflicts between decisions and alternative solutions. The decision making component

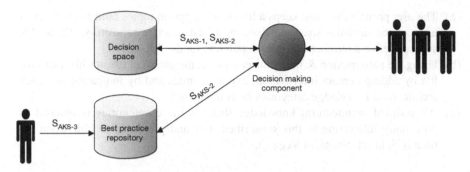

Fig. 10.2 Decision making component in relation to codified AK

manipulates (i.e., create, read, update, delete) AK stored in a decision space database
that keeps a data set for each project.
Scenario description (see Fig. 10.2):

(a) The architects use the decision making component as visual guide during their
discussions and negotiations about the architecture design.

Subscribe to architectural knowledge (Scenario $S_{AKS,4}$)

Situation: Architects would like to stay up-to-date.
Problem: How to inform architects of potentially available architectural knowledge
without flooding them with information?
Solution: An architect can use a subscription and notification service to subscribe to
specific AK topics. Based on this information the architect's user profile is created
or updated. The user profiles database connects to databases where the architectural
knowledge itself is being stored (i.e., the decision space database and best practice repository) to determine what types of architectural knowledge an architect can
subscribe himself to.
Scenario description (see Fig. 10.3):

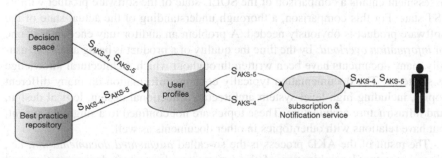

Fig. 10.3 Subscription and notification of AK

(a) The user profiles database keeps a list of subscription topics built from the contents of the decision space database and best practice repository. These AK sources define a number of topics dependent on the AK stored.
(b) Using the subscription & notification service, the architect creates his user profile by adding contact information, expertise areas and by indicating in which architectural knowledge categories he is interested.
(c) All codified architectural knowledge that fits these categories is marked as potentially interesting to this subscribed user and presented to him when the time is right (cf. Scenario $S_{AKS, 5}$).

Notify architects about architectural knowledge (Scenario $S_{AKS,5}$)

Situation: Architects would like to stay up-to-date.
Problem: How to inform architects of potentially available AK without flooding them with information?
Solution: An architect is notified by a subscription and notification service about potentially interesting AK depending on his user profile (for example using RSS feeds or email) as soon as new AK is stored in one of the databases. This notification mechanism enables the Just-in-Time AK requirement discussed in [12].
Scenario description (see Fig. 10.3):

(a) The subscription and notification service periodically scans for updated AK codified in one of the databases, and tries to match this with the user profiles stored.
(b) The AK (or a link to the source) is pushed to all users whose profiles indicate a match.

10.3.1.2 Virtual Spaces for AK Discovery

Although AK discovery has broader applications, it has originally been developed and piloted to support software quality audits. Discovery of AK from software product documentation is a typical activity that an auditor must perform to collect the information necessary for expressing an opinion on a product's quality. A quality assessment entails a comparison of the SOLL-state of the software product with its IST-state. For this comparison, a thorough understanding of the actual state of the software product is obviously needed. A problem an auditor may encounter is one of *information overload:* by the time the quality of a product is being assessed, usually many documents have been written throughout which architectural knowledge is scattered. The documentation typically contains information on many different topics, including high-level system architecture, functional design, logical design, and infrastructure architecture. These topics are not confined to a single document, but have relations with other topics in other documents as well.

The result of the AKD process is the so-called *augmented documentation*, i.e., a semi-structured combination of the (unstructured) product documentation and a (structured) quality ontology that defines generic quality criteria and relations between them. The documentation is augmented with *Latent Semantic Analysis*-inferred meaning (cf. [20]) and related to applicable quality criteria selected from the quality ontology. Parts of the documentation that have a meaning closely related to the meaning of a selected quality criterion have been identified. The selected quality criteria form an index to the product documentation.

Augmented documentation eases the "findability" of architectural knowledge and the comparison of IST-state product documentation with the SOLL-state evaluation frame. By using the LSA text analysis technique, the semantic structure underlying the product documentation can be found. This allows for suggestions regarding where to start reading when one is interested in a particular topic. It also allows for suggestions regarding how to continue reading such that the semantic difference between two consecutive documents is as small as possible, essentially providing a reading guide or a route through the documentation. Such a reading guide may for instance suggest a smooth trajectory from a high-level architectural overview to increasingly finer-grained specifications.

Some of the most important topics from a quality audit point of view are topics related to quality attributes and/or quality criteria. Therefore, in the discovery space the documentation is related to the quality criteria from the quality ontology. Parts of the documentation that have a meaning closely related to the meaning of a selected quality criterion are identified through LSA. The selected quality criteria form an index to the product documentation. Since the quality ontology defines relations between quality criteria, relations between product documentation parts can be inferred.

To carry out the AKD activities here described, the following scenarios have been supported by the AKD virtual spaces (shown in Fig. 10.4).

Selection of quality criteria (Scenario $S_{AKD,1}$)

Situation: Start of the audit, where quality attributes and their priorities (according to the customer) are known.

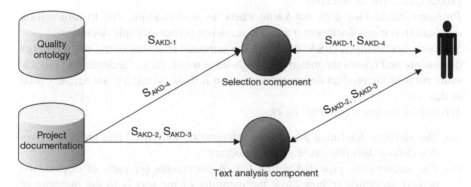

Fig. 10.4 AK discovery in quality audits

Problem: Which quality criteria to use to assess the product's compliance with the customer's requested level of quality? Since quality criteria are applicable in different product audits, auditors may read through previous audit reports to find out which quality criteria can be used. Obviously, such ad-hoc reuse is far from ideal, being time consuming and not transparent.

Solution: Codification in "quality ontology" of quality criteria and their relations according to generic AK structures (e.g., Kruchten's ontology [18]) makes them available for more systematic reuse. Intelligent visualization supports the auditor in deciding which criteria to use.

Scenario description (see Fig. 10.4):

(a) The auditor uses the Selection component to provide a list of prioritized quality attributes (e.g., 1=performance, 2=security, 3=usability).

(b) The auditor is presented with a list of measures that are known to favor those quality attributes (e.g., "use secure connections" for security) or to hinder them (e.g., "don't use passwords"). From those measures, auditors may derive quality criteria: measures that they expect to be in the product.

(c) The auditor indicates which measures should and should not be in the product, i.e., selects the quality criteria to be used in the audit. Since certain measures may be related (e.g., be in conflict or depend on each other) certain combinations are not allowed and some others are mandatory. The quality ontology identifies inconsistencies in the selected criteria and provides suggestions to solve them.

(d) Further decision support is provided through mining from previous audits latent relations that are not (yet) codified. This leads to suggestions such as "auditors who selected the criterion you just selected, also selected criterion X".

Accessing the body of knowledge (i.e., where to start reading, scenario $S_{AKD,2}$)

Situation: quality criteria have been selected; auditors need to read the product documentation to gain a certain level of knowledge about the product they are auditing. They want to gain a high-level understanding of the most important parts of the product, i.e., "the architecture".

Problem: the auditor does not know where to start reading, due to information overload (too many documents) and AK scattered across multiple documents.

Solution: Text analysis (LSA) discovers the semantic structure of the set of product documents and relates the meaning of high-level words (e.g., "architecture") to relevant parts in the product documentation, even if those words are not actually used in that text (cf. [10]).

Scenario description (see Fig. 10.4):

(a) The auditors determine the type of information they need and provide a term that denotes this interest (e.g., "architecture").

(b) The auditors are provided with a list of documents (or parts of documents) ranked according to how close the meaning of the text is to the meaning of the term the auditors provided (cf. [10]).

Guidance through the body of knowledge (Scenario $S_{AKD,3}$)

Situation: The auditors have read part of the documentation and want to continue gaining further insight for the audit.

Problem: The auditors want to have a smooth progression through the documentation, however, without any big jumps from e.g., high-level overview to low-level detail and back again.

Solution: Text analysis provides a distance measure between different text parts that is employed to guide the auditor through the documentation.

Scenario description (see Fig. 10.4):

(a) The auditors determine their subsequent information need and provide a corresponding term (e.g., the name of a module for further investigation).
(b) The auditors are provided with a list of documents ranked according to: how close the meaning of the text is to the meaning of the provided term; and how close the meaning of the text is to the meaning of the previously read text (cf. [10]).

Quality assessment (Scenario $S_{AKD,4}$)

Situation: The auditors have gained an overall understanding of the software product and now need to determine the product's compliance with the selected quality criteria.

Problem: Again, information overload: Too many documents and not all information regarding a particular product quality can be expected to be located at a single place.

Solution: By relating the meaning of the quality criterion (as defined in the quality ontology by its description and relation to other criteria) to the meaning of the software product documentation, parts of the documentation that talk about the criterion can be identified.

Scenario description (see Fig. 10.4):

(a) The auditors select a criterion that they want to investigate.
(b) The auditors are provided with a list of documents ranked according to how close the meaning of the text is to the meaning of the quality criterion.

10.3.1.3 Virtual Spaces for AK Traceability

In AK traceability, three concepts play an important role:

- *Concepts:* The classes of distinguished AK.
- *Relationships:* The relationships among these classes.
- *Knowledge Entities (KE):* Instances of a particular concept that can have relationships to one or more other instances.

The activities in a virtual space for AK traceability use these concepts. They include the following activities:

Identify AK and traceability needs. Codifying AK and providing traceability at the same time is a costly operation. Hence, it is important to minimize the required effort to do so. This is achieved in two ways: by focusing on the real AK needs and by reducing the effort of capturing of creating traceability.

Modeling the required AK and traceability information in a domain model. Based on the identified needs, the virtual space should assist an architect in defining a domain model for modeling the relevant AK concepts and relationships. This can take the form of suggesting (part-of) existing models based on the earlier identified needs.

Capture the knowledge according to this domain model. The virtual space should assist stakeholders with capturing the relevant AK in KEs. This is achieved by either automating the process (such as investigated in the discovery virtual space) or by offering intelligent integrated tooling in environments in which this knowledge is created or described.

Integrate captured knowledge with other sources. For the virtual space to offer optimal traceability, the captured knowledge should be integrated (i.e., related) to knowledge of other relevant sources. This activity is often intertwined with the capturing activity. There are several ways in which a virtual space could achieve this integration. First, a virtual space could automate this integration, e.g. by using text analysis techniques. Second, it could offer step-by-step suggestions on how this integration could take place, thereby guiding the integration process. Third, it could offer search functionality and associated suggestions to facilitate a manual integration process. Often, a combination of these three different possibilities is used for different concepts.

Consume the AK and its traceability. Once the needed AK has become traceable, this knowledge can be used for various purposes, including the production of additional AK and the identified AK and traceability needs. Some of example scenarios of this usage will be presented.

Evolve the knowledge. Typically, architecture is designed in multiple iterations. Hence, there is a need to not only evolve the architecture design, but also its associated knowledge and relations. A virtual space should support incremental updating of the KE and relationships, both in a reactive and proactive manner. For the former, a stakeholder wants to change some AK, and see the consequences of this change. For the latter, a virtual space should be able to detect certain changes and evolve related AK accordingly. For example, the removal of a requirement potentially invalidates the architectural decisions based on this requirement. With traceability, a virtual space could automatically determine such impacts.

Find specific AK to relate to (Scenario $S_{TA,1}$)

Situation: The software architect wants to find specific AK to relate to, so as to create traceability among the KE.

Problem: The number of KEs is typically very large and the specific KE might not be codified yet.

Solution: Based on the domain model, the virtual space makes a first selection of KE that could be related. Hence, it acts as a classification filter. In addition, the virtual space uses the traceability information of the starting KE as a way to guess what the context of the start point is and use this information to assist in the search process.

Scenario description:

(a) The software architect selects a KE as a starting point.
(b) Optionally, the architect selects a possible relationship (automatically inferred from the domain model) for the selected KE.
(c) Optionally, the architect can insert some keywords describing the KE to search for.
(d) The virtual space tries to find plausible candidate KE to relate to and orders the search results.
(e) The architect uses the traceability information to navigate through the search results.
(f) The architect selects one of the found KE and codifies the relationship or decides to manually create the missing KE.

Make an architectural decision (Scenario $S_{TA,2}$)

Situation: The software architect wants to make an architectural decision.

Problem: The software architect needs to rationalize this decision to convince stakeholders of its relevance and correctness.

Solution: The architect defines the traceability of the architectural decision to other AK. This makes the rationale of the decision traceable and helps in making the decision process more transparent.

Scenario description:

(a) The software architect, helped by the virtual space, scopes the problem space, thereby identifying the reason why an architectural decision has to be made.
(b) The software architect defines the alternative(s) considered.
(c) The architect captures the evaluation of the alternatives. The rationale for a particular choice is codified by providing traceability to specific AK from the problem space.
(d) The impact of the chosen alternative is considered for both the problem and domain space. New AK is created and related accordingly.

Design maturity assessment (Scenario $S_{TA,4}$)

Situation: The software architect wants to know how mature the software architecture design is. This includes the correctness, completeness, and consistency of the design and its description.

Problem: Judging the maturity of a design is not trivial, as it requires harmonizing subjective judgments of multiple experts on both individual and collections of KE. Again, information overload: Too many documents and not all information regarding a particular product quality can be expected to be located at a single place. *Solution:* The traceability provided by the codified AK allows for an automated assessment of the completeness of the AK. Since the defined domain model allows for assumptions about AK that should exist and their relationships. The explicit AK provides stakeholders the opportunity to assert and administrate the correctness of each individual KE. Consistency is improved, since navigating through and finding related AK becomes more easy thanks to increased traceability.
Scenario description:

(a) The software architect selects an architecture description the maturity should be assessed of.
(b) The virtual space identifies which parts of the AK are incomplete.
(c) The architect completes these AK omissions.
(d) The architect shares the architecture description and associated AK with relevant stakeholders.
(e) Each of these stakeholders asses the correctness and consistency of the AK and identify in the virtual space which parts are troublesome.
(f) The architect collects these remarks through the virtual space and resolves them in a new version of the architecture description.

10.3.1.4 Virtual Spaces for AK Compliance

The architecture of a software system guides the software development activities by providing the necessary direction for it. Architectural rules are the principles and statements on the software architecture that must hold at all times, and thus must be complied with [6]. Architectural compliance in global software development (GSD) environments poses additional challenges for sharing AK and complying with architectural rules.

The aim of compliance verification is that the resulting system is in line with the principles as expressed in architectural rules. A collaborative virtual space should allow for continuous compliance verification by promoting architectural knowledge to relevant stakeholders and development sites to reduce the gap between reality and the principles identified during compliance verification. Hence, the virtual space for AK compliance should not only support compliance verification in hindsight, but partly overlap with the virtual space for AK sharing.

To ensure compliance in GSD environments, the virtual space for AK compliance supports the following activities:

Identify architectural rules requires the virtual space to characterize a (possible sub-) set of architectural design decisions that are mandatory. The virtual space presents the architectural design decisions in a format which allows practitioners to perform compliance verification, by allowing to indicate entry criteria for e.g. the applicability of architectural rules for only part of the system, and criteria that allow practitioners to determine when architectural rules are satisfied, and when they are not.

The *inject architectural rules in company* practice is necessary to let the architectural rules sink in within the organization. The architectural rules need to be made known to the practitioners across the different development sites and their understanding should be verified explicitly.

Verify compliance supports matching designated parts of the implemented system with applicable architectural rules. The virtual space for AK compliance further supports a compliance officer in this process by running compliance checks automatically, when applicable. The compliance verification results in a list of non-compliance items that indicate what architectural rules are not complied with and where in the system this non-compliance occurred.

Address situations of non-compliance The results of the verification are interpreted by the compliance officer and presented to the software architect(s). The virtual space for AK compliance indicates the severity of the non-compliance which helps the software architect to take adequate follow-up measures. These follow-up measures can pertain to instructing or re-implementing architectural rules within the software architecture, or for adjusting the set of architectural design decisions which, in turn, will affect the set of architectural rules that hold.

The virtual space for AK compliance supports the following scenarios:

Identify architectural rules (Scenario $S_{AKC,1}$)

Situation: Architect(s) need to decide what architectural knowledge should be complied with in the software.
Problem: How does an architect indicate what architectural knowledge is mandatory? How can an architect be supported in providing the correct information that allows for both correct implementation and compliance verification?
Solution: Designate a subset of architectural design decisions as architectural rules.
Scenario description (see Fig. 10.5):

(a) The architect is provided with the set of architectural design decisions from the decision space.
(b) The architect selects a set of architectural design decisions that should be complied with.
(c) The architect augments the architectural design decisions with knowledge necessary to increase their "verifiability". This includes e.g.,

- Identification of the scope (both related to the system and the project) and the impact of non-compliance.
- Identification of the way compliance verification can take place (using e.g., automated tools or manual inspections).

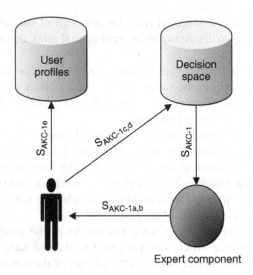

Fig. 10.5 Identify architectural rules

(d) The architect identifies a compliance verification method from a list of verification options provided to him.

(e) The architect identifies the stakeholders (per development site) that need to be informed of the AK to comply with.

Push architectural knowledge to relevant stakeholders (Scenario $S_{AKC,3}$)

Situation: Relevant stakeholders of architectural knowledge need to know what architectural rules are mandatory and need to be complied with.

Problem: How to ensure that all relevant stakeholders are informed of the architectural design decisions?

Solution: Use a notification system (see Scenario $S_{AKS,5}$) and ensure that stakeholders have consumed the architectural knowledge. The solution does not make use of

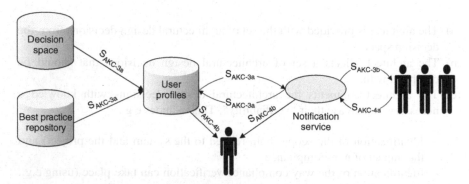

Fig. 10.6 Push architectural rules to stakeholders and verify their understanding

a subscription service (Scenario $S_{AKS,4}$) but uses a predefined set of stakeholders that must be informed.

Scenario description (see Fig. 10.6):

(a) The notification service matches architectural knowledge designated as architectural rules with the user profiles.
(b) Based on the user profiles that need to be informed, the notification service provides the architectural rules to the corresponding users.

Verify understanding with AK (Scenario $S_{AKC,4}$)

Situation: Relevant stakeholders need to understand the architectural knowledge.
Problem: How to ensure that all relevant stakeholders understand the architectural rules that must be implemented or complied with?
Solution: It is important to obtain feedback from the relevant stakeholders on their understanding of, or concerns regarding this architectural knowledge. When development sites are distributed, effective implementation of AK can only occur by collecting feedback from these development sites [5, 6, 7].
Scenario description (see Fig. 10.6):

(a) Practitioners who have received the architectural rules can indicate whether they are informed of the architectural knowledge.
(b) Feedback on the AK is solicited and transferred to the architect.

Address situations of non-compliance (Scenario $S_{AKC,6}$)

Situation: A system does not comply with the current architectural rules.
Problem: What are possible measures that the architect can take?
Solution: The architect can either identify if the current architectural rules must be modified to accommodate the current situation, or the practitioners of the responsible development sites need to change the system comply with the architectural rules.
Scenario description (see Fig. 10.7):

(a) The architect decides that certain architectural rules in its original form are no longer applicable and updates the architectural rules accordingly.
(b) The architect reinforces the existing architectural rules. The architect may use scenarios $S_{AKC,3}$ and $S_{AKC,4}$ as a minimum.

Fig. 10.7 Provide follow-up to compliance results

10.3.2 Towards a Virtual AK Sharing Community

The previous sections presented the conceptual scenarios supporting AK sharing, discovery, traceability, and compliance in a distributed virtual space. Let's imagine an AK sharing community of networked member organizations, each supporting one or more of such scenarios. In addition to their individual contribution, each scenario provides generic features that can further propel collaboration, which is called "social cognition" in [5] i.e., "the ability of a group of people to remember, think and reason".

For example (see Fig. 10.8) an auditing organization can locally carry out the quality audit of a product developed by a certain customer organization. The auditing organization, on its own, can locally annotate AK, which might be relevant for that audit. If the auditing organization and the customer organization connect their local virtual spaces and if relevant auditors can subscribe to and be notified of relevant new AK annotations, auditors are able to speed up the learning process about what knowledge is necessary to achieve an opinion about the product's

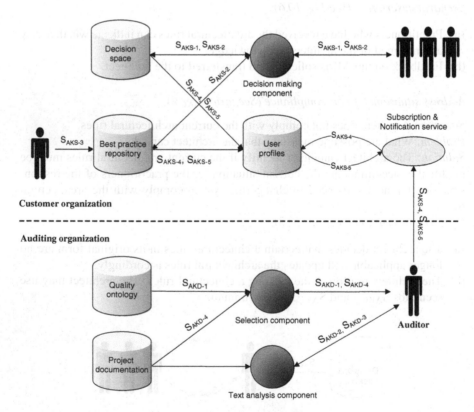

Fig. 10.8 Towards a community: connecting virtual spaces

quality. Further, experience and know-how can be improved, as well as the level of trust between the two partner organizations.

In order to provide more advanced AK management support we envision more of these scenarios that involve connecting virtual spaces of different organizations or departments of organizations. This will further enhance collaboration among different parties and will help in increasing the virtual community of architects.

10.4 Future Trends and Research Challenges

Building a virtual community into an organization is a long-term investment and introduces substantial change. We need to bring convincing arguments, backed by hard data, that such an investment is worthwhile. We also need ways to realize such migration. Also to ensure that new scenario combinations (such as the example discussed in Section 10.3.2) improve the state of the practice, a research challenge is to obtain a better understanding of what practitioners in the architecting process need.

A second research challenge is related to the different terminology used by different organizations. Different organizations speak their own "language" of AK. If AK is to be shared between organizations, then the virtual collaborative community needs to support appropriate translations from the AK meta-model of one to those of the other virtual spaces. This is a purely technical problem and can be resolved with different technologies, e.g., from the ontologies and the semantic web community. A cost-benefit analysis must be conducted, to make the right trade-off between the cost of the translation (especially with evolving AK meta-models) and the perceived benefit (quality of the translation).

Another – more technical – challenge is the visualization of AK in the different virtual spaces. There is no one-size-fits-all visualization solution. Therefore we need customizable solutions that can be tailored to the AK meta-model and even the intended usage.

Crowd sourcing is another trend that may have a large impact on virtual AK communities. The users of these communities may scale up to thousands, and may be given the power to define, on their own, requirements and use cases for AK; they may even design their own virtual spaces. This challenge needs to be addressed both technically (provide the right crowd sourcing technologies) and non-technically (showing people the benefits and leveraging their self-motivation).

Lastly, sharing AK through the virtual organizations raises many complicated legal issues, with respect to intellectual property rights. Of course sharing AK can happen both in open and in inner (closed consortia) communities. These aspects need to be thoroughly inspected before large corporations are convinced to contribute and share AK. Also, further research is needed about creating incentives for architectural knowledge sharing, since the success of the virtual community is largely determined by the amount of time and energy the users are willing to spend on it.

10.5 Conclusions

This chapter presented the conceptual view of the GRIFFIN collaborative community for AK management. This community consists of virtual spaces supporting four key AK management topics: AK sharing, discovery, compliance, and traceability.

We discussed how each of the scenarios has been designed in the GRIFFIN project. We further illustrated one example about how such scenarios can be potentially combined to implement more complex scenarios. In this way, scenarios can provide general solutions to common AK management problems and propel collaboration among individuals and across organizations.

We would like to especially encourage the industrial community to actively participate in addressing the challenges and forming the future virtual AK communities. We have come to the understanding that in the context of global software development, the industry of software-intensive systems faces these challenges intensively and with an increasing pace. There are still many problems that need to be resolved and there will be substantial research conducted before AK virtual communities become a reality. We hope that the industry will be keen in enthusiastically participating to this research and shape the way AK communities will collaborate in the future.

Acknowledgements This research has been partially sponsored by the Dutch Joint Academic and Commercial Quality Research & Development (Jacquard) program on Software Engineering Research via contract 638.001.406 GRIFFIN: a Grid for Information about architectural knowledge.

References

1. Ali Babar M et al. (2007) Architectural knowledge management strategies: Approaches in research and industry. 2nd Workshop on Sharing and Reusing architectural Knowledge – Architecture, rationale, and Design Intent (SHARK/ADI).
2. Bass L, Clements P, Kazman R (2003) Software Architecture in Practice. 2nd edn. SEI Series in Software Engineering. Boston, MA: Addison-Wesley.
3. Bosch J (2004) Software architecture: The next step. First European Workshop on Software Architecture (EWSA).
4. Capiluppi A, Lago P, Morisio M (2003) Characteristics of open source projects. European Conference on Software Maintenance and Reengineering.
5. Chi EH (2008) The social web: Research and opportunities. IEEE Computer (September) 41(9): 88–91.
6. Clerc V, Lago P, Van Vliet H (2007) Assessing a multi-site development organization for architectural compliance. 6th Working IEEE/IFIP Conference on Software Architecture (WICSA).
7. Clerc V, Lago P, Van Vliet H (2007) Global software development: Are architectural rules the answer? International Conference on Global Software Engineering (ICGSE).
8. Clerc V, Lago P, Van Vliet H (2007) The architect's mindset. 3rd International Conference on the Quality of Software Architectures (QoSA).
9. De Boer RC et al. (2007) Architectural knowledge: Getting to the core. 3rd International Conference on the Quality of Software Architectures (QoSA).

10. De Boer RC, Van Vliet H (2008) Architectural knowledge discovery with latent semantic analysis: Constructing a reading guide for software product audits. Journal of Systems and Software 81(9): 1456–1469.
11. Desouza KC, Awazu Y, Baloh P (2006) Managing knowledge in global software development efforts: Issues and practices. IEEE Software 23(5): 30–37.
12. Farenhorst R et al. (2008) A just-in-time architectural knowledge sharing portal. 7th Working IEEE/IFIP Conference on Software Architecture (WICSA).
13. Farenhorst R, Lago P, Van Vliet H (2007) EAGLE: Effective tool support for sharing architectural knowledge. International Journal of Co-operative Information Systems (IJCIS) 16(3/4): 413–437.
14. Hansen MT, Nohria N, Tierney T (1999) What's Your Strategy for Managing Knowledge? Harvard Business Review 77(2): 106–116.
15. Hofmeister C et al. (2007) A general model of software architecture design derived from five industrial approaches. The Journal of Systems and Software 80(1): 106–126.
16. Jansen A et al. (2007) Tool support for architectural decisions. 6th Working IEEE/IFIP Conference on Software Architecture (WICSA).
17. Jansen A et al. (2008) Sharing the architectural knowledge of quantitative analysis. 4th International Conference on the Quality of Software Architectures (QoSA).
18. Kruchten P (2004) An ontology of architectural design decisions in software-intensive systems. 2nd Groningen Workshop on Software Variability Management.
19. Lago P, Avgeriou P (2006) 1st Workshop on sharing and reusing architectural knowledge, Final Workshop Report. ACM SIGSOFT Software Engineering Notes 31(5): 32–36.
20. Landauer TK, Foltz PW, Laham D (1998) An introduction to latent semantic analysis. Discourse Processes 25: 259–284.
21. Nonaka I, Takeuchi H (1995) The Knowledge-Creating Company. New York: Oxford University Press.
22. O'Reilly T (2005) What is Web 2.0 – Design Patterns and Business Models for the Next Generation of Software. Sebastopol CA: O'Reilly Media.
23. Preece J (2000) Online Communities: Designing Usability, Supporting Sociability. Chichester: Wiley.
24. Yakovlev IV (2007) Web 2.0: Is it evolutionary or revolutionary? IT Professional, IEEE Computer Society 9: 43–45.
25. Zhuge H (2004) The Knowledge Grid. Singapore: World Scientific Publishing Co.

Chapter 11
Supporting Expertise Communication in Developer-Centered Collaborative Software Development Environments

Kumiyo Nakakoji, Yunwen Ye, and Yasuhiro Yamamoto

Abstract Looking at software development as a collective knowledge activity has changed the view of the role of communication in software development from something to be eliminated to something to be nurtured. Developer-centered collaborative software development environments (CSDEs) should facilitate software development in such a way, as individual software developers collaboratively develop information artifacts through social interactions. In this chapter, we identify two distinctive types of communication in software development, *coordination communication* and *expertise communication*, and argue that different sets of design guidelines are necessary in supporting each type of communication. We then describe nine design guidelines to support *expertise communication* based on the theories of social capital and models of supporting collective creativity.

11.1 Introduction

Software development is in essence information-intensive collaborative knowledge activity. It is about using information, generating information, and making information artifacts. The wide acceptance of agile processes and the success of many open source projects provide strong evidence that human aspects do matter in software development; cognitive and social processes play essential roles in successful software projects in which individuals' creative thinking in using and generating information are nurtured. We argue that software engineering environments must be designed to foster such individuals' creative knowledge processes, and that collaboration must be supported in the context of individuals' development activities. Collaborative software development environments (CSDEs) should be designed to facilitate and nurture individuals' creative knowledge processes. We call this approach *developer-centered CSDEs*.

K. Nakakoji (✉)
Research Centre for Advanced Science and Technology, University of Tokyo, Japan;
SRA Key Technology Laboratory Inc, Japan
e-mail: kumiyo@kid.rcast.u-tokyo.ac.jp

I. Mistrík et al. (eds.), *Collaborative Software Engineering*,
DOI 10.1007/978-3-642-10294-3_11, © Springer-Verlag Berlin Heidelberg 2010

Collaboration takes place with or without explicit communication. On the one hand, software developers regularly engage in collaboration through artifacts without explicit communication (e.g., by writing comments in code to be read by others). On the other hand, explicit communication becomes necessary when developers must ask their peers for information that is otherwise not obtainable. Existing studies have provided ample evidence that both collocated and distributed software development teams frequently engage in communication to acquire necessary information from peer developers [24, 30, 32].

Such studies have made us aware that there are two distinctive types of situations in which developers communicate with their peers: one is when they want to coordinate development activities, and the other is when they want to acquire knowledge and understanding of a particular aspect of the software artifact under investigation. A developer engages in communication with peer developers in both situations by using the same communication channels (such as face-to-face, email, or chat), but the nature of the communication in each is quite different. Despite the quintessential differences in the nature of the goals, challenges, and concerns between these situations, studies on supporting communication in software development have not clearly separated the two.

We distinguish the two types of communication by calling the former *coordination communication* and the latter *expertise communication*, and argue that communication support must be tuned to each type of communication based on their inherent differences. Different sets of design guidelines need to be developed for supporting each type of communication in developer-centered CSDEs.

In this chapter, we first briefly describe the historical context for the developer-centered CSDE approach in software engineering research and discuss why communication must be supported as a first-class object in CSDEs. We then elaborate the differences between *coordination communication* and *expertise communication* and describe why different guidelines are necessary for supporting each type of communication. We finally present nine design guidelines for supporting *expertise communication*. We have derived these guidelines based on the theories of social capital [17] and models of supporting collective creativity [37, 38] as well as existing tools in the research fields of intelligent support, groupware, knowledge management, and organizational memory. We outline each guideline with theoretical grounds and illustrate each with technical instruments introduced by the existing tools and environments.

11.2 Historical Context: Three Schools of Research Toward Developer-Centered CSDEs

Software engineering research has looked at humans and their collaborations from its very beginning. During the last few decades, however, its emphases have shifted several times. We identify three distinctive schools of research in this particular area. Table 11.1 illustrates the differences among these three schools.

Table 11.1 Three schools of human-oriented software engineering research

	School 1 Psychology-centered	School 2 Process-centered	School 3 Developer-centered
Focuses on:	Human programming skills	Artifacts evolving processes	Cognitive and social processes
Software development is viewed:	As an individual skillful task	As an information processing task	As a creative knowledge task
Primary research concern:	How to develop programming skills	How to manage a project	How to nurture creative collavborative development processes
Developers interact with:	Programming language	Documents and artifacts through step-by-step actions	Tools and environments
Looks at:	Expert-novice differences	Team-performance difference	Individual developer difference in terms of areas of expertise
Related disciplines:	– Cognitive psychology – AI (Knowledge-based) – CHI	– Organizational science – Operation research – Measurements	– Tool building – Knowlwdge community – CSCW
Key phrases:	Psychology of programming	Process programming	Creativity, motivation, collaboration, community
Research materials:	– Performance and productivity	– Products (things) and processes (humans) – Project management	– Peer programers as knowledge resources – Making information relevant to the task-at-hand – Social dependencies among developers – Globally distributed collaborative development

Table 11.1 (continued)

	School 1 Psychology-centered	School 2 Process-centered	School 3 Developer-centered
Beliefs:	There are two types of programmers: experts and non-experts (novices). Their interactions are of little relevance to the project performance.	All programmers perform tasks more or less equally as information processors (like assembly lines) but the team as a whole performs differently depending on the organizational maturity.	There are more than novice-expert differences among individuals. Each developer has his/her own area of expertise and are loosely tied together throught social interactions within a project.

The first school of research, which we call the *psychology-centered* approach, has investigated the inner cognitive process of programming by focusing on the differences between expert and novice (non-expert) programmers through a number of psychological studies. That was the time right after the 1975 publication of Frederick Brook's *The Mythical Man-Months,* which basically says that the man-month is not an appropriate measure of software development project performance. It was realized that there is a huge performance difference between good programmers and not-so-good programmers. This had motivated a large number of studies to explore what psychological/cognitive factors in programming distinguish experts from novices. The psychology of programming is a research area that primarily looks at the differences of programming productivity and efficiency between experts and novices, while studying the benefits as well as difficulties of mastering programming features (e.g., the *if* statement design), methods (e.g., object orientation), and usage (e.g., mnemonic variable names) [48, 49].

The second school of research, which we call the *process-centered* approach, has its focus on the collaborative and managerial aspects of a software development project. It views software development as a group activity, or teamwork, and studies how to improve the capability of a software development organization, such as process traceability and repeatability [26]. Interestingly, this second school of research is less concerned with the programming skills of individual developers. Instead, it focuses more on the skills of organization. This school advocates that a software development process is programmable, and software development should be treated as assembly lines in which developers produce software by following predefined process instructions [39]. Developers take specification documents and then test specifications as input and produce source code and test cases as output. Researchers in this second school have primarily focused on how to help project management in orchestrating and coordinating a number of work pieces that have been produced by a large number of developers.

The third school of research, which we call the *developer-centered* approach, is the focus of our research. It looks at both the cognitive and social aspects of software development as well as their mutual interactions. The focus has returned to an individual developer, who is now viewed as having his or her own area of expertise in terms of a specific context, such as, the expertise on a piece of source code, the expertise on a certain feature of the program, the expertise on a certain aspect of the application domain, or the expertise on a certain programming language. Thus, symmetry of ignorance, or asymmetry of knowledge, exists among project members. They often have to collaborate with peer developers to accomplish their own programming tasks, and the success of the whole team depends on such collaborations.

Researchers in the third school explore how to support developers in such a way that they collectively develop information artifacts. Project managers are expected to be concerned with how to ensure the creativity and productivity of individual developers by providing physically, organizationally, culturally, and computationally *right* environments, rather than to worry only about how to quantify project performances and how to keep an eye on the project milestones with regard to the produced artifacts.

Two major factors have fueled the third school of research: open source communities and agile development methods. Both demonstrate the great importance of an individual developer's motivation, engagement, and communication in software development.

Since a large number of open source software development projects have emerged – making openly available their source code, related documents, development history data, and mailing list archives – a number of field studies have examined how software artifacts evolve through intensive communicative activities. As Augustin et al. who operated SourceForge, noted, such data have revealed that successful open source community projects "employed a number of practices that were not well characterized by traditional software engineering methodologies" [4]. Their paper lists mobility of resources, culture of sharing, and peer review and peer glory as examples of such practices, and labels the practices as "collaborative software development, or CSD."

Many of the twelve practices of XP [5], a representative agile method, are concerned with human and social aspects. By embracing individuals and interactions over processes and tools in their manifesto, agile software development methods aim to achieve successful software development by nurturing developer's collective creative processes [52].

Communication has long been regarded as an important activity in software development. A software engineering textbook published in 1985 by Fairley, for instance, shows that 37% of developers' time is spent in job communication and email [16]. However, communication was then regarded as an overhead rather than a part of the fundamental activities in software development. The trend of open source and agile methods has strongly hinted that communication needs to be treated as a first-class activity to be supported. The third school of research now views communication as something to be nurtured, not to be avoided.

It is very important to note that communication costs in software development remain very expensive, even in the eyes of the third school of research. We argue that although supporting communication is important, encouraging more communication in general should not be the research goal. Communication problems are caused not only by the lack of communicative acts, but sometimes by too many communicative acts. For example, one case study reported that overwhelming incoming mail messages resulted in a significant coordination problem [11]. Studies have shown that programmers in general prefer to work in a solitary environment with long periods of uninterrupted time during which they can concentrate [13]. By engaging in creative knowledge work, developers embrace flow experience, which is a situation "in which attention can be freely invested to achieve a person's goals, because there is no disorder to straighten out, no threat for the self to defend against" [10].

A developer-centered CSDE should first ensure that a developer can focus on his or her own task itself, and then facilitate easy communication with peer developers only when it becomes necessary. An important and often overlooked aspect is that when a developer wants to have communication, the person who is the recipient of this communication is also a developer. Supporting communication must carefully balance one developer's needs for communication and the other developer's needs for a concentrated flow experience.

11.3 Coordination Communication and Expertise Communication in Software Development

Many studies have observed how and about what developers communicate with one another during software development. For instance, through a study on three well-known open source projects, Gutwin et al. have found that text-based communications (mailing lists and chat systems) are the developers' primary sources of acquiring both general awareness of the entire team and more detailed information about people's expertise and activities [21]. In an ethnographic study on an industrial project, Ko et al. have analyzed what information needs developers face during software development [30]. The findings of this study indicate that coworkers were the most frequent source of information for software developers, and they were most frequently sought for the questions, "What have my coworkers been doing?" and "In what situations does this failure occur?"

Such studies demonstrate that two distinctive types of communication are involved in software development. One is what we call *coordination communication*, in which a developer communicates with his or her peers to discuss and negotiate in order to resolve conflicts or to avoid possible conflicts among the software components on which they are working. The structural dependency of software components may reflect "social dependency" among the developers who work on the components in the sense that they have to coordinate their tasks through social interactions when it is necessary to resolve perceived conflicts [28, 56]. Tools for supporting coordination communication have been primarily studied in such research areas as coordinating programmers and programming tasks, through making developers aware of what other developers are doing; for instance, Ariadne [14], Palantir [47] or FastDASH [6].

The other type of communication is what we call *expertise communication*, in which a developer communicates with his or her peers to ask for information that is essential for performing his or her own task at hand [32, 33, 58]. This is usually for obtaining knowledge and understanding about the design and/or behavior of a particular part of the system under development. Tools for supporting expertise communication have been primarily studied in such research areas as knowledge sharing and expert finding, helping developers ask questions of other developers; for instance, Expertise Recommender [34], Expert Browser [35] and STeP_IN [58].

The rather obvious separation of the two research areas reflects the fact that these two types of communication have quintessential differences in nature: in their goals, challenges and concerns. However, existing studies have not clearly separated and compared the two types of communication in designing communication support for CSDEs. One of the reasons for this might have been the fact that developers engage in both types of communication through the same communication channels: by sending email messages, by starting a chat, or by walking to a coworker's desk. However, different types of computational support mechanisms are necessary for the two types of communication due to their different natures.

For instance, a mechanism to find communication partners must be different in coordination communication and expertise communication because the relation between the developer who starts the communication and those with whom he or she communicates is different. In coordination communication, there is a symmetric or reciprocal relation between those who initiate communication and those who are sought for communication, with roughly equal amounts of interest and expected benefit. Coordination communication is a part of impact management, which is "the work performed by software developers to minimize the impact of one's effort on others and at the same time, the impact of others into one's own effort" [15].

In contrast, expertise communication is characterized by an asymmetric and unidirectional relation between the one who asks a question and the one who is asked to help [58]. The benefit is primarily for the information-seeking developer, while the costs are primarily paid by the information-provider. Such costs include the cost of paying attention to the information request, that of stopping his or her own ongoing development task, that of composing an answer for the information-seeking developer while collecting relevant information when necessary, and that of then going back to the original task.

We argue that different types of communication demand different sets of guidelines in designing communication support in developer-centered CSDEs. Redmiles et al. presented the continuous coordination paradigm for supporting software development [42]. The paradigm contains four principles: (1) to have multiple perspectives on activities and information; (2) to have nonintrusive integration through synchronous messages or through the representation of links between different sites and artifacts; (3) to combine socio-technical factors by considering relations between artifacts and authorship so that distributed developers can infer important context information; and (4) to integrate formal configuration management and informal change notification via the use of visualizations embedded in integrated software development environments [42]. Part of this paradigm supports coordination communication, and some, but not all, of its principles may also apply to support expertise communication.

In the remainder of this chapter, we present design guidelines for supporting expertise communication in software development. By "expertise communication," we do not mean knowledge exchange or knowledge transfer in a general sense. We use the phrase to refer to activities of a software developer who seeks, from his or her peer software developers, information that is essential yet not readily available in existing artifacts to accomplish his or her task, right in the middle of software development. The developer communicates with coworkers and asks for information not for the sake of increasing general knowledge in the abstract but to perform his or her own immediate task.

11.4 Nine Design Guidelines for Supporting Expertise Communication

This section presents nine design guidelines for supporting expertise communication.

Guideline #1: Expertise communication must be seamlessly integrated with other development activities.
A need for expertise communication emerges during the development activity when a software developer finds his or her task in need of information that is available only through other developers. The developer must be able to acquire the necessary information in a timely fashion so that he or she can carry out the current task more effectively and productively in a fluid manner [57]. Communication with peer developers to seek expertise should be supported as a continuum of information search tasks from an information-seeking software developer's point of view. It needs to be integrated with the software development environment to minimize the cognitive cost of conscientiously switching to a different application that supports expertise communication.

Not many existing tools supporting expertise communication consider this guideline. One of few tools that follow this guideline is STeP_IN_Java [58]. STeP_IN_Java has the "Ask Expert" feature embedded within the Java document-browsing interface. Each Java method is accompanied with the "Ask Expert" button; by pressing the button, the user is connected to a message-composing interface to write a question about the Java method, which is then delivered to those developers who have expertise about the method. The system thus makes expertise communication a natural extension of browsing Java documents.

Guideline #2: Expertise communication mechanisms should be personalized and contextualized for the information-seeking developer.
Information seeking in software development is an in situ and highly individualized action. A developer's needs for acquiring information from his or her coworkers arise when he or she is dealing with a specific task in a development environment. Integration with the development environment provides the context of the problem with which a developer is dealing. Such context should be utilized by an expertise communication mechanism to customize its support to the context and the background knowledge of the developer [12, 57].

Identification of experts should be tuned for who is looking for what. Expertise is not an absolute attribute but a relative attribute of a developer, and it changes over time. Answer Garden [2] is an early attempt to identify UNIX experts based on predefined expertise profiles. The Expertise Recommender system [34] mines configuration management logs to identify experts based on organizational relations to support software maintainers. The developmental histories of developers (such as activities recorded in Concurrent Versions System (CVS) repositories, mailing archives, and written programs) should be used to identify who has the needed expertise about a particular problem at the particular moment [35, 55]. Having temporal information of the socio-technical context allows the information-seeker to understand whether a developer has the expertise being sought, and how he or she has gained it. Such information is not only useful for identifying the expertise being sought, but also valuable for understanding the information-seeker's background so that the system can locate those who have mental models similar to those of the information-seeking developer [55].

Guideline #3: Expertise communication should be minimized when other types of information artifacts are available.
Resorting to peers as information resources involves not only the information-seeking developer but also those developers who are asked to provide information [27]. Expertise communication is therefore an expensive means to get a developer's work done. It should not be promoted as the first choice; rather, it should be avoided when code, documents, development history records, archived previous communications, and/or other artifacts that satisfy the information needs are available.

Two mechanisms have been explored to consider this guideline in existing research: (1) initially leading users to artifacts before providing the means of expertise communication; and (2) archiving communication results to avoid unnecessarily repeated communications.

One example is Answer Garden and Answer Garden 2 [1, 2] which first allow a user to browse a database of commonly asked questions; if the sought answer is not present, the system "automatically sends the question to the appropriate expert, and the answer is returned to the user as well as inserted into the branching network, thus evolving the organizational memory [1]."

STeP_IN_Java [58] takes a similar approach by first guiding a developer in attending to the search and browsing interface of Java source code, documents, and communication archives. Only from the browsing interface does the system allow the developer to compose a question and ask other developers for information about the browsed artifact. The communication is again archived and associated with the artifact.

Other mechanisms, such as TagSEA, which is a shared waypoints mechanism to mark specific locations in Java source code elements or documents by using social tagging [50], are also useful in guiding developers to access previously communicated information.

Guideline #4: Expertise communication mechanisms should take into account the balance between the cost and benefit of an information-seeking developer and the group productivity.
From the project team's perspective, expertise communication is a two-edged sword in solving collaboration problems in software development. Broadcasting a question allows a developer to find the right people by letting other developers decide for themselves whether to respond [21]. However, if developers are frequently interrupted to offer help, their productivity is significantly reduced, resulting in lower group productivity for them [59].

Attention has been rapidly becoming the scarcest resource in our society [20]. Attention economy is concerned with the use or the patterns of allocation of attention for the best possible benefits. Following this thread of thought, the concept of collective attention economy has been proposed and used as an instrument to analyze the effective use of the sum of the attentions of the members in a group [59].

Our rough estimate of how much attention (in terms of time) is collectively spent in expertise communication in the mailing list of the open source project Lucerne is that more than 60,000 min (more than 1,000 h) were collectively spent every month [59]. In an organizational setting, this collective cost might even outweigh the benefits of knowledge collaboration; it certainly decreases the overall productivity of the whole project [41].

Some studies have looked into this problem. Both the Answer Garden approach [2] and the STeP_IN approach [58] try to reduce the cost incurred by expertise providers by limiting the recipients of the question only to those who are both able (through the expert identification process) and very likely to be willing (through the expert selection process) to answer the question.

Guideline #5: Expertise communication support mechanisms should consider social and organizational relationships when selecting developers for communication.
Favorable interpersonal relationships help in communicating expertise due to pre-existing trust and mutual understanding [1]. An arduous relationship between an information seeker and an information provider often leads to the failure of expertise sharing [9]. People have very nuanced preferences concerning how and with whom they like to share expertise and how they like to maintain control of their social interactions [22].

The theory of social capital provides an analytic framework to understand this decision-making process [17]. Social capital is the "sum of the actual and potential resources embedded within, available through and derived from the network of relationships possessed by an individual or social unit" [36]. Social capital manifests itself in forms of obligations, expectations, trust, norms of generalized reciprocity, and reputations.

The feelings of expectation and obligation play important roles during the process of deciding whether and when to help. Researchers see obligations and expectations as complementary features [8] incurred during prior interactions that create value for the community in the future [44]. In other words, when B helps A, B would have a reasonable expectation that A will do something for B sometime down the road, and that A would feel obliged to help B [8].

Answer Garden 2 [1] uses organizational and physical proximities in the selection process. STeP_IN [58] uses social relationships and nuanced perception of individual relationships. Table 11.2 illustrates the different strategies used in the selection steps.

Similar to STeP_IN, some tools give high priority to the individual preferences for expertise communication. For instance, ReachOut [45] takes into consideration factors such as the helper's motivation to answer questions on the topic or

Table 11.2 Selection strategies reported in Answer Garden 2 [1], STeP_IN [58] and other strategies

Answer Garden 2 strategy	STeP_IN strategy	Other strategies
1. Organizational criteria 1-1 Keeping it local 1-2 Cross department 1-3 Last resort 2. Load on the sources 2-1 Selection based on regular workload 2-2 Selection based on workload over time 3. Performance 3-1 Problem comprehension 3-2 Providing a suitable explanation 3-3 Attitude	1. Inter-personal preferences of an individual 1-1 Exclude 1-2 Include 2. Obligation 2-1 Inter-personal obligation (has been helped by the information seeking developer) 2-2 Total-social obligation (has been helped by others in the group) 3. External communication history (has previously communicated via email) 4. Random selection	– Communication regency – Organizational hierarchy (relative significance and impact of the information-seeking developer to potential helpers) – Institutional secrecy – Eager helper (very motivated to help others) [54]

to participate at this very moment, as well as the helper's history of participation. The availability of choices and options helps the development of favorable attitudes toward expertise communication [46] and this favorable attitude is critical for expertise communication.

Guideline #6: Expertise communication support mechanisms should minimize the interruption when approaching those who are selected for communication.
When being approached to provide information for the benefit of another developer, developers are likely to feel interrupted. Answering or providing help consumes the time and attention of the helping developers and distracts them from their own tasks.

An interruption is regarded as an unexpected encounter initiated by another person, which disturbs "the flow and continuity of an individual's work and brings that work to a temporary halt to the one who is interrupted" [51]. The cost of interruption includes not only the attention spent on the interrupting event, but also the disruption of flow and continuity of the ongoing work [29] and the accompanied work resumption efforts [28].

Expertise communication support tools, therefore, need to feature mechanisms that would minimize interruption when approaching potential helping developers. ReachOut [45], for instance, a chat-based tool for peer support, collaboration, and community building, invites potential helpers to join a conference chat by pushing the question to a nonintrusive client on their computer screens. Incoming questions fade in and out until the user decides to answer.

The field of human-computer interaction has long been studying how to model interruption between humans and computer agents [25]. Some parts of the models and findings of such studies should be taken into account to achieve more effective, less disruptive communication channels in support of expertise communication in software development.

In an attempt to minimize interruption for other developers by reducing the number of those who are asked to help, one may not be able to get the needed information. To address this issue, Answer Garden 2 has proposed the idea of escalation of support [1]. When no answers are provided from the selected group for a predefined period of time, the system automatically expands the recipients of the question to involve more people, larger groups, and a wider range of areas.

Guideline #7: Expertise communication support mechanisms should provide ways to make it easier for developers to ask for help.
Developers feel different levels of difficulty and ease, depending on to whom they ask and through what communication channels. It is easy for developers to ask peers for information through face-to-face communication because they know each other, know how to approach each other, and have a good sense of how important their question is in relation to what the experts seem to be doing at the moment [23].

As Gerstberger and Allen report, "engineers, in selecting among information channels, act in a manner which is intended not to maximize gain, but rather to minimize loss. The loss to be minimized is the cost in terms of effort" [19]. Thus, developers tend to choose face-to-face communication because it would be less likely to be turned down, and to ask for help from coworkers whom they feel are easy to access rather than from the most appropriate person in some cases. This might end up in the wasteful use of a small set of "nice" people who keep helping others even if they do not have the appropriate expertise.

Developers may immediately get the necessary information or may never get any useful information, depending on how they ask. Rhetorical strategies, linguistic complexity, and wording choice all influence the likelihood of others responding [31] and replying to a question [3, 9].

Studies show that information-seekers demonstrate different asking behaviors, depending on whether they are in public, in private, communicating with a stranger, or communicating with a friend, due to the different levels of perceived psychological safety in admitting a lack of knowledge [9]. If every question asked would always go to all members of the mailing list, the information-seeker would risk giving colleagues the impression that he or she is rather ignorant and incompetent [18].

The perceived social burden on a potential information-provider may affect how easy it is for an information-seeker to ask a question. A field study of Answer Garden reports that because the information-seeker's identity was not revealed in Answer Garden, the information-seeker felt less pressure in asking questions and bothering experts [2]. It might also become easier for an information-seeking developer to ask a question when he or she knows that the recipients have the option and freedom to ignore the request.

Reder and Shwab have noted that tactical skill in selecting communication channels "often determines an individual's ability to influence and sometimes control the course and direction of group tasks and impact the success of particular projects" [41]. Expertise communication support mechanisms, therefore, need to consider social factors that affect expertise-seeking behaviors and help software developers in their expertise communication if they do not have the tactical skill to select the right communication channel.

Guideline #8: Expertise communication support mechanisms should provide ways to make it easier for developers to answer or not to answer the information request.
Developers who receive the request for help in expertise communication need to decide whether to answer. They may feel different levels of social pressure, depending on from whom and through which communication channel the request is coming. For instance, in direct emails, the receiver bears the interruption cost of the reply or the social burden of taking no action [53].

The success of expertise communication should not come at the price of developers' reluctance for further participation in future collaboration. Some developers might get bored by answering repeatedly asked questions that they deem too simple to be worth their time and expertise, and some might want to guard their unique expertise to retain their "market value" in the organization [43]. The goodwill and limited attention of developers should be economically utilized to achieve sustainable and long-term success. They should not be forced into helping just for fear of causing unnecessary disruptions to the social cohesion and norms of the project team, which is unlikely to be sustainable.

Unwillingness also leads to lower quality of communication. When workers are forced into sharing expertise without much willingness, they often use "verbal and intellectual skills as a defense to keep a person with a problem from consuming too much of their time," and their answers are often "impressive-sounding" but not helpful [9] resulting in a waste of time for both parties.

Developers may respond to a question not because they want to answer it, but because they do not want to ignore it. Even though helping is costly, taking no action may incur a social cost. Saying "no" untactful to an information-seeking developer deteriorates the expert's relation with the seeker and negatively affects the expert's social reputation among other peers because such behavior deviates from social norms [40].

The STeP_IN framework provides a communication mechanism called a *dynamic mailing list*; a temporal mailing list is created every time an information-seeking developer posts a question, with the recipients decided dynamically [58]. Whereas the sender's identity is shown to the recipients, the recipients' identities are not revealed unless they reply to the request. If some of the recipients do not answer, for whatever reasons, nobody will know it; therefore, refusing to help becomes socially acceptable, similar to "hiding out to get some work done" [13]. If one of the recipients answers the question, his or her identity is revealed to all members of the dynamic mailing list. This asymmetrical information disclosure is meant to reinforce positive social behaviors without forcing others into collaboration.

Guideline #9: Expertise communication channels must be socially aware.
Socially aware communication [40] refers to the transmission of information or signals that does not violate social norms. Existing communication channels include

face-to-face, direct email, mailing lists, wikis, bulletin boards, Internet relay chat (IRC), telephone, or video conferences.

Different communication channels give various degrees of control to either the information-seeking developer or those who are asked to provide information. Decisions need to be made, depending on the goals and social context, about who should gain the social control of communication.

One prime example of such control is the disclosure of identities of information-seekers and information-providers. Different tools take different approaches in designing such disclosure of identities. In a field study of Answer Garden that had an information-seeker's identity hidden and an information-provider's identity revealed, the seekers felt easier asking and the information-providers felt more "obliged" and tended to "show off" their expertise [2]. STeP_IN [58] in contrast, makes a seeker's identity revealed to those who receive the question, whereas the receivers' identities remain hidden unless they answer in a dynamically formulated temporal mailing list. This design decision is based on the viewpoint that the information-provider should be granted more control because the information-seeker is the main beneficiary and the information-provider is the benefactor.

Cohen et al. have investigated, through field studies of a legal firm, the phenomena of adversarial collaboration, in which peers who are adversaries having opposing goals nonetheless have to collaborate to get their tasks done [7]. They argue that adversarial collaborations are "the sine qua non of situations that call for the selective dissemination of information." Although software developers in a project are by no means adversaries and have no opposing goals, they may have different interests and motivations in their own specific contexts, especially when a project is inter-organizational or involves subcontracted members. Mechanisms for supporting asymmetric disclosure of information may need to be designed within expertise communication channels.

11.5 Concluding Remarks

This chapter has argued for a developer-centered CSDE where communication is considered as a first-class activity in software development. We identified two distinctive types of communication in software development, *coordination communication* and *expertise communication*, and elaborated on their differences.

Communication support mechanisms have features that imply suitable communication genres [41]. Such features include whether the communication is one-to-one or one-to-many; whether the communication happens synchronously or asynchronously; whether the sender and the recipients are anonymous or identified; whether all the relevant information is disclosed symmetrically or asymmetrically among the sender, recipients, and others; whether the social control of communication is granted to the sender or to the recipient; whether the mechanism makes it easier for the information-seeker or the recipient; and what media should be used, such as text, voice, video, or other types of multimedia, each of which demonstrates different degrees of achievability and searchability.

Taking the above features into total consideration as well as the distinctive nature of expertise communication in software development, we have presented a list of nine design guidelines for supporting expertise communication in software development. These guidelines are interdependent: following one guideline may also lead to following a few other guidelines, or following one guideline may conflict with following another guideline. Each guideline is important in some particular context. In designing expertise communication support mechanisms, one needs to understand what corporate and organizational culture exists and what types of collaboration their software projects want to nurture.

Although this chapter has argued to distinguish coordination communication from expertise communication for supporting communication in developer-centered CSDEs, it has not been our intention here to develop two different communication interfaces for developers. Developers presently do not and probably will not want to distinguish the two; they simply want to communicate with their peers for a variety of reasons. After identifying different sets of design guidelines in support of coordination and expertise communications, the forthcoming research agenda would involve how to integrate the two mechanisms so that developers would be able to seamlessly engage in different types of communications without consciously switching between the two.

References

1. Ackerman MS, McDonald DW (1996) Answer Garden 2: Merging organizational memory with collaborative help. Proceedings of CSCW'96, ACM Press, New York, pp. 97–105.
2. Ackerman MS (1998) Augmenting organizational memory: A field study of Answer Garden. ACM Transactions on Information Systems 16(3): 203–224.
3. Arguello J, Butler BS, Joyce E, Kraut R, Ling KS, Rose C, Wang X (2006) Talk to me: Foundations for successful individual-group interactions in online communities. In: Grinter R, Rodden T, Aoki P, Cutrell E, Jeffries R, Olson G (Eds.) Proceedings of CHI'06, April 22–27, ACM, New York, pp. 959–968.
4. Augustin L, Bressler D, Smith, G (2002) Accelerating software development through collaboration. Proceedings of ICSE'02, ACM, New York, pp. 559–563.
5. Beck K (1999) Extreme Programming Explained: Embrace Change. Reading, MA: Addison-Wesley.
6. Biehl JT, Czerwinski M, Smith G, Robertson GG (2007) FASTDash: A visual dashboard for fostering awareness in software teams. Proceedings of CHI'07, ACM, New York, pp. 1313–1322.
7. Cohen AL, Cash D, Muller MJ (2000) Designing to support adversarial collaboration. Proceedings of CSCW'00, ACM, New York, pp. 31–39.
8. Coleman JC (1988) Social capital in the creation of human capital. American Journal of Sociology 94: S95–S120.
9. Cross R, Borgatti SP (2004) The ties that share: Relational characteristics that facilitate information seeking. In: Huysman M, Wulf V (Eds.) Social Capital and Information Technology. Cambridge, MA: The MIT Press, pp. 137–161.
10. Csikszentmihalyi M (1990) Flow: The Psychology of Optimal Experience. New York: HarperCollins.

11. Damian D, Izquierdo L, Singer J, Kwan I (2007) Awareness in the wild: Why communication breakdowns occur. Proceedings of ICGSE'07, IEEE Computer Society, Washington, DC, pp. 81–90.
12. Davor Cubranic C, Murphy GC (2003) Hipikat: Recommending pertinent software development artifacts. Proceedings of ICSE'03, Portland, OR, pp. 408–418.
13. DeMarco T, Lister T (1999) Peopleware: Productive Projects and Teams. New York: Dorset Housing Publishing.
14. de Souza CRB, Quirk S, Trainer E, Redmiles D (2007) Supporting collaborative software development through the visualization of socio-technical dependencies. Proceedings of GROUP'07, Sanibel Island, FL, pp. 147–156.
15. de Souza CRB, Redmiles D (2008) An empirical study of software developers management of dependencies and changes. Proceedings of ICSE'08, pp. 241–250.
16. Fairley R, (1985) Software Engineering Concepts. New York: McGraw-Hill College.
17. Fischer G, Scharff E, Ye Y (2004) Fostering social creativity by increasing social capital. In: Huysman M, Wulf V (Eds.) Social Capital and Information Technology. Cambridge, MA: The MIT Press, pp. 355–399.
18. Flammer A (1981) Towards a theory of question asking. Psychiatry Research 43: 407–420.
19. Gerstberger PG, Allen TJ (1968) Criteria used by research and development engineers in the selection of an information source. Journal of Applied Psychology 52(4): 272–279.
20. Goldhaber MH (1997) The attention economy. First Monday 2(4).
21. Gutwin C, Penner R, Schneider K (2004) Group awareness in distributed software development. Proceedings of CSCW'04, ACM, New York, pp. 72–81.
22. Halverson CA, Erickson T, Ackerman MS (2004) Behind the help desk: Evolution of a knowledge management system in a large organization. Proceedings of CSCW'04, ACM, New York, pp. 304–313.
23. Herbsleb J, Grinter RE (1999) Splitting the organization and integrating the code: Conway's law revisited. Proceedings of ICSE'99, pp. 85–95.
24. Herbsleb J, Mockus A (2003) An empirical study of speed and communication in globally-distributed software development, IEEE Trans Software Engineering 29(3): 1–14.
25. Horvitz E, Apacible J (2003) Learning and reasoning about interruption. Proceedings ICMI'03, ACM, New York, pp. 20–27.
26. Humphrey W (1989) Managing the Software Process. Reading, MA: Addison-Wesley Professional.
27. Illich I (1971) Deschooling Society. New York: Harper and Row.
28. Iqbal ST, Bailey BP (2006) Leveraging characteristics of task structure to predict the cost of interruption. CHI'06, ACM, New York, pp. 741–750.
29. Jackson T, Dawson R, Wilson D (2001) The cost of email interruption, Journal of Systems and Information Technology 5: 81–92.
30. Ko AJ, DeLine R, Venolia G (2007) Information needs in collocated software development teams. International Conference on Software Engineering (ICSE), 20–26 May, pp. 344–353.
31. Kraut R, Kiesler S, Mukhopadhya T, Scherlis W, Patterson M (1998) Social impact of the internet: What does it mean? Commun ACM 41(12): 21–22.
32. LaToza TD, Venolia G et al (2006) Maintaining mental models: A study of developer work habits. Proceedings of ICSE'06, Shanghai, pp. 492–501.
33. McDonald DW, Ackerman MS (1998) Just talk to me: A field study of expertise location. Proceedings of CSCW'98, Seattle, WA, pp. 315–324.
34. McDonald DW, Ackerman MS (2000) Expertise recommender: A flexible recommendation system architecture. Proceedings of CSCW'00, pp. 101–120.
35. Mockus A, Herbsleb J (2002) Expertise browser: A quantitative approach to identifying expertise. Proceedings of ICSE'02, Orlando, FL, pp. 503–512.
36. Nahapiet J, Ghoshal S (1998) Social capital, intellectual capital, and the organizational advantage. Academy of Management Review 23: 242–266.

37. Nakakoji K (2006) Supporting software development as collective creative knowledge work. Proceedings of KCSE2006, Tokyo, pp. 1–8.
38. Nakakoji K, Ohira M, Yamamoto Y (2000) Computational support for collective creativity. Knowledge-Based Systems Journal, Elsevier Science 13(7–8): 451–458.
39. Osterweil L (1987) Software processes are software too. Proceedings of ICSE'87, pp. 2–13.
40. Pentland A (2005) Socially aware computation and communication. Computer 38(3): 33–40.
41. Reder S, Schwab RG (1988) The communication economy of the workgroup: Multi-channel genres of communication. Proceedings of CSCW'88, ACM, New York, pp. 354–368.
42. Redmiles D, Hoek Avd, Al-Ani B, Hildenbrand T, Quirk S, Sarma A, Filho RSS, de Souza C, Trainer E (2007) Continuous coordination: A new paradigm to support globally distributed software development projects. Wirtschaftsinformatik 49: S28–S38.
43. Reichling T, Veith M (2005) Expertise sharing in a heterogeneous organizational environment. Proceedings of ECSCW'05, Springer-Verlag, New York, pp. 325–345.
44. Resnick P (2002) Beyond bowling together: Sociotechnical capital. In Carroll JM (Ed.) HCI in the New Millennium. Reading, MA: Addison-Wesley, pp. 247–272.
45. Ribak A, Jacovi M, Soroka V (2002) Ask before you search: Peer support and community building with Reach out. Proceedings of CSCW'02, ACM, New York, pp. 126–135.
46. Salancik GR, Pfeffer J (1978) A social information processing approach to job attitudes and task design. Administrative Science Quarterly 23: 224–253.
47. Sarma A, Noroozi Z, Hoek Avd (2003) Palantir: Raising awareness among configuration management workspaces. Proceedings of ICSE'03, pp. 444–454.
48. Shneiderman B (1980) Software Psychology: Human Factors in Computer and Information Systems. Cambridge, MA: Winthrop.
49. Soloway E, Ehrlich K (1984) Empirical studies of programming knowledge. IEEE Transactions on Software Engineering 10(5): 595–609.
50. Storey M, Cheng L, Bull I, Rigby P (2006) Shared waypoints and social tagging to support collaboration in software development. Proceedings of CSCW'06, ACM, New York, pp. 195–198.
51. Szoestek AM, Markopoulos, P (2006) Factors defining face-to-face interruptions in the office environment. Proceedings of CHI'06, ACM, New York, pp. 1379–1384.
52. Tomayko JE, Hazzan O (2004) Human Aspects of Software Engineering (Electrical and Computer Engineering Series). Rockland, MA: Charles River Media, Inc.
53. Tyler JR, Tang JC (2003) When can I expect an email response? A study of rhythms in email usage. Proceedings of ECSCW'03, Helsinki, pp. 239–258.
54. Van den Hooff B, De Ridder JA, Aukema EJ (2004) Exploring the eagerness to share knowledge: the role of social capital and ICT in knowledge sharing. In: Huysman M, Wulf V (Eds.) Social Capital and Information Technology. Cambridge, MA: The MIT Press, pp. 163–186.
55. Vivacqua A, Lieberman H (2000) Agents to assist in finding help. Proceedings of CHI'00, ACM, New York, pp. 65–72.
56. Wagstrom P, Herbsleb J (2006) Dependency forecasting. Communications of the ACM 49(10): 55–56.
57. Ye Y, Fischer, G (2002) Supporting reuse by delivering task-relevant and personalized information. Proceedings of ICSE'02, Orlando, FL, pp. 513–523.
58. Ye Y, Yamamoto Y, Nakakoji K (2007) A socio-technical framework for supporting programmers. Proceedings of ESEC/FSE'07, ACM, New York, pp. 351–360.
59. Ye Y, Yamamoto Y, Nakakoji K (2008) Understanding and improving collective attention economy for expertise sharing. Proceedings of CAiSE'08, June, Lecture Notes in Computer Science 5074, Springer, Berlin Heidelberg, pp. 167–181.

Part III
What We Know (and Do not Know) About Collaborative Software Engineering

John Grundy

Software engineering must be practiced by people within organizations. Recent trends in software engineering practice have resulted in much more complicated issues around collaboration than in its historical context. Traditionally software engineering was practiced by small teams – with a large problem decomposed via divide-and-conquer methods into smaller teams – that were co-located, shared a common methodology, used common techniques and tools, and could communicate if not directly face-to-face then via leaders and managers face-to-face. While collaborative software engineering in such a context is still very challenging, the homogeneous team, process, method, tool and management structures greatly help.

New models of software engineering have made collaboration issues much less straightforward. Multi-site software teams are very common to large organizations [8]. Even smaller organizations may use outsourcing or use/contribute to open source software projects [1], resulting in multi-site issues. Agile processes require much more iterative build processes and higher levels of inter-team communication. Many tasks conducted by teams may involve techniques and tools that need to be shared [5]. An example is analysis tasks whereby a code base is analyzed to assist understanding, fault-finding and/or evolution. Studies of practices in these domains have greatly enhanced our understanding of collaboration issues [7]. However many open questions exist in this domain.

A number of process models have been studied for their fit for multi-site, global software engineering [9]. These have generally been characterized as light-weight, medium-weight and heavy-weight in terms of centralized control and rigidity of process. A variety of factors impact on an organizations choice of process approach including size, culture, language, nature of project and size of project.

Two fundamentally different ways of decomposing multi-site process models are Extended Workbench [8] and System of Systems [1]. In the extended workbench approach a centralized management structure assigns remote teams units of work – usually scoped design/code/test. In the system of systems approach, decentralized teams work on different phases of a project e.g., a testing team, coding team, and requirements team. Despite numerous studies of multi-site software teams it is still unclear when to chose different models for the overall organization. In fact, carrying out empirical studies for such multi-site teams to better inform us about team organization is itself still an area of ongoing research.

Communication and co-ordination models in software teams have been studied for many years [2]. Many studies have looked at the very interesting area of free/open source software development [2]. Around an open source software product grows a community of shared interest. A range of determinants exist as to whether the project will be "successful" in terms of its outcomes. Socialization must be supported among group members along with more traditional issues of group communication and co-ordination of work. Open source/free software communities have particular approaches developed to support these activities. Again, despite numerous careful studies, it is still very unclear how to best foster socialization in such communities via best practice communication and co-ordination strategies. Further analysis of co-ordination and communication and tool support for proactively understanding these are areas of continuing research.

Many tasks must be distributed when undertaking collaborative software engineering. Analysis tasks are often not those one thinks of when considering collaboration but are becoming more important to support in collaborative software engineering contexts. Examples include mining histories of changes, versions, faults and communication [6]. While more traditional software development techniques have been supported by collaboration tools e.g., testing, requirements, architecture and coding, traditionally analysis tasks have been limited to single-site and team-owned artifacts.

Many analysis techniques are amenable to sharing across team boundaries and/or results being used in a more collaborative fashion. How we go about identifying tasks suitable for such collaborative support is still unclear. How we go about making data suitably available for collaborative analysis is a challenge both in terms of technical support and organizational artifact management. How analysis tools and the techniques they embody can be effectively developed, shared and evolved in cross-team and even cross-organizational boundaries is an area of active research and emerging practice.

The three chapters in Part III consider various aspects relating to organizational as well as team impact of collaborative Software Engineering practices. These range from analysis tasks relating to (mostly) low-level software artifacts; communication and co-ordination analysis and understanding relating to high-level communication and organizational structures in open source software development projects; and development processes applied to multi-site software engineering projects. Each contribution tackles a different level of abstraction in collaborative software engineering.

Chapter 12 by Ghezzi and Gall addresses the issue of supporting low-level artifact analysis in order to abstract higher level structures and thereby understanding. They describe a scenario of cross-task and cross-organizational artifact analysis support. They pose questions around how can a team effectively roll out such analysis tools and share these tools between teams and organizations. A tool platform is presented which addresses this domain and allows cross-team and cross-organizational analysis technique and support tool development and sharing. A service-oriented approach supports analysis technique access and composition.

Chapter 13 by Pinzger and Gall addresses the issue of understanding communication and collaboration structures in open source software projects. They propose a workbench to assist in the extraction, analysis and visualization of collaboration/communication relationships to support open source projects. This takes data relating to collaboration and communication and enables teams to represent this with a meta-model, extract appropriate data, carry out analysis of the data and present it via a dashboard-style visualization platform. An evaluation of the approach is presented.

Chapter 14 by Avritzer and Paulish reviews a set of commonly used software processes for the domain of multi-site software engineering. They detail two process models in particular and compare and contrast their relative characteristics and merits. These are the workbench model whereby teams are assigned scoped work by centralized control and a system of systems model whereby teams are organized vertically according to expertise. A long running project is studied demonstrating how these process models can be rolled out and evaluation of the approaches presented. Directions for future multi-site software team organization are discussed.

References

1. Avritzer A, Cai Y, Paulish D (2008) Co-ordination implications of software architecture in a global software development project. Proceedings of WICSA 2008.
2. Damian D, Williams L, Layman L, Bures H (2006) Essential communication practices for extreme programming in a global software development team. Information & Software Technology 48(9): 781–794.
3. Ducheneaut N (2005) Socialization in an open source software community: A socio-technical analysis. Computer Supported Co-operative Work 14: 323–368.
4. Fogel K (2005) Producing Open Source Software: How to Run a Successful Free Software Project. Sebastopol, CA: O'Reilly Media.
5. Gall HC, Fluri B, Pinzger M (2009) Change analysis with evolizer and change distiller. IEEE Software 26(1): 26–33.
6. Livshits B, Zimmermann T (2005) Dynamine: Finding common error patterns by mining software revision histories. Proceedings of the European Software Engineering Conference, pp 296–305.
7. Mockus A, Fielding RT, Herbsleb JD (2002) Two cases studies of open source software development: Apache and Mozilla. ACM Transactions on Software Engineering and Methodology 11(3): 309–346.
8. Sangwan R, Bass M, Mullick N, Paulish D, Kazmeier J (2007) Global Software Development Handbook. Boca Raton, FL: Auerbach Publications.
9. Prikladnicki R, Audi J, Damian D, Oliveira T (2007) Distributed software development: Practices and challenges in different business strategies of offshoring and onshoring, Proceedings of the International Conference on Global Software Engineering.
10. Ying AT, Murphy GC, Ng R, Chu-Carroll MC (2004) Predicting source code changes by mining change history. IEEE Transactions Software Engineering 30(9): 574–586.

Chapter 12
Distributed and Collaborative Software Analysis

Giacomo Ghezzi and Harald C. Gall

Abstract Throughout the years software engineers have come up with a myriad of specialized tools and techniques that focus on a certain type of software analysis such as source code analysis, co-change analysis or bug prediction. However, easy and straight forward synergies between these analyses and tools rarely exist because of their stand-alone nature, their platform dependence, their different input and output formats and the variety of data to analyze. As a consequence, distributed and collaborative software analysis scenarios and in particular interoperability are severely limited. We describe a distributed and collaborative software analysis platform that allows for a seamless interoperability of software analysis tools across platform, geographical and organizational boundaries. We realize software analysis tools as services that can be accessed and composed over the Internet. These distributed analysis services shall be widely accessible in our incrementally augmented *Software Analysis Broker* where organizations and tool providers can register and share their tools. To allow (semi-) automatic use and composition of these tools, they are classified and mapped into a software analysis taxonomy and adhere to specific meta-models and ontologies for their category of analysis.

12.1 Introduction

A common feature of many software analysis tools is that they focus on just a particular kind of analysis to produce the results wanted. If different analyses are required, an engineer needs to run several tools, each one specialized on a particular aspect, ranging from pure source code analysis, duplication analysis, co-change analysis, bug prediction, to bug fixing patterns and visualization. All these techniques have their own explicit or implicit meta-model which dictates how to represent the input

G. Ghezzi (✉)
Software Evolution and Architecture Lab, Department of Informatics, University of Zurich,
8050 Zürich, Switzerland
e-mail: ghezzi@ifi.uzh.ch

I. Mistrík et al. (eds.), *Collaborative Software Engineering*,
DOI 10.1007/978-3-642-10294-3_12, © Springer-Verlag Berlin Heidelberg 2010

and the output data. Thus the sharing of information between tools is only possible by means of a cumbersome export towards files complying with a specified exchange format. Also, if there exist several analyses of the same kind (e.g., code duplication analysis) there is hardly any way to compare the results or integrate them other than manual investigation. Tool interoperability is hampered even more by their stand-alone nature as well as their platform and language dependence. As a consequence, distributed and collaborative software analysis scenarios are severely limited.

12.1.1 Tools and IDEs

Lately, many software companies have been putting a lot of effort in tool integration to keep track and collect data on software development projects to enable and promote seamless collaboration in all the development phases. The main goal is to create a powerful and successful software development team collaboration platform to integrate work across the phases of the development life-cycle done by different actors. Examples for such IDEs are *IBM's Jazz*[1] or *Microsoft's Visual Studio Team System 2010.*[2] Among the much functionality, they fully integrate work item management with source control, team processes, build and test case management. For example, for a piece of code, change set information is provided why changes were made (the associated work items), when it had some test problems, when it finally made it into a release, who has been working on it, or what source code changes were involved. But software analysis, and in particular release histories, are being left out of the picture. Thereby, these IDEs gather a huge amount of data on the development process but only a very little portion of it is then effectively used for analysis purpose.

From a research perspective, throughout the years, we have developed several tools to extract and analyze different types of data about a software project: its CVS release history and Bugzilla data [7] its FAMIX model [5] its fine-grained source code changes [9] its change types and couplings [8] and its developer networks [28]. All these tools are integrated into our software evolution platform called *Evolizer* which allows them to communicate and share their data [10]. But what if we want to add an external, already existing analysis, say a code clone detector? Not only we would have to deal with language and platform dependency issues but even more, we would have to take care of inter-domain integration of the data produced by the new tool and the one already shared in our platform.

We argue that these challenges can be solved by means of service orientation. In this chapter we present our approach towards a *distributed and collaborative*

---

[1] http://jazz.net

[2] http://msdn.microsoft.com/en-us/vstudio/bb725993.aspx

software analysis platform that allows for interoperability of different soft-ware analyses across platform, geographical and organizational boundaries. Particular analyses are represented in software analysis taxonomy and adhere to specific meta-models and ontologies for their category. They offer a common web service interface that enables their composite use on the Internet. These distributed analysis services are accessible through an incrementally augmented *Software Analysis Broker*, where organizations and tool builders can register and share their analyses.

Allowing disparate analyses to be available as web services and interoperate by sharing their data would be highly beneficial for three reasons: (1) it can speed up the collaboration of software engineers by being able to share their analyses and use each others analyses with only little overhead; (2) not only tool builders but also analyses itself could collaborate as web services and they could be composed into chains of services or into more complex services with the web service composition language such as BPEL4WS; and (3) it would facilitate the uncovering of new meaningful analyses based on a *Software Analysis Broker*.

12.1.2 A Scenario for Collaborative Software Analysis Across Organizational and Tool Boundaries

Before going deeper into detailing our work, we briefly illustrate the challenges we want to address and the potential impact of our work with the following software analysis collaboration scenario:

> Alice has developed a tool extracting the detailed CVS history of software projects to gain better insights on the development process. Bob has a tool doing the same but with Bugzilla data, and Charlie's tool extracts the Famix model of a given object-oriented software project by parsing its entire source code to obtain an unambiguous and precise language indepen-dent representation of it. Each tool works on a specific platform and requires its own settings and parameters.
>
> Alice, Bob, and Charlie do not work for the same institution. They decided to unify their efforts to thoroughly analyze the history of Foozilla; multi-million lines of code system, but the communication overhead due to different data-models, different result data formats, and storage media are too cumbersome to follow-up on their exciting plan. A unified software analysis platform that would allow them to easily get a detailed holistic view of the history of Foozilla: it would tell them for example for each release which bugs are related to specific files revisions, thus providing a clear link between a bug and some specific source code files. Bug prone parts, bug fixing and other source code change patterns would then be easy to spot.
>
> Based on this, new and additional analyses could be produced and offered on the same platform. For example, Jane could then develop the analysis she always wanted to imple-ment but lacked the right expertise and tool support. That analysis calculates source code metrics (through its Famix model, without thus having to deal with the actual source code) for each CVS release to spot code smells to both show their trend over time and their relation to reported bugs and eventually show that into some nice navigable graphical interface.

12.2 State-of-the-Art in Software Analyses

Software analysis is one of the key activities in software evolution as it allows one to extract the most diverse and extensive information regarding a software system. The classic analyses have been around for years targeting models and source code [16]. In the last years many research groups have shifted their attention to software evolution and the community of reverse engineering, reengineering, and program understanding has actually acknowledged that evolution is indeed the umbrella of their research activities. There is a plethora of research on software analysis, but it is not our intention to give a complete picture of the state of the art. We just want to sketch the type and range of analyses that can be integrated in our proposed service platform. In this way we want to better contextualize our approach and show its potential.

Approaches focusing on the software evolution either study its source code change history, bug history, its underlying dynamics or a combination of them. Fischer et al. [7] developed a release history database, combining information from version control and bug tracking systems, namely CVS and Bugzilla to facilitate further analysis. Draheim et al. [6] had a similar approach but only worked with version control data from CVS. Many other works detect and track changes made on the source code during the software lifetime. Zou et al. [35] used origin analysis to detect merging and splitting while S. Kim et al. [20] used it to track function name changes. M. Kim et al. [21] focused on code clone evolution and built a clone genealogy tool to extract code clones history from a project CVS repository. Works by Zimmermann et al. [34] and Ying et al. [33] predict future source code changes given past source revision history of a project stored into CVS repositories to then recommend potentially relevant source code for a particular modification task. Source revision history is analyzed to extract also other kinds of information. Livshits et al. [24] combine that with dynamic analysis techniques to identify application-specific patterns and find pattern violation. Hipikat [3] forms an implicit group memory combining CVS source repository data, Bugzilla data, messages posted on developer forums and other project documents to recommend artifacts that are relevant to a particular task that a developer is trying to perform. Gall et al. [11] extracted change couplings of software modules by analyzing CVS data, in particular check in and check out time and the authors of those actions; from that they were able to discover design flaws without analyzing a single line of code. Fluri et al. [8] focused on the extraction of several fine-grained source code change types and the assessment of their significance in terms of their impact on other source code entities and whether they may be functionality-modifying or functionality-preserving. Then, Nagappan et al. [27] predicted defect density for a system using code churn metrics fetched from its change history.

Similarly to the works on source code change, bug analysis addressed extraction of data from a bug repository (as in [7]), its prediction or its analysis. For that,

Hassan et al. [14] developed a dynamic cache of the ten mostly error prone subsystems (directories). Kim et al. [22] proposed a similar approach, but they dynamically cached the most likely fault prone source code locations. Sliwerski et al. [29] related version history and a bug database to detect, as Kim et al. code locations whose changes had been risky in the past and annotated them with color bars to show their risk rate. While much effort has been spent on software cost/effort prediction, very little has been done on bug fixing effort prediction. As for example the work by Weiss et al. [32] in which, for every new bug report in a issue tracking system, similar earlier reports are fetched and their average time is used as a prediction for the new one.

Not only has the history of a software development process been addressed, but also its underlying dynamics. In particular, a lot of research has also been performed on the role of the developers in evolutionary processes. For example, Čubranić et al. [4] and Anvik et al. [1] both developed approaches for bug triaging that recommend a list of developers with the appropriate expertise to solve a particular bug by applying machine learning techniques on bug reports fetched from a bug repository (i.e., Bugzilla). Mockus et al. [26] located people with desired expertise not using bug reports but by analyzing data from change management systems. Gîrba et al. [12] analyzed CVS logs to reconstruct code ownership to help in answering which authors are knowledgeable in which part of the system and also reveal behavioral patterns: when and how different developers interact in which way and in which part of the system.

The use of web services and ontologies for software analysis and evolution has been addressed only recently. A few works have used software analysis data and concept representations with ontologies. Hyland-Wood et al. [15] presented OWL ontology of software engineering concepts including classes, tests, metrics and requirements. Happel et al. [13] in their KOntoR approach stored and retrieved meta-data about software artifacts to foster software reuse. What is interesting for us is that they proposed various ontologies to provide background knowledge about software components, such as the programming language and licensing models. Highly related to our approach is the work by Kiefer et al. [19] which proposed EvoOnt, a software repository data exchange format including software, release and bug related information based on OWL. To effectively mine software systems represented in that OWL format and find, for example, code smells, they introduced iSPARQL; a query engine supporting similarity joins. From their work we borrow the idea of using ontologies to represent software analysis data to facilitate data exchange and automatic reasoning. Jin and Cordy [17] with their Ontological Adaptive Service-Sharing Integration System (OASIS) are the first and so far only researchers that studied ontology based software analysis tool integration system that employs domain ontology and specifically constructed external tool adapters. They also implemented a proof of concept with three reverse engineering tools that allowed them to explore service-sharing as a viable means for facilitating interoperability among tools.

12.3 The Software Service Platform

There is a huge variety of tools and techniques offering the most disparate analyses of a software system, but it is impossible for researchers and software companies to easily and effectively shares, combine and integrate them. What follows is the description of how we tackle the problem.

12.3.1 The Software Analysis Broker Infrastructure

Figure 12.1 gives an overview of our approach, which is made up by four main constituents: software analysis web services, an analysis services catalog, a *Software Analysis Broker* and ontologies. Software analysis web services "wrap" already existing analysis tools exposing their functionalities and data through a web service. The analyses catalog classifies all the registered analysis services with respect to specific software analysis taxonomy. The *Software Analysis Broker* web service acts as the interface between the catalog and the users. Specific ontologies are used to define and represent the data consumed and produced by the different analysis services, while upper ontologies define much more generic concepts common to several specific ontologies. Thus, they provide semantic links between them, which otherwise would remain decoupled.

In the following, we explain these constituents in greater detail.

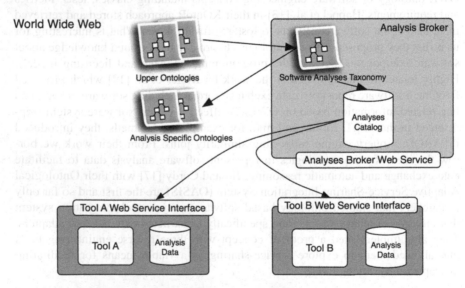

Fig. 12.1 Overview of our software analysis service platform

12.3.1.1 Software Analysis Services

Our solution proposes software analyses to be available as web services. We decided to leverage this paradigm over other competing middleware technologies as it is a well known standard and it was devised to overcome some of the problems we also face and thus already offers many of the features we need, namely: language, platform and location independence and service composition.

Independence is achieved with the use of XML-based languages to describe the services (WSDL) and a simple, lightweight communication protocol (SOAP) intended for exchanging structured information, formatted into XML-based messages, in a decentralized, distributed environment, normally using HTTP/HTTPS. Composition and orchestration is provided by BPEL4WS (Business Process Execution Language for Web Services), an XML-based language designed to enable task sharing for a distributed computing – even across multiple organizations – using a combination of Web services. Moreover, because of these characteristics of loose coupling, published interfaces and a standard communication model, existing applications can expose their functionalities through web services without significant changes. The internal logic, the input and output formats used, the platform and language under which the original tool runs remain the same but are hidden behind the web service not being a burden for interoperability anymore [2, 31]. At last, with the use of semantical annotated web services, they can be seamlessly integrated with ontologies, whose usefulness and significance in our solution will be explained later.

12.3.1.2 Software Analyses Catalog and Taxonomy

With web services, we can easily share, use and combine different analyses across organizational, geographical, platform and language boundaries through the Net. But these services alone are not enough; they need to be kept track of and classified in some sort of registry. This is why we created the *Analyses Catalog*, which is used to store and classify all the registered analysis services so that any user can automatically discover analysis services she is interested in, invoke them and then fetch the results. To do that, a clear and univoque classification is essential. Based on the existing software analysis techniques we developed specific software analysis taxonomy to systematically classify the existing and future services. This taxonomy divides the possible analyses into three main categories based on what aspect of a software system they focus on:

- the development process,
- the underlying models, or
- the actual source code.

Software development analyses are further divided into those targeting the development history (extraction, prediction and analysis of source code changes and bugs), its underlying process (its dynamics and metrics, as the ones defined by Lorenz et al. [25]) and the teams involved in it (their dynamics and metrics), as shown in Fig. 12.2.

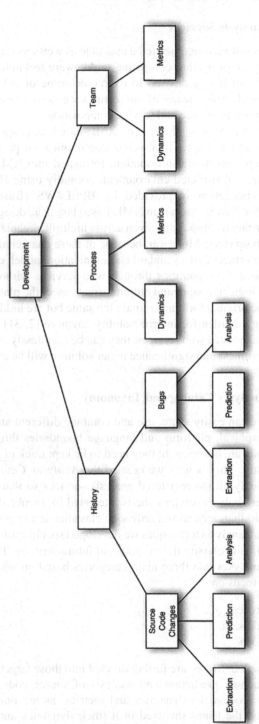

Fig. 12.2 A view of the software development analysis branch

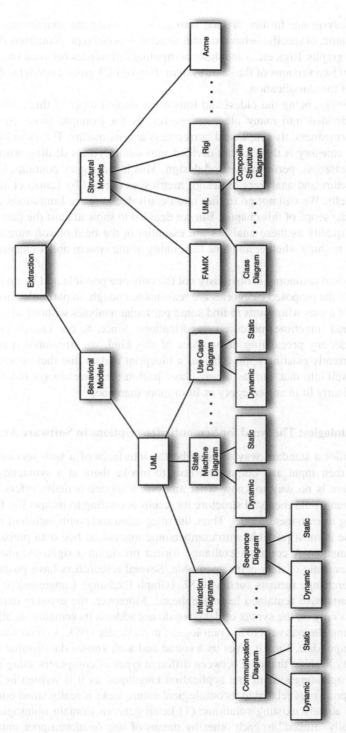

Fig. 12.3 A compact view of the software model extraction branch

Model analyses are further divided into those targeting the extraction, either dynamic or static, of specific behavioral and structural model representations (UML, FAMIX, call graphs, Rigi, etc.,) and those computing differences between two models, usually of two versions of the same system. Figure 12.3 gives a condensed view of this part of the classification.

Code analyses, being the oldest and thus most studied topic of this taxonomy, are further divided into many other categories, as for example those checking code well-formedness, its syntactical correctness and its quality. For example, the code quality category is then further divided into subcategories dealing with code security, conciseness, performance and design. This last category contains, among others, extractors and analyzers of design metrics, as defined by Lanza et al. [23] and code-smells. We will not go further into details due to space limitations and as it is beyond the scope of this chapter. But we decided to show at least the part about code design quality as these analyses are essential in the field of software evolution analysis to study whether and how the quality of the system under examination evolved.

This proposed taxonomy is obviously not the only one possible and by no means complete. But the proposed categories are reasonable enough, in particular from the perspective of a user who wants to find some particular analyses without struggling with many and sometimes obscure categorizations. Since, to our knowledge, the literature lacks any preexisting taxonomies of this kind, we structured it mainly using the currently existing approaches as a blueprint and so that they would "fit" reasonably well into that, but, as in any classification there are always individuals that do not clearly fit in any category or fit in more than one.

12.3.1.3 Ontologies: The Need for Semantic Descriptions in Software Analysis

WSDL specifies a standard way to describe the interfaces of a web services, the structure of their input and output and how to invoke them at a syntactic level. However, there is no way to know what analysis a service actually offers. Each specific service would then still structure its results according to its specific format and following its own meta-model. Thus, the integration and combination of results would still be at most possible with cumbersome manual ad-hoc data preparation and transformation. A common exchange format providing a rigorous, univoque syntax and semantic of data is indispensable. Several researchers have pushed for common interchange formats such as GXL (Graph Exchange Language) or XMI, but their efforts have remained largely unheard. Moreover, the existing exchange formats focus only on the syntax of data, but do not address its semantic at all.

A promising alternative is to use ontologies, in particular OWL, to represent both results and input data. First it gives us a sound and well known data format to use and the ability to share that data between different types of computers using different types of operating system and application languages, as it is written in XML. Second, the properties related to its ontological nature make it really stand out from all the other already existing solutions: (1) heterogeneous domain ontologies can be semantically "linked" to each other by means of one or more upper ontology, which describe general concepts across a wide range of domains. In this way it is possible to reach interoperability between a large numbers of ontologies accessible "under" some upper ontology. In terms of software analysis services, it means that results from the most disparate type could be automatically combined given that they share some common concepts; (2) with the OWL Description Logic foundation it is possible to perform automatic reasoning and derive additional knowledge; (3) we can use a powerful query language such as SPARQL or its extension iSPARQL [18] that uses similarity operators to query for similar entities; and (4) in contrast to XML and XQuery that operate on the structure of the data, OWL treats data based on its semantics. This allows for an extension of the data model with no backward compatibility problems with existing tools.

Moreover, thanks to the recently introduced Semantic Annotations for WSDL and XML Schema, web services and ontologies can be effectively integrated together to create *semantic web services*. Semantic annotations can be attached to any part of a web service definition, adding semantic meaning to it, as it is shown in Fig. 12.4 (the semantic annotations are bold and circled).

The example highlights the reasons why this approach is useful for our purposes. First the service itself can be declared to represent a particular concept of ontology, in our case a CVS release history data extractor. Second, its inputs and outputs can be declared of being concepts of specific ontologies and thus have a clear semantical meaning. In the example of Fig. 12.4, since the service itself offers a CVS release history, the output is then declared of representing a CVS history, as defined in the ontology (we will show more details in Section 12.4). In this way we know precisely what the service returns and what that means. Moreover, with all this information

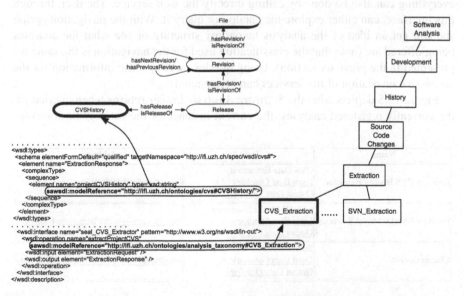

Fig. 12.4 An example of a semantical annotated web service definition

we can then check, for every new service being registered in our analyses catalog, whether it supports inputs and provide results conforming to ontologies specific to the analysis it is declared to implement (e.g., every CVS extraction service has to return a CVS history).

12.3.1.4 Software Analysis Broker Web Service

The *Software Analysis Broker* acts as a "layer" between the catalog and the users, through which they can query, update, manage the catalog (namely register, update and unregister analysis services). They can even expand the taxonomy, as new types of analyses that were not yet classified, or some modification to the already existing classification, could come up in the future. More precisely, the *Software Analysis Broker* can be queried to get the content of the analyses catalog (in other words, the registered analyses) and if one or more specific analyses have been performed on some project. We decided to offer just these two functionalities because those two pieces of information are what a user might want to know in this context. Furthermore, any additional information can then be fetched from a combination of them. Those two queries are offered through a web service interface and the results formatted into a standardized machine readable format, more precisely OWL. In this way tools of any kind can (semi-) automatically fetch the analyses they need to then call them without any human intervention. However, this makes the results hardly readable by humans. So, we chose to let the *Software Analysis Broker* be queried in the same way through a website, which will format and present the results in a much more understandable form for human users. Therefore we will show the *Software Analysis Broker* functionalities through its website interface, keeping in mind that everything can also be done by calling directly the web service. The user, through this interface, can either explore the catalog or query it. With the navigation option she can get an idea of the analysis taxonomy structure or see what the analyses being offered are (note that the classification used for the navigation is the same we presented in the previous section). Using queries more specific information for the successive invocation of the services can be gathered.

Figure 12.5 depicts what the *Software Analysis Broker* returns when queried for the currently registered analyses: the current instance of the catalog. So for every

Name	Type	Address
Evolizer CVS History Extractor	CVS Data Extraction Input Data Ontology Output Data Ontology	http://localhost:8080/Webolizer/CVS
Evolizer FAMIX Model Extractor	FAMIX Model Extraction Input Data Ontology Output Data Ontology	http://localhost:8080/Webolizer/FAMIX
ChangeDistiller	Source Code Changes Detection Input Data Ontology Output Data Ontology	http://localhost:8080/ChangeDistillerWeb

Fig. 12.5 The registered analysis services

service is reported the name, the address through which it can be invoked and the type of analysis offered. Knowing the latter gives the user all the information on the service input and output. In fact, as we explained in the previous section, every analysis type is associated with ontologies to which the input and output of the service offering that must conform. Thus with this query it is possible to know what analyses can be performed and gather all the information needed to then call the desired ones. So it will be used when a user or a tool, given a project, wants to conduct some analysis and has to know who is currently offering it.

Figure 12.6 shows what the *Software Analysis Broker* returns when queried to find out if one or more types of analysis were performed on some projects. Note that for all the projects is displayed whether or not every single requested analysis has been already performed, without explicitly showing what is the actual service that did it. In fact, as long as it is performed, it does not really matter who performed the analysis since, as explained before, all the services offering it will comply to a common output (both syntactically and semantically). Nevertheless the address of the actual service offering the analysis is simply hidden by the HTML representation behind the "check" symbol. So it can be immediately invoked to get the available data without having to query the *Software Analysis Broker* for any other information.

All this information allows one to see what data about a project is already available to then fetch it or trigger the analysis to produce it. Furthermore, it can be handy for tools and users that need case study data from existing projects to then run their own analysis. For example, a tool extracting some newly defined software project metrics might need CVS history data of software projects for case studies and proofs of concept for validation. So, instead of finding suitable projects and extracting their CVS data by itself, it could take advantage of the previous analyses and thus just fetch the data that has already been extracted by the registered services offering CVS data extraction. Moreover, with the *Software Analysis* Broker web service, we can add more complex functionalities, such as service composition, on top of the analyses catalog which would allow us to fully exploit our platform. For example, if a user wants a series of analyses performed on a project, she would have two options. She could search the catalog for the desired analyses, compose them through a web interface and then execute them; or she could let the *Software Analysis Broker* take care of finding, composing, executing them (for example with BPEL) and then just get the final results once the whole process is done.

Project	CVS Data Extraction	Bugs Data Extraction	Famix Model Extraction	Source Code Changes Detection
argouml	✓	✗	✓	✗
azureus	✓	✓	✓	✓
org.eclipse.compare	✓	✗	✓	✗
org.eclipse.jdt	✓	✗	✗	✗

Fig. 12.6 *Software Analysis Broker* list of analyses and projects

12.4 Software Analysis Services at Work

Now we present an excerpt of software analysis services that we have implemented
and show how they can be orchestrated to solve the task outlined in our analysis
scenario. All services exploit techniques and tools that have been implemented by
our group comprising the CVS importer, Bugzilla importer, and FAMIX parser. For
each service we show its semantical annotated definition and the ontologies of the
needed input and generated output data.

12.4.1 CVS History Extractor Service

This service extracts the versioning information comprising release, revision, and
commits information from a CVS repository. Figure 12.7 shows the definition of
the web service. The service belongs to the "CVS_Extraction" category of our taxonomy, as it is declared by the WSDL element framed by box number 2. As such it
needs a URL as input that specifies the location of the CVS repository. When running it connects to the repository, obtains and processes the CVS information and
outputs the resulting data model in the format specified by the CVSHistory ontology
(see WSDL element marked with 1).

The core concepts of the CVS History ontology are depicted in Fig. 12.8. In
addition to the directory structure, the importer obtains, for each file, all its revision information and corresponding modification reports. They basically contain

```
<wsdl:types>
  <schema elementFormDefault="qualified" targetNamespace="http://ifi.uzh.ch/spec/wsdl/cvs#">
    <element name="ExtractionRequest">
      <complexType>
        <sequence>
          <element name="repositoryUrl" type="xsd:string"/>
        </sequence>
      </complexType>
    </element>
    <element name="ExtractionResponse">
      <complexType>
        <sequence>
1         <element name="projectCVSHistory" type="xsd:string"
            sawsdl:modelReference="http://ifi.uzh.ch/ontologies/cvs#CVSHistory/">
        </sequence>
      </complexType>
    </element>
</wsdl:types>

  <wsdl:interface name="seal_CVS_Extractor" pattern="http://www.w3.org/ns/wsdl/in-out">
2   <wsdl:operation name="extractProjectCVS"
      sawsdl:modelReference="http://ifi.uzh.ch/ontologies/analysis_taxonomy#CVS_Extraction">
      <wsdl:input element="ExtractionRequest" />
      <wsdl:output element="ExtractionResponse" />
    </wsdl:operation>
  </wsdl:interface>
</wsdl:description>
```

Fig. 12.7 Excerpt of the WSDL definition of the CVS Importer service

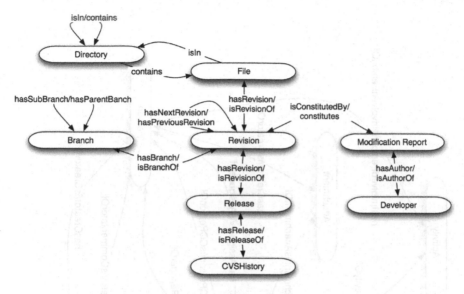

Fig. 12.8 High-level view of the CVS history ontology

the information on who changed when/which source file and how many lines have been inserted/deleted. That data is stored as RDF triples and a reference is provided to the user for accessing it. The reference can be queried from the *Software Analysis Broker* so that the processing of particular CVS repositories needs to be done only once. Any subsequent request can use the saved triple store.

12.4.2 Bugzilla Extractor Service

This service extracts problem reports and change requests from a Bugzilla repository. Due to space limitations, we cannot show its WSDL definition, which is similar to the one we just showed for the CVS importer. The service belongs to the "Bugzilla_Extraction" category which is a subcategory of generic bug extraction services. Similar to the CVS Importer service, it needs a string denoting the URL of the location of the Bugzilla repository as input. When run, the service accesses the Bugzilla repository to derive the problem reports and change requests in XML format, parses them and stores the result as RDF triples. The triples conform to the ontology shown in Fig. 12.9.

Optionally, the client of the service can provide a reference to an already imported CVS model. When the reference is given, the service runs a procedure that establishes the links between CVS Revision and Issue entities. As no standard to report a bug fix or a reference to a bug in the CVS commits is enforced (usually the developers add the related bug reference number in the commit message), in order to effectively reconstruct those links, some heuristics are needed. Our service

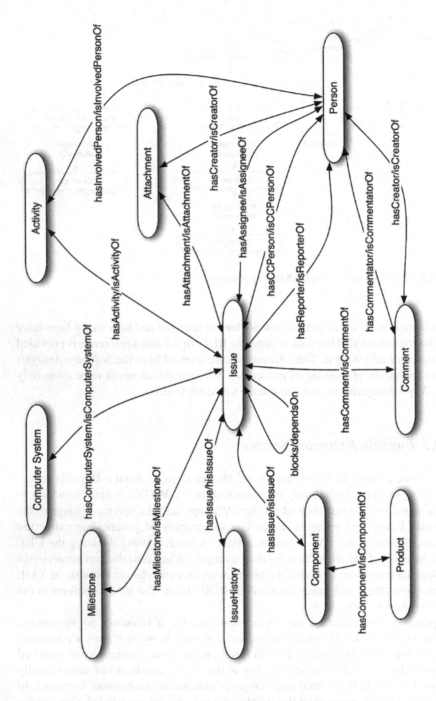

Fig. 12.9 High-level view of the issue tracking history ontology

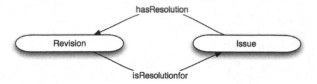

Fig. 12.10   High-level view of the Issue Tracking-Cvs links ontology

can be configured to use several of them, from very simple to more structured ones, such as the one proposed by Sliwerski et al. [30]. That inferred linking data is structured as an instance of the simple ontology shown in Fig. 12.10, which basically associates each extracted Bugzilla issue to all its related CVS revisions of the CVS History that was passed as input and vice versa. Also these links are stored as RDF triples with the ontology referenced by the element marked 3.

12.4.3 Famix Model Extractor Service

Like the Bugzilla Extractor, this service requires as input a project CVS history data. Given that information, it then fetches, for each project release, its source code and parses it to get the related Famix model and transforms it into a specific Famix ontology, shown in Fig. 12.11. That data is then returned as the output of the service and stored as RDF triples. The CVS history this service requires as input is not only used to know and fetch all the releases of the project of interest, but it is used also to create links between the CVS history and the Famix Model created. This information is represented using the ontology shown in Fig. 12.12. The links keep track of all the CVS revisions in which a Famix Class (which represents the generic OO class concept) was modified and vice versa. From the Class entity all the remaining information on its related Famix Model can be easily fetched and in the same way, from its linked Revision, all the associated CVS information can be gathered. As before, the data is returned as part of the service output and stored as RDF triples.

12.4.4 An Interoperability Scenario

If we come back to the analysis scenario we presented in Section 12.1, the services we introduced before are more or less the ones that Alice, Charlie and Bob agreed to offer after their meeting. So, what happens when they are integrated in our *Software Analysis Broker* platform and a user, in our case the fourth person of the scenario, Jane, comes into play?

As a first step she needs to check what is available on the catalog and in particular whether services offering the required analyses exist and are registered. In order to do that she queries the *Software Analysis Broker* to see whether some CVS history,

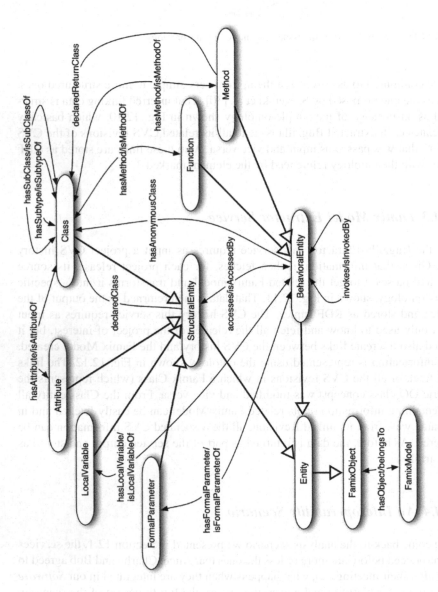

Fig. 12.11 High-level condensed view of the Famix model ontology

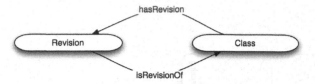

Fig. 12.12   High-level view of the Famix-Cvs links ontology

Bugzilla history and Famix extraction services are available. Then, by fetching the semantically annotated WSDL file for each of them, Jane can learn what input data needs to be supplied and what is their expected output. So in this case she finds out that in order to get all the data she wants, first she needs to call the CVS History Extractor and then, once the results are ready, provide them to the Bugzilla Extractor and the Famix Model Extractor so that they can carry out their analyses, as they require CVS History data to perform their analyses. She can do this all by herself by getting the reference to the services and invoking them in the required order and with the right inputs. Or, even better, she instructs the Software Analysis Broker to compose those three services into a BPEL workflow and have it run on a BPEL engine, which will actually take care of the whole flow, passing the data from one service to another, as we mentioned in Section 12.3.1. In this way she only needs to specify how to compose and run the different services without having to deal with and know BPEL itself. In this case the whole execution of the services is more or less automated. This is useful for the combination of time consuming analyses, either for the type of the analysis itself or for the analyzed system size.

In Jane's case, the body of knowledge that she's eventually able to get is shown in Fig. 12.13. Note how all the ontologies are linked thanks to the links between the CVS and Bugzilla data and the CVS and Famix data. She can then proceed to examine that huge amount of data and fetch all the information needed for her analysis using SPARQL queries or any other approach of her choice. By querying the Famix data of every project release she can extract all the source code metrics she needs to spot possible code smells and then get all "smelly" classes. Due to the links established between the Famix and the CVS data she can get for any of those classes all their revisions and from there, with the links between the Issue Tracking and the CVS data, get all the issues associated to them. With that data she can then run her own analysis on the relation between code smells and bugs: to see whether code smells caused the emergence of bugs and/or bug fixing reduces the amount of code smells.

The same job, without our platform would have required the installation and configuration of at least three different tools, the ad-hoc transformation to and from the different formats used by them and the manual linking of that different data (or developing an ad-hoc tool to do that). On the other hand, with our solution, it boils down to the invocation of just a few web services and some SPARQL queries, with no tedious and error prone data preparation, code modification, etc.

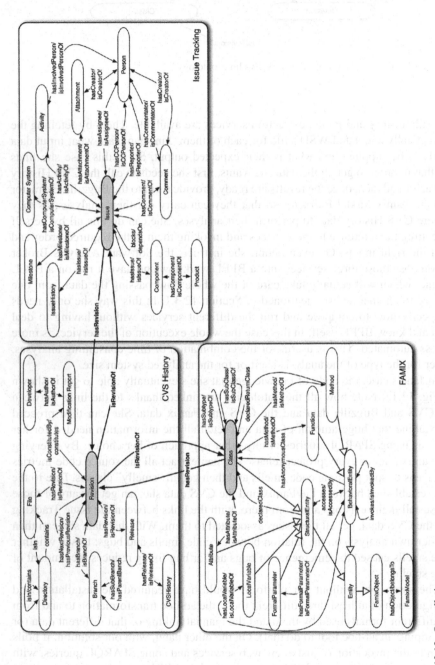

Fig. 12.13 Overall view

12.5 Conclusions

The combination and integration of different software analysis tools is a challenging problem when we need to gain a deeper insight into a software system's evolution. For every required analysis a specialized tool, with its own explicit or implicit meta-model dictating how to represent the input and the output has to be installed, configured and executed. Even if different analyses of the same kind exist, the only way to compare them is to do it manually.

Our approach solves that problem with *a combination of ontologies and web services for software analysis*. Using web services to expose the functionalities offered by the analysis tools gives us independence from platform, language and location. Further we can apply well-known mechanisms of service composition and orchestration (*e.g.*, BPEL4WS) of several analysis services. OWL ontologies specific to distinct types of analyses allow us to have standard formats to define and represent the data consumed and produced by the analysis services, which can then be integrated with each other based on semantic "links". These links are provided by generic, upper ontologies. With semantically annotated web services, we can formalize for each service the actual ontological concepts and its input and output by just adding a few annotations in the service definition. Moreover, it is then possible to support (semi-) automatic composition of services based on the semantics of their input and output. And due to OWL's powerful query language SPARQL and its Description Logic foundation, data can be extracted and additional knowledge can be inferred with existing tools.

Allowing disparate analysis tools to collaborate with each other and share their information via a service platform can be highly beneficial. Research groups and individuals can share and exploit each other's expertise and knowledge on software analysis with only little overhead, in a standard, unambiguous way, thus avoiding reinventing the same wheels over and over again. Moreover, from a software engineer point of view, not only it will enhance and speed up the work by providing access to a big amount of information without the need to install several tools and to cope with many output formats, but it would also promote the uncovering of new meaningful and interesting metrics deriving from the most diverse types of analysis that can finally "talk" and collaborate with each other.

The work we have presented is a major endeavor and as such still work in progress. However, everything shown here is part of already existing prototypes that we developed. The *Software Analysis Broker* and the services, along with all their related ontologies, have been realized and extended into full-fledged web services so that they can be used by outside users. The (semi-) automatic composition of services using semantics has not been implemented yet but we have started to address it. This is because first we wanted to have an initial version of the whole infrastructure up and running with just a few services registered. This should point out the possible problems and issues to guide subsequent improvements and to show the feasibility and usefulness of the approach. In this way also external users could start using our own analyses to see how it works, grasp its potentials and may be integrate their own tools. In fact, since it is a platform for distributed and collaborative software analysis, we would like to have other research groups share their analysis approaches through our platform, and thereby leveraging it.

References

1. Anvik J, Hiew L, Murphy GC (2006) Who should fix this bug? Proceedings of the International Conference on Software Engineering, pp. 361–370.
2. Canfora G, Fasolino A, Frattolillo G, Tramontana P (2006) Migrating interactive legacy systems to web services. Proceedings of the European Conference on Software Maintenance and Reengineering, pp. 36–46.
3. Čubranić D, Murphy GC (2003) Hipikat: Recommending pertinent software development artifacts. Proceedings of the International Conference on Software Engineering, pp. 408–418.
4. Čubranić D, Murphy GC (2004) Automatic bug triage using text categorization. Proceedings of the International Conference on Software Engineering and Knowledge Engineering (SEKE) pp. 92–97.
5. Demeyer S, Tichelaar S, Steyaert P (2000) FAMIX 2.0 – The FAMOOS information exchange model. Technical Report.
6. Draheim D, Pekacki L (2003) Process-centric analytical processing of version control data. Proceedings of the International Workshop on Principles of Software Evolution, p. 131.
7. Fischer M, Pinzger M, Gall H (2003) Populating a release history database from version control and bug tracking systems. Proceedings of the International Conference on Software Maintenance, pp. 23–32.
8. Fluri B, Gall HC (2006) Classifying change types for qualifying change couplings. Proceedings of the International Conference on Program Comprehension, pp. 35–45.
9. Fluri B, Würsch M, Pinzger M, Gall HC (2007) Change distilling – Tree differencing for fine-grained source code change extraction. IEEE Transactions on Software Engineering 33(11): 725–743.
10. Gall HC, Fluri B, Pinzger M (2009) Change analysis with evolizer and change distiller. IEEE Software 26(1): 26–33.
11. Gall H, Jazayeri M, Krajewski J (2003) CVS release history data for detecting logical couplings. Proceedings of the International Workshop on Principles of Software Evolution (IWPSE 2003), pp. 13–23.
12. Gîrba T, Kuhn A, Seeberger M, Ducasse S (2005) How developers drive software evolution. Proceedings of the International Workshop on Principles of Software Evolution, pp. 113–122.
13. Happel H, Korthaus A, Seedorf S, Tomczyk P (2006) KOntoR: An ontology-enabled approach to software reuse. Proceedings of the International Conference on Software Engineering and Knowledge Engineering.
14. Hassan A, Holt R (2005) The top ten list: Dynamic fault prediction. Proceedings of the International Conference on Software Maintenance, pp. 263–272.
15. Hyland-Wood D, Carrington D, Kaplan S (2006) Toward a software maintenance methodology using semantic web techniques. Proceedings of the International Workshop on Software Evolvability, pp. 23–30.
16. Jackson D, Rinard M (2000) Software analysis: a roadmap. Proceedings of the International Conference on the Future of Software Engineering, pp. 133–145.
17. Jin D, Cordy JR (2005) Ontology-based software analysis and reengineering tool integration: The OASIS service-sharing methodology. Proceedings of the International Conference on Software Maintenance, pp. 613–616.
18. Kiefer C, Bernstein A, Stocker M (2007) The fundamentals of iSPARQL – A virtual triple approach for similarity-based semantic web tasks. Proceedings of the International Semantic Web Conference, pp. 295–309.

19. Kiefer C, Bernstein A, Tappolet J (2007) Mining software repositories with iSPARQL and a software evolution ontology. Proceedings of the International Workshop on Mining Software Repositories.
20. Kim S, Pan K, Whitehead E (2005) When functions change their names: Automatic detection of origin relationships. Proceedings of the Working Conference on Reverse Engineering, pp. 23–32.
21. Kim M, Sazawal V, Notkin D, Murphy G (2005) An empirical study of code clones genealogies. Proceedings of the European Software Engineering Conference, pp. 23–32.
22. Kim S, Zimmermann T, Whitehead EJ Jr, Zeller A (2007) Predicting faults from cached history. Proceedings of the International Conference on Software Engineering, pp. 489–498.
23. Lanza M, Marinescu R (2005) Object-Oriented Metrics in Practice. Secaucus, NJ: Springer-Verlag New York, Inc.
24. Livshits B, Zimmermann T (2005) Dynamine: Finding common error patterns by mining software revision histories. Proceedings of the European Software Engineering Conference, pp. 296–305.
25. Lorenz M, Kidd J (1994) Object-Oriented Software Metrics: A Practical Guide. Upper Saddle River, NJ: Prentice-Hall, Inc.
26. Mockus A, Herbsleb J (2002) Expertise browser: A quantitative approach to identifying expertise. Proceedings of the International Conference on Software Engineering, pp. 503–512.
27. Nagappan N, Ball T (2005) Use of relative code churn measures to predict system defect density. Proceedings of the International Conference on Software Engineering, pp. 284–292.
28. Schwarz B (2007) SNA-cockpit – Master's thesis, University of Zurich, Department of Informatics.
29. Sliwerski J, Zimmermann T, Zeller A (2005) HATARI. Raising risk awareness. Proceedings of the European Software Engineering Conference, pp. 107–110.
30. Sliwerski J, Zimmermann T, Zeller A (2005) When do changes induce fixes? Proceedings of the International Workshop on Mining Software Repositories, pp. 1–5.
31. Sneed HM, Sneed S (2003) Creating web services from legacy host programs. Proceedings of the International Workshop on Web Site Evolution, pp. 59–65.
32. Weiss C, Premraj R, Zimmermann T, Zeller A (2007) How long will it take to fix this bug? Proceedings of the International Workshop on Mining Software Repositories, p. 1.
33. Ying AT, Murphy GC, Ng R, Chu-Carroll MC (2004) Predicting source code changes by mining change history. IEEE Transactions on Software Engineering 30(9): 574–586.
34. Zimmermann T, Weissgerber P, Diehl S, Zeller A (2004) Mining version history to guide software changes. Proceedings of the International Conference on Software Engineering, pp. 563–572.
35. Zou L, Godfrey M (2003) Detecting merging and splitting using origin analysis. Proceedings of the Working Conference on Reverse Engineering, pp. 146–154.

Chapter 13
Dynamic Analysis of Communication and Collaboration in OSS Projects

Martin Pinzger and Harald C. Gall

Abstract Software repositories, such as versioning, bug reporting, and developer mailing list archives contain valuable data for analyzing the history of software projects and its dynamics. In this chapter, we focus on the analysis of the communication and collaboration in software projects and present an approach that works on software archives with social network analysis techniques. Our tool called STNA-Cockpit provides both, a meta-model to represent communication and collaboration and a graph visualization technique to interactively explore instances of the meta-model. These instances are reconstructed from CVS, Bugzilla, and mailing list data. In a case study with the Eclipse Platform Core project data we demonstrate that with STNA-Cockpit one can observe project dynamics for certain periods of time. This allows, for example, project managers to early identify communication bottlenecks, contributor and expertise networks, or to understand how newcomers can be integrated fast and efficiently into their team.

13.1 Introduction

Communication and collaboration among team members are key success factors for large, complex software projects. In addition to industry, examples of such projects can be found in the Open Source Software (OSS) community, for example, the Mozilla, Apache, Eclipse projects. OSS projects are of particular interest for communication and collaboration research because their developers rarely or never meet face-to-face.

Findings of previous research showed that OSS developers coordinate their work almost exclusively by three information spaces: the implementation space, the documentation space, and the discussion space [6]. Typically, in OSS projects a versioning system, such as, the concurrent versions system (CVS), provides the

M. Pinzger (✉)
Software Engineering Research Group, Delft University of Technology, Netherlands
e-mail: M.Pinzger@tudelft.nl

I. Mistrík et al. (eds.), *Collaborative Software Engineering*,
DOI 10.1007/978-3-642-10294-3_13, © Springer-Verlag Berlin Heidelberg 2010

backend of the implementation space. It keeps track of changes made to projected related files and corresponding versions. The World Wide Web is used as the primary documentation space. Because of the distributed and informal nature of OSS projects, discussions between project members, project associates, and users are done and tracked in mailing lists and bug reporting systems. This results in a representative data set that enables communication and collaboration analysis. The representative data in OSS projects as well as its public availability motivated us to develop the Socio-Technical Network Analysis (STNA)-Cockpit. However, our approach is not limited to OSS projects. It can also be applied in industrial settings in which such data is available.

STNA-Cockpit provides means and techniques to obtain a deeper insight into the communication and collaboration structure of software projects. In particular, we use STNA-Cockpit to address the following research questions:

- Who owns or is working on which components?
- Who are the key personalities (e.g., leading developers) in the project?
- Are there deviations in the developer contribution structure?

We address these questions by analyzing the communication and collaboration structure that is reconstructed from versioning archives (implementation space), bug tracking and mailing list archives (discussion space). We leave out the documentation space whose analysis is out of scope for this chapter.

In summary, the chapter makes three contributions, of which the first one is a meta-model for representing communication and collaboration in OSS projects. We briefly describe the set of techniques and tools for importing the data and further present the heuristics that are used by STNA-Cockpit to integrate the various data sources into the communication and collaboration network.

The STNA-Cockpit approach is our second contribution. STNA-Cockpit uses a graph-based visualization technique to analyze the communication and collaboration structure. Properties of the communication between developers and collaboration on software components are mapped to graphical attributes in the graph. This results in a number of graph structures that form *visual patterns* which indicate, for example, team organization, the key personalities in the project, or the owners of source code components. Furthermore, these patterns also indicate violations in the communication and collaboration structure, such as, isolated developers or alien commits. In addition, STNA-Cockpit provides facilities to dynamically browse the communication and collaboration network over time. It uses a sliding time window approach that allows the user to navigate back and forth in the project history. This enables the observation of changes in the communication and collaboration structure. For example, it shows how newcomers get involved in the project, or how leading developers hand over their job to their successors.

We demonstrate the benefits of our integrated meta-model and the STNA-Cockpit approach in a case study with the Eclipse Platform Core project. This is our third and last contribution. Results of the study show how STNA-Cockpit can be used to find out, for example, the roles of different developers, such as, communicators and connectors, and how a new developer got socialized. The STNA-Cockpit approach proves useful to aid project leaders in observing and controlling the communication and collaboration structure in software projects and can provide an integral part in collaborative software engineering.

The remainder of the chapter is structured as follows: The next section presents related work of social network analysis in the software engineering domain. Section 13.3 describes the concepts for modeling communication and collaboration in OSS projects and the techniques to reconstruct them from raw data available for OSS projects. Section 13.4 introduces the STNA-Cockpit approach and its graphical language. The evaluation of STNA-Cockpit with the Eclipse Platform Core project is presented in Section 13.5. And, in Section 13.6 we draw conclusions and outline future work.

13.2 State-of-the-Art in Socio-technical Network Analysis

The public availability of project data made OSS projects to one of the most studied subjects in the software engineering research community. In [7] Karl Fogel presents a number of guidelines to manage and the technical infrastructure to run OSS projects. In the context of this chapter, the technical infrastructure of OSS projects is of particular interest. It basically consists of a versioning system, bug tracking system, and mailing lists for the communication and co-ordination of work. Communication between developers and users takes place in discussion forums and the bug tracker. Topics range from bug fixes, feature requests, to hints for the installation and usage of an application. The source code typically is managed with a versioning system, such as, CVS or subversion. They keep track of changes in the source files and project documents and are also used to mark software releases. While the "large" projects, such as, Eclipse and Mozilla provide their own infrastructure many OSS projects are hosted by development web sites, such as, SourceForge.net. Recent research results and emerging opportunities in OSS development are presented by Scacchi in [20]. We would like to refer the reader to this publication to get a deeper insight into OSS development.

The various data sources available from OSS development web sites formed the input to several studies of organization, communication, and co-ordination aspects in software projects. For example, Crowston et al. [5] used data from developer mailing lists and online forums of three active projects to analyze co-ordination mechanisms of OSS communities. The analysis is based on the Co-ordination Theory Approach framework [15]. They found similarities between OSS groups and reported practices of proprietary projects in the co-ordination mechanisms used to manage task-task dependencies. Differences were found in the co-ordination of task-actor dependencies. In particular, "self-assignment" was the most common mechanism used in OSS projects. Later on, Howison et al. [11] took a closer look at the dynamics of the social structure by applying social network analysis over time. They used data obtained from the SourceForge.net bug tracking repository. Results of their analyses showed that most of the participants are involved in the project for only a short period while few participants are involved for longer periods.

Similar to our approach, Ducheneaut [6] analyzed the socialization of newcomers to the OSS community of Python, showing that the integration of a new member is not only depending on her technical skills but also on her ability to learn how to participate and to build an identity for that her ideas will get accepted and integrated. He combines the social network built from the mailing list archive with the material structure based on CVS log. To visualize the project's evolution he implemented the OSS Browser, which provides a dynamic view of the social network, built on the Conversation Map of Sack [18].

Sack et al. [19] continued this research field with an analysis across the three information spaces that build the socio-technical network: discussion, implementation, and documentation. They tried to answer the questions how power is distributed, how links evolve between people, and how the cognitive activity of discussions is influenced by the social and governance structures of the project. Mails, CVS logs, and enhancement proposals of the Python project served as data basis. Similarly, Bird et al. presented a study in which they analyzed the process by which people join open source projects [3]. Results support their hypotheses that the rate of immigration is non-monotonic, and that technical skill and social reputation has an impact on becoming a developer. In our approach we reuse several of the ideas presented by these approaches

Several other studies used data from OSS projects to analyze communication and co-ordination aspects. For example, Ghosh showed that many open source projects hosted at SourceForge.net are organized as self-organizing social networks [9]. Similarly, Xu et al. studied the development community at SourceForge.net and classified contributors into project leader, core developer, co-developer, and active user [21]. Huang et al. used version histories to identify core and peripheral development teams [12]. Ohira et al. used social networks and collaborative filtering to support the identification of experts across projects [17]. Lopez et al. explored statistics and social network properties of the development community at SourceForge.net to find collaborations and topological properties [14]. In particular, they found small world phenomenon and scale free behaviors and also that weakly associated but contributing co-developers and active users may be important factors in open source software development.

Network visualization is a well-researched field and there exist a number of sophisticated frameworks and tools to visualize social networks, for example, Pajek [2] or Net Draw which is an integral part of the social network analysis tool Ucinet [4]. While these tools can visualize various kinds of social networks including also socio-technical networks, none of them takes into account evolution. Similar to our approach, Ogawa et al. [16] presented a visualization technique to analyze the evolution of the communication and collaboration activities of software projects. They used data from CVS repositories and mailing list archives. The visualization is based on combining the repository view and the mailing list view via people. The repository is represented using the Windows Explorer tree visualization and the mailing lists are displayed as clusters within Sankey diagrams.

Aberdour [1] addressed the question on how to achieve OSS quality by comparing best practices of OSS development with closed-source software development. He reported that high-quality OSS relies on having a large and sustainable community that has to be fully understood by the community members. The final guidelines to high-quality OSS imply high code modularity, rapid release cycles and many bug finders. His findings on quality justify our aim at providing means for a better understanding of software project dynamics, in both open and closed source software projects.

13.3 Modeling Communication and Collaboration in OSS Projects

In this section, we outline the motivation and present the means and techniques to analyze the interactions of a software project team. The main focus is on the question about the inner life of the project that consists of people playing different roles and of the products they develop. The collaborative interaction among the project members is reflected in the organization and has an influence on the project's outcome and its environment. The social structure of a community, based on communication, is combined with collaboration information representing working teams. This integration enables to further investigate the activities going on inside the project. The developed means and techniques are based on analyses of OSS communities, but they can be adapted to commercial projects as well.

13.3.1 Communication in OSS Projects

Open source software projects typically have no formal organization and pre-assigned command and control structure. Team members can join projects and contribute as they wish. This demands organizational instruments to share and exchange information. Bug tracking systems, such as Bugzilla, are used to manage bug reports and development tasks. Internet mailing lists are instruments to address information to a dynamically changing community. A mailing list has a list of subscribers receiving the messages processed by the reflector address. We assume that most of the core developers of the community interact using such designated tools. This section shows how we derive a model of the communication in OSS projects from Bugzilla and mailing list data.

13.3.1.1 Deriving Communication Paths from Mail Traffic

Communication in mailing lists happens on a subject/topic between a sender and at least one receiver at a certain point in time with a given content. Discussions arising from an initial mail can be grouped into threads – mails referring to the same subject are kept together. Within mailing list threads, the messages can grow in a dendritic

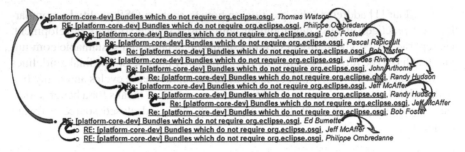

Fig. 13.1 Communication paths extracted from the Eclipse Platform Core developer mailing list

way. Figure 13.1 shows an excerpt of a mail thread from the online mailing list archive of Eclipse Platform Core.

A mail addressed to a mailing list is processed by the reflector and sent to all subscribers. This means that the *To:* address is always the mailing list address itself; hence, there is no explicit receiver address. In our example this address is *platform-core-dev*. To model the communication path between sender and receiver, the receiver needs to be reconstructed from subsequent answering mails. The identification of the sender is given by the *From:* field which is denoted by the name on the right side of a message. For determining the receivers of emails we analyze the tree structure of a mail thread and compute the *To:* and *Cc:* paths.

Figure 13.1 illustrates the two paths in our example thread whereas gray arrows denote the *To:* path and light gray arrows the *Cc:* path. A gray arrow is established between an initial mail and its replies. For example, Philippe Ombredanne is first replying to the mail of Thomas Watson, so in this case Philippe Ombredanne is the sender and Thomas Watson is the receiver of the mail. To derive *Cc:* receivers we consider the person answering a mail as an intended receiver of this mail. In case this person is already the *To:* receiver (as it applies with the mails number 3–5 between Bob Foster and Pascal Rapicault) no additional path is derived, because we assume that a mail is not sent to a person twice.

For importing the data from the mailing lists archives we extended the iQuest tool. iQuest is part of TeCFlow,[1] a set of tools to visualize the temporal evolution of communication patterns among groups of people. It contains a component to parse mailing lists and import them into a MySQL database. Our extension aims at including the *follow-up* information of mails to fully reconstruct the structure of a mail-thread. The sample thread shown above consists of 15 mails that result in 25 communication paths.

13.3.1.2 Deriving Communication Paths from Bug Reports

The second source outlined for modeling communication paths is a bug tracking repository, such as, Bugzilla. Bugzilla users create reports and comments and give

---

[1] http://www.ickn.org/ickndemo/

answers to former editors or commentators. Within a Bugzilla bug report, a person can play different roles: (1) the reporter that opens and describes a problem; (2) the assigned developer who takes over the ownership or current responsibility; (3) a developer on the *Cc:* list who wants to be kept informed; or (4) a person that comments on the report.

Similar to mailing lists, communication in bug reports consists of a sender, at least one receiver, a time stamp, the subject, and the content of the message. For the reconstruction of communication paths we consider two actions: creating a bug report and writing a comment. The communication emerging from report creation is the assignment of the task to the assignee by the reporter and the notification of the persons registered as *Cc:* The subject of the communication is the short description and the content is the long description of the bug report.

Comments result in further communication. Each commentator addresses their comment to the reporter, the assignee, and all former commentators. This approach differs to the one of Howison et al. [11] where only a communication to the immediate previous poster was assumed. The subject of communication is denoted by the short description and the content by the comment. Regarding communication with *Cc:* addressees, we assume that if somebody is concerned he or she will get involved as a commentator.

We use the Bugzilla importer of Evolizer [8] to obtain the bug report data from Bugzilla repositories. Given the URL of the Bugzilla repository the importer downloads the bug reports in XML format, parses them and stores the results into the Evolizer database. We next query each bug report from the database and reconstruct the communication paths as illustrated before. Regarding our example we reconstructed 36 communication paths, including three *Cc:*'s. In general, we expect more communication paths in bug reports than in mailing lists archives.

13.3.2 Collaboration in OSS Projects

To model the collaboration in a project, we need to know who is or was working on which component of the system. Versioning repositories, such as CVS, provide details about code revisions that enable to derive this information. The minimal information required is the author of the modification and the affected file. For each revision the time stamp of the CVS commit, the corresponding commit message and the extent of the file modification (number of lines added and deleted) are extracted from the CVS log. We use the Evolizer CVS importer plug-in to obtain the CVS log information from online repositories. The importer parses the CVS log of each source file and stores the extracted information into the Evolizer database.

In addition to the collaboration of developers on source files, we are interested in the ownership of source files. This enables the analysis of the interaction between the developer and the owner of a file, and, in particular, how the communication between the two proceeds. Girba et al. propose a measurement for the notion of code ownership by evaluating the CVS log [10]. They define the owner of a source file as being the developer that contributed the most code lines to it. For each source files revision and author the difference between the number of lines added and number of lines deleted is computed. The sum of these deltas presents the contribution of a developer.

We extend the approach by Girba et al. by also taking into account the initial files size that refers to the initial contribution of the first developer. Experiments with CVS information from the Eclipse project showed that, when taking into account the initial number of lines of code, the number of owner changes is reduced by around 88%. With this we can more realistically reflect code ownership relationships.

13.3.3 Integrating Communication and Collaboration Data

The *person* is the central entity in communication and collaboration data as obtained from mailing lists, Bugzilla and CVS data. Therefore, we use the person to link the three data sources to obtain a consistent view on the communication and collaboration in software projects. The underlying data sources, however, have different approaches regarding the identification and characterization of a person. The personal information appearing within CVS logs, bug reports, or emails are the name of the person, the email address and the CVS user name. The objective of the integrated data model is to unify this person information so that each person is represented by exactly one entity in the model. Figure 13.2 depicts the meta-model to represent the integrated CVS, Bugzilla, and mailing list data.

The person entity is in the center of the model and links CVS with Bugzilla and mailing list data. The possible roles of a person are highlighted by arc labels which are author of source code contributions, owner of source files, reporter of a bug, assignee, and person on the *Cc:* list, and commenter of a bug report, and sender, receiver of an email. Furthermore, we establish a link between Issues and affected source file revisions.

In the virtual world of the Internet it is easy to create different identifiers for a single person. For CVS, Bugzilla, and mailing lists archive data this concerns the use of different email addresses. For example, *Chris McGee* uses *cbmcgee@ca.ibm.com*, *jeffl@informaldata.com* and *sirnewton_01@yahoo.ca* as his email addresses. The mapping of these addresses to a single person is a non-trivial task.

We follow a semi-automatic approach: For each person entity extracted from an email, CVS log, or bug report, the matching algorithm first looks up the email address in the database. If a person with the same email address exists, the person is assigned to the corresponding revision, issue, comment, or email. If not, the email address is analyzed to extract the person's name. Our algorithm assumes that a name consists of at least two words and that they are separated by a dot or underscore within an email address prefix. In some cases such a name cannot be derived from the prefix, because, for example, it denotes an email distributor address, an alias, or a nickname. In case the name could be extracted, the algorithm searches the corresponding person in the object model. For this our algorithm uses the Levenshtein string similarity measure [13]. If a person object with a similar name is found in the object model, the new email address is added to the list of email addresses of this

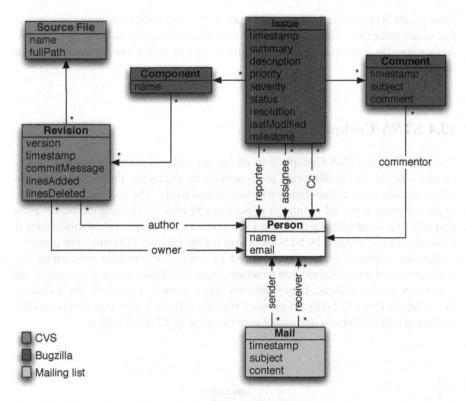

Fig. 13.2 Integrated model for representing communication and collaboration data in OSS projects

person. In every other case the person is assumed to be unknown and a new person entity is added to the database.

While this algorithm works fine for person information obtained from Bugzilla and mailing lists, there are problems with matching persons obtained from CVS log data. Typically, the author stored in CVS logs indicates the CVS user name, but not the real name of a person. Because of the high number of false matches, the mapping of these persons is done manually.

In addition to the information of a person, email addresses contain domain information that, for example, denotes the business unit of a developer. We use this information to assign developers to teams. We obtain email addresses that have been generated with *MHonArc*.[2] The problem is that MHonArc provides a spam mode which deters spam address harvesters by hiding the domain information of email addresses. For example, the email address of *Chris McGee* is displayed as

---

[2] http://www.mhonarc.org/

cbmcgee@xxxxxxxxx. In such cases our matching algorithm searches the alternative email addresses of a person to reconstruct the missing domain information. We furthermore do a manual inspection of the results to assure the correctness of the matching's.

13.4 STNA-Cockpit

The objective of STNA-Cockpit is to enable an understandable perception of the project's set-up and to illustrate its dynamics by exploring the evolution of the communication and collaboration structure interactively. The user can either investigate a particular period in time or move through time by shifting the observation period forward and backward. Figure 13.3 shows a sample view of a socio-technical network graph as created by STNA-Cockpit for the Eclipse Platform Core project.

Various graphical features are utilized to convey information concerning the communication and collaboration structure. Basically, nodes in the graph represent persons or work packages. Edges illustrate the communication between people or the collaborations of developers on work packages. In the following, we present the various graphical features and visual patterns used by STNA-Cockpit.

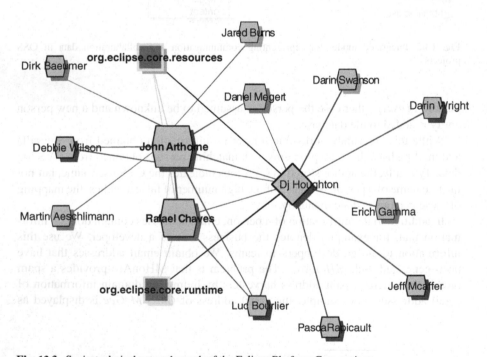

Fig. 13.3 Socio-technical network graph of the Eclipse Platform Core project

13.4.1 Actors

An actor can play different roles within the project: project member, source file owner, new source file owner. A project member is illustrated by a gray actor node and labeled with the person's name. The color of the shadow of a node illustrates the domain (i.e., business unit) to which the actor belongs. The default shape is a hexagon and the border color is always black (see Fig. 13.4a). The size of an actor node is proportional to the number of incoming and outgoing communication paths. The bigger the node is the more this actor has communicated with other team members. The owner of a source file is illustrated by shaping the node as diamond (see Fig. 13.4b).

A node label with a frame indicates that the developer took over the ownership of a source file in the corresponding work package. The change of the ownership comes along with an alien commit that is represented by drawing the actor name in bold face (see Fig. 13.4c).

| (a) Project member | (b) Owner | (c) Owner change |

Fig. 13.4 Shapes and graphical features to represent actors in the STNA-Cockpit graph

13.4.2 Work Packages

A work package is illustrated by a gray rectangle. The default color of the border is light gray and the default color of the shadow is also light gray (see Fig. 13.5a). The border color indicates the number of bug reports that have been associated with committed revisions (i.e., the number of commits that contained a bug report number in the commit message). The color gradient is from light to dark gray. The darker the color the fewer commits referenced bug reports (see Fig. 13.5b). In addition, the shadow of a node indicates the total number of problems reported for the work package. The color gradient ranges also from light to dark gray, whereas dark gray indicates a work package that has been affected by many problems. Similar to actor

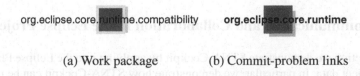

| (a) Work package | (b) Commit-problem links |

Fig. 13.5 Shapes and graphical features to represent work packages in the STNA-Cockpit graph

nodes, changes in the ownership of source files are indicated by drawing the label of the affected work package in bold face.

13.4.3 Communication and Collaboration

Ties (i.e., edges) in the graph either represent an interaction that occurs or is valid within the selected observation period. Possible interactions are: sending an email to a mailing list, opening a bug report, commenting on a bug report, committing source code changes to the versioning repository, and owning source code.

The communication between actors is colored gray. The width of an edge indicates the amount of communication between the associated actors (see Fig. 13.6a). A commit of source code changes to the versioning repository is indicated by a gray edge between the developer and the work package the modified source file belongs to (see Fig. 13.6b). Also for these edges, the width indicates the number of commits. In case of an alien commit, the font of the two node labels denoting the developer and affected work package are changed to bold face as described above. The ownership of source files contained by work packages is represented by a black edge between owners and work packages.

(a) Email and bug communication   (b) Developer contribution

Fig. 13.6 Shapes and graphical features to represent communication and collaboration in the STNA-Cockpit graph

Applying these patterns to the network graph of Fig. 13.3 we can see that most of the communication has been between John Arthorne, Dj Houghton, and Rafael Chaves. The represented communication was on bug reports solely. During the selected observation period these three authors committed changes to source files contained by the two packages *org.eclipse.core.resources* and *org.eclipse.core.runtime*. Dj Houghton owns source files in these packages while John Arthorne and Rafael Chaves performed alien commits.

13.5 Communication and Collaboration in the Eclipse Project

In this section we demonstrate STNA-Cockpit by applying it to the Eclipse Platform Core project data. In particular, we demonstrate how STNA-Cockpit can be used to answer the following questions:

- Who owns or is working on which source code package?
- Who are the key personalities in the Eclipse Platform Core project?
- Can we identify shortcomings in the communication and collaboration structure in the project, meaning alien commits?

We use the Eclipse Platform Core project as an example to illustrate the benefits of our integrated data model and the STNA-Cockpit approach. Analysis results are interpreted in the context of this project and should not be generalized. The following section briefly outlines the Eclipse Platform Core project and the data sources we used in the case study.

13.5.1 The Eclipse Platform Core Project

Eclipse.org is an open source community whose projects are focused on building an integrated and extensible development platform. The Eclipse Project is the top-level project dedicated to providing a robust, full-featured, commercial-quality, and freely available platform for the development of integrated tools. In this case study, we focus on the Eclipse Platform Core component that is a main component of the Eclipse Platform project. In January 2007, the Eclipse Platform project comprised 18 mailing lists, 34 different classified Bugzilla components and more than 350 plug-ins. To know which part of the source code is affected by a discussion within an email or bug report the different data sources had to be mapped. Table 13.1 shows the set of the plug-ins, mailing lists, and Bugzilla components that concern Eclipse Platform Core. The mapping was obtained from the Eclipse Platform Core project website.[3]

In total the source code of Eclipse Platform Core component consists of 17 plug-ins. Communication between the developers of the component takes place in the mailing list *platform-core-dev*. In Bugzilla, two components were used to report problems and enter change requests for the Eclipse Platform Core project. In a first

Table 13.1 Plug-in sources, mailing list, and Bugzilla components of the Eclipse Platform Core project

Name	Plug-ins	Mailing list	Bugzilla
Platform.Core	org.eclipse.core.contenttype	platform-core-dev	Platform.Runtime
	org.eclipse.core.expressions		Platform.Resources
	org.eclipse.core.filesystem.*		
	org.eclipse.core.jobs		
	org.eclipse.core.resources.*		
	org.eclipse.core.runtime.*		
	org.eclipse.core.variables		

---

[3] http://www.eclipse.org/eclipse/platform-core/

step, we retrieved the CVS, Bugzilla, and mailing list data of mentioned data sources up to November 2006. From CVS we retrieved 7,479 change log entries from 997 source files. 7,907 bug reports have been imported from Bugzilla and 102 emails were retrieved from the *platform-core-dev* mailing list.

After importing the data, the Evolizer database contained 2,581 persons, 101 email and 11,081 Bugzilla communication paths. 2,536 person entities were imported from the Bugzilla data, 132 are mailing list users of which 73 have been matched to Bugzilla users. Contributions to the source code were from 27 developers. All of them have been mapped to Bugzilla users. Because we were mainly interested in the communication and collaboration of Eclipse developers, we concentrated our analysis on the 27 developers. While all these developers participated in Bugzilla reporting; only 14 of them wrote emails to the mailing list.

In the following we show a number of applications of STNA-Cockpit and the benefits of our integrated data model and visualization approach.

13.5.2 Ownership and Alien Commits

Assume a scenario in which a project manager wants to find out that owns or is working on which plug-in of the Eclipse Platform Core project, and whether there have been violations in the developer contribution structure. For this, the project manager selects the observation period and has STNA-Cockpit draw the collaboration graph that represents only the CVS information. We did this for the Eclipse Platform Core project for the time period from 14th to 28th February 2005 and obtained the collaboration graph depicted in Fig. 13.7.

The black edges in the graph denote the ownership of source files at that time. For example, the graph shows that Jeff Mcaffer, Pascal Rapicault, and Dj Houghton are the owners of source files of the *org.eclipse.core.runtime.compatibility* plug-in. In general, the graph shows several owners of source files per plug-in. Most interesting, however, is that John Arthorne contributed to this plug-ins, though; he is not an owner of source files of any of this plug-ins. All his contributions were so called alien commits that are indicated by the bold labels of the nodes representing John Arthorne and the modified plug-ins. The dark gray border of work packages further indicates that almost zero of the commits reference a Bugzilla bug report. Moreover, the shadows of two rectangles are painted in dark gray indicating that the two corresponding plug-ins were affected by a high number of problems. In summary, such a view provides the project manager with an overview about the commit and bug reporting activities within the selected observation period. Alien commits might indicate shortcomings in the code or team organization, depending on whether or not strict code ownership has been followed in a project.

13.5.3 Communicators

STNA-Cockpit can aid project managers in identifying the key personalities in her project. The *communicator* is such a key personality who knows where the

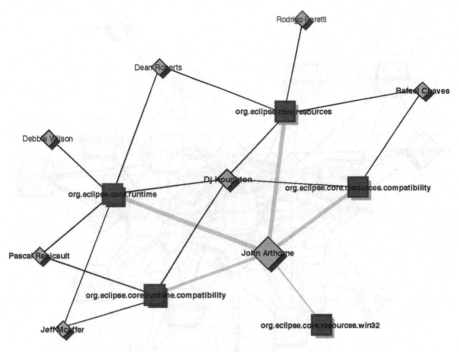

Fig. 13.7 Collaboration in the Eclipse Platform Core project observed in the time from 14th to 28th February 2005

information ideally gets processed. Figure 13.8 illustrates the communication via the developer mailing list and Bugzilla data over 21 months. The amount of communication (i.e., the number of communication paths reconstructed from bug reports and emails) is illustrated by the width of edges. The wider the edges of a person's node are, the more this person communicated with other developers.

The graph in Fig. 13.8 shows the core development team whose members frequently communicate with each other. Rafael Chaves, Dj Houghton, Jeff Mcaffer Thomas Watson, John Arthorne, and Pascal Rapicault form the core team. They are the communicators who keep the network together and play an important role within the project. Interesting is that they all belong to either the group *@ca.ibm.com* or *@us.ibm.com* as indicated by the shadows of rectangles representing these developers. Another highly connected group is formed by the Swiss team (*@ch.ibm.ch*) whose members are represented by the nodes on the right side of the graph. Almost each developer of the Swiss team is in touch with the US team; however, Markus Keller and Daniel Megert turn out as the main communicators between the two teams during that time.

Another interesting finding concerns the environment via which the developers communicated. Most of the communication was via Bugzilla bug reports indicated by the gray edges. Only the core team also used the mailing list to discuss Eclipse

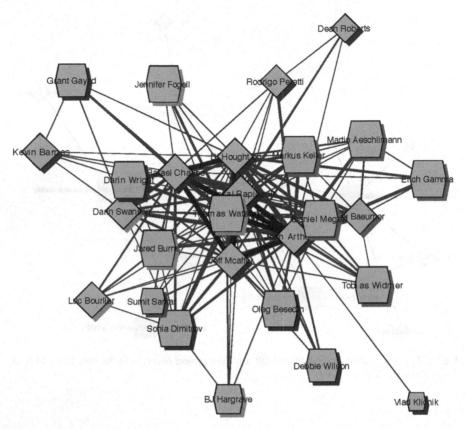

Fig. 13.8 Communicators of the Eclipse Platform Core project as from May 2004 to February 2006

Platform Core relevant issues. Such findings are of particular interest when new ways of communication are considered.

13.5.4 Project Dynamics

Newcomers should be integrated fast into development teams to rapidly increase productivity and foster synergy among team members. With STNA-Cockpit the project manager can observe how newcomers actually are integrated into their teams. For this, the project manager selects the starting observation period and uses the time-navigation facility of STNA-Cockpit to investigate the evolution of the communication and collaboration network over time. The graph animation allows the project manager to observe how the newcomer behaves concerning communication and collaboration with other team members. In particular, she looks for communication paths that tell her the newcomer gets actively involved

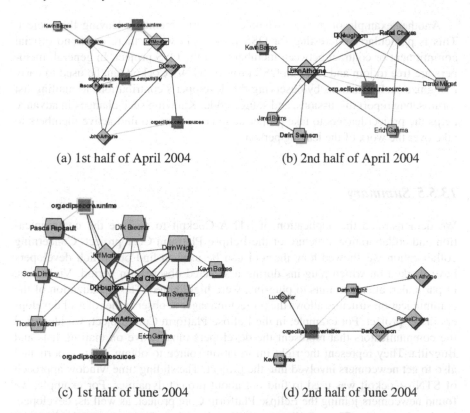

(a) 1st half of April 2004   (b) 2nd half of April 2004

(c) 1st half of June 2004   (d) 2nd half of June 2004

Fig. 13.9 Socialization of Kevin Barness in the Eclipse Platform Core project

in discussions on the developers mailing lists and bug reports. In addition, she observes whether the newcomer contributes to the plug-ins and finally takes over responsibility of portions of the source code.

Consider the following scenario in which Kevin Barness is entering the US team *@ca.ibm.com* of the Eclipse Platform Core project in April 2004. Figure 13.9 depicts various snapshots taken from the network created for subsequent points in time. Kevin Barness is starting as a developer in the Eclipse Platform Core team at the beginning of April 2004. His first action is to get in touch with some key person-alities of the project, namely Rafael Chaves and John Arthorne. His first contacts are visualized by the graphs depicted by (Fig. 13.9a, b). In the following weeks he com-municates also with other project members to get more involved into the project (see Fig. 13.9c), namely Darin Wright and Darin Swanson. As (Fig. 13.9d) illustrates, Darin Wright is a developer and Darin Swanson the owner of the files that are going to be modified by Kevin. Rafael Chaves seems to play the role of the connector who introduces the new developer Kevin Barness to the responsible persons. According to the graph, he is communicating with two senior developers.

Another example of project dynamics concerns members leaving the project. This is particularly interesting for OSS projects in which there exists no official commitment or contract between members and the OSS project. In general, members are free to join and leave an OSS project. STNA-Cockpit can be used to early recognize such situations by observing the developer's contributions to mailing list forums, bug report discussions, and source code. Knowing such changes in advance helps the project leaders to take proper actions, such as, to find active members to take over the work of the leaving person.

13.5.5 Summary

We demonstrated the application of STNA-Cockpit to analyze the communication and collaboration structure of the Eclipse Platform Core project. Concerning collaboration we showed how the tool can be used to find out which developers have worked on which plug-ins during a selected observation period. Violations, in particular, alien commits to plug-ins, were highlighted. The visualization of the communication structure allows the project manager to observe the roles of developers in her project. For example, in the Eclipse Platform Core project, we identified the communicators that represent the developers most active on mailing lists and Bugzilla. They represent the right information source to obtain status reports and also to get newcomers involved into the project. The sliding time window approach of STNA-Cockpit was used to find out about project dynamics. For example, we found newcomers joining the Eclipse Platform Core project, as well as, developers leaving the project. These findings underline the value of our integrated communication and collaboration data model and visualization techniques as implemented by STNA-Cockpit.

13.6 Conclusions and Future Work

Software repositories, such as versioning, bug reporting, and developer mailing lists contain valuable data for analyzing the communication and collaboration structure of software projects. We presented a meta-model to represent communication and collaboration in OSS project and showed how an instance of such a model can be obtained from CVS, Bugzilla, and mailing list data. We also introduced our STNA-Cockpit tool to interactively explore the integrated model by means of graph visualizations. With this tool the user can observe project dynamics in a software project at any point in time and over time using the data provided by Evolizer.

Getting awareness of communication and collaboration in a project can be very valuable for the project manager: (1) understanding how newcomers can be integrated fast and efficient; (2) knowing the key contributors and communicators in the different teams; and (3) being able to replace or add expertise holders in project phases and in software parts. Of course all this requires the data to be available in a processable form but the key issue for that is the identity management. As long as email and Bugzilla identities can be matched to people such an analysis can work mostly automated. Such mapping data for identities should be easy to keep up-to-date and then can be fed into tools, such as, STNA-Cockpit that then can compute the communication and collaboration network of a project automatically. The time-window browsing further allows one to zoom into particular phases of the project and learn about collaboration patterns of developers.

Still, there are limitations of the current approach that are due two facts. First, in many OSS projects such identity mapping data does not exist and has to be reconstructed with quite some manual effort. Second, the analysis of collaboration patterns is not yet reflected on software releases, features or software phases, such as, testing or refactoring. But from our analysis we have seen a great potential of investigating communication and collaboration data for project steering ranging from the role of a developer to the role of a project manager.

References

1. Aberdour M (2007) Achieving quality in open source software. IEEE Software 24: 58–64.
2. Batagelj V, Mrvar A (2003) Pajek – Analysis and visualization of large networks. Graph Drawing Software, Springer, pp. 77–103.
3. Bird C, Gourley A, Devanbu P, Swaminathan A, Hsu G (2007) Open borders? Immigration in open source projects. Proceedings of the International Workshop on Mining Software Repositories, IEEE Computer Society Press.
4. Borgatti SP, Everett MG, Freeman LC (2002) Ucinet for Windows: Software for Social Network Analysis. Harvard, MA: Analytic Technologie.
5. Crowston K, Wei K, Li Q, Eseryel UY, Howison J (2005) Co-ordination of free/libre open source software development. Proceedings of the International Conference on Information Systems, Association for Information Systems, pp. 181–193.
6. Ducheneaut N (2005) Socialization in an open source software community: A Socio-technical analysis. Computer Supported Cooperative Work 14: 323–368.
7. Fogel K (2005) Producing Open Source Software: How to Run a Successful Free Software Project. Sebastopol, CA: O'Reilly Media.
8. Gall HC, Fluri B, Pinzger M (2009) Change analysis with evolizer and change distiller. IEEE Software 26: 26–33.
9. Ghosh RA (2003) Clustering and dependencies in free/open source software development: Methodology and tools. First Monday 8(4).
10. Girba T, Kuhn A, Seeberger M, Ducasse S (2005) How developers drive software evolution. Proceedings of the International Workshop on Principles of Software Evolution, IEEE Computer Society Press, pp. 113–122.
11. Howison J, Inoue K, Crowston K (2006) Social dynamics of free and open source team communication. Proceedings of the International Conference on Open Source Software, Boston, Springer, pp. 319–330.
12. Huang SK, Min Liu K (2005) Mining version histories to verify the learning process of legitimate peripheral participants. Proceedings of the International Workshop on Mining Software Repositories, ACM Press.
13. Levenshtein VI (1966) Binary codes capable of correcting deletions, insertions and reversals. Soviet Physics Doklady 10: 701–710.
14. Lopez-Fernandez L, Robles G, Gonzalez-Barahona JM (2004) Applying social network analysis to the information in cvs repositories. Proceedings of the International Workshop on Mining Software Repositories.

15. Malone TW, Crowston K (1994) The interdisciplinary study of co-ordination. ACM Computing Surveys 26: 87–119.
16. Ogawa M, Ma KL, Bird C, Devanbu P, Gourley A (2007) Visualizing social interaction in open source software projects. Proceedings of the International Asia-Pacific Symposium on Visualization, IEEE Computer Society Press, pp. 25–32.
17. Ohira M, Ohsugi N, Ohoka T, Matsumoto K (2005) Accelerating cross project knowledge collaboration using collaborative filtering and social networks. Proceedings of the International Workshop on Mining Software Repositories, ACM Press.
18. Sack W (2001) Conversation map: An interface for very large-scale conversations. Journal of Management Information Systems 17: 73–92.
19. Sack W, Detienne F, Ducheneaut N, Burkhardt JM, Mahendran D, Barcellini F (2006) A methodological framework for socio-cognitive analysis of collaborative design of open source software. Computer Supported Co-operative Work 15: 229–250.
20. Scacchi W (2007) Free/open source software development. Proceedings of the Joint Meeting of the European Software Engineering Conference and the Symposium on the Foundations of Software Engineering, ACM Press, pp. 459–468.
21. Xu J, Gao Y, Christley S, Madey G (2005) A topological analysis of the open source software development community. Proceedings of the Proceedings of the Annual Hawaii International Conference on System Sciences, IEEE Computer Society Press.

Chapter 14
A Comparison of Commonly Used Processes for Multi-Site Software Development

Alberto Avritzer and Daniel J. Paulish

Abstract This chapter describes some commonly used multi-site software development processes and compares them with respect to the amount of coordination that they support across locations. Specifically, two common processes, called the "Extended Workbench Model" and "System of Systems Model" will be compared based on our experience. The processes have each been experimentally applied over several years to a global development project, called the "Global Studio Project" (GSP) in which university students around the world have simulated the processes used for an industrial multi-site development project. Lessons learned will be discussed and guidance given for multi-site development projects based on our experience from experimental and real projects.

14.1 Motivation

For the past few years, Siemens has been experimenting with software development processes and practices for globally distributed projects using student-based development teams located at different universities around the world. The students who make up the Global Studio Project (GSP) simulate an industrial software development project using common practices for collaboration among distributed sites. Experiences with this project have been reported in a number of papers [2] and it has been documented as a case study (GSP 2005) within [21].

The motivation for studying multi-site software development processes is driven by the business needs. A number of questions were raised, and they are still being investigated.

A. Avritzer (✉)
Siemens Corporate Research, Inc., Princeton, NJ 08540, USA
e-mail: alberto.avritzer@siemens.com

I. Mistrík et al. (eds.), *Collaborative Software Engineering*,
DOI 10.1007/978-3-642-10294-3_14, © Springer-Verlag Berlin Heidelberg 2010

- What can we do better to get products faster to the global market?
- Which software engineering technologies & processes can we apply? e.g., Requirements Engineering, Requirements Patterns, Domain Modeling, Business Object Modeling, Model Analysis Tools, Product Line Engineering, Software Architecture.
- What software management techniques can we apply? e.g., Global Development, Agile Team Processes, Rapid Application Development.
- How do we integrate products acquired from multiple divisions distributed around the world with local market requirements?
- How can we best utilize the globally distributed workforce by exploiting diversity, local creativity, and domain expertise?
- How can we reduce overall development costs by exploiting local labor rates?

Communication and cultural differences have been reported as the most common non-technical barriers that are usually encountered in global software development projects [6, 11]. The selection of a global software development process methodology for the development and testing of a software project introduces new challenges to project management. Project managers of global software development projects must address issues related to several time zones, large geographical distances, conflicts generated by lack of cultural sensitivity among team members, lack of frequent communications, and the resulting lack of trust among members of remote teams [8, 15].

In [7], Damian et al. raise the issue of the more formal nature of the communications among remote team members, as contrasted to the more informal nature of communications within a collocated team. It's more likely that strong personal relationships will form within a collocated team leading to more opportunities for communication among team members for the informal exchange of information related to the project. Therefore, collocated projects benefit from the informal exchange of information, while globally distributed software development projects are more likely to encounter communications challenges.

In [20], Sa and Maslova introduced a unified framework that was designed to enable physically separated teams engaged in a global software development project to define their own software development processes using several notations. The objective of the proposed framework is to create a unique process representation for the project to facilitate communication and synchronization among the teams.

In [3], Braun described a set of categories that were used to categorize projects that are likely to perform well in a global software development environment. The proposed classification was used to suggest an off-shoring process to enable a physically separated workforce to work seamlessly in an industrial environment. The proposed process for global work attempts to integrate physically separated teams by taking advantage of locally available skills, individual team structures, and team communication.

In [4], Carmel and Agarwal discuss the impact of geographical distances on coordination and control of global software development projects. In [13], and [14], Herbsleb et al. recommend that remote software development teams have frequent face-to-face meetings to increase the levels of communications. Furthermore, it was recommended that team members should be able to identify and contact the correct person to address questions and issues. In [15], Layman reports that several global software development challenges could be overcome by increased informal communication among the remote team members.

For many years, software project organizations have often been structured in accordance with the system architecture design of the product being developed [1, 2]. For globally distributed software development projects, coordination and communication among the development teams are more complex than for collocated projects due to time, distance, and cultural differences. For multi-site software development projects, it is especially important to minimize the need for communication between teams that are not collocated and to maximize the communication within a local team. In general, more loosely coupled architectures with well defined interfaces for which components are distributed across development sites are more amenable to reduce communications between the remote teams.

In [23], Setamanit et al. present a discrete-event simulation model that is designed to help project managers assess global software distributed processes. The discrete-event simulation model was applied to a simple example project to model several project phases. The paper evaluates the impact of several global software development dimensions on project performance, defined as effort, duration, and latent defects.

In [5], Cusumano et al. present an analysis of global software development practices that was based on a survey of 104 projects. Most of the projects were custom or semi-custom software development projects with medium reliability requirements to be deployed at business workstations. It was observed that conventional water-fall software development processes were very popular in India, Japan and Europe, while the use of formal specifications was less common in the US.

In [9], Ebert and De Neve provide detailed recommendations for successful global software development projects that are based on the authors' analysis of Alcatel's switching and routing division's global software development experiences. They recommend splitting the work according to feature content and building collocated teams to work on specific features. This approach is called *coherent and collocated teams of fully allocated engineers;* i.e., engineers that are not distracted by other tasks. They recommend that all development locations working on a specific product line shall use the same processes, methodologies, and terminology. They conclude that managing global software development is not easy and entails several risks to the projects involved. However, they observed as an important benefit of global software development projects the increased level of innovation that is created by engineers with very different cultural backgrounds.

In [16] Nguyen et al. present an empirical study aimed at showing that the introduction of new collaborative environments has greatly diminished the impact of physical distribution on task delay and task resolution times. Wikis and social networking sites provide the ability to asynchronously track and comment on work items by teams that are physically separated.

In [12] Herbsleb and Moitra outlined several of the impacts that physical separation can have on global software development projects: strategic issues related to work assignment to different sites, cultural issues related to the close interaction of team members from several backgrounds, inadequate communication related to physical separation of team members, knowledge management of project assets, and process issues. Specifically, the authors have identified the criticality of synchronizing process steps among physically separated teams and have pointed out that concurrent software development in global projects is extremely difficult because of requirements volatility and the lack of informal communications. In the "system of systems" process introduced in this chapter, we describe our experience with concurrent development in a global software development project and the use of domain experts that are physically separated to overcome the difficulties introduced by requirements volatility and the lack of informal communications among the physically separated teams.

14.2 Comparison of Different Business Processes for Global Software Development

In [18] Prikladnicki et al. report on an empirical case study of distributed software development processes in five large industrial companies. Data for the case study was obtained by interviews of managers and technical leaders in these companies and document reviews. The companies reported on three main types of software processes used for global software development projects:

1. Lightweight processes defined by eliminating some steps from standard processes.
2. Standard well documented processes.
3. Heavyweight processes defined by adding additional requirements to the standard processes.

The authors report on several dimensions for analysis of the distributed software development processes used by these five companies. The authors proceed to simplify the control dimensions into build or buy, and the geographic dimensions into onshore and offshore. The companies reported several challenges in applying these distributed software development processes. In the following, we describe the most common challenges encountered in this case study, for the four combinations of distributed software development processes:

- *Onshore-Buy process* – The definition of a common software development process, including coding standards, configuration management and knowledge management between the central site and the vendor companies was a very difficult challenge for these companies.
- *Onshore-Build process* – The outsourcing of work to a supplier within close geographical distance that worked for the same company created informality in change requests that impacted the software quality and tracking of defects. This

company identified as a difficulty the definition of a formal software development process.

- *Offshore-Buy process* – The main problem identified by this company was the lack of a common software development process between the central site and the vendor. For example, in the requirements engineering phase a common process for requirements elicitation was not in place. Problems were identified in the requirements engineering phase that were later diagnosed as related to miscommunication or lack of requirements documentation.

- *Offshore-Build process* – The difficulties found by this company were related to cultural and language differences and the lack of trust between the central site and the remote sites as the remote sites were asked to integrate into the architecture, coding standards, and processes defined by the central site.

14.3 Example Processes

Processes for multi-site software development are optimized for the communications patterns among the software engineers working at different physical locations. Team members working at multiple locations often must overcome communications and intercultural barriers caused by time zones and distance as compared to engineers working in a collocated project. Multi-site development projects are often larger than collocated projects; thus, processes used at one site will often have difficulty scaling up for large distributed teams. Furthermore, development processes are usually not easily portable due to differing working habits, conditions, and culture such that what works well in Boston may not work so well in Bangalore.

Processes for multi-site software development are often based on an approach where requirements and designs are decomposed such that components can be developed by a collection of small teams working at different locations. Thus, the system architecture is a key factor for the success of the multi-site development project. For such projects, loosely coupled architectures are more amenable for splitting up the development work to be done across the multiple sites. Sub-processes for requirements engineering, design, testing, quality assurance, and project management must be modified for multi-site work. For example, the use of requirements models described in UML are often better than text-based specifications for multi-site projects, since the software engineers at some of the sites may not have adequate reading comprehension skills for specifications that are not written in their native language.

Software project managers can use many processes and organizational structures for developing software products across multiple development sites. Some of the project approaches that could be considered include organizing by: *product structure, process steps, release, competence center,* and *open source.* In a *product structure* organizational approach, the requirements engineers and architects allocate features to components and the components are allocated as work packages to the different sites. In a *process steps* structure, work is allocated across the sites in accordance with the phases of the software development process; e.g., requirements engineering may be done at one site, development at another site(s), and testing at yet another site. In a *release* based organization approach, the first product release is developed at one site, the second at another site, etc. Often, the releases will be overlapped to meet time-to-market goals; e.g., one site is testing the next release, another site is developing a later release, and yet another site is defining the requirements for an even later release. In a *platform* structure, one site may be developing reusable core assets of the product line and other sites may be developing application-level software that uses the platform. In a *competence center* organizational approach, project work is allocated to sites depending on the technical or domain expertise located at that site. For example, perhaps all user interface design is done at a site where usability engineering experts are located with experience designing similar products. In an *open source* structure, many independent contributors develop the software product in accordance with a technical integration strategy. Centralized control is minimal except when an independent contributor integrates his code into the product line. These organizational approaches may change over time. For example, components may be allocated at first with the intent that the remote site will develop the skills over time to become a competence center in the functionality that component provides [8].

We will illustrate two example processes that were used on the Global Studio Project (GSP). During the first two years of the GSP, a product structure approach was used to organize the project and an "extended workbench model" development process was used [21]. This resulted in a hub and spoke organizational structure (Fig. 14.1) in which the remote component development teams communicated mostly with the central team roles (e.g., chief requirements engineer, chief architect, project manager) at the headquarters or central site.

This hub and spoke organization is typically used when a central organization is utilizing remote development sites for the first time. It often will take a year or more to be able to develop the domain expertise, RE, and development skills in the staff in the remote teams [21]. Thus, the central team transfers some of their know-how to the remote teams over time such that they are able to take on a bigger

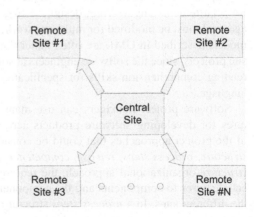

Fig. 14.1 Example extended workbench model multi-site software development organization

role in the development project. We recommend to organizations starting distributed development for the first time to take a long-term view, since there will be a substantial learning curve time necessary for the remote teams to become productive contributors to the development project.

During the third and fourth years (versions 3.0-4.0) of the Global Studio Project, a "system of systems" process was used for distributed development [2]. With this approach, the software development process is still defined and managed centrally, but the architecture and requirements engineering teams are extended with key domain experts who are resident at the remote sites. The specialized domain knowledge drives the overall requirements and software architecture specification efforts as early phase activities. Frequent communication between the central and remote teams and among the remote teams is encouraged. Unlike the extended workbench model approach, the central team is not required to co-ordinate the communications among the distributed teams.

Figure 14.2 compares the extended workbench model with the system of systems model, with respect to the technical skills and domain knowledge needed. In practice, central organizations working with a remote development site for the first time will likely apply the extended workbench model and then migrate to the system of systems model as the domain and technical expertise of the remote site team members increases. It should be noted that a continuum of processes could be used depending on the organizational, product, and project needs. The extended workbench and system of systems process models are quite different, and any specific project will require process tailoring to define its unique process.

The motivation for comparing these different processes was twofold. We learned that the extended workbench model required significant upfront work by the central team before the remote teams could be productively engaged. This upfront work by the central team consisted of early phase tasks such as requirements specifications and architecture definition, and they took several staff months to complete.

In addition, for GSP version 3.0, the central team staff size was significantly reduced as compared to GSP version 2.0. Therefore, we realized that we needed a fully distributed development process, where remote teams could hit the ground running and not have to wait for the central team requirements specification effort. We also realized that if we defined a common interface for component

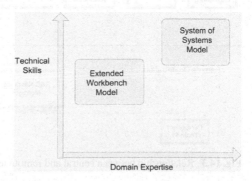

Fig. 14.2 Extended workbench vs. system of systems process models

integration, we could get the development teams started immediately with their code development activities.

Although the team size for the GSP (version 3.0-4.0) was smaller than that for (version 1.0-2.0), we strongly suspect that the system of systems model will work better for very large projects than the extended workbench model. This is because for larger projects the key roles at the central site tend to get overloaded with communications from the remote sites (see Fig. 14.1). Therefore, in a system of systems model, domain experts for each individual system are identified upfront, such that they are reachable by the local team members for addressing questions. Thus a project with more distributed expertise should be able to better scale upward.

We have suggested that the maximum size for a project using the extended workbench model is approximately 15 M lines of C++ code (LOCs) [21]. This is based on rules-of-thumb where a maximum of 150 components are defined in the system architecture and each component is less than 100 K LOCs.

14.3.1 Extended Workbench Model

Figure 14.3 gives an example organization showing the relationship between the central and remote teams for the extended workbench model. The product manager has the overall responsibility for the life cycle of product development. The chief requirements engineer and chief architect have major responsibility for technical decisions affecting the product's functionality and performance. The members of the remote component development teams report to a local R&D resource manager at their site. The remote teams report to the project manager at the central location, primarily through their assigned supplier manager, who serves as a bridge between the sites.

Figure 14.4 provides a process description for the extended workbench model.

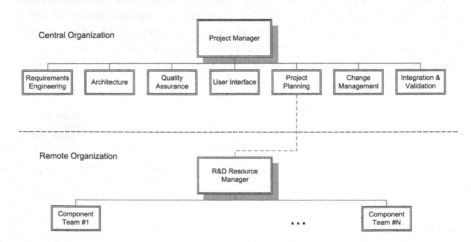

Fig. 14.3 Relationship between central and remote teams

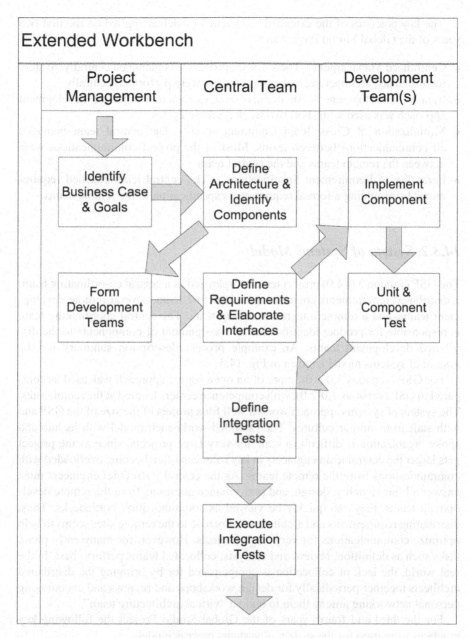

Fig. 14.4 Example extended workbench process model

The key practices of the extended workbench model as applied on the first two years of the Global Studio Project are:

- Centralized Management – The software process was managed centrally. System requirements, architecture, and system testing were performed centrally.
- Iterative Development – An iterative and incremental software development approach was used with short two week iteration cycles.
- Minimization of Cross Team Communication – The central team managed all communications between teams. Most of the project communications were between the remote teams and the central team.
- Formality of Requirement Specifications – The central team clarified requirements by providing a formal requirements specification to the remote teams.

14.3.2 System of Systems Model

The GSP (version 3.0-4.0) project team is organized as a central co-ordinating team, a distributed requirements engineering/architecture team, several remote development teams, and a remote integration testing team. The central coordinating team is responsible for product identification and assignment of components to the distributed development teams. An example process description summary for the system of systems model is given in Fig. 14.5.

For GSP (versions 3.0-4.0), more of an open source approach was used as compared to GSP (versions 1.0-2.0), with competence centers located at the remote sites. The system of systems approach worked well for a project of the size of the GSP and with staff from similar cultures. The extended workbench model with its hub and spoke organization is difficult to scale for very large projects, since as the project gets larger the central team engineers in key roles can often become overloaded with communications from the remote teams. As the central team chief engineers must answer all functionality, design, and performance questions from the remote development teams, they can quickly be viewed as communication bottlenecks. Thus, distributing requirements and architecture expertise to the remote sites seems to help optimize communications for very large projects. However, for many early phase tasks such as definition, review, and analysis, collocated teams perform best. In the real world, the lack of collocation is compensated for by bringing the distributed architects together periodically for design workshops and reviews and encouraging personal networking among them to build a "virtual architecture team".

For the third and fourth years of the Global Studio Project the following key practices were used for the system of systems process model.

- Hybrid centralized/distributed management – The software process is still developed and managed centrally. However, an architecture/requirements team composed of members of the central team and key members of the remote teams is formed. The objective is to use domain knowledge about the large existing software components to help steer the overall requirements and system

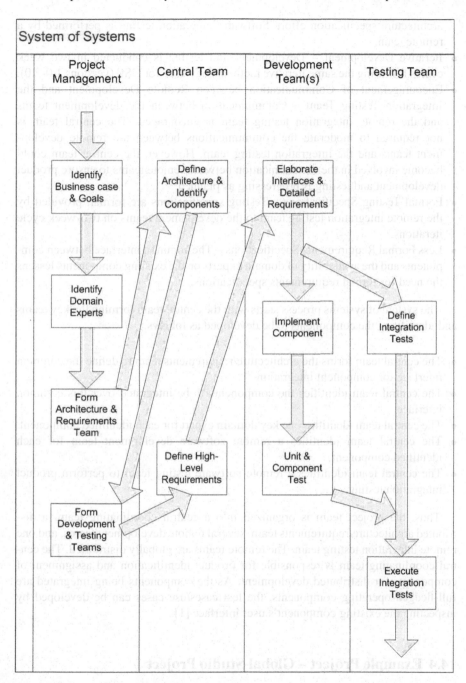

Fig. 14.5 Example system of systems process model

architecture specification effort. Software integration testing is performed by a remote team.

- Iterative Development – Development and testing is conducted in two week cycles following the same iterative methodology used for GSP (versions 1.0-2.0).
- Encouragement of Communication between Remote Development and the Integration Testing Team – Communication between the development teams and the remote integration testing team is encouraged. The central team is not required to moderate the communications between the remote development teams and the integration testing team. However, the central team could become involved in the communication between remote teams to ensure product development and testing is progressing as planned.
- Formal Testing Specifications – Testing specifications are formal, provided by the remote integration testing team to the development teams on two-week cycle iterations.
- Less Formal Requirements Specifications – The common interface between components and the availability of domain experts on the existing components lessens the need for formal requirements specifications.

The system of systems process starts with the central team forming the key teams and identifying the components to be developed as follows:

- The central team forms the architecture/requirements team to define the common interface for component integration.
- The central team identifies the components to be integrated over this common interface,
- The central team identifies one key domain expert for each identified component,
- The central team identifies a remote software development team for each identified component,
- The central team identifies a remote software testing team to perform product integration testing.

Thus, the project team is organized into a central coordinating team, a distributed architecture/requirements team, several remote development teams, and one remote integration testing team. The remote teams are globally distributed. The central coordinating team is responsible for product identification and assignment of components for distributed development. As the components being integrated are full-fledged operating components, the test cases/use cases can be developed by inspecting the existing component's user interface [1].

14.4 Example Project – Global Studio Project

In 2004, Siemens Corporate Research (SCR) initiated an experimental software engineering project called the Global Studio Project (GSP) which was set up using university student teams in 6 universities across 4 continents (see Fig. 14.6) [21].

Fig. 14.6 Global studio project

The student teams simulated an industrial distributed software development project in order to help increase the understanding of practices that could be used to successfully execute global projects and avoid some of the pitfalls of such projects. Although Siemens had much experience with globally distributed software development, both good and bad, the lessons learned working with student teams were insightful.

Development teams were set up at 6 universities with about 30 developers within 5 countries in 4 continents spread across 11 time zones. The students implemented a "light" version of a Siemens software product, and they developed and delivered 67.5 KLOCs of operational product and test code in two years.

In the first two years of the project, the students used the extended workbench model and developed a building management station. In the third and fourth year of the project, the students used the system of systems model and developed a performance engineering tools set. In addition to providing the research team with experimental project data, the students generally believed that working on a simulated industrial project was beneficial to their software engineering education [19].

The Global Studio Project created an experimental distributed software engineering project where students were used to simulate the roles described in the multi-site development processes used. Thus, there was a lack of the business risk normally associated with an industrial software development project. The advantage was that researchers could observe the best and not so good practices of the development team as they attempted to develop a product with staff spread out across multiple countries and continents. In most cases, the distributed team members didn't know each other and communicated with each other without face-to-face meetings. The communications among the team members were monitored by applying social network analysis (SNA) surveys.

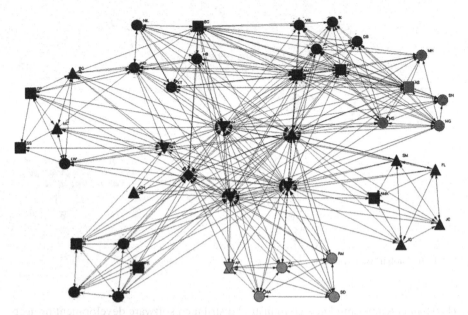

Fig. 14.7 Social network analysis

Social network analysis [22] has been useful for measuring and understanding the communications patterns among team members in the Global Studio Project. As illustrated in (Fig. 14.7), the nodes represent team members and the lines represent the communications between them. Note that the three teams at the bottom of (Fig. 14.7) communicate only among their own team members and with the central team, while the top four teams communicate with each other. For this project, the top four teams were collaborating on a subsystem development and they were at two locations within the same time zone. The bottom three teams were working on components that were loosely coupled from each other. Misalignment between the SNA diagram and the system architecture module diagram may indicate that project problems may be developing; for example, the system architecture is changing or inefficient or costly communications are negatively impacting productivity.

14.5 Lessons Learned

Some of the lessons learned during the Global Studio Project are summarized below.

Communications: Distributed projects typically have more complex communication and coordination problems than collocated projects, since much informal communication is lost (e.g., water cooler talk) due to distance and time zones. The GSP compensated for this lack of informal communications using collaboration tools such as wikis and videoconferencing and with more formal specifications, but what was surprising to the researchers observing the project was the very large amount of communications necessary to execute the project. Software development is still largely a social activity, and the social network analysis surveys done during the GSP showed high degrees of communication interaction across the team members.

Team Size: Agile development processes were encouraged for the GSP, but today's methods work best for smaller teams. Thus, the GSP became a collection of small teams. During the course of development iteration, a 4-person student team at one university usually learned to work well together, but they also needed to interface with other teams made up of students whom they never met. Keeping the individual team sizes small was achieved with the architecture design where smaller components were allocated as work packages to remote teams with standard interfaces that were centrally defined.

Cultural Differences: The students in different countries had different working habits. Some of these were imposed by the university (e.g., part-time or full-time, holidays, vacations), but some habits appeared to be culturally driven. Basic characteristics such as timeliness, directness, friendliness, meeting processes, attention to details were diverse enough that students were often "surprised" by the behaviors of students in remote teams. Ultimately, members of remote teams must "trust" each other to be able to confidently execute the project. We observed that the cultural differences contributed to the relatively long start-up times for new teams to become productive as well as the learning curves for the application domain and common development tools.

Project Management: The factors for success for project management are usually dependent on the teams, communication, and environment. For GSP (versions 3.0-4.0), the objective of team building activities was to build a high-performing team with a feeling of partnership. The project was initiated by having one face-to-face kickoff meeting, where the key team members were present. After three weeks, a face-to-face architecture meeting was held at the central team's site. The project manager followed-up with a face-to-face meeting with one key team member that could not be present at the kick-off meeting. In addition, the leader of Integration Testing was resident at the central site for one month. The project used a shared document and code repository, and had weekly telecoms to address issues. All project members were invited to attend the weekly telecoms, and most telecoms were well attended. We believe the high level of commitment observed throughout the project was due to the strong personal relationships that were created by the team building activities. We observed an evolution of the communication patterns among team members, depending on the actual phase the project. Initially, most of the communication was among co-located team members and among the members visiting the central team. We concluded that the reason for this pattern of communication was the lack of knowledge of the work and expertise located in the remote teams. As the project gathered momentum we saw a shift in the pattern of communications from site-based to task-based communications depending on need. Finally, as the project reached the critical milestone for delivery we saw even greater communications based on need and less communications based on site. The project had several micro-cultures of a few similar cultural domains, so cultural shock was not as it is usually found when team members are from very distinct cultures. In the few instances that cultural problems did occur, it was quickly resolved through intensive communication.

Architecture: A key feature of the system of systems process used for GSP (versions 3.0-4.0) is that the architects were distributed at remote sites and competence centers, each having different expertise and responsible for a different component. This is different from previous the extended workbench model used for GSP (versions 1.0-2.0), where all the architects were located at the central site. We observed the benefit of having a focal architect within each remote site. When the software architecture is well-modularized after the design rules are stabilized, a team member can obtain all the information he/she needs to accomplish their task within the local team, and does not need to send inquiries to members of another remote team.

Viewing software architecture design as a decision making process, we hypothesize that the dependency structure among design decisions implies the potential needs for communication. Therefore, it is important to make the potential communication requirements between modules explicit early in the architecture development process such that tasks could be assigned to global teams to maximize the project communication efficiency. To achieve this purpose, we need an appropriate representation of the modular structure of the design to reveal the potential needs for communication among architects and developers.

14.6 Conclusions

Future software systems will clearly become larger and provide increased functionality. We have assumed that the organizations required to develop these ultra-large-scale software systems will necessarily become larger. For practical space and staffing reasons, these future development organizations will likely be widely spread across multiple sites, spanning nations, time zones, and continents. Distance, time, language, and cultural differences will make communications among team members more difficult.

Our ultra-large-scale software systems of the future will likely be developed by strangers who may never have worked together before. Informal communications among team members around the water cooler or in the company lunch room will cease to exist. We envision that the agile processes trend will continue such that individual component development teams will remain small and be part of a large coordinated project; i.e., a team of teams. This will require new multi-site development processes and organizational models that compensate for the loss of informal communications and exploit the advantages of new system architectures, tools, and technologies.

We conclude that global software development projects could be structured to take advantage of domain expertise located in remote sites to create a more scalable environment, as the central site experts would not be so overwhelmed by remote site requests. This additional scalability is achieved because our processes enable the distribution of important tasks to remote sites.

14.7 Future Extensions to the System of Systems Global Software Development Process

The introduction of global software development practices was motivated, initially, by the price differential of software engineering between North America and Western Europe from India, China, and Eastern Europe [10]. However, the recent successes of global software development initiatives in India, China and Eastern Europe, and the relative increase in the proportion of science and engineering degrees awarded in Asia and Eastern Europe [17] seem to indicate that system of systems global software development processes, where domain experts are located at all the physically distributed sites will have increased acceptance in the future.

According to the National Science Foundation (NSF) [17] in 2004 about 4 million students were awarded first degrees in Science and Engineering: 700,000 in Asia, 1 Million in Western and Eastern Europe including Russia, and 600,000 in the US. Moreover, while about 5% of all US awarded bachelor degrees are in Engineering, Asian countries award more than 50% of all first degrees in Science and Engineering.

Therefore, we are currently involved with a new experimentation with a "system of systems" software development process, where the objective is to have access to domain experts that are physically distributed. We envision a process where several project reviews are performed to elicit requirements and identify areas where the project team lacks in-house domain expertise. These areas would then be farmed-out to domain experts for detailed specification of system components, algorithms, and methodologies for validation of correctness. These domain experts would work closely with the developers at the development sites providing leadership and guidance to the local developers.

References

1. Avritzer A, Hasling W, Paulish D (2007) Process investigations for the global studio project version 3.0. Proceedings of the International Conference on Global Software Engineering (ICGSE 2007), IEEE Computer Society.
2. Avritzer A, Cai Y, Paulish D (2008) Co-ordination implications of software architecture in a global software development project. Proceedings of WICSA 2008.
3. Braun A (2007) A framework to enable offshore outsourcing, Proceedings of the International Conference on Global Software Engineering (ICGSE 2007), IEEE Computer Society.
4. Carmel E, Agarwal R (2001) Tactical approaches for alleviating distance in global software development. IEEE Software 18(2): 22–29.
5. Cusumano M, MacCormack A, Kemerer C, Crandall W (2003) A global survey of software development practices. MIT Sloan School of Management, Paper 178, June 2003, http://ebusiness.mit.edu.

6. Damian D (2002) Workshop on global software development. International Conference on Software Engineering (ICSE'02), USA, IEEE Computer Society, pp. 19–25.
7. Damian D, Williams L, Layman L, Bures H (2006) Essential communication practices for extreme programming in a global software development team. Information & Software Technology 48(9): 781–794.
8. Ebert C, Parro C, Suttels R, Kolarczyk H (2001) Improving validation activities in a global software development. 23rd International Conference on Software Engineering, CA, IEEE Computer Society, pp. 545–554.
9. Ebert C, De Neve P (2001) Surviving global software development. IEEE Software 18(2): 62–69.
10. Hazzan O, Dubinsky Y (2006) Can diversity in global software development be enhanced by agile software development?, Proceedings of the 2006 International Workshop on Global Software Development for the Practitioner, May 23–23, 2006, Shanghai, China, pp. 58–61.
11. Herbsleb J, Mockus A, Finholt T, Grinter R (2000) Distance, dependencies, and delay in a global collaboration. 2000 ACM Conference on Computer Supported Co-operative Work (CSCW'00), USA, ACM.
12. Herbsleb J, Moitra D (2001) Global software development. IEEE Software 18(2): 16–20.
13. Herbsleb J, Mockus A, Finholt T, Grinter R (2001) An empirical study of global software development: Distance and speed. Proceedings of the. *23rd International Conference on Software Engineering (ICSE'01)*, USA, IEEE Computer Society, pp. 81–90.
14. Herbsleb J, Bass M, Paulish D (2005) Global software development at Siemens: Experience from nine projects. Proceedings of the 27th International Conference on Software Engineering (ICSE'05), USA, IEEE Computer Society, pp. 524–533.
15. Layman L (2006) Changing students' perceptions: Analysis of the supplementary benefits of collaborative development. 19th Conference on Software Engineering Education and Training, IEEE Computer Society, pp. 159–166.
16. Nguyen T, Wolf T, Damian D (2008) Global software development and delay: Does distance still matter? Proceedings of the International Conference on Global Software Engineering (ICGSE 2008), IEEE Computer Society.
17. NSF (2008) Science and Engineering Indicators http://nsf.gov/statistics.seind08/c2/c2s5.htm.
18. Prikladnicki R, Audi J, Damian D, Oliveira T (2007) Distributed software development: Practices and challenges in different business strategies of offshoring and onshoring. Proceedings of the International Conference on Global Software Engineering (ICGSE 2007), IEEE Computer Society.
19. Richardson I, Moore S, Paulish D, Casey V, Zage D (2007) Globalizing software development in the local classroom. Proceedings of the 20th Conference on Software Engineering Education & Training (CSEET'07), IEEE Computer Society.
20. Sa J, Maslova E (2002) A unified process support framework for global software development. Proceedings of the 26th International Computer Software and Applications Conference on Prolonging Software Life: Development and Redevelopment (COMPSAC'02), IEEE Computer Society.
21. Sangwan R, Bass M, Mullick N, Paulish D, Kazmeier J (2007) Global Software Development Handbook. Boca Raton, FL: Auerbach Publications.
22. Scott J (1991) Social Network Analysis: A Handbook, 2nd edn. Thousand Oaks, CA: Sage Publications.
23. Setamanit S, Wakeland W, Raffo D (2003) Planning and improving global software development process using simulation. Proceedings of the Global Software Development Workshop, Shangai, China.

Part IV
Emerging Issues in Collaborative Software Engineering

John Grundy

In recent years a number of new areas of software engineering practice have emerged that bring new challenges to collaboration on large scale software projects. These include, though are not limited to, the rise in open source software projects, outsourcing of substantive parts of software projects, improving knowledge management and sharing in software development, and better identifying, capturing and using rationale in software development projects.

Free and open source software projects have become a major player in research and commercial software development [8]. However, open source software engineering introduces a range of new challenges that "closed source" projects do not normally have to contend with. This includes the need to co-ordinate work across a diverse community of – usually voluntary and often unpaid contributors; the adoption of a workable software process and collaboration tools to support the diverse, highly distributed team; various collaboration support features ranging from version control and repositories, to bug tracking and release management software [8]. Because of the complexity of relationships evident in open source projects – both technical and social – a range of studies have been carried out in this domain. Most analysis of various socio-technical relationships in free and open source software projects aim to better understand how these work and can support collaboration in this emerging domain [2]. Tools to support understanding and management of these relationships have begun to be developed and deployed [4]. Open questions include what sorts of collaboration affordances in free/open source projects will best support different aspects of project work at different times between different team members for different purposes.

Open source software is most commonly carried out by distributed teams and individuals. This is one example of geographically distributed software development. Another example is offshore development where an organisation carries out parts of its software development in highly distributed geographic locations [3]. Such projects introduce many challenges around communication, collaboration and co-ordination. A further complication can come from outsourcing software development to an offshore provider [9]. This introduces yet another challenge of inter-company collaboration between software teams. A major area of project failure in this domain is the challenge of distance. Some aspects of a project may be suitable for offshore outsourcing while others not. Some teams and organisations may be adept at providing offshore outsourcing but others not. How does management determine which aspects of a project to offshore outsource? How do they determine suitable providers? Capability Maturity Models have been developed to assist process improvement – can similar approaches assist with offshore outsourcing capability assessment?

A key area of challenge in collaborative software development is the architecting of a system. Of particular interest in recent times has been the desire to better capture knowledge about the architecture and the architecting process itself, in order to improve communication, understanding and decision making [1]. To date while much interest has been generated in this area, there are limited approaches and tools to support collaborative architecting via knowledge sharing [6]. Key challenges include how to manage the process; what knowledge to capture and how; how to share the knowledge effectively; and evolution of the knowledge base as the software evolves. Distributed software development compounds these challenges, for example in the open source software domain where a highly distributed developer base needs to understand the architecture of a complex system.

A new and emerging domain of software engineering is product line engineering where a "product line" of software products is produced from a variable core [7]. A key challenge is in describing and managing the variability aspects of software product lines [5]. Collaboration problems are introduced particularly in the domain of requirements engineering for product lines. These are compounded even further if a geographically distributed product line engineering project, such as in an offshore outsourcing project. One promising approach to addressing the challenges is rationale management to better describe and manage variability.

Chapter 15 by Scacchi looks at the issue of "affordances" in open source and/or free software development projects. These affordances include such issues as community dynamics, development process selection, collaborative work practices and related socio-technical relationships. The focus is around what sorts of collaboration affordances best assist collaborative work in this increasingly important domain of software engineering. The work analyses a range of studies of open source software projects and provides insights into collaboration practices and opportunities for future research and practice.

Chapter 16 by Mäkiö et al looks at the issue of decision making around outsourcing of software development. More and more outsourcing projects are being undertaken, many of which include an "off shore" component. Distance is a major factor in the failure of outsourcing projects and the authors argue that risk mitigation should be undertaken early on such projects. To this end they have developed an "Outsourcing Maturity Model" (OMM) to assist in the determination of suitability and readiness for offshore outsourcing on complex software development projects.

Chapter 17 by Liang et al looks at knowledge sharing issues in the domain of collaborative software architecting. A key focus is supporting the use of architectural knowledge when collaborating on software development. They present a two-part solution to this problem: a collaborative architecting process using architectural knowledge as a key foundation, and a supporting tool.

Chapter 18 by Thurimella investigates the role of rationale in the emerging domain of product line engineering, specifically around the requirements engineering process. A range of collaboration problems present due to the separation of domain and application engineering in this domain. The authors propose a new methodology of issue-based variability management. This uses rationale management to extend variability management in product line engineering.

References

1. Avgeriou P, Kruchten P, Lago P, Grisham P, Perry D (2007) Architectural knowledge and rationale: Issues, trends, challenges. ACM SIGSOFT Software Engineering Notes 32(4): 41–46.
2. Bergquist M, Ljungberg J (2001) The power of gifts: Organizing social relationships in open source communities. Information Systems Journal 11: 305–320.
3. Carmel E, Agarwal R (2002) The maturation of offshore sourcing of information technology work. MIS Quarterly Executive 1(2): 65–78.
4. de Souza CRB, Quirk S, Trainer E, Redmiles D (2007) Supporting collaborative software development through visualization of social and technical dependencies. Proceedings of the ACM Conference on Supporting Group Work (Group07), Sanibel, Island, FL, pp. 147–156.
5. Dutoit A, McCall R, Mistrik I, Paech B (Eds.) (2006) Rationale Management in Software Engineering. Berlin, Heidelberg, New York: Springer.
6. Farenhorst R (2006) Tailoring knowledge sharing to the architecting process. ACM SIGSOFT Software Engineering Notes 31(5): 15–19.
7. Pohl K, Boeckle G, van der Linder F (2005) Software Product Line Engineering Foundations, Principles, and Techniques. Berlin, Heidelberg, New York: Springer.
8. Scacchi W (2006) Understanding free/open source software evolution. In: Madhavji NH, Ramil JF, Perry D (Eds.) Software Evolution and Feedback: Theory and Practice. New York: John Wiley and Sons Inc., pp. 181–206.
9. Tho I (2005) Managing the Risks of IT Outsourcing. Oxford: Elsevier Butterworth-Heinemann.

Chapter 15
Collaboration Practices and Affordances in Free/Open Source Software Development

Walt Scacchi

Abstract This chapter examines collaborative work practices, development processes, project and community dynamics, and other socio-technical relationships in free and open source software development (FOSSD). It also describes what kinds of collaboration affordances facilitate collaborative work in FOSSD projects. It reviews a set of empirical studies of FOSSD that articulate different levels of analysis. Finally, there is discussion of limitations and constraints in understanding what collaboration practices and affordances arise in FOSSD studies and how they work, and then to emerging opportunities for future FOSSD studies.

15.1 Introduction

This chapter examines and compares collaborative work practices, processes, and affordances that emerge in empirical studies of free/open source software development (FOSSD) projects. FOSSD is a way for building, deploying, and sustaining large software systems on a global basis, and differs in many interesting ways from the principles and practices traditionally advocated for software engineering (SE) [63]. Hundreds of FOSS systems are now in use by thousands to millions of end-users, and some of these FOSS systems entail hundreds-of-thousands to millions of lines of source code. So what's going on here, and how are collaborative FOSSD processes used to build and sustain these projects, and how might differences with SE be employed to explain what's going on with FOSSD?

One of the more significant features of FOSSD is the formation and enactment of collaborative software development practices and processes performed by loosely coordinated software developers and contributors. These people may volunteer their time and skill to such effort, and may only work at their personal discretion rather than as assigned and scheduled. Further, FOSS developers are generally expected

W. Scacchi (✉)
Donald Bren School of Information and Computer Sciences, Institute for Software Research, University of California, Irvine, CA 92697-3455, USA
e-mail: Wscacchi@ics.uci.edu

I. Mistrík et al. (eds.), *Collaborative Software Engineering*,
DOI 10.1007/978-3-642-10294-3_15, © Springer-Verlag Berlin Heidelberg 2010

(or prefer) to provide their own computing resources (e.g., laptop computers on the go, or desktop computers at home), and bring their own software tools with them.

FOSS developers often work on global software projects that do not typically have a corporate owner or management staff to organize, direct, monitor, and improve the software development processes being put into practice on such projects [cf. 29]. Does the absence or limited presence of corporate authorities or sponsors encourage or facilitate collaboration in FOSSD, or do collaborative practices and affordances supporting FOSSD reduce the need to rely on traditional corporate authority or project management regimes? Is collaborative practice a defining feature of FOSSD, is FOSSD a causal attribute of collaboration, or does collaborative practice more readily produce FOSS? What motivates software developers participate in FOSSD projects? Is volunteerism and personal discretion key to collaboration in FOSSD projects? Why and how are large FOSSD projects sustained through collaborative practices and affordances? How are large FOSSD projects coordinated, controlled or managed without a traditional project management team? Why and how might answers to these questions change over time? These are the kinds of questions addressed in this chapter.

15.1.1 What Is Free/Open Source Software Development?

FOSSD is mostly not about SE, at least not as SE is portrayed in modern SE textbooks [cf. 63]. FOSSD is also not SE done poorly. It is instead a different approach to the development of software systems where much of the development activity is openly visible, and development artifacts are publicly available over the Web. Furthermore, substantial FOSSD effort is directed at enabling and facilitating collaboration among developers (and also end-users), but generally there is no traditional SE project management regime, budget or schedule. FOSSD is also oriented towards the joint development of an ongoing community of developers and users concomitant with the FOSS system of interest.

FOSS developers are typically end-users of the FOSS they develop [57, 58, 65, 69] and other end-users often participate in and contribute to FOSSD efforts as non-developers. There is also widespread recognition that FOSSD projects can produce high quality and sustainable software systems that can be used by thousands to millions of end-users [44]. Thus, it is reasonable to assume that FOSSD processes are not necessarily of the same type, kind, or form found in modern SE projects [63]. Subsequently, what is known about collaborative SE processes may not be equally applicable to FOSSD practices without some explicit empirical justification. Thus, it is appropriate to review what is known about FOSSD and where collaboration practices and affordances emerge along the way.

15.1.2 What Are Affordances Supporting Collaborative Software Development?

Affordances refer to situated, interactional properties between objects and actors that facilitate certain kinds of social interactions in a complex environment. The concept of affordances appears in the studies that employ the construct to characterize aspects of complex work settings that facilitate how people interact though computing systems [1, 47]. Computer-supported work environments, when effective, afford new ways and means for collaborative learning [36]. Subsequently, the focus in this chapter is on the interactions that facilitate collaborative activities between FOSS developers who are geographically dispersed but share access to online artifacts, networked information repositories and communication infrastructures, such as Web pages, Web sites, source code version servers, distributed file servers, virtual private networks, and the like. Consider the example in Fig. 15.1, a screenshot of an excerpt from the "Code of Conduct" that helps inform participants and communicate social norms on how to "be collaborative" in the K Development Environment (KDE) FOSS project.

This collaboration affordance includes a narrative inscription on a KDE project Web page (an object in a complex online environment) that encourages and guides project participants (actors – developers or users of KDE) for how to collaborate (via certain kinds of social interaction) in the KDE project. Collaboration affordances in FOSSD may emerge in online venues and workspaces for FOSSD work, and may differ by the kind or type of FOSS being developed (e.g., operating system utility program versus network computer game), the project web site or multi-project Web portals in use, as well as by the infrastructure of online tools participants use in FOSSD work.

What makes software development in general, or FOSSD in particular, collaborative? Is collaborative software development work natural and obvious, or challenging, perplexing, and sometimes problematic? What can be done to facilitate or encourage opportunities to make software development work more collaborative, or even more fun and playful [cf. 46]? Do all multi-user software development tools, interfaces, or repositories automatically enable collaboration, or are some more effective than others? Questions like these help ground our interest in reviewing what kinds of affordances are found in empirical studies of FOSSD work, and how they facilitate collaborative software development activities with online software artifacts.

15.1.3 Results from Recent Studies of FOSSD

The remainder of this chapter provides a review of empirical studies of FOSSD that articulate different levels of analysis, and each level is examined in a separate section. Emphasis is directed at identifying affordances that facilitate collaborative software development activities found in different studies of FOSSD participants, practices, and projects. Section 15.2 provides a brief background on what motivates people to participate and contribution to FOSSD projects. Section 15.3 examines the different resources and capabilities that FOSS developers bring to their projects. Section 15.4 examines practices in co-operation, co-ordination, and control that arise within self-organizing FOSSD projects. Section 15.5 examines how multiple FOSSD projects give rise to alliances and inter-project network communities. Section 15.6 examines how clusters of diverse projects form FOSS ecosystems that can exhibit collective patterns of sustained exponential growth. Finally, there is a discussion of limitations and constraints in the FOSSD studies so far, followed by conclusions that highlight emerging opportunities for future studies of collaborative FOSSD work practices, development processes, information artifacts, and project communities.

15.2 Individual Participation in FOSSD Projects

One of the most common questions about FOSSD projects to date is why will software developers join and participate in such efforts, as well as engage in sometime difficult and challenging technical work, often without pay, for sustained periods of time. Surveys of FOSS developers [e.g., 23, 27, 28] have posed and investigated such questions. There are complex motivations for why FOSS developers are willing to allocate their time, skill, and effort by joining a FOSS project [28, 66]. Some FOSS developers are motivated to see their contribution of time, effort, and code as gifts they provide to a project community [3]. Other motivations include a developer's ability to acquire skill and sustained experience from working in multiple or different roles [34, 53, 66]. It can also include a desire to work on software systems that the developer finds personally interesting, a desire to work with well-regarded FOSSD experts, or to be recognized by project peers as a valued and frequent contributor to a highly visible FOSS project [28, 25]. Similarly, it can be that the developer routinely uses the FOSS system of interest, and wants it to implement some additional feature or capability, or wants to reinvent processing capabilities found in other software systems, or to add innovative system features [64, 65, 58]. These conditions represent different ways for how participants learn to collaboratively develop FOSS in different projects and different application domains.

Motivations for participating in FOSSD stand in contrast to the traditional view of software project management. Software project managers are suppose to design technical work activities in ways that are satisfying and thus motivating to developers [5]. Project managers are also responsible for insuring developers collaborate with one another when needed, and where developers are able to participate in setting project development goals and providing process feedback/improvement. Software project managers are expected to make SE work interesting, rewarding, and satisfying, and if they cannot do this, then the SE project may fail or produce low quality and hard to maintain software [5].

In contrast, the most frequently cited reason why software developers participate and contribute to FOSSD projects is *to learn* [23]. In other words, participating developers come to believe FOSSD projects of interest are expected to provide ways and means for individual and collaborative learning [cf. 14, 36]. Consequently, when developers no longer value or lose interest in what can be learned from a FOSSD project in which they participate, they may choose stop contributing to the project and move on. In traditional SE, project managers shape working conditions and thus the basis for collaborative work, while in FOSSD projects, individual participates must take responsibility for learning how to organize and manage themselves so as to fulfill their personal motivations when working with other FOSS developers currently participating in the projects. Thus, in this regard, the different ways and means for FOSS developers to learn things of greatest personal interest serve as individual level affordances for engaging in collaborative FOSSD project work. Conversely, developers who do not want to collaborate with the FOSS project developers at hand will not be able to realize or appropriate the common FOSSD collaborative learning affordances they find motivational, and thus they may move on to search for another project of interest.

15.3 Resources and Capabilities Supporting FOSSD

What kinds of resources or development capabilities are needed to help make FOSS efforts collaborative and successful? Based on what has been observed and reported across many empirical studies of FOSSD projects, the following kinds of socio-technical resources (or social capital) enable the development of both FOSS software and ongoing project that is sustaining its evolution, application and refinement, though other kinds of resources may also be involved [57, 59]. The following sub-sections examine collaborative practices and affordances centered on different resources and capabilities found in FOSSD projects.

15.3.1 Personal Software Development Tools and Networking Support

FOSS developers, end-users, and other volunteers often provide their own personal computing resources in order to access or participate in a FOSS development project. They similarly provide their own access to the Internet, and may even host personal Web sites or information repositories. It is not uncommon that a FOSS developer works on a project from a room at home, or on a laptop PC while traveling. FOSS developers bring their own choice of software development tools and methods to a project, and sometimes the number of tools employed ranges into dozens. The mobility of tools and laptop computers also enables the organization and enactment of collaborative FOSS *hackathons*[1] – marathon FOSS development experience involving dozens of developers at a chosen destination for the purpose of collaboratively analyzing, modifying, and rebuilding a given FOSS system. Participation in such events often entails travel and related expenses often borne out of pocket by each participant, though they also find such events personally and professionally rewarding, convivial, and fun, even though involving long hours of difficult and technically challenging work.

---

[1] Description and examples of FOSS hackathons at http://en.wikipedia.org/wiki/Hackathon.

Sustained commitment of personal resources helps *subsidize* the emergence and evolution of the ongoing project, its shared (public) information artifacts, and resulting open source code. It spreads the cost for creating and maintaining the information infrastructure of the virtual organization that constitute a FOSSD project [7, 48]. These in turn help create recognizable shares of the FOSS *commons* [2, 49, 50] that are linked (via hardware, software, Internet and Web) to the project's information infrastructure. So personal computers, FOSS tools, and hackathons are affordances that help enable collaborative FOSSD.

15.3.2 Beliefs Supporting FOSS Development

Why do software developers and others contribute their skill, time, and effort to the development of FOSS and related information resources? Though there are probably many diverse answers to such a question, it seems that one such answer must account for the belief in the freedom to access, study, modify, redistribute and share the evolving results from a FOSS development project [11, 12, 25]. However, it also includes *freedom of expression* and *freedom of choice* [18, 60]. Neither of these freedoms is explicitly declared, assured, or protected by copyright or commons-based intellectual property rights, nor by end-user license agreements. However, these freedoms are realized in choices for what to develop or work on (e.g., choice of work subject or personal interest over work assignment), how to develop it (choice of method to use instead of a corporate standard), and what tools to employ (choice over which personal tools to employ versus only using what is provided). They also are expressed in choices for when to release work products (choice of satisfaction of work quality over schedule), determining what to review and when (modulated by ongoing project ownership responsibility), and expressing what can be said to whom with or without reservation.

The enactment of beliefs, values, and norms for why and how to develop FOSSD, which constitute part of a FOSS developer's mental model [cf. 20], that are represented in FOSS licenses and project narratives (Fig. 15.1.), serve as affordances that enable collaborative FOSSD projects and teamwork. Similarly, failure to enact and sustain such beliefs can lead to participants being challenged by others regarding their commitment to collaboratively develop FOSS in a proper manner, so the absence or failure of such an affordance can drive FOSS developers apart [15, 17, 19].

15.3.3 FOSSD Informalisms

Software informalisms [57] are the information artifacts that participants use as resources to describe, proscribe, prescribe, or question what's happening in a FOSSD project. They are informal narrative resources that are comparatively easy to use, and publicly accessible to those who want to join the project, or just browse around. They are generally supported with lightweight tools [4, 68]. Nonetheless,

Be collaborative

The Free Software Movement depends on collaboration: it helps limit duplication of effort while improving the quality of the software produced. In order to avoid misunderstanding, try to be clear and concise when requesting help or giving it. Remember it is easy to misunderstand emails (especially when they are not written in your mother tongue). Ask for clarifications if unsure how something is meant; remember the first rule - assume in the first instance that people mean well.

As a contributor, you should aim to collaborate with other community members, as well as with other communities that are interested in or depend on the work you do. Your work should be transparent and be fed back into the community when available, not just when KDE releases. If you wish to work on something new in existing projects, keep those projects informed of your ideas and progress.

It may not always be possible to reach consensus on the implementation of an idea, so don't feel obliged to achieve this before you begin. However, always ensure that you keep the outside world informed of your work, and publish it in a way that allows outsiders to test, discuss and contribute to your efforts.

Contributors on every project come and go. When you leave or disengage from the project, in whole or in part, you should do so with pride about what you have achieved and by acting responsibly towards others who come after you to continue the project.

As a user, your feedback is important, as is its form. Poorly thought out comments can cause pain and the demotivation of other community members, but considerate discussion of problems can bring positive results. An encouraging word works wonders.

Fig. 15.1 An excerpt from a FOSSD project Web page that both encourages and guides how and why project participants can collaborate. Source: http://www.kde.org/code-of-conduct/, accessed October 2008

these artifacts serve as both workspaces where collaborative FOSSD work activities (including reading, reviewing, writing, and learning) occurs, as well as the products of such collaborations [14, 16, 37, 54, 57].

The most common informalisms used in OSSD projects include (i) communications and messages within project Email [68], (ii) threaded message discussion forum, bulletin boards, or group blogs, (iii) news postings, and (iv) instant messaging or Internet relay chat. These enable developers and users to converse with one another in a lightweight, semi-structured manner, and now use of these tools is global across applications domains and cultures. As such, the discourse captured in these tools is a frequent source of OSS requirements. A handful of OSSD projects have found that summarizing these communications into (v) project digests [16] helps provide an overview of major development activities, problems, goals, or debates. These project digests represent multi-participant summaries that record and hyperlink the rationale accounting for focal project activities, development problems, current software quality status, and desired software functionality. Project digests (Fig. 15.2) record the discussion, debate, consideration of alternatives, code patches and initial operational/test results drawn from discussion forums, online chat transcripts, and related online artifacts [16].

Other common informalisms include (vi) scenarios of usage as linked Web pages or screenshot galleries, (vii) how-to guides, (viii) to-do lists, (ix) Frequently Asked Questions, and other itemized lists, and (x) project Wikis, as well as (xi) traditional system documentation and (xii) external publications [e.g., 24, 25]. OSS

1. Further trouble-shooting with the wx 2.6 drivers

20 Jun – 21 Jun Archive Link: "[IRC] 20 Jun 2006 "
Summary By Peter Sullivan
Topics: Forms, Common
People: Reinhard Muller, James Thompson, Johannes Vetter, Peter Sullivan

Further to Issue #117, Section #2   (**22 May :** Layout in GNUe Forms with wx 2.6 driver), Reinhard Muller (reinhard) suggested to James Thompson (jamest) **"if you are bored, you can try again the wx26 uidriver"**, as Johannes Vetter (johannesV) had done **"some massive changes and it might be that your issues with fscking up the boxes are solved"**. James said that, although he was busy, **"i really need to get that tested, as the dropdown box issues in 2.4 are preventing some selections from being allowed"**. So he was keen to have a version of GNUe Forms that worked with the user interface driver for wx 2.6 as soon as possible.

Trying Johannes' new code for GNUe Forms with his existing GNUe Forms Definitions, James found problems - **"none of which are due to anything wrong with what you've done - it's all in my forms"**, where he had been relying on 'features' (such as overlapping text boxes) that Johannes had treated as 'bugs' and now fixed. Johannes confirmed that "overlaping is now being checked ... not only for boxes but for all widgets" . He added, **"if you click the detail-button you'll see the offending line in your XML-File - this makes debuging"** a GNUe Form Definition (gfd) "a lot easier". James reported that all five of his existing GNUe Form Definitions were not working with the new code - but **"i would still imagine it's something funky I'm doing in the form"** rather than a problem with Johannes' code. He noted that, on the last one, the problem that he had been having with the dropdown menu had been fixed, but the form now **"aborts on query"** .

(ed. [Peter Sullivan] Note that the lack of any guarantees on backward compatability, even with 'features'/'bugs' is one of the reasons why GNUe Forms remains at a version number below 1.0 as of time of writing, as discussed further in Issue #112, Section #4   (**13 Apr :** Forms approaching version 1.0?) .)

Fig. 15.2 A project digest that summarizes multiple messages including those hyperlinked (indicated by highlighted underlined text) to their originating online sources.
Source: http://www.kerneltraffic.org/GNUe/latest.html, accessed July 2006

(xiii) project property licenses (whether to assert collective ownership, transfer copyrights, insure "copyleft," or some other reciprocal agreement) are documents that also help to define what software or related project content are protected resources that can subsequently be shared, examined, modified, and redistributed. Finally, (xiv) open software architecture diagrams, (xv) intra-application functionality realized via scripting languages like Perl and PhP, and the ability to either (xvi) incorporate externally developed software modules or "plug-ins," or (xvii) integrate software modules from other OSSD efforts, are all resources that are used informally, where or when needed according to the interests or actions of project participants.

All software informalisms are found or accessed from (xix) project related Web sites or portals. These Web environments are where most OSS software informalisms can be found, accessed, studied, modified, and redistributed [57]. A Web presence helps make visible the project's information infrastructure and the array of information resources that populate it. These include FOSSD multi-project Web sites (e.g., SourgeForge.net, Savanah.org, Freshment.org, Tigris.org, Apache.org, Mozilla.org), community software Web sites (PhP-Nuke.org), and project-specific Web sites (e.g., www.GNUenterprise.org), as well as (xx) embedded project source code Webs (directories), (xxi) project repositories (CVS [24] or Subversion), and (xxii) software bug reports [31] and (xxiii) issue tracking data base like Bugzilla (http://www.bugzilla.org/). Last, giving the growing global interest in online social networking, it is not surprising to find increased attention to documenting various kinds of social gatherings and meetings using (xxiv) social media Web sites (e.g., YouTube, Flickr, MySpace, etc.) where FOSS developers, users, and interested others come together to discuss, debate, or work on FOSSD projects, and to use these online media to record, and publish photographs/videos that establish group identity and affiliation with different FOSSD projects.

Software informalisms as online artifacts which developers employ as their online workspaces are where and in what FOSSD is organized, captured, reviewed, and managed. Accordingly, these informalisms serve as affordances that facilitate, enculturate, and document collaborative work in FOSSD projects.

15.3.4 Skilled, Self-organizing, and Self-managed Software Developers

Developing complex software modules for FOSS applications requires skill and expertise in a target application domain. For example, contributing to a FOSSD project like Filezilla (http://filezilla.sourceforge.org) requires knowledge and skill in handling file transfer states, actions, and protocols. Developing FOSS modules or applications in a way that enables an open architecture requires a base of prior experience in constructing open systems. The skilled use of project management tools for tracking and resolving open issues, and also for bug reports contribute to the development of such system architecture [51].

FOSS developers organize their work as a virtual organizational form [7, 18, 48] that seems to differ from what is common to in-house, centrally managed software development projects, which are commonly assumed in traditional SE textbooks. In the decentralized virtual organization of a large ongoing FOSSD project like the Apache.org or Mozilla.org, a hierarchical role/skill-based meritocracy [22, 6, 34] can arise. In such a meritocracy, there is no proprietary software development methodology or standard tool suite that all developers must employ, but critical decisions for what to do (e.g., overall system design) and how to do it will follow from respected core developers [cf. 51]. Similarly, there are few explicit rules about what development tasks should be performed, who should perform them, when, why, or how. However, this is not to say there are no rules that serve to govern the project or collective action within it.

FOSS project participants self-organize around the expertise, reputation, and accomplishments of core developers, secondary contributors, and tertiary reviewers and other peripheral users [9, 38]. FOSSD participants nearer the core have greater control and discretionary decision-making authority, compared to those further from the core [cf. 6, 9, 38]. Subsequently, core developers are expected to provide guidance, example artifacts, routinely use FOSSD coordination tools (e.g. CVS/Subversion, Bugzilla), and make critical decisions meritocratically. Together these afford collaborative FOSSD. Similarly, other participants must be able to both learn from and contribute to the efforts of the core developers. Together these realize a virtual, meritocratic, or self-managed form of decentralized software project management [7, 58].

15.3.5 Discretionary Time and Effort of Developers

Are FOSS developers working for "free" or for advancing their career and professional development? Following the survey results of Hars and Ou [28] and others [23, 27], there are many personal and professional career oriented reasons for why participants will contribute their time and effort to the sometimes difficult and demanding tasks of software development. Results from case studies in free software projects like GNUenterprise.org appear consistent with these observations [18, 19, 60]. These include self-determination, peer recognition, project affiliation or identification, and self-promotion, as well as belief in the inherent value of free software [cf. 11, 12, 25]. Core developers are expected to provide example through their own work practices, artifact contributions, and virtual project management style that other participants can observe, acknowledge, and learn from in ways that continue to afford collaborative FOSSD over time. Accordingly, the discretionary time, skill and effort of FOSS developers commit to their FOSSD project give rise to increased opportunity to collaborate, and increased collaborative activity can give rise to increased commitment of discretionary time and effort.

15.3.6 Trust and Social Accountability Mechanisms

Developing complex FOSS source code and applications requires trust and accountability among project participants. Though trust and accountability in a FOSSD project may be invisible resources, ongoing software and project development work occur only when these intangible resources and mechanisms for social control are present. Actions that embody trust and accountability arise in many forms. They include (a) assuming ownership or responsibility of a project software module, (b) voting on the approval of individual action or contribution to ongoing project software [22], (c) shared peer reviewing [2, 11, 12], and (d) contributing gifts [3] that are reusable and modifiable common goods [49]. They also arise through the project's recognition of a developer's status, emerging reputation, and migration from peripheral roles to core contributor [34]. The ways and means through which FOSS developers exercise trust and social accountability mechanisms act to afford, build, and sustain collaborative work practices in FOSSD projects.

15.4 Co-operation, Co-ordination, and Control in FOSS Projects

Getting software developers to work together, even when they desire to cooperate is not without its challenges for coordinating and controlling who does what when, and to what they do it to. Conflicts arise in both FOSSD [18, 33] and traditional software development projects [56], and finding ways to resolve conflicts becomes part of the cost (in terms of social capital) that must be incurred by FOSS developers for development progress to occur. Minimizing the occurrence, duration, and invested effort in such conflicts quickly becomes a goal for the core developers in an FOSSD project. Similarly, finding tools and project organizational forms that minimize or mitigate recurring types of conflicts also becomes a goal for experienced core developers. Focus of this section is thus directed to examining how different tools, artifacts, and socio-technical interaction practices are employed to enable FOSS developers to self-organize and govern project activities in an effective and adaptive manner.

Software version control tools such as the concurrent versions system, CVS – itself an FOSS system and document base [24] – have been widely adopted for use within FOSS projects [cf. 11, 12, 21, 25]. Tools like CVS are being used as both (a) a logically centralized mechanism for coordinating and synchronizing FOSS development, as well as (b) an online venue for mediating control over what software enhancements, extensions, or architectural revisions will be checked-in and made available for check-out throughout the decentralized project as part of the publicly released version. In addition, the FOSS architecture the project organizes itself about may commonly be expressed through informal access/update rules and file/directory archiving schemes that are coded and agreed to by FOSS code contributors [cf. 51].

FOSSD projects teams can take the organizational form of a meritocracy [cf. 22, 58] operating as a dynamically organized virtual enterprise [7, 18, 48]. A layered meritocracy is a hierarchical organizational form that centralizes and concentrates certain kinds of authority, trust, and respect for experience and accomplishment within the team [cf. 6]. Such an organizational form also makes administrative governance more tractable and suitable, especially when a FOSS project seeks to legally constitute a non-profit foundation to better address its legal concerns and property rights [49]. However, it does not necessarily imply the concentration of universal authority into a single individual or directorial board, since decision-making may be shared among core developers who act as peers at the top layer, and they may be arrayed into overlapping groups with other project contributors with different responsibilities and interest areas [cf. 34].

Traditional software project management stresses planning, staffing, budget and schedule control activities. Virtual project management exists within FOSS communities, for example within projects developing FOSS-based computer games [58], to enable control via project decision-making, Web site administration, and administration of CVS/Subversion repositories (or other similar source code control tools). VPM requires multiple people to act in the roles of team leader, sub-system manager, or system module owner in a manner that may be short-term or long-term, based on their skill, accomplishments, availability and belief in ongoing project development. The implied requirement for VPM can be seen within Fig. 15.3, from the FOSS project developing *Planeshift*, a free massively multiplayer online role-playing game. Similarly, VPM exists to mobilize and sustain the use of privately owned resources (e.g., Web servers, network access, site administrator labor, skill and effort) that are made available for shared use or collective reuse by the ongoing project [cf. 2, 60].

To be a leader you must pass the approval of the direc-
tor. Before that you will be considered a W.T.B. (Want
To Be) Leader and only after proving that you have the
right skills and dedication to the project you will of-
ficially become a leader.

There's one leader for each department and he can have
also one co-leader helping in his job. He will ensure
progress in his department completing the most important tasks in his area and will organize work of other
members. He is the primary reference for development.
Required Skills:
    * Strong commitment to the project.
    * Good skill to organize work of the Team.
    * Team leadership.
    * Good knowledge of the area in which he applies
The leader is the most important contributor of his department! He will complete critical tasks, he will always have job to do. His tasks are similar to the ones
of the members (see below in the section of a specific
department). He will also manage work of other guys.

Fig. 15.3 Description of virtual project management skills implied for a team leader
Source: http://www.planeshift.it/recruitment.html, accessed October 2008

Many FOSSD projects also post guidelines for how to report and discuss bugs,
unintended features, or flaws in the current FOSS system release. These guidelines
are embodied in online artifacts that developers follow in ways that suggest they
have elevated certain informalisms into community norms (Fig. 15.1) that act to
encourage or control appropriate behavior within FOSSD projects.

Thus, a variety of socio-technical arrangements are put into motion in a
FOSSD project in ways that encourage developers to cooperate, coordinate,
and control their development activities through tools, informalisms, shared
resources, and contribution practices. These collectively afford a lightweight centralized project management scheme through decentralized collaborative FOSSD
practices.

15.5 Alliance Formation, Inter-project Social Networking and Community Development

How does the gathering of FOSS developers give rise to a more persistent self-
sustaining organization or project community? Through choices that developers
make for their participation and contribution to a FOSSD project, they find that
there are like-minded individuals who also choose to participate and contribute
to a project. These software developers find and connect with each other through
FOSSD Web sites and online discourse (e.g., threaded discussions on bulletin
boards) [45], and they find they share many technical competencies, values, and

beliefs in common [7, 18, 20]. This manifests itself in the emergence of an alliance of collaborating FOSSD projects that share either common interests or development methods in projects that adopt a given FOSS system for subsequent application development, or in a occupational network of FOSS developers [18].

Examples of FOSS multi-project alliances are readily recognized. First, there are those that have established non-profit corporations or foundations like Apache, Mozilla, Gnome, Perl, Eclipse, NetBeans, or Free Software Foundation [49]. Second, there are those organized and supported by for-profit corporations by Sun Microsystems (e.g., OpenOffice), Hewlett-Packard, IBM, Nokia, and others [13, 52]. Third, other FOSS multi-project networks arise as the result of the architectural integration of multiple, disparate FOSS systems into larger, more encompassing system of systems [60]. Fourth, some FOSS projects produce systems that are platforms, frameworks or libraries of components which in turn give rise to application projects which are developed using these core systems. The Open Graphics Rendering Engine (OGRE at http://www.ogre3d.org), for instance, serves as the basis for dozens of user-led projects that build applications (like computer games) using OGRE. These projects both depend on OGRE project, as well as the network of other application projects, for FOSS code, updates, development expertise and advice. In turn, the peripheral participation of FOSS developers in these application projects can supplement the base of collaborating developers and users of the core systems.

Becoming a central node in a social network of software developers that interconnects multiple FOSS projects is also a way to accumulate social capital and recognition from peers. However, it also enables the merger of independent FOSS systems into larger composite ones that gain the critical mass of core developers to grow more substantially and attract ever larger user-developer communities [42, 59]. Multi-project clustering and interconnection enables small FOSS projects to come together as a larger social network with the critical mass [43] needed for their independent systems to be merged and experience more growth in size, functionality, and user base. It also enables shared architectural dependencies to arise (perhaps unintentionally) in the software components or sub-systems that are used/reused across projects [cf. 9, 32, 51]. FOSSD Web sites also serve as hubs that centralize attention for what is happening with the decentralized development of the focal FOSS system, its status, participants and contributors, discourse on pending/future needs, etc. Subsequently, there is growing research interest in understanding, modeling, and analyzing the social and technical networks of FOSS developers [9, 30, 41, 42]. Fig. 15.4 provides an example of a social network of FOSS developers spanning five projects, but interlinked by just two developers.

Other studies [28, 35] indicate that upwards of two out of three OSS developers contributes to two or more FOSSD projects, and perhaps as many as 5% contribute to 10 or more FOSSD projects. The density and interconnectedness of this social networking characterizes the membership and in-breeding of the FOSS movement [15, 17, 19], but at the same time, the multiplicity of projects reflects its segmentation into specific socio-technical FOSSD domains.

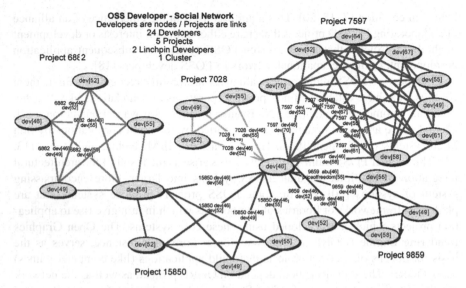

Fig. 15.4 A social network linking 24 FOSS developers in five projects through two "linchpin" developers into a larger multi-project community [42]

All of these conditions for inter-project networking and alliance formation point to new kinds of requirements for collaborative software development – for example, network community building requirements, community software requirements, and community information sharing system (Web site and interlinked communication channels for email, forums, and chat) requirements [46, 57]. These requirements may entail both functional and non-functional requirements, but they will most typically be expressed using FOSS informalisms, rather than using formal notations based on some system of mathematical logic known by few. Similarly, sharing beliefs, values, communications, artifacts and tools among FOSS developers enables not only cooperation, but also provides a basis for "common ground," shared mental models and experiences, camaraderie, and learning [cf. 20, 31, 38].

As such, the emergence of alliances among multiple, internetworked FOSSD projects helps to sustain and expand the viability of each participating project, along with the community of contributing developers (who are also users) and peripheral users. Together, they collectively afford collaborative software development connections and opportunities that transcend the boundaries of the constituent FOSSD projects.

15.6 FOSS as a Multi-project Software Ecosystem

As noted above, many FOSSD projects have become interdependent through the networking of software developers, development artifacts, common tools, shared Web sites, and computer-mediated communications. What emerges from this is

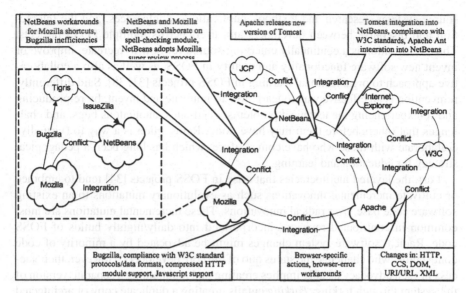

Fig. 15.5 A depiction of a multi-project software ecosystem that supports Web-based information infrastructures [33]

a kind of *multi-project software ecosystem*, whereby ongoing development and evolution of one FOSS system gives rise to propagated effects, architectural and integration dependencies, functional conflicts, or vulnerabilities in one or more of the projects linked to it [33]. Fig 15.5 depicts part of the FOSS ecosystem that supports a Web-based information infrastructure that interlinks Mozilla/Firefox Web browsers (and also Internet Explorer), Apache Web servers, NetBeans interactive development environment, Java development community (JCP), and others.

Interdependencies that span a software ecosystem are most apparent when FOSSD projects share source code modules, components, or sub-systems. In such situations, the volume of source code of an individual FOSSD project may appear to grow at an *exponential rate* when modules, components, or sub-systems are integrated in whole into an existing FOSS system [8, 35, 59, 62, 67]. Such an outcome, which economists and political scientists refer to as a "network externality" [50], may be due to the import or integration of shared components, or the replication and tailoring of device, platform, or internationalization specific code modules. Such system growth patterns therefore seem to challenge the well-established laws of software evolution [39, 40]. Thus, software evolution in a multi-project FOSS ecosystem is a collaborative evolution ("co-evolution") process spanning interrelated FOSSD projects, people, artifacts, tools, code, and project-specific activities [59, 69].

It may also be useful to characterize a key evolutionary dynamic of FOSS as *reinvention* [cf. 58]. Reinvention is enabled through the sharing, examination, modification, and redistribution of concepts and techniques that have appeared in closed source systems, research and textbook publications, conferences, and the interaction and discourse between developers and users across multiple FOSS projects. Thus, reinvention is a continually emerging source for how to recreate, improve or invent new software functionality and quality in FOSS, as well as also a collaborative approach to organizational learning in FOSS projects [31, 38]. Said differently, reinvention is an effective way to learn how to innovate and invent, by re-producing and re-experiencing the technical problems, dead-ends, anomalous bugs, and challenges that others before them may have done. Reinvention is a way to (virtually) collaborate with those who have come before, which has long been a pedagogical strategy for education and learning.

Last, the layered meritocracies that arise in FOSS projects [34] tend to embrace or cultivate incremental innovations such as evolutionary mutations to an existing software code base, over radical innovations. These incremental mutations are most common in contributed revisions incorporated into daily/nightly builds of FOSS code. Radical software system changes might be advocated by a minority of code contributors who challenge the status quo of the core developers. However, their success in such advocacy usually implies creating and maintaining a separate version of the system through forking. *Forking* entails creating a duplicate copy of architected source code, then modifying or refactoring into a distinct new architectural configuration. Such forking may split/fragment a FOSSD project team into distinct sets of collaborators, which may results in no group having a sufficient critical mass of core developers. Thus, incremental FOSS mutations tend to win out over time since they more easily afford and sustain current collaboration patterns. Such affordance limits major FOSS system changes to arise slowly through meritocratic coordination and consensus building that give rise to new system versions with alternative architectural configurations [cf. 51, 58, 59].

15.7 Discussion

One discussion topic that immediately may come to mind is whether the collaboration affordances found in the FOSSD studies cited above might also be found in SE projects. At least four views of this topic can be considered.

First, we do not yet have in hand such a review of empirical studies of SE projects that identifies the collaboration affordances found therein, though such studies are starting to appear [cf. 29]. Though it might be an academic exercise to examine common SE textbooks to see what affordances for collaborative SE they might suggest or the reader might hypothesize, the point of this chapter was to focus review and examination of empirical studies of FOSSD to find what collaboration affordances are observed in these studies. So a fair and balanced comparison grounded in empirical studies is not yet possible due to a lack of such studies of SE projects.

Second, it is unclear to what extent such affordances found in SE projects that build proprietary (closed source) software systems in a centrally managed and controlled way, would be readily comparable to FOSSD projects that are self-organized and self-managed in a decentralized way. In traditional SE projects,

developers are generally assumed to be collocated (although there are exceptions, like subcontracted, outsourced, or offshore development), while in FOSSD
projects, developers are generally assumed to not be collated (with few exceptions like hackathons). Thus, while such an investigation might produce some
sharp comparisons and keen insights, this is a matter that requires further empirical
study.

Last, it is unclear whether there are studies of closed source SE projects that are
organized as internetworked alliances, though it seems likely that networked multi-
projects exist, though perhaps within the boundaries of a large corporate framework,
or behind the corporate firewall [cf. 13].

15.8 Conclusions

This chapter provides a multi-level analysis of collaboration affordances that support free/open source software development work, through a review of dozens of
empirical studies of FOSSD. Various kinds of collaboration affordances were identified with respect to individual participation in FOSSD projects, resources and
capabilities that FOSS developers bring to a project, how FOSS developers cooperate and coordinate decentralized development activities, how multiple FOSSD
projects coalesce into inter-networked alliances, and how FOSS ecosystems give
rise to co-evolutionary patterns of growth and diversity. FOSSD can be understood
as a socio-technical approach to collaborative software development supported
through an array of collaboration affordances. The development of FOSS systems
entails both the collaborative development of a networked project community, as
well as the collaborative development of a network of software components and
online artifacts. Consequently, some topics for further study can also be identified
from this review.

First, it is possible to engage in systematic case studies of collaboration affordances that arise in comparable set of FOSSD projects. The findings reviewed
in this chapter span multiple studies with different research methods, tools, data
sets, and discipline-specific analytical lens [cf. 26, 30]. As collaboration affordances supporting software development are a relatively new topic of study, then
it is appropriate to consider examining multiple FOSSD projects close up and in-
depth to determine what affordances enable different kinds of collaborative activities
in different development task situations. Case studies indicate such studies may
rely more on qualitative, ethnographic field study and participant observation (i.e.,
become an active participant in one or more FOSSD projects to observe or discover
collaboration affordances in action) [26, 55, 61].

Second, it may be possible to develop ways and means for mapping, visualizing,
or animating collaboration affordances in action. As affordances associate properties of objects and actors that give rise to interactions in a situated environment, then
it may be possible to identify and graphically portray these data elements in various
kinds of networked representations [61]. There is a growing trend in studies focusing on social networks or technical dependencies within FOSSD projects to render

their data and associations as different kinds of networks [10]. As such, how best to visualize collaboration affordances would be an intriguing avenue for exploration.

Last, as suggested in the Discussion section, there are numerous opportunities to study collaboration affordances within traditional software engineering projects. Similarly, there is need to systematically compare collaboration affordances found in FOSSD and SE projects so as to see what's similar, what's different, and why. The study of collaboration affordances in projects that seek to actively embrace and practice both FOSSD and SE is mostly unexplored territory, and many such projects can be found at the Tigris.org "open source software engineering" Web portal. Finally, as the review in this chapter indicates that affordances for collaborative software development can be analyzed at different/multiple levels of analysis, then multiple analytical lenses are now available to help focus new studies of collaborative software engineering. This chapter marks a starting point for further study.

Acknowledgments The research described in this chapter has been supported by grants #0534771 and #0808783 from the National Science Foundation; also grants from the Center for the Edge, and the Acquisition Research Program, at the Naval Postgraduate School. No endorsement implied. Contributors to this research include Chris Jensen, Margaret Elliott, John Noll, Mark Ackerman, and others at the Institute for Software Research at the University of California, Irvine.

References

1. Anderson R, Sharrock W (1992) Can organizations afford knowledge? Computer Supported Cooperative Work 1(3): 143–616.
2. Benkler Y (2006) The Wealth of Networks: How Social Production Transforms Markets and Freedom. New Haven, CT: Yale University Press.
3. Bergquist M, Ljungberg J (2001) The power of gifts: Organizing social relationships in open source communities. Information Systems Journal 11: 305–320.
4. Churchill EF, Bly S (1999) It's all in the words: Supporting work activities with lightweight tools. Proceedings of the ACM Conference Supporting Group Work, Phoenix, AZ, pp. 40–49.
5. Couger JD, Zawacki RA (1980) Motivating and Managing Computer Personnel, New York: John and Wiley and Sons.
6. Crowston K, Howison J (2006) Hierarchy and centralization in free and open source software team communications. Knowledge Technology & Policy, Winter 18(4): 65–85.
7. Crowston K, Scozzi B (2002) Open source software projects as virtual organizations: Competency rallying for software development. IEE Proceedings – Software 149(1): 3–17.
8. Deshpande A, Riehle D (2008) The total growth of open source. IFIP International Federation for Information Processing, Vol. 275; In: Russo B, Damiani E, Hissan S, Lundell B, Succi G (Eds.) Open Source Development, Community and Quality. Boston, MA: Springer, pp. 179–209.
9. de Souza CRB, Froehlich J, Dourish P (2005) Seeking the source: Software source code as a social and technical artifact. Proceedings of the ACM International Conference on Supporting Group Work (GROUP 2005), Sanibel Island, FL, pp. 197–206.
10. de Souza CRB, Quirk S, Trainer E, Redmiles D (2007) Supporting collaborative software development through visualization of social and technical dependencies. Proceedings of the ACM Conference on Supporting Group Work (Group'07), Sanibel Island, FL, pp. 147–156.
11. DiBona C, Cooper D, Stone M (2005) Open Sources 2.0. Sebastopol, CA: O'Reilly Media.
12. DiBona C, Ockman, Stone M (1999) Open Sources: Voices from the Open Source Revolution. Sebastopol, CA: O'Reilly Media.
13. Dinkelacker J, Garg PK, Miller R, Nelson D (2002) Progressive open source. Proceedings of the 24th International Conference on Software Engineering, Orlando, FL, pp. 177–184.

14. Ducheneaut N (2005) Socialization in an open source software community: A socio-technical analysis. Computer Supported Cooperative Work 14(4): 323–368.
15. Elliott M (2008) Examining the success of computerization movements in the ubiquitous computing era: Free and open source software movements. In: Elliott M, Kraemer KL (Eds.) Computerization Movements and Technology Diffusion. Medford, NJ: Information Today, Inc.
16. Elliott M, Ackerman M, Scacchi W (2007) Knowledge work artifacts: Kernel cousins for free/open source software development. Proceedings of the ACM Conference on Support Group Work (Group'07), Sanibel Island, FL, pp. 177–186.
17. Elliott M, Kraemer KL, (Eds.), (2008) Computerization Movements and Technology Diffusion. Medford, NJ: Information Today, Inc.
18. Elliott M, Scacchi W (2005) Free software development: Cooperation and conflict in a virtual organizational culture. In: Koch S (Ed.) Free/Open Source Software Development. Hershey, PA: IGI Publishing, pp. 152–172.
19. Elliott M, Scacchi W (2008) Mobilization of software developers: The free software movement. Information, Technology and People 21(1): 4–33.
20. Espinosa JA, Kraut RE, Slaughter SA, Lerch JF, Herbsleb JD, Mockus A (2002) Shared mental models, familiarity, and coordination: A multi-method study of distributed software teams. International Conference on Information Systems, Barcelona, Spain, December, pp. 425–433.
21. Feller J, Fitzgerald B, Hissam S, Lakhani K (2005) Perspectives on Free and Open Source Software. Cambridge, MA: MIT Press.
22. Fielding RT, (1999) Shared leadership in the apache project. Communications of the ACM 42(4): 42–43.
23. FLOSS (2002) Free/libre and open source software: Survey and study, FLOSS Final Report, http://www.flossproject.org/report/.
24. Fogel K (1999) Open Source Development with CVS. Scottsdale, AZ: Coriolis Press.
25. Fogel K (2005) Producing Open Source Software: How to Run a Successful Free Software Project. Sebastopol, CA: O'Reilly Press.
26. Gasser L, Scacchi W (2008) Towards a global infrastructure for multidisciplinary studies of free/open source software. IFIP International Federation for Information Processing, Vol. 275; In: Russo B, Damiani E, Hissan S, Lundell B, Succi G (Eds.) Open Source Development, Community and Quality. Boston, MA: Springer, pp. 143–158.
27. Hann IH, Roberts J, Slaughter S, Fielding R (2002) Economic incentives for participating in open source software projects. Proceedings of the Twenty-Third International Conference on Information Systems, pp. 365–372.
28. Hars A, Ou S (2002) Working for free? Motivations for participating in open source projects. International Journal of Electronic Commerce 6(3): 25–39.
29. Herbsleb JD, Paulish DJ, Bass M (2005) Global software development at Siemens: Experience from nine projects. Proceedings of the 27th International Conference on Software Engineering, St. Louis, MO, pp. 524–533.
30. Howison J, Conklin M, Crowston K (2006) FLOSS mole: A collaborative repository for FLOSS research data and analyses. International Journal of Internet Technology and Web Engineering 1(3): 17–26.
31. Huntley CL (2003) Organizational learning in open-source software projects: An analysis of debugging data. IEEE Transactions on Engineering Management 50: 485–493.
32. Iannacci F (2005) Beyond markets and firms: The emergence of open source networks. First Monday 10(5).
33. Jensen C, Scacchi W (2005) Process modeling across the web information infrastructure. Software Process – Improvement and Practice 10(3): 255–272.
34. Jensen C, Scacchi W (2007) Role migration and advancement processes in OSSD projects: A comparative case study. Proceedings of the 29th International Conference on Software Engineering, ACM, Minneapolis, MN, pp. 364–374.

35. Koch S (2005) Evolution of open source software systems – A large-scale investigation. Proceedings of the 1st International Conference on Open Source Systems (OSS2005), Genoa, Italy.
36. Kreijns K, Kirschner PA (2001) The social affordances of computer-supported collaborative learning environments. Proceedings of the 31st ASEE/IEEE Frontiers in Education Conference, TIF 12–17, Reno, NV.
37. Lanzara GF, Morner M (2005) Artifacts rule! How organizing happens in open source software projects. In: Czarniawska B, Hernes T (Eds.) Actor-Network Theory and Organizing. Malmo, Sweden: Libre & Copenhagen Business School Press, pp. 197–206.
38. Lave J, Wenger E (1991) Situated Learning: Legitimate Peripheral Participation. Cambridge: Cambridge University Press.
39. Lehman MM (1980) Programs, life cycles, and laws of software evolution. Proceedings of the IEEE 68: 1060–1078.
40. Lehman MM (2002) Software evolution and software evolution processes. Annals of Software Engineering 12: 275–309.
41. Lopez-Fernandez L, Robles G, Gonzalez-Barahona JM, Herraiz I (2006) Applying social network analysis to community-driven libre software projects. International Journal of Information Technology and Web Engineering 1(3): 27–28.
42. Madey G, Freeh V, Tynan R (2005) Modeling the F/OSS Community: A quantitative investigation. In: Koch S (Ed.) Free/Open Source Software Development. Hershey, PA: IGI Publishing, pp. 203–221.
43. Marwell G, Oliver P (1993) The Critical Mass in Collective Action: A Micro-Social Theory. Cambridge: Cambridge University Press.
44. Mockus A, Fielding R, Herbsleb JD (2002) Two case studies of open source software development: Apache and Mozilla. ACM Transaction on Software Engineering and Methodology 11(3): 309–346.
45. Monge PR, Fulk J, Kalman ME, Flanagin AJ, Parnassa C, Rumsey S (1998) Production of collective action in alliance-based interorganizational communication and information systems. Organization Science 9(3): 411–433.
46. Mynatt ED, O'Day VL, Adler A, Ito M (1998) Network communities: Something old, something new, something borrowed. Computer Supported Cooperative Work 7(1): 123–156.
47. Norman D (1999) Affordances, conventions, design. Interactions 6(3): 38–43.
48. Noll J, Scacchi W (1999) Supporting software development in virtual enterprises. Journal of Digital Information 1(4), February, http://jodi.tamu.edu/Articles/v01/i04/Noll/.
49. O'Mahony S (2003) Guarding the commons: How community managed software projects protect their work. Research Policy 32(7): 1179–1198.
50. Ostrom E, Eggertssons T, Calvert R (1990) Governing the Commons: The Evolution of Institutions for Collective Action. Cambridge: Cambridge University Press.
51. Ovaska P, Rossi M, Marttiin P (2003) Architecture as a coordination tool in multi-site software development. Software Process – Improvement and Practice 8(3): 233–247.
52. Robles G, Duenas S, Gonzalez-Baharona JM (2007) Corporate involvement in libre software: Study of presence in debian code over time. In: Feller J, Fitzgerald B, Scacchi W, Sillitti A (Eds.) Open Source Development, Adoption and Innovation, IFIP Vol. 234. Boston, MA: Springer, pp. 121–132.
53. Robles G, Gonzalez-Baharona JM (2006) Contributor turnover in libre software projects. In: Damiani E, Fitzgerald B, Scacchi W, Scott M Succi G (Eds.) Open Source Systems, IFIP Vol. 203. Boston, MA: Springer, pp. 273–286.
54. Robles G, Gonzalez-Baharona JM, Merelo JJ (2006) Beyond source code: The importance of other artifacts in software development (a case study). Journal of Systems and Software 79(9): 1233–1248.
55. Sack W, Detienne F, Ducheneaut B, Mahendran D, Barcellini FA (2006) Methodological framework for socio-cognitive analyses of collaborative design of open source software. Computer Supported Co-operative Work 2(3): 229–250.

56. Sawyer S (2001) Effects of intra-group conflict on packaged software development team performance. Information Systems Journal, 11: 155–178.
57. Scacchi W (2002) Understanding the requirements for developing open source software systems. IEE Proceedings – Software 149(1): 24–39.
58. Scacchi W (2004) Free/open source software development practices in the computer game community. IEEE Software 21(1): 59–67.
59. Scacchi W (2006) Understanding free/open source software evolution. In: Madhavji NH, Ramil JF, Perry D (Eds.) Software Evolution and Feedback: Theory and Practice. New York: John Wiley and Sons Inc., pp. 181–206.
60. Scacchi W (2007) Understanding the development of free e-commerce/e-business software: A resource-based view. In Sowe SK, Stamelos I, Samoladas I (Eds.) Emerging Free and Open Source Software Practices. Hershey, PA: IGI Publishing, pp. 170–190.
61. Scacchi W, Jensen C, Noll J, Elliott M (2006) Multi-modal modeling, analysis and validation of open source software development processes. International Journal of Internet Technology and Web Engineering 1(3): 49–63.
62. Schach SR, Jin B, Wright DR, Heller GZ, Offutt AJ (2002) Maintainability of the linux kernel. IEE Proceedings – Software 149(1): 18–23.
63. Sommerville I (2006) Software Engineering, 8th edn. New York: Addison-Wesley.
64. Von Hippel E (2005) Democratizing Innovation. Cambridge: MIT Press.
65. Von Hippel E, Von Krogh G (2003) Open source software and the "private-collective" innovation model: Issues for organization science. Organization Science 14(2): 209–223.
66. Von Krogh G, Spaeth S, Lakhani K (2003) Community, joining, and specialization in open source software innovation: A case study. Research Policy 32(7): 1217–1241.
67. Weiss M, Moroiu G, Zhao P (2006) Evolution of open source communities. In Damiani E, Fitzgerald B, Scacchi W, Scotto M, Succi G (Eds.) Open Source Systems, IFIP Vol. 203. Boston, MA: Springer, pp. 21–32.
68. Yamauchi Y, Yokozawa M, Shinohara T, Ishida T (2000) Collaboration with lean media: How open-source software succeeds. Proceedings of the Computer Supported Cooperative Work Conference (CSCW'00), ACM Press, Philadelphia, PA, pp. 329–338.
69. Ye Y, Nakajoki K, Yamamoto Y, Kishida K (2005) The co-evolution of systems and communities in free and open source software development. In Koch S (Ed.) Free/Open Source Software Development. Hershey, PA: IGI Publishing, pp. 59–82.

Chapter 16
OUTSHORE Maturity Model: Assistance for Software Offshore Outsourcing Decisions

Juho Mäkiö, Stafanie Betz, and Andreas Oberweis

Abstract Offshore outsourcing software development (OOSD) is increasingly being used by the Software Industry. OOSD is a specific variant of Geographically Distributed Software Development (GDSD). Compared to the traditional mode of software development (i.e., in-house) GDSD is more edgy and puts at risk the attainment of the expected results. Although the failure of an offshore outsourcing software project may be caused by a variety of factors, one major complication is geographical distance. Consequently we argue that risk avoidance in outshore software development should be undertaken well in advance of the development launch. This could be done by testing the offshore outsourcing relevance of each software project and then the offshore outsourcing company involved. With this in mind we have developed the OUTSHORE Maturity Model – OMM.

16.1 Introduction

The outsourcing of software development implies that an organization wholly or partially contracts out software development to another organisation. If the partner organisation is located abroad, this might be termed "an offshore outsourcing of software development". If the development takes place in physically far-flung locations, it is called "Global Software Development" (GSD) [32] or "Distributed Software Development" (DSD) [13]. Whether domestic or foreign, outsourcing can be an uncertain undertaking. Nonetheless many companies use offshore outsourcing to reduce time-to-market, to tap global resources, to profit from round-the-clock development, and to reduce costs.

The goal of OOSD must always be to uphold competitiveness in the global market. This goal should be promoted by the concise and purposeful employment of every resource – information technology, talent and competence to assure a thriving

J. Mäkiö (✉)
Forschungszentrum Informatik FZI, 76131 Karlsruhe, Germany
e-mail: juho.maekioe@gmx.de

I. Mistrík et al. (eds.), *Collaborative Software Engineering*,
DOI 10.1007/978-3-642-10294-3_16, © Springer-Verlag Berlin Heidelberg 2010

offshore outsourcing project. All of which helps the company maintain ongoing global penetration. However, global distribution of the development raises a number of knotty questions concerning accomplishment and implementation. Often there is a huge disparity between targets and the results attained. Outsourcing studies reveal that 47% of buyers terminated their offshore outsourcing relationship prematurely [39]. In 45% of cases the reason was poor provider performance and in 47% absent cost benefits [39]. Studies carried out in German SMU's report that the quality of work being done by the offshore outsourcing team tends to be inferior to that of in-house development projects; consequently only around 45% are found passable, yet prove unusable in 9–15% of cases [30]. Other studies revealed similar results. For example, [31] reports on a survey of 414 engineers and development managers working in partially or wholly offshore outsourced projects (US based) which reveals almost half (45%) of the work performed by the offshore team was of quite low quality and that 11% of it was unusable or actually a hindrance to progress.

Risk is inherent in business decision-making. This is clearly the case in OOSD. Boehm states that post-mortems on the most unsuccessful software projects indicate that failure might have been avoided if there had been explicit and early concern with identifying and resolving the high-risk elements [6].

The technical, strategic or financial advantages of software offshore outsourcing and GSD might be contrasted to the number of risks widely published in the scientific and management literature (e.g., [22, 27, 29, 34, 35, 38]) where a number of varying risks are debated. One list of specific software outsourcing risks is presented in [35]. Based on a literature study, the authors identify ten distinct risk areas: the risk of dependence, risk of loss of control over the activity, risk of loss of know-how, risk of performance, social risk, risk of failure of the beneficiary, hidden cost risks, risk of irreversibility, risk of conflict and disparity of culture, and the overall global economic risk. Still, the authors do not diagnose technical aspects as being so risky. Above all they stress pliable factors, such as a dependency growing on the outsourcing partner and evolving events being seen as a risk.

One further aspect is considered by [29]. This author considers the company's aptness and readiness for outsourcing. To deal with this aspect, he classifies the inherent risks into four groups: outsourcing experience, technology, the business situation and management approach. Outsourcing potential is measured via a questionnaire consisting in 120 five-scored questions on the risk factors in an OOSD project. Based on this result, a prediction is made of how likely outsourcing failure or success will turn out to be. This approach judges the status quo before the project starts. But, it does not contemplate process.

However, risk avoidance during software development is directly coupled to the software development process and the risks factors [5]. This may prove inadequate in offshore outsourcing projects. We agree with Boehm that risk avoidance, or at least risk limitation, in a distributed software development project should be initiated before the project is even launched. This could be brought about by assessing the offshore outsourcing competence of the software project together with the offshore outsourcing company's suitability. With this in mind we have developed the OUTSHORE Maturity Model – OMM.

16.2 Related Works

In the software industry, maturity models are employed to improve process, technology and personnel to ensure better performance. Generally these models assess the startup maturity level of an organization and assess how a higher level might be reached (cf. [16, 25]). The importance of maturity models is established by the fact that product quality rests squarely on process maturity. Consequently a number of maturity models have been developed to support a process upgrade in software development and to describe the evolution of large and complex IS organizations (e.g., [18, 21]). Contingent on the avowed purpose, a number of maturity models focus on various aspects of software development. The common goal, however, is to help organizations improve their software engineering management practice. Table 16.1 offers an overview of the history of the commonly-applied maturity model CMMI resting on the software development process.

Table 16.1 An overview of maturity models

Maturity model	Focus
P-CMM (People Capability Maturity Model)	The level of attention team members should get from management during the systems development process [16].
DMM (Documentation Maturity Model)	Assessment of the quality of software system documentation used in aiding program understanding [33].
MMAST (Maturity Model for Automated Software Testing)	The enhancement of effective software verification and validation [25].
SE-CMM (Systems Engineering Capability Maturity Model)	Assistance in coordinating and publishing a model that would foster improvement in the systems engineering process [9].
SA-CMM (Software Acquisition Capability Maturity Model)	The software acquisition capability of an organization [15] defining five maturity levels and several Key Process Areas (KPAs) for consideration.
CMMI (Capability Maturity Model Integration)	Defines goals to be reached by a set of processes in the organization to boost the productivity of software development as it becomes more disciplined and controlled. CMMI consists of five maturity levels and twenty-two process areas [14].
CMMI-DEV (Capability Maturity Model Integration for Development)	Assistance in product and service development processes [10].
CMMI-ACQ (Capability Maturity Model Integration for Acquisition)	Assistance in supply chain management, acquisition, and outsourcing processes in government and industry [11].

Customary in maturity models is that they assist software organizations progressing along the evolutionary path from ad hoc, chaotic processes to mature, disciplined software processes [23]. Note that the focus is clearly on process improvement. See also for example SPICE (Software Process Improvement and Capability Determination) an assessment of single software development processes with process attributes [3].

It is well known that software project management is moulded by a multiplicity of factors, such as communications, project schedules plus planning, and personnel, as stated in [6]. Further, attention is required on well-defined, -managed and -documented software processes in the organization as they are thought to have a significant payoff in terms of project success [17]. Therefore a total development process encompassing individual perspectives that span all organizational levels is to be recommended (cf. [17]). For, beyond software processes, communication and co-ordination mechanisms should play a central role as success co-ordinates in distributed software development [12, 26] because they reduce project uncertainty and improve performance. We would argue that problems in both communication and co-ordination are not only related to the ongoing process. Such problems depend as well on a given buyer maturity and the given project suitability for offshore outsourcing. The other relevant factor is the ability of the participating organizations to perform at the structural level.

Software offshoring maturity models are used to measure the competence of vendors to deliver the performance promised. Some work has already been done covering the maturity of the buyer of distributed development services. The Sourcing of IT Work Offshore (SITO) stage model [8] and the model presented in [28] likewise describe a four-stage migration path for organizations performing offshore IT work. For them, the subject matter will be the buyer's organization itself. However, only a few studies have been done assessing the buyers' ability to co-operate offshore, while assessing the capability of any one project for offshoring. The aim of the OUTSHORE Maturity Model, OMM, is to fill this gap.

16.3 The OUTSHORE Maturity Model (OMM)

The OMM is based on an empirical study carried out to broaden understanding of the risk components of offshore software development. Twenty-nine experts in the field of distributed software development projects came to be interviewed. The semi-structured interviews lasted about one and a half hours and took place from October 2006 to October 2007. The interviews were partly recorded and partly noted down. The collected data was analyzed using Grounded Theory [19]. Based on the results from the interviews risk factors were formulated. These risk factors were subsequently evaluated with respect to their value in offshore software development and with reference to the literature (cf. [2, 1, 20, 31, 30, 36, 35, 34, 27, 29, 28, 7]). Based on this, 20 risk factors (e.g., knowledge management, socio-cultural distance,

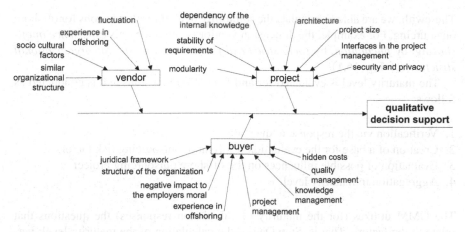

Fig. 16.1 Dimensions and risk factors of the OMM for the qualitative decision support of software development projects

experience in offshoring, process maturity (cf. [2, 23, 24, 30]) became formulated in order to be applied in the OMM (cf. Fig 16.1).

Generally we came to the conclusion that companies are quite aware of the existing distributed software development project risks. Nonetheless, companies, especially in the first few projects, were not in a position to identify or calculate the existing problem, or the inherent risks in the prevailing situation. As stated in [8] and in [28] offshore IT sourcing follows a stage model based on the increasing maturity of the offshore outsourcing effort. At the beginning the buyer possesses no comprehensive development skills – at the highest level, global sourcing becomes a core competence.

The aim of the OMM is to help organizations decide whether they are capable of executing successfully a software development project in a distributed environment in co-operation with one or several partners. In the assessment of maturity, three main dimensions are considered: the buyer, the supplier(s) and the project to be developed within a distributed environment. Each dimension comprises a number of factors used in the entire maturity calculation for that very dimension. Calculated maturity is embodied in a single number from one to five (ajar to the five maturity levels of CMMI). High maturity means that the risk for successful project execution with respect to that single dimension will be low, and vice versa. Simultaneously, it delivers a maturity level for every risk factor, while delivering hints on required improvements.

16.3.1 The Calculation of OUTSHORE Maturity

As already mentioned, OUTSHORE maturity is calculated by means of risk factors. These factors are mapped into three OMM dimensions: *vendor*, *project* and *buyer*.

Therewith, we are able to calculate the suitability of all three dimensions for offshore outsourcing. For example, the dimension vendor is defined by his *experience in offshoring*, by *fluctuation*, by *socio-structural factors* and *any similar organizational structure* (cf. Fig. 16.1).

The maturity level is evaluated for and from all dimensions and is conducted as follows:

1. Verification via the response to questions
2. Creation of a base for the evaluation of offshore outsourcing risk factors
3. Evaluation of possible influences on the offshore outsourcing project
4. Aggregation to maturity level.

The OMM utilizes (for the maturity of calculation responses) the questions that relate to the factors. That is, Step One of the calculation of the maturity level: verification via the response to the questions. Each factor is linked to one or more questions. The answers are scored on a scale from one to five, signifying that the higher the score, the higher the measured maturity involving that single factor. The maturity of factors with more than one answer is calculated from the score average.

Expressed formally, for each risk factor csf_d the base of the maturity B_d is calculated separately as the sum of the maturity of singular risk factors f_d divided by the number of questions belonging to that risk factor ($\#f_d$) of that dimension:

$$B_d = \sum \frac{f_d}{\#f_d} \qquad (16.1)$$

As an example, questions are given that lie within the dimension of the *buyer* and the factor *knowledge management*. Eleven questions belong to that one risk factor. Some of the questions are as follows:

- Have you established a project independent structural knowledge transfer?
- Do you support the communication by employing formal modeling languages (e.g., UML)?
- Do you plan a recirculation of the knowledge transfer from your vendor to your company?
- Do you consider the technical documentation will suffice for the operation and maintenance of software?

The calculation of B_d is Step Two of the calculation of the OUTSHORE Maturity: Creation of a base for the evaluation of the offshore outsourcing risk factors: the B_d provides information on the suitability of an organisation for distributed software development with respect to the risk factors. As some risk factors are more important than others, the factors are weighted with the aid of expert opinion. Table 16.2 depicts the OMM dimensions, the mapped risk factors, and the weight of the risk factors. As already mentioned, the risk factors are based on an empirical study.

Table 16.2 Weight of the influence on the offshore outsourcing development project

Dimension (d)	Risk factor (csf$_d$)	Weight (w$_f$)
Vendor	Experience in offshoring	3.6
Vendor	Fluctuation	4.0
Vendor	Socio-cultural factors	3.0
Vendor	Similar organizational structure	2.0
Project	Modularity	2.66
Project	Project size	3.0
Project	Stability of requirements	1.8
Project	Architecture	1.3
Project	Dependency of the internal knowledge	3.5
Project	Security and privacy	1.3
Project	Interfaces in the project management	2.4
Buyer	Hidden costs	2.2
Buyer	Experience of offshoring	3.6
Buyer	Project management	4.5
Buyer	Knowledge management	4.5
Buyer	Quality management	3.3
Buyer	Juridical framework	3.3
Buyer	Structure of the organization	2.7
Buyer	Negative impact on employers' moral	2.0

The weighting is also empirically based. Experts have been asked to value each risk factor from the buyer's point of view in a scale from one to five. Expert interviews concerning weighting were conducted with our industrial partners from the project OUTSHORE (cf. Acknowledgements). The weighting is assessed as being the average of the valuation provided by the experts.

For example, for the buyer the vendor's experience in offshoring is more important than the comparable organizational structure (4.0 > 2.0). Within the dimension *buyer*, the culture of the company is more significant than its experience in offshoring or distributed software development.

We offer the weighting factor for the risk factors within the OMM as a default setting. But, as it is a default setting, it can be adjusted according to the preferences of the user of the OMM. The influence of each factor varies according to the timing of its appearance and depending on the prevention of its negative effects. This is indicated through the weighting. The weighting itself is Step Three of the calculation of maturity level: Evaluation of the possible influence on the offshore outsourcing project: for each dimension d the maturity M_d can be calculated separately as the sum of the base of the maturity of the singular risk factors B_d multiplied with the weighting factor w_f of that risk factor, and divided by the sum of the weighting factor w_f:

$$M_d = \frac{\sum B_f{}^* w_f}{\sum w_f} \tag{16.2}$$

Next is Step Four: aggregation to maturity level is carried out by calculating the overall maturity M. M is calculated as the sum of the maturities of all dimensions as follows:

$$M = \sum M_d, d \in \{buyer, project, vendor\} \tag{16.3}$$

However, a distributed software development project passes through certain phases. Not only the maturity of the dimensions is important, but also the project process phases. Yet to gain the maximum benefit from the OUTSHORE maturity calculation, the questions need to be mapped into the OMM phase model that is presented in the following section.

16.3.2 The OMM Phase Model

As already mentioned, the dimensions are classified by the questions. The OMM should ease assessment of the risk factors of an OOSD project. On this account we developed the OMM phase model. The OMM phase model is a classical software development process model augmented by an even more vast preparation phase and a transition phase (cf. Fig. 16.2). The process depicted is based upon our empirical study and literature review (e.g., [1, 3, 37]).

Within the OMM, the risk factors are assigned to distributed software development process phases so the maturity of the buyer, vendor and project will be measured. This eases the offer of advice on the specific areas requiring improvement and on the identification of responsible persons or areas of competence. In the following we introduce the phases a distributed software development process passes through.

The process consists of seven major phases (cf. Fig. 16.2) and a comprehensive phase-wide project management containing the phases and linking them thereafter into a chain of major project management activities. The first above-mentioned question of the risk factor knowledge management ("Have you established a project independent structural knowledge transfer?") belongs to this phase.

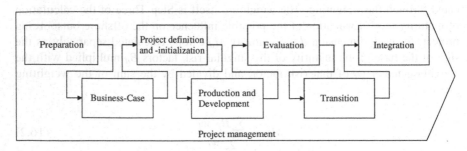

Fig. 16.2 The OMM phase model

In each phase different tasks demanding diverse kinds of resources, roles and activities are to be executed.

The first phase, "Preparation", is devoted to project preparation. The preparation concludes the search for a suitable project partner, a checking of the internal structures of the buyer organization in respect of its abilities to start a distributed project, a checking of the communication structures and skills of employees, as well as a clear formulation of expected results. Furthermore, the main motivation for outsourcing/offshoring needs to be clarified and the employees have to be informed. Moreover, metrics to measure the success must be defined.

The second phase, "Business Case", functions as a self examination for the buyer. The development processes are checked in respect of their capability to be executed by the vendor, the availability of personal skills within the buyer's organization and the suitability of the project for outsourcing are similarly to be checked. The required roles and responsibilities will need to be clarified.

During the third phase, "Project definition and initialization", both project deadlines and teams are defined, along with the outshore partner and the functional and non-functional software requirements to be communicated. The communication structures within the project are defined and, if possible, face-to-face meetings arranged (with sufficient time allowed to get to know all relevant people) will be structured in this phase. The main focus is on the breaking down of social barriers. The second above-mentioned question of the risk factor knowledge management ("Do you support the communication with the use of formal modeling languages (e.g., UML)?") belongs to this phase.

The following phase "Production and development" is devoted to software development. During this phase control mechanisms and communication structures involving the outsourcing partner, as well as clear functioning communication links between the two teams, will have to be checked iteratively.

During the "Evaluation" phase the results of the development phase are evaluated and tested. The information flow from developers to buyers (and vice versa) has to function properly. Lack of trust between the teams complicates this phase.

The "Transition" phase directs knowledge transfer from outshore provider to the buyer and it serves the buyer to avoid dependency on the outshore provider. The knowledge transfer requires working communication mechanisms and trust between the employees. The third above-mentioned question ("Do you plan a recirculation of the knowledge transfer from your vendor to your company?") belongs to this phase.

During the "Integration" phase the developed software is to be integrated into the existing systems. The integration contains a final testing of the new software and therefore requires careful planning. The fourth above-mentioned question of the risk factor knowledge management ("Do you think the technical documentation will be sufficient for the operation and maintenance of the software?") belongs to this phase.

In linking the risk factors to the process we seek to ease and improve the planning of the Global Software Development Process. The model supports communication between various stakeholders (e.g., manager, process owner, business analyst, risk manager, buyer, and vendor).

Table 16.3 Level – buyer, vendor and project maturity

Level	Buyer maturity	Project suitability	Vendor maturity
Level 1: *Initial*	Almost no distributed software development project experience	Very complex and mission-critical projects	Grand cultural and geographical distance and no domain knowledge, almost none distributed software development project capability
Level 2: *Started*	Some exposure to distributed software development projects	Complex and critical projects	A lot of cultural and geographical distance, ad-hoc capabilities
Level 3: *Aware*	Distributed software development projects mechanism emerge	Non-core projects	cultural and geographical distance, strong capabilities
Level 4: *Managed*	Distributed software development projects are understood and controlled	Mitigation or isolated new development	Some cultural and geographical distance, domain knowledge
Level 5: *Mature*	Global player, distributed developments a core competence	Simple, independent and large projects	Marginal cultural and geographical distance, none fluctuation, multi-shore supplier

The OMM phase model specifies major phases for distributed software development and indicates tasks for each phase. However, the phase model does not say anything about the dimensions of the maturity: buyer maturity, vendor maturity and project maturity (cf. Table 16.3). In the following section this aspect of OMM is discussed in more detail.

16.3.3 The Levels of the OUTSHORE Maturity Model

The OMM targets the assessment of the company's offshore outsourcing capability with respect to its suitability for the vendor and the suitability of the project being offshore outsourced. The OMM might be used to measure both offshore and onshore outsourcing. The OMM provides a tool for risk management [4]. OMM rates the buyers' maturity using the dimensions – *strategy, experience in offshoring, project management; knowledge management, hidden costs, quality management, juridical framework, operational structuring, and negative impact on morale* (cf. Fig. 16.1). The project maturity is measured using the dimensions *modularity, size, duration, requirements stability, number of interfaces, type of the project, dependency of the company's internal knowledge, security, plus privacy* as well as *architecture*. The third aspect – vendor – is measured by *socio-cultural distance, experience in offshoring/outsourcing, and fluctuation*.

The goal of the OMM is to predict by means of various criteria whether a planned project that is to be offshore outsourced might be completed successfully and to if offshore outsourcing will be executed to ease and improve the planning of the Global Software Development Process. A successful completion means that the resulting software functions as expected and the development is finished punctually without financial overrun. An offshore outsourcing specific maturity model is needed when the risks of offshore development differ sharply from in-house or onshore development. As mentioned above, the OMM measures the maturity in three dimensions. Each dimension contains elements that are essential for a successful offshore project. The OMM is organized into five maturity levels for each dimension, as depicted in Table 16.3. The calculated value indicates the ability of an organisation to offshore outsource software projects in respect of that dimension. In so doing we believe that the organisation gets a better overview of its weaknesses. The identification of the risk factors is often the problem, as stated in our interviews. The values may be summarised into a combined OMM maturity.

16.4 Summary and Outlook

In this chapter we described the OMM – a novel maturity model to support software offshore outsourcing, which offers companies a decision support system that checks their preparation for offshore outsourcing development projects. The OMM is developed using expert opinion and reference to the literature on outsourcing, offshoring, global and distributed software development as well as to maturity models. Additionally, we have conducted a case study with German SMUs to evaluate the OMM. Thus, we can deliver practical guidelines for practitioners to minimize risks in offshore outsourcing development projects.

The OMM is based on a set of risk factors for successful OOSD, which are extracted from interviews and literature studies. The OMM facilitates the delivery of advice on specific areas requiring improvement and the identification of responsible persons or areas of competence. A decision matrix on the planned project, as well as on vendor preferences (in addition to the buyers' maturity level) is needed to provide a qualitative decision support tool that surveys all relevant risk factors of an offshore outsourcing decision (cf. [1]). The dimensions and risk factors of this decision matrix are depicted in (Fig. 16.1). The OMM provides a rigorous basis for a priori detection of the risk factors of the three dimensions *vendor, project* and *buyer* within the software development process. It offers an objective evaluation tool for OOSD projects, thus providing a stable fundament for further studies of software offshore outsourcing.

Acknowledgements This research was developed within the co-operation project OUTSHORE funded by the German Federal Ministry of Education and Research (bmb+f). OUTSHORE is a collaboration of the Forschungszentrum Informatik (FZI), the institute AIFB of the Universität Karlsruhe (TH) and several industrial partners. The research project has a runtime of 30 months. The goal of the OUTSHORE project is to determine the effect of risk factors on an offshore software development project. A decision model, based on these criteria, will be created for the project run-time simulation to enable risk analysis on distributed software development projects.

References

1. Amberg M, Wiener M (2005) Kritische Erfolgsfaktoren für Offshore Softwareentwicklungsprojekte – eine explorative Studie. Friedrich-Alexander-University, Erlangen-Nürnberg.
2. Aubert BA, Dussault S, Patry M, Rivard S (1999) Managing the risk of IT outsourcing system sciences. Proceedings of the 32nd Annual Hawaii International Conference (HICSS) 32(7): 10–20.
3. Balzert H (2008) Softwaremanagement: Lehrbuch der Softwaretechnik. Spektrum Akademischer Verlag.
4. Betz S, Mäkiö J (2008) Applying the OUTSHORE approach for risk minimisation in offshore outsourcing of software development projects. Multikonferenz Wirtschaftsinformatik (MKWI) 2008, München, Germany.
5. Boehm B (1991) Software risk management: Principles and practices. Piscataway: IEEE Software, 8: 32–41.
6. Boehm BW (1981) Software Engineering Economics. Englewood Cliffs, NJ: Prentice-Hall Inc.
7. Boos E, Iealniesks J, Moczadlo R, Rohfels M, Schmidt C, Simmen J (2005) BITKOM – Leitfaden Offshoring. Bundesverband Informationswirtschaft, Telekommunikation und neue Medien e.V., Berlin.
8. Carmel E, Agarwal, R. (2002) The maturation of offshore sourcing of information technology work. MIS Quarterly Executive 1(2): 65–78.
9. Carnegie Mellon University (1995) Software Engineering Institute. A Systems Engineering Capability Maturity Model VersionSM 1.1. available on: http://www.sei.cmu.edu/pub/documents/95.reports/pdf/mm003.95.pdf. Accessed May 2008.
10. Carnegie Mellon University (2006) CMMI® for Development, Version 1.2, Software Engineering Institute CMMI for Development, available on: http://www.sei.cmu.edu/publications/documents/06.reports/06tr008.html. Accessed May 2008.
11. Carnegie Mellon University (2007) Software Engineering Institute. CMMI® for Acquisition, Version 1.2 available on: http://www.sei.cmu.edu/publications/documents/07.reports/07tr017.html. Accessed May 2008.
12. Casey V, Richardson I (2006) Uncovering the reality within virtual software teams. Workshop on Global Software Development for the Practitioner, Shanghai, China, pp. 66–72.
13. Cataldo M, Herbsleb, JD (2008) Communication patterns in geographically distributed software development and engineers' contributions to the development effort. Proceedings of the 2008 International Workshop on Co-operative and Human Aspects of Software Engineering, Leipzig, Germany, pp. 25–28.
14. Chrissis MB, Konrad M, Shrum S (2006) CMMI. Guidelines for Process Integration and Product Improvement. Reading, MA: Addison-Wesley.
15. Cooper J, Fischer M (2002) Software Aquisition Capability Maturity Model® Version 1.03., Technical Report available on: http://www.sei.cmu.edu/pub/documents/95.reports/pdf/mm003.95.pdf. Accessed May 2008.
16. Curtis B, Hefley WE, Miller SA (1995) People Capability Maturity Model [P-CMM]. UK: Addison-Wesley.
17. Curtis B, Kellner MI, Over J (1992) Process modeling. Communications of the ACM 35(9): 75–90.
18. Galliers R, Sutherland AR (2003) The Evolving Information Systems Strategy, 3rd edn. Oxford: Strategic Information Management, Elsevier.
19. Glaser B, Strauss A (1967) The discovery of Grounded Theory: Strategies of Qualitative Research. New York: Aldine.
20. Gold T (2005) Outsourcing Software Development – Making it Work. Boca Raton, FL: Auerbach Publications.

21. Greiner LE (1972) Evolution and revolution as organizations grow. Harvard Business Review 50(4): 37–46.
22. Herbsleb J, Mockus A, Finholt T, Grinter R (2000) Distance, dependencies, and delay in a global collaboration. Proceedings of the 2000 ACM Conference on Computer Supported Co-operative Work, pp. 319–328.
23. Herbsleb J, Zubrow D, Goldenson D, Hayes W, Paulk M. (1997) Software quality and the capability maturity model. Communications of the ACM 40(6): 30–40.
24. Herbsleb JD, Moitra D (2001) Global software development. IEEE Software, March/April 18(2): 16–20.
25. Humphrey WS (1989), Managing the Software Process. Reading, MA: Addison-Wesley.
26. Kraut RE, Streeter LA (1995) Co-ordination in large scale software development. Communications of the ACM 38(7): 69–81.
27. Lientz B, Larssen L (2006) Risk Management for IT-Projects: How to Deal with over 150 Issues and Risks. Oxford: Elsevier.
28. McCarthy J, Ferrusi Ross C, Schwaber CE (2003) Users' Offshore Evolution and Its Governance Impact. Forrester Research, December.
29. Mezak S (2006) Software Without Borders – A Step-by-Step Guide to Outsourcing Your Software Development. Los Altos, CA: Earthrise Press.
30. Moczadlo R (2005) Chancen und Risiken des offshore-Development – Empirische Analyse der Erfahrungen deutscher Unternehmen, Germany, available on: http://www.competencesite.de/offshore.nsf/8FB68EAB823EF285C1256D72005BBCD1/$File/studie_offshore_prof_moczadlo.pdf.
31. Morales AW (2004) Outshore by Numbers, available on: http://www.ddj.com/architect/184415074.
32. Paasivaara M, Lassenius C (2004) Collaboration practices in global inter-organizational software development projects. Software Process: Improvement and Practice 8(4): 183–199.
33. Pierce R, Tilley S (2002) Automatically connecting documentation to code with rose. Proceedings of the 20th Annual International Conference on Systems Documentation, ACM Press, New York, pp. 157–163.
34. Ramesh G (2007) Managing Global Software Projects. New Delhi: Tata McGraw-Hill Publishing Company Limited.
35. Salma B, Lyes K, Abderrahman E, Younes B (2007) Quality risk in outsourcing. Proceedings of International Conference on Service Systems and Service Management, pp. 1–4.
36. Schaaf J, Weber M (2005) Offshoring-Report 2005: Ready for Take-off, Economics – Digitale Ökonomie und struktureller Wandel, 52, Deutsche Bank Research.
37. Sommerville I (2006) Software Engineering: Update. Amsterdam: Addison-Wesley Longman.
38. Tho I (2005) Managing the Risks of IT Outsourcing. Oxford: Elsevier Butterworth-Heinemann.
39. Weakland T (2005) DiamondCluster 2005 Global IT Outsourcing Study. Chicago, IL: DiamondCluster International, Inc.

Chapter 17
Collaborative Software Architecting Through Knowledge Sharing

Peng Liang, Anton Jansen, and Paris Avgeriou

Abstract In the field of software architecture, there has been a paradigm shift from describing the outcome of the architecting process to documenting architectural knowledge, such as design decisions and rationale. Moreover, in a global, distributed setting, software architecting is essentially a collaborative process in which sharing and reusing architectural knowledge is a crucial and indispensible part. Although the importance of architectural knowledge has been recognized for a considerable period of time, there is still no systematic process emphasizing the use of architectural knowledge in a collaborative context. In this chapter, we present a two-part solution to this problem: a collaborative architecting process based on architectural knowledge and an accompanying tool suite that demonstrates one way to support the process.

17.1 Introduction

According to a recent paradigm shift in the field of software architecture [3, 4, 24], the product of the architecting process is no longer only the models in the various architecture views, but the broader notion of Architectural Knowledge (AK) [23]: the architecture design as well as the design decisions, rationale, assumptions, context, and other factors that together determine architecture solutions. Architectural (design) decisions are an important type of AK, as they form the basis underlying software architecture [19]. Other types of AK include concepts from architectural design (e.g., components, connectors) [35], requirements engineering (e.g., risks, concerns, requirements), people (e.g., stakeholders, organization structures, roles), and the development process (e.g., activities) [10].

P. Liang (✉)
Department of Mathematics and Computing Science, University of Groningen, 9747 AG Groningen, Netherlands
e-mail: liangp@cs.rug.nl

I. Mistrík et al. (eds.), *Collaborative Software Engineering*,
DOI 10.1007/978-3-642-10294-3_17, © Springer-Verlag Berlin Heidelberg 2010

The entire set of AK needs to be iteratively produced, shared, and consumed during the whole architecture lifecycle by a number of different stakeholders as effectively as possible. The stakeholders in architecture may belong to the same or different organization and include roles such as: architects, requirements engineers, developers, maintainers, testers, end users, and managers etc. Each of the stakeholders has his/her own area of expertise and a set of concerns in a system being developed, maintained or evolved. The architect needs to facilitate the collaboration between the stakeholders, provide AK through a common language for communication and negotiation, and eventually make the necessary design decisions and trade-offs.

However, in practice, there are several issues that hinder the effective stakeholder collaboration during the architecting process, which diminishes the quality of the resulting product. One of these problems is the lack of integration of the various architectural activities and their corresponding artifacts across the architecture lifecycle [17]. The different stakeholders typically have different backgrounds, perform discrete architectural activities in a rather isolated manner, and use their own AK domain models and suite of preferred tools. The result is a mosaic of activities and artifacts rather than a uniform process and a solid product.

This chapter focuses on how to integrate stakeholder-specific approaches and tools related to the individual architecting activities. We propose a two-part solution to this problem: a process and an accompanying tool suite. The first part integrates requirements engineering (RE) and the various architecting activities (e.g., analysis, synthesis, evaluation, maintenance etc.,) and their consumed and produced AK, as well as the related stakeholders, into a single process model based on the principle of sharing AK. Note that we have decided to take RE into account: even though it is technically not part of the architecting process, they are closely intertwined and affect one another [31].

The second part is the Knowledge Architect tool suite that supports the collaborative architecting process by realizing and integrating different tools that correspond to the various activities of the process. The tool suite demonstrates one way to support the process, which is derived from the requirements of our industrial partner; there are other ways to support the same activities depending on the organization, the domain, and the specific project at hand. Currently, the tool suite consists of the following tools: the Document Knowledge Client supporting architects writing an architecture document; the Excel and Python Plug-ins supporting system analysts performing quantitative architectural analysis; the Knowledge Repository acting as the central location to store all the relevant AK; the Knowledge Explorer allowing other stakeholders to search, inspect, and trace AK; the Knowledge Translator translating AK from one language to the other for easy understanding. An important feature of the tool suite is that the individual tools share their AK for specific activities through a central knowledge repository, thus providing traceability of the AK and automated checking across a wide range of architecting activities.

Section 17.2 of this chapter discusses collaboration in software architecting and the role of AK. Section 17.3 presents the integrated process for collaborative architecting, while Section 17.4 introduces the accompanying tool suite. Section 17.5

elaborates on the details of collaboration by applying the process and tooling, exemplified through a running example . The paper ends with a discussion on related work, followed by conclusions and directions for future work.

17.2 Theoretical Background

17.2.1 Collaboration in Software Architecting

Architecting is an inherently collaborative process between architects and several stakeholders, who have various concerns and viewpoints. Software architecture:

- Allows stakeholders to work together, communicate, negotiate, and eventually agree upon the architectural decisions and rationale [34].
- Defines the partition of both the technical architecture and the organizational teams building the system [5].
- Resolves errors and deals with risks throughout the system [5].
- Documents the explicit AK of the organization and the project to facilitate future evolution [4].

In [17] the authors of five industrial architecture design methods propose a common model for architecting, comprised of three fundamental architecting activities: architectural analysis, synthesis, and evaluation. They identify the problem of lack of integration between these activities and their corresponding artifacts, and they propose to deal with this problem through the concept of a *backlog*: a collection of needs, issues, problems, ideas, which binds the 3 architecting activities together. Therefore, the backlog acts as a central knowledge artifact that is both produced and consumed by the 3 activities, facilitating their integration. In a collaborative setting, this integration problem is aggravated due to the distribution of stakeholders who have different backgrounds and expertise. In our approach, we also propose knowledge sharing as a promising solution, but at a larger scale: an elaborate set of AK is shared and reused across the proposed architecting process. The shared AK provides a common language for the distributed stakeholders to communicate, reason, and ensure their concerns are being addressed.

The general goals of collaboration in software engineering identified in [38] include: "Driving convergence towards a final architecture and design", "Managing dependencies among activities, artifacts, and organizations", "Identifying, recording and resolving errors", and "Recording organizational memory". We specialize these goals for collaboration in architecting and restate them as follows:

- Producing an integrated and consistent architecture document that has emerged from iterative stakeholder negotiation and agreements.
- Managing the dependencies and establishing traceability among architecting activities, artifacts and involved stakeholders.

- Identifying, recording and resolving architectural conflicts, risks, inconsistency, and incompleteness.
- Recording the knowledge which is relevant to the whole architecting process.

To evaluate how the proposed process and tool achieve these goals, we revisit them in the Conclusions section.

17.2.2 Knowledge Management for Collaborative Architecting

A distinction is often made in Knowledge management (KM) between two types of knowledge [30]: *tacit* (personalized) knowledge that resides in people's head, versus *explicit* knowledge that is codified in some form. The latter is often further characterized as documented or formalized knowledge. Documented knowledge is expressed in natural languages or drawings, e.g., Word and Excel documents that contain architecture description and analysis models. Formal knowledge is expressed (or annotated) in formal languages or models with clearly specified semantics. Typical examples of this form include AK ontologies [22] or AK domain models [2, 9, 10, 20, 21, 35, 36] that formally define concepts and relationships (e.g., *Design Decision* related to *Concern*). They aim at providing a common language for unambiguous interpretation by stakeholders. Formal AK can better facilitate activities for architectural collaboration than documented or tacit AK [10]. However, formal AK entails additional cost and effort [8].

Based on the knowledge types, Hansen et al. classify KM in two strategies [16]: *codification* aims at codifying knowledge and making it available for anyone through knowledge repositories; *personalization*, helps people to communicate knowledge instead of storing it. Both KM strategies are employed in software engineering activities [33]: most research and industry practice has been associated with codification [11], while personalization has been given less attention. In this chapter, we mainly focus on codified AK in collaborative architecting. Personalization is also valuable, and will be further investigated in our future work.

17.3 A Process for Collaborative Software Architecting

The architecting process involves several stakeholders due to its cross-cutting nature from requirements to implementation. For large projects, several teams may work simultaneously on different parts or in different development stages of the whole system, and exchange information. AK is the most important part of the exchanged information and is of paramount importance to the architecting process.

To investigate the role of AK in the architecting process, we have closely cooperated with our industrial partner, Astron (the Dutch radio astronomy institute), which develops large and complex software systems for radio telescopes. What makes these systems interesting from a collaborative AK perspective is: (1) the development consortium consisting of multiple international partners, (2) the long development time of nearly a decade, (3) the long required operational lifetime of at least 20 years.

In this context, we first identified and described the requirements to manage AK in the architecting process of Astron through a number of use cases using our earlier work [37]. We subsequently identified the AK needed to execute these use cases and expressed this knowledge in a domain model [20]. Using both the domain and the use cases, we derived and generalized a collaborative architecting process that integrates the different architecting activities. To support this general process within Astron, we developed a tool suite, which is presented in Section 17.4.

Figure 17.1 illustrates this derived process in terms of activities and AK produced and consumed. Furthermore, it visualizes the close interaction between architecture (solution space) and requirements (problem space), as they are closely intertwined [31]. Every architecting activity can provide feedback to the RE activity, as new insights, acquired during architecting, lead to a better understanding of the problem domain. It is noted that the AK-based architecting process is not sequential, but highly iterative and incremental: achieving an acceptable architecture requires an iterative design and evaluation process that allows refinement to address new

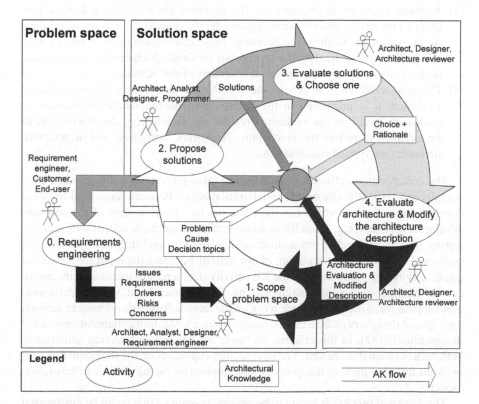

Fig. 17.1 The architecting process from an AK perspective

requirements and trade-offs. The architecting activities and the related RE activity are briefly described as follows:

(0) *Requirements engineering.* This activity fuels the architecting process with different elements (e.g., requirements, drivers, decision topics, risks, and concerns) from the problem space. These form the main input for the activity of scoping the problem space. Requirements engineers, customers and end-users are typical stakeholders.

(1) *Scope problem space.* The architect selects the architecturally significant elements from the problem space and distills them into a concrete problem. To put the problem in perspective, a cause (e.g., from technical aspects) of the problem is described as well. This scoping is needed, as the problem space is usually too big, thereby forcing the architect to focus only on the key issues. Typical stakeholders of this activity are: architects, analysts, designers, and requirements engineers.

(2) *Propose solutions.* The architect uses the existing architecture description and the problem of the previous step, in order to come up with one or more solutions that (partially) address the problem. Architects, analysts, designers, and programmers are typical stakeholders in this activity.

(3) *Evaluate solutions & choose one.* The architect evaluates the solutions, and makes a design decision by selecting among the proposed solutions (according to the evaluation results). The decisions may entail making one or more trade-offs and is accompanied by the appropriate rationale. Architects, designers, and architecture reviewers are typical stakeholders of this activity.

(4) *Evaluate architecture & modify the architecture description.* Once a solution is chosen, it is integrated in the architecture and the whole architecture is evaluated. Based on the evaluation results, the architecture description has to be modified to reflect the new status. Architects, designers, and architecture reviewers are typical stakeholders.

The collaboration activities in architecting takes place in two dimensions: horizontally and vertically. Horizontal collaboration occurs between sequential software development activities, which can be in the macro- or micro-level of the software development phases, e.g., from RE to architecting (the macro-level), or within architecting (the micro-level) from architectural analysis to architectural synthesis. In horizontal collaboration, the output, of one activity becomes the input for the subsequent activity, e.g., the output of the RE activity (i.e., a requirements specification), acts as the input of the architecting activity. On the other hand, vertical collaboration happens when different people work on the same software development activity, e.g., several designers make a class diagram using a UML tool collaboratively in the design activity [32]. In this chapter, we cover the RE and architecting activities in both collaboration dimensions. The next section elaborates on the tool suite that supports the different parts of this process, and emphasizes on the various collaboration aspects.

The proposed process is meant to be generic enough so that it can be customized and adapted into specific architecting processes used in organizations. As an example, we describe how it can be mapped to the generalized model of architecting proposed in [17]: architectural analysis maps to the scoping of the problem space (activity 1); architectural synthesis maps to proposing solutions (activity 2); architectural evaluation maps to evaluating alternative solutions and selecting the optimal one (activity 3), as well as evaluating the architecture with the integrated design decisions (activity 4). The advantage of this general applicability is that it does not conflict with established architecting processes in the organizations. The disadvantage is that it does not contain enough details to be applied on its own; it has to be refined before it can be applied in practice.

17.4 The Knowledge Architect Tool Suite

To support the collaborative architecting process described in the previous section, we implemented the Knowledge Architect (KA): a tool suite[1] for creating, using, translating, sharing, and managing AK. The process itself is described in a generic way and does not delve into details about the various aspects of collaboration, as it is meant to be as broadly applicable as possible. On the contrary, the KA tool suite entails specialized support for integrating the various process activities and supporting collaboration between the stakeholders. In specific, the tool suite implements the following features to serve the collaboration purposes:

- A central *knowledge hub*. In a large project, multiple stakeholders are involved in the different process activities and typically manage and maintain their part of the relevant AK. The knowledge hub is critical for gathering all the AK in one resource, and providing an interface to all involved stakeholders to manage and evolve it;
- *Traceability management*. In a collaborative architecting process, AK entities are produced by various stakeholders. Traceability needs to be established between these collaboratively produced artifacts (e.g., a requirement leads to a design decision and when one changes the other needs to be updated). This is of paramount importance during the architecture iterations, but also for the architecture evolution;
- *Knowledge translation among different stakeholders*. Typically stakeholders come from different backgrounds and have their own perspectives on architecture, usually limited to individual AK entities (see Fig. 17.2). Effective knowledge translation (dashed arrows in Fig. 17.2) enables various stakeholders to understand each other and speak through a "common language". Furthermore, knowledge translation provides the ability to present the "big picture", and especially the complex relationships between different parts of the knowledge;
- *Automated checking*. Different stakeholders working at varied activities and at different times may touch upon the same or related AK entities. Automated

---

[1] Part of the tool suite can be downloaded from http://search.cs.rug.nl/griffin

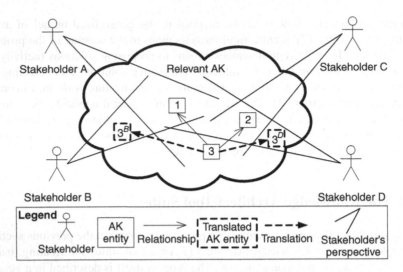

Fig. 17.2 AK sharing from the perspectives of different stakeholders

checking may help to identify the conflicts, inconsistencies, and incompleteness in the collaboratively produced AK entities. Especially, when the amount of knowledge increases, this type of automated support is the only way to effectively manage it.

Currently, the tool suite consists of 6 tools, which are presented in Fig. 17.3: Knowledge Repository, Document Knowledge Client, Excel Plug\-in, Python Plug-in, Knowledge Explorer, and Knowledge Translator. The figure illustrates how these tools are mapped onto the architecting process and its associated activities (see Fig. 17.1).

A brief outline of each tool is provided here. A more elaborate description is presented in the next subsections, while the exact details can be found in [28]. In short, these tools are the followings:

- *Knowledge Repository* is at the heart of the tool suite: a central location, which provides various interfaces for other tools to store and retrieve AK.
- *Document Knowledge Client* is a Word plug-in that supports capturing (anno-tating) and using (storing and retrieving from the Knowledge Repository) AK within architecture and requirement documents inside Microsoft Word.
- *Analysis Model Knowledge Clients* support capturing (annotating) and using (storing and retrieving from the Knowledge Repository) AK of quantitative analysis models. This type of analysis concerns the investigation of alternative architectural solutions by delivering (scenario-based) quantifications of one or more quality attributes of these solutions. Specifically, two knowledge clients are developed (Excel and Python Plug-in):

  - *Excel Plug-in* supports capturing and using AK of quantitative analysis models inside Microsoft Excel [20].

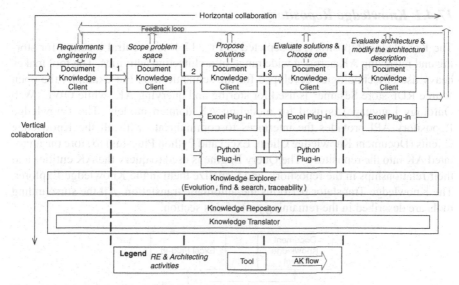

Fig. 17.3 Mapping the KA tool suit onto the requirements engineering and architecting activities

- *Python Plug-in* supports capturing AK from quantitative analysis models described in Python.
- *Knowledge Explorer* analyzes the relationships between AK entities. It provides various visualizations to inspect AK entities and their relationships.
- *Knowledge Translator* (semi-)automatically translates the formal AK based on one AK domain model into the AK based on another, so that various stakeholders can understand each other when they use different AK domain models to document AK.

We have mentioned before that the KA tool suite was built in the context of the Griffin project[2] for use within our industrial partner: Astron. Therefore certain tools of the suite are aimed at integrating with the tools already used at Astron. In particular this covers Microsoft Word for architecture documentation, Microsoft Excel and Python for architecture analysis models. This is only one way to support the architecting activities (see Fig. 17.3); various other tools could be potentially built on the same underlying ideas of annotating AK on documentation and analysis models.

In this section, we first introduce these tools, including the motivations of (why) and functions provided by (what) these tools. In the next section, we present the RE and architecting activities in a collaboration perspective by using these tools in a concrete running example.

---

[2] GRIFFIN: a GRId For inFormatIoN about architectural knowledge, http://griffin.cs.vu.nl/

17.4.1 Knowledge Repository

The Knowledge Repository, as depicted in Fig. 17.4, is a central location for storing and retrieving AK across a wide range of architecting activities. The tool makes heavy use of technologies developed for the semantic web. For example, the open source RDF store Sesame[3] is used for storing and querying AK, while OWL (Web Ontology Language) is used for modeling AK domain models. The Knowledge Repository API provides the interfaces to communicate with all the Knowledge Clients (Document Knowledge Client, Excel and Python Plug-ins) to store the annotated AK into the repository. The Query Engine is used to query the AK entities and their relationships in the repository, and visualize them in the Knowledge Explorer. The Knowledge Translator performs the automatic translation. All the surrounding tools are described in the remaining part of this section.

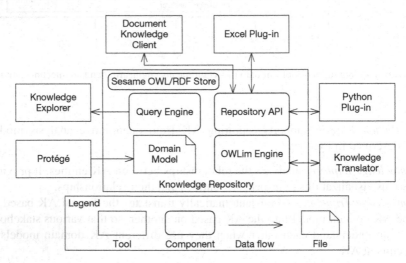

Fig. 17.4 The Knowledge Repository with other tools in the KA tool suite

17.4.2 Document Knowledge Client

The Document Knowledge Client is a plug-in to capture and use explicit AK inside Microsoft Word 2003. Various AK domain models can be deployed in the Knowledge Repository for different users (stakeholders), who annotate the AK using the AK domain models they can understand. Hence, the tool can be reused with other AK domain models. The tool offers three basic functions:

AK capturing: Knowledge can be captured in a Word document by selecting a piece of text and right clicking and choosing the appropriate option from the pop-up menu. When adding a new AK entity, a menu appears which allows the

---

[3] http://www.openrdf.org/

user to provide additional information about the entity, e.g., *Name, Type, Status* and *Connections*.

AK traceability: The relationships among AK entities comprise critical traceability information in collaborative architecting. For example, to find out "who (stakeholders) are concerned with a design decision". The AK traceability can be easily created or removed by pop-up menus in the Document Knowledge Client.

Design maturity assessment: One of the advantages of formalized (annotated) AK is automatic reasoning support based on the underlying formal models. The Document Knowledge Client supports the architect in assessing the completeness of the architecture description. Based on the AK domain model, the tool performs model checks using conformity rules to identify incomplete parts.

17.4.3 Excel Plug-In

The Excel Plug-in implements a domain model for quantitative architecture analysis models in Microsoft Excel. The tool supports analysts in making the AK produced during architecture analysis explicit. The aim is to facilitate the sharing of AK to other analysts and the analysis results in a transparent manner to other stakeholders. The tool offers the following three basic functions:

AK capturing: The major part of the AK of an architectural analysis model in Excel is found in the cells. Often labels surrounding the cell denote the semantic meaning of a cell. The tool allows analysts to make special annotations to cells. For reviewing purposes, the tool also tracks the review state of each cell and allows for comments.

AK traceability: An important feature of the tool is that it is capable of automatically inferring the dependencies among the cells (AK entities). Hence, the traceability relationships between AK entities are automatically captured.

AK visualization: To facilitate manual verification, the tool offers a visualization of the AK dependency graph, which corresponds to the cells in the Excel worksheets.

17.4.4 Python Plug-In

Similar to the Excel Plug-in, the Python Plug-in provides functionality to codify the AK of analysis models. In this case, the analysis models are expressed using the Python programming language. Both the Excel and the Python Plug-in assume quite similar domain models. Hence, the concepts and functionality discussed in the previous section also apply here.

17.4.5 Knowledge Explorer

Typically, the size of an AK repository will be considerable containing thousands of AK entities. Finding the right AK entity, or even worse a number of related AK

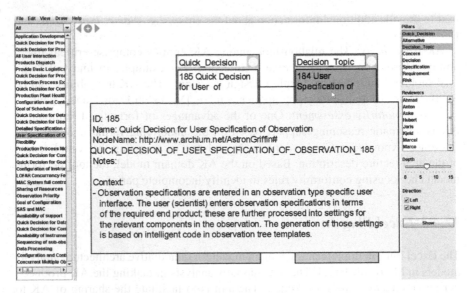

Fig. 17.5 The screenshot of the Knowledge Explorer

entities, from such a big collection is not trivial. Hence, there is a need for a tool to assist in exploring an AK repository. The Knowledge Explorer can support users in visualizing AK entities and their relationships. Figure 17.5 presents a screenshot of the tool. It provides search functionality on the left hand side. The resulting AK entities of this search action are shown in the list on the left hand side. The results can be filtered using the drop down box on the left, thereby reducing the size of the found results. The filtering is based on the type of the AK. The available options are taken from the used AK domain model. Double clicking on one of the search items results in illustrating a number of related AK entities in columns.

17.4.6 Knowledge Translator

The purpose of the Knowledge Translator is to translate the AK in various AK domain models from one to the other and vice versa. This allows various users to understand the AK codified in different AK domain models. This is critical for stakeholders from different backgrounds to understand each other in a collaborative architecting process. For example, a requirements engineer and an architect use different AK domain models to produce and consume requirements (part of AK), but need to have a common understanding. Currently, we employ the core model proposed in [10] as a central model for the AK translation by an indirect translation approach [27].

The AK translation can be done manually or automatically. Both ways have their respective advantages and disadvantages on translation cost and quality, and stakeholders can select an appropriate manner by trading off quality and cost in their own context. The initial cost-benefit analysis about the AK translation cost and quality has been investigated in [27].

17.5 Collaboration Within the Process with KA

In this section, we present the collaboration within the proposed architecting process, as it is supported by the KA tool suite. We discuss both horizontal and vertical collaboration and demonstrate them through a running example. The context of this running example originates from the architecting process used at our industrial partner, Astron (see Section 17.3). In their projects, there is a large and complex body of knowledge that needs to be shared frequently among the distributed stakeholders. However, the different backgrounds and expertise of these stakeholders restrains them from achieving a common understanding and thus hinders the integration of collaborative architecting activities. We have worked closely with Astron for the software architecture of two projects that concern the next generation of radio telescopes. The stakeholders involved with the architecting process in these projects include end-users (scientists), requirements engineers, architects, analysts, designers and architecture reviewers.

17.5.1 Requirements Engineering

17.5.1.1 Horizontal Collaboration

In a traditional software development scenario, a requirements engineer produces the software requirements specification in a document, e.g., in a Word file. The requirements engineer subsequently delivers the requirements documentation to the architect for the architecture design. Within this process, the requirements engineer, architect, and other related stakeholders will closely interact with each other. This close interaction is needed to ensure common document understanding [6], conciliate requirements [31], and improve the architecture design, etc. In a distributed development environment or in a long-term development project, this intensive interaction between the requirements engineer and the architect is quite challenging. The geographical distance between the two actors hinders effective interaction, while staff reassignment in a long-term project would result in knowledge vaporization [19]. In such cases, the Knowledge Repository acts as the project requirements knowledge center: the repository provides valuable requirements information according to established AK domain models[4], and it helps the architect to understand the requirements correctly and unambiguously.

---

[4] If there is no explicit specification, we assume that the AK domain model employed in various requirements engineering and architecting activities for producing and consuming AK is the same one, so that all stakeholders can communicate the AK in a common language.

Running example: a requirements engineer[5] specifies the requirements (including *architectural significant requirements*, *concerns* and *risks*, etc.,) in the requirements document through discussion with customers. Afterwards, the requirements engineer uses the Document Knowledge Client to annotate the knowledge about requirements in this document, e.g., "The user (scientist) uses these interfaces to propose and specify observations." (an AK entity of concept *Requirements*), and "This flexibility is of great importance especially for the high performance applications." (an AK entity of concept *Concerns*). In the end, all the annotated AK entities are stored into the Knowledge Repository. The architect retrieves the requirements information from the Knowledge Repository, and scopes the problem (architectural analysis) by choosing only the architecturally-significant ones (e.g., scoping the *decision topics* from the *requirements*). The architect subsequently stores the newly produced AK entities into the Knowledge Repository for further collaboration.

The whole collaboration process is illustrated in Fig. 17.6. The numbers in this figure represent the actions sequence. The KA tool suite offers features to support these collaboration activities. For example, the design maturity assessment function based on formal AK can help the architect to find out whether all the *requirements* have been considered or not. Another example is that the traceability of formal AK can help the architect to trace from the design space (e.g., a *design decision*) back to the original cause in the problem space (e.g., a *requirement*).

17.5.1.2 Vertical Collaboration

The typical scenario in RE is that all the system stakeholders can propose their individual *requirements*, *concerns*, and *risks* from different perspective and at different levels (business goals, product features, user requirements, etc.). Inevitably, there are always conflicts (e.g., conflict business goals, concerns) and mismatch

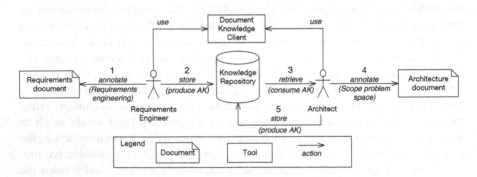

Fig. 17.6 AK sharing process between requirements engineer and architect

---

[5] The collaboration between other stakeholders is also critical, e.g., between the telescope user and requirements engineer, but we focus on the requirements engineer and architect in the scope of this chapter.

(e.g., no user requirements relating to a product feature) in the candidate requirements. The collaboration among all the requirements stakeholders is needed to form a clear and unambiguous requirements specification using negotiation and reaching compromises. Another situation is that different requirements engineers work on the requirements specification for different part of the system at same time. In this case, they also have to understand the requirements, which have been elicited and documented by other requirements engineers for consistency. Hence, collaboration among these requirements engineers is a necessity to achieve a coherent and consistent requirements specification.

Running example: Customer *A* specifies the requirement "The flow of information, either control or monitoring metrics, is in the vertical direction.", and then the requirements engineer uses the Document Knowledge Client to annotate this *requirement* and store this AK entity into the Knowledge Repository. Customer *B* uses the Document Knowledge Client to retrieve the latest *requirements* from the Knowledge Repository. After this, Customer *B* finds out that the *requirement* "The flow of information in the vertical direction" is not desirable. The customer wants "The flow of information is in the horizontal direction". In this situation, Customer *B* adds his/her requirement, annotates, and stores this requirement as a conflict requirement with the requirement proposed by Customer *A*. Eventually, the requirements engineers will try to negotiate and resolve the conflict with all the other requirements stakeholders (e.g., through voting) or just inquire the high level project decision maker to choose one.

17.5.2 Scope Problem Space

17.5.2.1 Horizontal Collaboration

"Scope problem space" is the first activity in the architecting process, aimed at refining the problem space by selecting the architecture significant problem elements. The results of this activity are a set of *architectural significant requirements*, e.g., *problem, cause,* and *decision topic*s, which are further used in the following activity to produce *alternative architectural solutions*. The architect uses the Document Knowledge Client to annotate these *architectural significant requirements*, which he/she has identified, using the AK domain model, and stores them into the Knowledge Repository. After this, the analyst can retrieve this AK from the Knowledge Repository, understand it based on the AK domain model, and propose *alternative architectural solutions*.

Running example: An architect analyzes an *architectural significant requirement*, e.g., "In this (data) view on the system software, we focus on the control over the data processing pipelines.", and gets a *decision topic*, e.g., "the control method over the data processing pipelines", which has to be addressed by a *design decision*. After that, the architect annotates and stores this *decision topic* into the Knowledge Repository. The *decision topics* can be retrieved by the analyst from the Knowledge Repository for further collaboration, e.g., in the proposing solutions activity.

17.5.3 Propose Solutions

17.5.3.1 Horizontal Collaboration

Once the scoping of the problem space is complete and a clearer picture of the problem at hand is created, the architect has to define one or more alternative solutions to (partially) address the problem. These alternatives need to be shared in some shape or form, e.g., using a textual description, figures, presentation, or a conversation, in order to be evaluated. For important decisions, the alternatives are shared with the stakeholders: (1) to validate whether the alternative is indeed addressing the problem (2) to create understanding and support among the stakeholders for the choice made in the next step.

Furthermore, thinking up alternative solutions often leads to new insights in the problem space. For example, it is not uncommon to find requirements unclear on key aspects or find out that a particular concern is being overlooked. Hence, close collaboration with a requirements engineer (and perhaps other stakeholders as well) is needed to sort out these aspects.

Running example: Following the running example from the previous activity, the analyst retrieves this *decision topic* from the Knowledge Repository, and proposes several *alternative architectural solutions*, e.g., "use real-time control method", "use batch control" and "use real-time or batch control depending on the data characteristics". After this, the analyst annotates these *alternative architectural solutions* in the architecture document and stores these newly produced AK entities into the Knowledge Repository. The architecture reviewer retrieves the corresponding *concerns, decision topic*, and its *alternative architectural solutions* from the Knowledge Repository. Based on this AK, the reviewer evaluates the *alternative architectural solutions* against related user *concerns*. It is noted that there is a bidirectional traceability relationship created automatically between a *decision topic* and an *alternative architectural solution*, as dictated by the relationships in the AK domain model. With the bidirectional traceability relationship, when the architect changes (removes, modifies) the *decision topic*, then the analyst will be notified to reconsider the *alternative architectural solutions* which have been proposed.

17.5.3.2 Vertical Collaboration

For two reasons the proposed alternatives need to be shared among architects as well. Firstly, sharing alternatives among each other inspires architects to consider new solution directions. Often this takes the form of creatively combining existing alternatives into a new one. Secondly, this sharing prevents architects from redoing work already done by their peers. For analysts, sharing the alternatives is important as well. The analysis of different experts has to be reconciled to evaluate a single alternative. However, this requires a shared understanding among the analysts what this alternative exactly entails. Consequently, the knowledge of what these alternatives are should be shared.

Running example: The analysts use the Knowledge Explorer to find out what kind of assumptions their fellow analysts have made in their analysis about the alternatives. Based on this knowledge, they can update their own analysis models. Software architects can share a software architecture document to facilitate vertical collaboration. Using the Document Knowledge Client, an architect can trace from a *Decision Topic* to the proposed alternatives and read their description.

17.5.4 Evaluate Solutions and Choose One

17.5.4.1 Horizontal Collaboration

The horizontal collaboration in this activity takes place between the software architect/analyst and other stakeholders. It involves sharing four different types of AK. The first type is the evaluation criteria that should be used to judge the various alternative solutions. An important criterion is the extension to which a proposed alternative solution addresses the defined decision topic. In addition, the captured concerns during RE provides good candidates for evaluation criteria. Additional horizontal collaboration with the requirements engineers is needed when the evaluation criteria are not clear.

The second type is the relative importance of the aforementioned criteria. Typically, there are differences among how the stakeholders perceive the importance of the criteria. Hence, the architect has to reach an acceptable compromise, and through horizontal collaboration, communicate this compromise to the stakeholders.

The third type is the perceived pros and cons of each alternative, i.e., the ranking of each proposed alternative solution on the defined criteria. Often conflicts arise among stakeholders due to differences in the perception of these pros and cons and their associated likelihood and strength. Since this knowledge forms the basis of the rationale of the choice, it is of paramount concern to reach consensus among the stakeholders about these properties. One of the goals of analysts is providing detailed information about these properties in an objective manner to facilitate this ranking.

The fourth type is the choice made among the alternatives. The associated rationale is based on the three earlier introduced elements. In practice, only this last element is typically communicated. In this situation, the rationale and the three other elements are only shared when asked for.

Running example: In the previous step, three *alternative architectural solutions* were proposed and documented in a document: "use real-time control method", "use batch control" and "use real-time or batch control depending on the data characteristics". In this step, the architect writes down the choice made (e.g., for the use real-time control method) and provides a small explanation for this choice, e.g., reducing costs by not requiring additional storage. Selecting this piece of text and pressing the add AK entity (KE) button of the Document Knowledge Client adds the text as a *Decision* to the Knowledge Repository. To provide traceability, the architect relates the newly created *Decision* KE to the chosen *Alternative*. Indirectly, this also relates the *Decision* to the other considered alternatives through their common *Decision Topic*.

To provide rationale, the tool suite provides two options. The first one is found in the Document Knowledge Client and allows the architect to relate an analysis result from one of the Analysis Model Clients (Excel and Python Plug-ins) as either a *Pro* or *Con* to an *Alternative*. For example, the predicted cost of the real-time alternative. The second option is to use the Knowledge Explorer to find suitable concerns (e.g., cost) that could be an evaluation criterion.

17.5.4.2 Vertical Collaboration

Among analysts the vertical collaboration for this activity mostly consists of unifying the analysis results of different experts in one consistent picture. In this way, evaluating the alternatives becomes relatively easy. Vertical collaboration among architects is about the knowledge sharing covering the aforementioned four AK types, since it is this knowledge that makes up the reasoning behind the architecture.

Running example: To present an objective basis for decision making analysts make a four column table in the architecture document with the first column being the criteria used and the other three columns representing the three alternatives considered. The rows present for each criterion the analysis result for each alternative. Using the Document Knowledge Client, the analyst creates the traceability between the document and his/her quantitative analysis from Python or Excel. By sharing this document with other analysts, each adding their own row, a complete unified picture for the evaluation is created. Architects use a similar approach.

17.5.5 Evaluate Architecture and Modify the Architecture Description

This evaluation activity is similar to the previous evaluation activity, but has a larger scope. The previous activity focuses on the evaluation of alternative architecture solutions while this activity evaluates the entire architecture with the incorporated new design decision (chosen solution). Consequently, the collaborations through AK sharing of these two evaluation activities are quite similar. Hence, we do not repeat them again. We focus on the activity "modify the architecture description".

17.5.5.1 Horizontal Collaboration

Collaboration in this activity happens between sequential activities, i.e., horizontal collaboration from architecture description to detailed design. In this collaboration, the Knowledge Repository can also act as the hub in which the architects and designers share the architecture description information.

Running example: An architect makes a *design decision* "use real time control during data taking and processing", annotates, and stores this AK entity into the Knowledge Repository. A designer retrieves the latest *design decisions* from the Knowledge Repository and makes a detailed design which is based on this *design decision*.

17.5.5.2 Vertical Collaboration

Based on the evaluation results, an architect modifies the design and documents the outcome of design, using natural language or special notations (e.g., Architectural Description Language or UML) in a document. The architecture description can be completed by a single architect in a small project, but for a large project, several architects will be working together for the various parts of the system. The collaboration among them is essential to produce an integrated and consistent architecture document in the end. The Knowledge Repository acts as the hub in which all the architects share the architecture description information with each other.

Running example: One of the user *concerns* about the system is stated as "Performance issue is in a higher priority than cost in this system". Architect *A* makes a *design decision* to address this *concern* as "use real time control during data taking and processing", and annotates and stores this AK entity into the Knowledge Repository. Architect *B* makes another *design decision* to address the same *concern* as "limit the data payload during data taking and processing", annotates, and stores this AK entity into the Knowledge Repository as well. Architect *C* retrieves the latest *design decisions* from the Knowledge Repository and uses the design maturity assessment function provided by Document Knowledge Client to verify the architecture design. The design maturity assessment function detects that these two *design decisions* address the same *concern* and are actually in conflict with each other. Therefore, Architect *C* tries to negotiate with Architects *A* and *B* to come up with a single *design decision*, e.g., "use real time control during data taking and processing". Other defects or weak points can also be detected by the design maturity assessment, such as incompleteness. Architect *C* annotates the new *design decision* and stores (updates) the Knowledge Repository for further collaboration with other architects.

17.5.6 Feedback Loop

Feedback can be provided from any architecting activity to the RE activity, as for example new user *concerns*, *solutions* and *design decisions* pose new *requirements*. Architecting is a highly iterative process. In each iteration, the requirements are revisited until all the *architectural significant requirements* are satisfied and all *risks* are mitigated. The Knowledge Repository is the central storage of AK produced in all activities, and supports feeding this knowledge back to the RE activity.

Running example: An example of collaboration that concerns providing feedback to RE is the following: the architect makes a *design decision* "use SAS (a software package for data visualization) for data observation", annotates, and stores this *design decision* into the Knowledge Repository. A requirements engineer retrieves this *design decision* from the Knowledge Repository and finds that this *design decision* results in a new *requirement* "the data observation should be visualized in GUI". The requirements engineer annotates and stores this newly-produced requirement into the Knowledge Repository. In this way, (other) requirements engineers

can retrieve the updated requirements from the Knowledge Repository and validate
the consistency between the new requirement and the existing ones.

17.5.7 Architectural Knowledge Translation

AK translation is a common function in all activities (both RE and architecting),
since the involved stakeholders typically use different AK domain models to produce and consume the AK. It is comparable to human language translation, were
people from different countries speaking different languages try to communicate. A
translator is needed for effective communication between them, as he or she translates from one language to another and vice versa. The quality of the translation
depends on the quality of the translator, i.e., how correctly the translator can translate
knowledge. In AK translation, various translation methods can be employed with
their specific advantages and disadvantages depending on the translation context
(number of involved AK domain models and AK entities, etc.,) [26, 27].

Running example: A requirements engineer working at branch *A* of Astron uses
the AREL AK domain model [35] to annotate knowledge about *requirements* e.g.,
"The user (scientist) uses these interfaces to propose and specify observations" (an
AK entity of AREL concept *Functional requirement*), and "The new user (scientist)
shall know how to use these interfaces to propose and specify observations in 2 h"
(an AK entity of AREL concept *Non-functional requirement*). These two AK entities are subsequently stored into the Knowledge Repository. An architect working
at branch *B* of Astron uses the LOFAR AK domain model [18] to consume and produce AK. In particular, the architect uses the concept *Requirement* from the LOFAR
AK domain model to retrieve all the requirements information from the Knowledge
Repository which has been produced by the requirements engineer of branch *A*. Due
to the different requirement concepts being used by the AK producer (requirements
engineer at branch *A*) and consumer (architect at branch *B*), knowledge translation
is needed. The Knowledge Translator uses the defined AK concept mapping relationship to translate AK entities. For example, the AREL AK concept *Functional
requirement* and *Non-functional requirement* are both the *subClassOf* the LOFAR
AK concept *Requirement*. Using this relationship, the Knowledge Translator translates the two AK entities annotated in the AREL domain model into the AK entities
in the LOFAR domain model and stores translated AK entities into the Knowledge
Repository. After this translation, the architect at branch *B* can retrieve all the
requirements information from the Knowledge Repository.

17.6 Related Work

Computer Supported Cooperative Work (CSCW) in software engineering comprises all software engineering methods, norms, and tools that support teamwork
flexibly and effectively [7]. CSCW concentrates on improving the efficiency of

groupware [25] for software development. It focuses on the vertical collaboration in the software development lifecycle, e.g., the collaboration among requirements engineers or among designers. One such example is ProjectIT-Studio, an integrated environment that supports collaborative RE by combining wikis with CASE tools for requirements specification and validation [14]. This tool can assist non-technical stakeholders during the requirements specification and help requirements engineers for a seamless integration with dedicated RE CASE tools. ProjectIT-Studio fosters the stakeholders' involvement in collaborative RE from a socio-technical perspective. Another example is the UML profile UML-G for cooperative UML modeling in the design activity [32]. It supports software modeling by explicitly representing shared data, roles and actors in cooperative sessions. UML-G stresses the sharing of design outcomes (i.e., models), but does not pay attention to the rationale underneath the design.

A CSCW approach for architecting was proposed in [15] addressing the collaborative architecture modeling of complex component-based systems. A collaborative modeling tool was provided for the architecture design team in which several architects design architecture cooperatively. Multiple architects are able to concurrently access and manipulate the software architecture information stored in a server machine. The shared software architecture information in this tool is mostly the design artifacts (e.g., components, data flows, external entities, etc.). There is no support to store information about design decisions and rationale.

Similarly, Maheshwari and Teoh implemented a web-based tool for collaborative software architecture evaluation, supporting the Architecture Tradeoff Analysis Method (ATAM) [29]. They argue that the ATAM method has its limitations in an increasingly globalized software industry in which the distribution of development teams is extensive. Their web-based tool provides a mental mapping from the physical world to the internet world. For example, their tool set provides communication tools, such as chatting, brainstorming, voting tool, etc. The tool set also provides some assistant tools for ATAM, such as Utility Tree Viewer/Editor, Features Evaluator, etc.). Most of the knowledge exchanged by their tool set is personalized knowledge, which is often difficult to understand by users who come from different backgrounds.

Farenhorst et al. use wikis to support collaboration, communication, and consensus decision making in the architecting process of distributed development by sharing AK [13]. They suggested that, for successful AK sharing, it is necessary to tailor the types and content of AK for sharing according to the concrete architecting process [12]. Their work focuses on personalized (e.g., by using yellow pages) and documented AK and not on formal AK.

PAKME (Process-centric Architectural Knowledge Management Environment) is a web-based tool aimed at providing knowledge management support for the architecting process [1]. PAKME focuses on various collaborative features (e.g., collaborative decision making) for distributed stakeholders involved in the architecting process by managing codified AK (pattern, decision etc.,) and personalized AK (contact management, online collaboration, etc.). Other related work on AK sharing and reusing can be found in the SHARK workshop series [3, 4, 24].

17.7 Conclusions and Future Work

AK is widely accepted and recognized to be of paramount importance for the success of software architecting. However, the collaboration among the stakeholders involved in the architecting process is hindered by the lack of integration of architecting activities and the corresponding AK. This has severe implications for the quality of both the architecting process and the product. This chapter presented a collaborative architecting process and the accompanying tool suite that integrate the architecting activities through AK sharing.

The process and the accompanying tool suite address the four goals of collaboration in software architecting identified in Section 17.2.1:

(1) Using the central Knowledge Repository and Knowledge Client tools, an integrated and consistent architecture document can be produced through stakeholders collaboration;
(2) Using various AK domain models to capture (annotate) AK in the Knowledge Clients, dependencies and especially traceability among architecture artifacts can be effectively managed in the Knowledge Repository;
(3) Using the functions provided by the Knowledge Client tools (e.g., design maturity assessment of the Document Knowledge Client), the architectural conflicts, risks, inconsistency and incompleteness can be identified, recorded and resolved based on the formal relationships defined in the AK domain model and semantic web inference;
(4) Using the central Knowledge Repository, all the knowledge which is relevant to the whole architecting process (AK) is recorded.

Although the proposed approach (process and tool suite) was derived from a specific organization, it is generally applicable to other organizations: as explained in Section 17.3, the proposed collaborative architecting process is orthogonal to current architecting processes. Due to its generic nature, it has to be adapted and customized into an existing architecting process before it is put into practice. For the accompanying tool suite, some general tools (Knowledge Repository, Document Knowledge Client, Knowledge Explorer, and Knowledge Translator) can be adjusted and employed to the architecting processes mentioned above since they follow closely the proposed process. The Excel and Python Plug-ins have been developed according to Astron's needs, and can only be used if other organizations have similar needs (quantitative analysis).

The KA tool suite has been used and (empirically) validated in two industrial case studies at Astron for quantitative analysis of architecture design [20] and enrichment of architecture documentation [18]. In [20] the tool suite was deemed effective for facilitating AK sharing for verification and validation of quantitative architectural solutions. In [18] we proved that the tool suite helps to partially address the shortcomings of current architecture documentation approaches of large and complex systems.

In the future, the integrated collaborative architecting process with the tool suite should be further validated in a larger industrial project with a cost-benefit analysis.

The tool suite needs to be further improved with respect to its usability and scalability. Finally, we plan to extend this suite with other tools for a wider application of AK sharing (e.g., UML/ADL modelers, Email Plug-in, and other quantitative analysis tools).

Acknowledgments This research has been partially sponsored by the Dutch Joint Academic and Commercial Quality Research & Development (Jacquard) program on Software Engineering Research via contract 638.001.406 GRIFFIN: a GRId For inFormatIoN about architectural knowledge. The authors would like to thank Astron for their support and access to the LOFAR software architecture documents.

References

1. Ali-Babar M, Gorton I (2007) A tool for managing software architecture knowledge. Proceedings of the 2nd Workshop on Sharing and Reusing architectural Knowledge – Architecture, rationale, and Design Intent (SHARK/ADI 2007), 20–26 May, pp. 11–17.
2. Ali-Babar M, Gorton I, Kitchenham B (2006) A framework for supporting architecture knowledge and rationale management. In: Dutoit AH et al. (Eds.) Rationale Management in Software Engineering. Berlin: Springer-Verlag, pp. 237–254.
3. Avgeriou P, Lago P, Kruchten P (2008) Third International Workshop on Sharing and Reusing Architectural Knowledge (SHARK 2008). ICSE Companion, pp. 1065–1066.
4. Avgeriou P, Kruchten P, Lago P, Grisham P, Perry D (2007) Architectural knowledge and rationale: Issues, trends, challenges. ACM SIGSOFT Software Engineering Notes 32(4): 41–46.
5. Bass L, Clements P, Kazman R (2003) Software Architecture in Practice, 2nd edn. Boston, MA: Addison-Wesley Professional.
6. Bhat JM, Gupta M, Murthy SN (2006) Overcoming requirements engineering challenges: Lessons from offshore outsourcing. IEEE Software 23(5): 38–44.
7. Bischofberger WR, Kofler T, Mätzel KU, Schäffer B (2002) Computer supported cooperative software engineering with beyond-sniff. Proceedings of the 7th Conference on Software Engineering Environments (SEE 1995), 5–7 April, pp. 135–143.
8. Capilla R, Nava F, Carrillo C (2008) Effort estimation in capturing architectural knowledge. Proceedings of the 23rd IEEE/ACM International Conference on Automated Software Engineering (ASE 2008), 15–19 September, pp. 208–217.
9. Capilla R, Nava F, Pérez S, Dueñas J (2006) A web-based tool for managing architectural design decisions. ACM SIGSOFT Software Engineering Notes 31(5): 20–27.
10. de Boer RC, Farenhorst R, Lago P, van Vliet H, Clerc V, Jansen A (2007) Architectural knowledge: Getting to the core. Proceedings of the 3rd International Conference on the Quality of Software Architectures (QoSA 2007), 12–13 July, pp. 197–214.
11. Dingsøyr T, Conradi R (2002) A survey of case studies of the use of knowledge management in software engineering. International Journal of Software Engineering and Knowledge Engineering 12(4): 391–414.
12. Farenhorst R (2006) Tailoring knowledge sharing to the architecting process. ACM SIGSOFT Software Engineering Notes 31(5): 15–19.
13. Farenhorst R, van Vliet H (2008) Experiences with a wiki to support architectural knowledge sharing. Proceedings of the 3rd Workshop on Wikis for Software Engineering (Wikis4SE 2008), 8–10 September.
14. Ferreira D, da Silva AR (2008) Wiki supported collaborative requirements engineering. Proceedings of the 3rd Workshop on Wikis for Software Engineering (Wikis4SE 2008), 8–10 September.
15. Guo J, Liao Y, Parviz B (2006) A collaboration-oriented software architecture modeling system – JarchiDesigner. Proceedings of the 13th Annual IEEE International Symposium

and Workshop on Engineering of Computer Based Systems (ECBS 2006), 27–30 March, pp. 481–482.

16. Hansen MT, Nohria N, Tierney T (1999) What's your strategy for managing knowledge? Havard Business Review 77(2): 106–116.

17. Hofmeister C, Kruchten P, Nord RL, Obbink H, Ran A, America P (2005) A general model of software architecture design derived from five industrial approaches. Journal of Systems and Software 80(1): 106–126.

18. Jansen A, Avgeriou P, van der Ven JS (2009) Enriching software architecture documentation. Journal of Systems and Software 82(8): 1232–1248.

19. Jansen A, Bosch J (2005) Software architecture as a set of architectural design decisions. Proceedings of the 5th Working IEEE/IFIP Conference on Software Architecture (WICSA 2005), 6–10 November, pp. 109–120.

20. Jansen A, de Vries T, Avgeriou P, van Veelen M (2008) Sharing the architectural knowledge of quantitative analysis. Proceedings of the 4th International Conference on the Quality of Software Architectures (QoSA 2008), 14–17 October, pp. 220–234.

21. Jansen A, van der Ven J, Avgeriou P (2007) Tool support for architectural decisions. Proceedings of the 6th Working IEEE/IFIP Conference on Software Architecture (WICSA 2007), 6–9 January, pp. 44–53.

22. Kruchten P (2004) An ontology of architectural design decisions in software intensive systems. Proceedings of the 2nd Groningen Workshop on Software Variability Management (SVM 2004), 2–3 December, pp. 54–61.

23. Kruchten P, Lago P, van Vliet H (2006) Building up and reasoning about architectural knowledge. Proceedings of the 2nd International Conference on the Quality of Software Architectures (QoSA 2006), 27–29 June, pp. 43–58.

24. Lago P, Avgeriou P (2006) First workshop on sharing and reusing architectural knowledge. ACM SIGSOFT Software Engineering Notes 31(5): 32–36.

25. Li J, Li T, Lin Z, Mathur AP, Kanoun K (2004) Computer supported co-operative work in software engineering. Proceedings of the 28th International Computer Software and Applications Conference (COMPSAC 2004), 27–30 September, pp. 328–328.

26. Liang P, Jansen A, Avgeriou P (2008) Selecting a high-quality central model for sharing architectural knowledge. Proceedings of the 8th International Conference on Quality Software (QSIC 2008), 12–13 August, pp. 357–365.

27. Liang P, Jansen A, Avgeriou P (2009) Sharing architecture knowledge through models: Quality and cost. The Knowledge Engineering Review 24(3): 225–244.

28. Liang P, Jansen A, Avgeriou P (2009) Knowledge architect: A tool suite for managing software architecture knowledge. Technical Report RUG-SEARCH-09-L01, University of Groningen, http://www.cs.rug.nl/~liangp/download/liang2009kat.pdf.

29. Maheshwari P, Teoh A (2005) Supporting ATAM with a collaborative web-based software architecture evaluation tool. Science of Computer Programming 57(1): 109–128.

30. Nonaka I, Takeuchi H (1995) The Knowledge-Creating Company: How Japanese Companies Create the Dynamics of Innovation. New York: Oxford University Press.

31. Nuseibeh B (2001) Weaving together requirements and architectures. IEEE Computer 34(3): 115–117.

32. Rubart J, Dawabi P (2004) Shared data modeling with UML-G. International Journal of Computer Applications in Technology 19(3): 231–243.

33. Rus I, Lindvall M (2002) Knowledge management in software engineering. IEEE Software 19(3): 26–38.

34. Tang A, Ali-Babar M, Gorton I, Han J (2006) A survey of architecture design rationale. Journal of Systems and Software 79(12): 1792–1804.

35. Tang A, Jin Y, Han J (2007) A rationale-based architecture model for design traceability and reasoning. Journal of Systems and Software 80(6): 918–934.

36. Tyree J, Akerman A (2005) Architecture decisions: Demystifying architecture. IEEE Software 22(2): 19–27.

37. van der Ven J, Jansen A, Avgeriou P, Hammer D (2006) Using architectural decisions. Short Papers of the 2nd International Conference on the Quality of Software Architectures (QoSA 2006), 27–29 July.
38. Whitehead J (2007) Collaboration in software engineering: A roadmap. Proceedings of Future of Software Engineering (FOSE 2007), 20–22 March, pp. 214–225.

Chapter 18
Collaborative Product Line Requirements Engineering Using Rationale

Anil K. Thurimella

Abstract Variability management is the central part of software product line engineering. Due to the separation of domain and application engineering, product line requirements engineering encounters several collaboration problems during variability management. These collaboration problems have an additional layer of complexity, in case, product line organizations are geographically distributed. To address the collaboration problems, we propose a new methodology called issue-based variability management, which is based on the extension of variability management using rationale management. In particular, variability meta-model is viewed as a part of rhetorical rationale model. The methodology is explained and evaluated based on a combination of orthogonal variability model (OVM) and a rationale management approach based on questions, options and criteria (QOC).

18.1 Introduction

Software product line engineering [17] enables customization of products for various market-segments from an abstraction called a *product line platform*. The set of products are developed from a product line platform is termed as a *software product line*. Software product line engineering provides several advantages based on reuse; quicker time-to market, improved cost savings and defect rates. Using software product lines several companies have recorded success stories. For example, Siemens AG Medical Solutions has achieved a 57% reuse of test cases by adopting product lines. Before the adoption of product lines, no reuse was recorded [17].

A product line platform is made up of several assets. An asset could be a system model element (artifacts that are used in software development such as use cases,

A.K. Thurimella (✉)
Harman/Becker Automotive Systems, 76307 Karlsbad, Germany
e-mail: anil_98ee601@yahoo.com

I. Mistrík et al. (eds.), *Collaborative Software Engineering*,
DOI 10.1007/978-3-642-10294-3_18, © Springer-Verlag Berlin Heidelberg 2010

classes, test cases etc) or a variability model element, an abstraction for variability. Variability is introduced in product line platform to allow customization and reuse of artifacts to address the needs of different market segments. Variability management involves several activities. Variability identification covers identification and representation of variability; product instantiation which deals with the resolution of variability for individual products of a product line; and variability evolution, which addresses the change of variability itself. Product line evolution includes the evolution of system model elements and variability model elements.

Software product line engineering involves two activities, domain engineering and application engineering. *Domain engineering* is an activity in which assets of a product line platform are identified, implemented and maintained. Another activity, *application engineering* is responsible for instantiating products from a product line platform. In product line requirements engineering, the activities of variability management are to be performed based on collaboration of domain and application engineering. Therefore, supporting collaboration between domain and application engineering is critical. The communication problem between conflicting views exists from the level of single system requirements engineering. To address the collaboration between domain and application engineering, in this contribution, variability management is extended using rationale management in order to enable *issue-based collaboration*[1] between domain and application engineers. The collaboration supported by a rhetorical model is termed as issue-based collaboration. *Rationale* is defined as the reasoning that leads to a system model [6]. Rationale management is viewed as a special branch of collaborative software engineering.

This chapter is organized as follows. The collaboration problems during variability management are presented and discussed in Section 18.2. Background information, in particular orthogonal variability modeling (OVM) and rationale-based unified software engineering model (RUSE) are covered in Section 18.3. Related work is described in Section 18.4. The methodology is presented and illustrated in Section 18.5. The empirical evaluation is presented in Section 18.6 and the paper is concluded in Section 18.7.

18.2 The Communication Problems

Damian and Zowghi raised that lack of collaboration between remote stakeholders is a major problem in distributed requirements engineering of single system development [3]. As product line organizations involve more stakeholders than single system development, collaboration between remote stakeholders is even more problematic in software product line engineering.

In a product line organization, domain and application engineering are separated and are realized by a domain engineering team and several application engineering

---

[1] Previously, it was viewed as informal collaboration [26, 27].

teams. Due to this separation, their tasks are also different. The task of domain engineering team is to introduce and maintain variation points, while the task of an application engineering team is to instantiate variation points. Furthermore, the clients of a domain engineering team are several application engineering teams, where as the clients of an application engineering team are the customers from a market segment. This leads to the projects with different timelines, milestones and stress factors for these teams. These factors could contribute to inconsistencies in a product line system: A domain engineering team might be busy in maintaining the product line platform, while an application engineering requires to perform product instantiations. In this context, application engineering teams tend to develop artifacts from scratch instead of instantiating variation points. This leads to redundant development of artifacts, which is an inconsistency in a product line system. The inconsistent product line system is a result of weak coupling between domain and application engineering.

Let us consider an example (refer Fig. 18.1), where a product line platform has a variation point, Routing with the following variants: Traffic congestion, Rerouting, Automatic routing and Multi-destination routing. In application engineering, Traffic congestion is instantiated from Routing for P1. But in the case of P2, Automatic routing is instantiated, while Traffic congestion is developed from scratch within the application engineering team. This is a redundant development of Traffic congestion, which is an inconsistency in product line system. To achieve a strong coupling between domain and application engineering, issue-based collaboration is to be supported during product instantiations between domain and application engineering. This is a new collaboration pattern in software product line engineering, which does not exist in single system development.

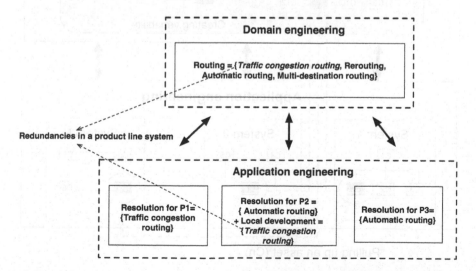

Fig. 18.1 Redundancies during product instantiation, in a weakly coupled product line system

In the scenario of pulling up an asset (refer Fig. 18.2), domain engineers pull-up artifacts that are developed by various application engineering teams. An application engineering team focuses only on the development of their product, but does not care about other products. Because of lack of time for communication and competition between product teams, the participants of an application engineering team tend to hide artifacts from the other application engineering teams. But, pulling out reusable artifacts developed by application engineering teams and creating variability is a major concern for domain engineering team. In this context, because of conflict of interests, domain engineers fails to pull-up artifices which again leads to inconstancies in a product line system. To achieve a strong coupling between domain and application engineering, issue-based collaboration is to be supported during product line evolution. This is another collaboration pattern specific to software product line engineering.

The new collaboration problems exit from the stage of co-located domain and application engineering. When transitioning to distributed product line development, achieving a strong coupling between domain and application engineering is even more challenging. Currently, many product line organizations are developing products for global markets [16]. In this context, a domain engineering team can work in one country (e.g., Germany) while the application engineering teams are

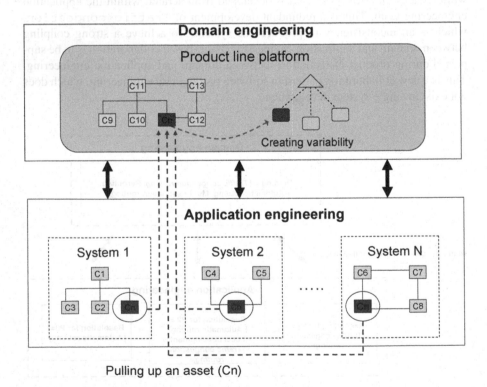

Pulling up an asset (Cn)

Fig. 18.2 Pulling up an asset, a collaboration pattern during product line evolution

present in several different cultures (e.g., US, India & China). Furthermore, in large product line organizations, domain engineering could be distributed. Therefore, issue-based collaboration for the two collaboration problems is to be supported across geographically distributed locations. As product line organizations involve more stakeholders when compared with single system development organizations, all discussions and decisions may not happen in face-to-face meetings. In this prospective, issue-based collaboration is to be supported between remote stakeholders in product line organizations to perform variability management.

Traditionally variability is identified by re-engineering artifacts based on data-mining [11]. The re-engineering based approach generates an initial variability model, which has to be adopted by the collaboration of domain experts. Therefore, collaboration is to be supported for variability identification as well. As collaboration is to be supported for various activities like, variability identification, product instantiation and product line evolution, it is collaboration is an aspect that crosscuts various activities of variability management.

18.3 Background

To address the collaboration problems, which are characterized with conflicts-of-interests between domain and application engineering, negotiations are to be supported. Fischer and Ury proposed the Harvard negotiation model to effectively draw agreements on business deals, union disputes and hostage situations [7]. They focus on the interests and mutual gain participants. This is also called a win–win approach. Later, Kunz and Rittel triggered the use of rationale models to support negotiations [13].

Rationale models are rhetorical models, which have been used to support collaboration between project participants. Issue-based information systems (IBIS) is the early rationale approach and supports collaboration between stakeholders for resolving wicked-problems [13]. A *wicked-problem* is an issue, which cannot be solved algorithmically, but could be solved using discussions and debates. The initial research of rationale management, IBIS, is in planning theory and not in the software engineering community. But, its research has migrated into software engineering community. The first was n-dim, which is proposed by Subrahmanian et al. [19] n-dim supports collaboration during software design.

Questions options and criteria is another rationale approach, which is proposed by Mac Lean et al. [14]. According to Dutoit [5], the criterion of QOC could be a goal or non-functional requirement. Based on this enhancement, he uses QOC to support collaborative work in product management meetings. Later, QOC has been used to support issue-based collaboration in globally distributed projects. The rationale-based unified software engineering model (RUSE) [27] combines system models, collaboration model and a model of the organization and its meta-model is shown in Fig. 18.3. RUSE supports System Models based on the concepts such as Feature, Document, Use Case, Class and Test Case. The

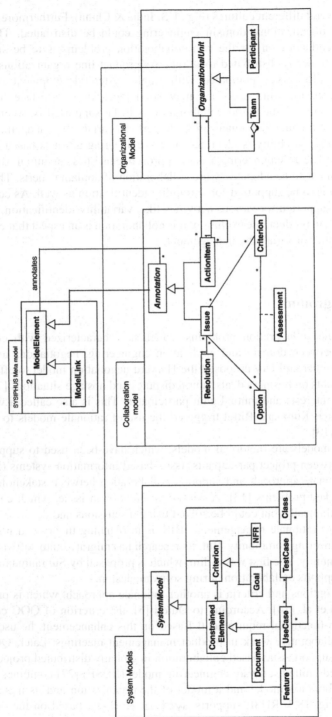

Fig. 18.3 The meta-model for RUSE [27]

Collaboration model of RUSE is a rhetorical model with classes Issue, Option, Criterion and Assessment, which is called the issue model (same as the QOC). An object of ModelElement, can be linked to many objects of Issue, the rationale discussions are initiated. During the rationale discussions stakeholders (distributed in a multi-site environment), propose options, criteria and assessments collaboratively. All this information is organized and visualized in the form of a justification matrix and resolutions (also called decisions) are made. Each Resolution is linked to an ActionItem, which is assigned to a Participant in the OrganizationalUnit. RUSE has been implemented in Sysiphus [20].

A simplified version of OVM's meta-model [17] is shown in Fig. 18.4. *Variability Model Element* is an abstraction used for variability modeling, which has concrete classes Variation Point and Variant. A Variation Point presents the reason and location of variation and a Variant presents possibility of variation. A variation Point is associated with a variant using *Variability Dependency*, which can be Optional, i.e., the variant could be selected during a product instantiation or Mandatory, i.e., the variant must be selected during product instantiation. Optional variability dependencies can be constrained using Alternative Choice, which provides maximum and minimum number of variants that could be instantiated for products.

All combinations of variation point and variant are constrained using *Constraint Dependency*, which are Requires and Excludes. Requires implies that the selection of a variation point/variant supports the selection other

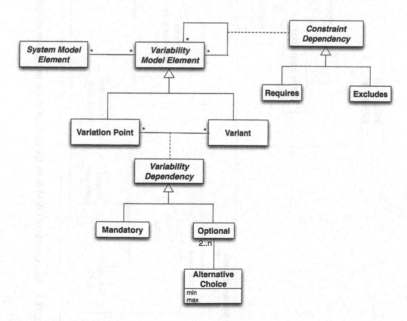

Fig. 18.4 A simplified version of OVM meta-model

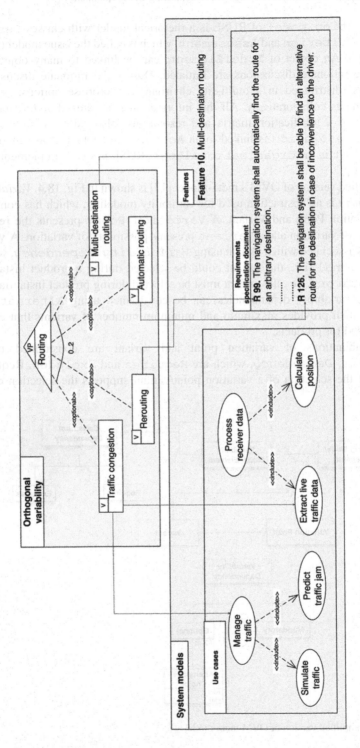

Fig. 18.5 An example of OVM from the domain of car navigation systems

variation point/variant. Excludes semantically mean that the selection of variation point/variant contradicts the selection of other variation point/variant. Variability modeling is related to system modeling as well. The many-to-many association between *System Model Element* and *Variability Model Element* is the traceability between system models and variability models. This is the concept behind orthogonal variability modeling, which means that variability modeling is done externally to system modeling.

Figure 18.5 shows an instance of the meta-model. Here `Routing` variation point is associated with variants such as `Traffic congestion routing, Rerouting, Automatic routing` and `Multi-destination routing`. The variability model is linked various requirements engineering models as a part of `System` models like `features, use case diagrams` and `Requirements specification document`.

18.4 Related Work

Traditional product line requirements engineering approaches does not address the collaboration between stakeholders for variability management very well. For example, existing product instantiation approaches based on configuration techniques [10] focus on the part of the product that could be derived using dependency analysis. However, there is less support for resolving variation points based on the collaboration of domain and application engineers. Furthermore, conventional variability modeling based on feature modeling [12], UML extensions [8] and orthogonal variability modeling (OVM) [17] are concerned with representing variability dependencies and constraints. However, they do not focus on relating collaboration models for variability management in requirements engineering.

Santos et al. raised that there is a tradeoff between domain and application engineering during product instantiation [18]. Their approach focuses to support domain and application engineering at the architecture level. In contrast, issue-based variability modeling addresses domain and application engineering for the complete software lifecycle based on a common meta-model as well as supports negotiations between participants during variability management. Berenbach identifies collaboration problems between participants for requirements reviews; between analysis and design as well as design and development teams; and change management [1]. His contribution does not identify the conflicts of interests and collaboration problems between domain and application engineering. Existing distributed requirements engineering approaches such as distributed requirements negotiations based on EasyWinWin [9], awareness support in distributed software development [2] and collaboration approach based on information models [15] do not address the inconsistencies of artifacts between domain and application engineering.

Deelstra et al. raise artifact redundancies as a problem in software product lines [4]. According to them, lack of proper documentation could lead to redundancies. This contribution describes that lack of negotiations between domain and application engineering could lead to redundancies as well.

Lago and van Vliet [21] addressed the capture of rationale for product line architecture. Their contribution focuses only on architectural design decisions but does not focus on representing rationale for an orthogonal variability model, which could be used for the whole development process.

18.5 Issue-Based Variability Modeling

A meta-model for issue-based variability modeling [23] is shown in Fig. 18.6, which is on the combination of RUSE and OVM. The combination is based on several "similarities" [26, 24] between rationale and variability management:

- Variation point and variant of variability are similar to issue and option of rationale management.
- Similar to variability management, rationale management uses concepts like variability dependencies and constraint dependencies.
- Rationale modeling is done orthogonal to system models, which is another similarity with variability modeling.

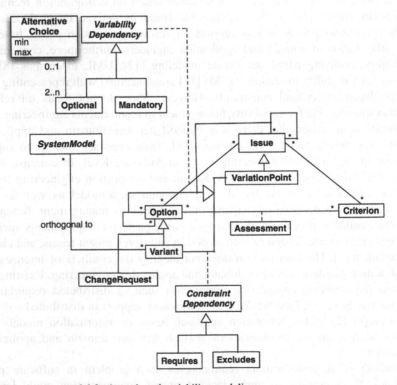

Fig. 18.6 A meta-model for issue-based variability modeling

Exploiting the similarities, variability meta-model is viewed as a special type of collaboration model. Based on this new vision, issue-based collaboration could be effectively used for variability management. In particular the collaboration aspects during product instantiation, variability identification and product line evolution are explained in the subsequent sub-sections.

18.5.1 Collaboration for Product Instantiation

In domain engineering, a variability model is viewed as a partial issue network of variation points (issues) and variants (options). Therefore, the variability model sits in the Collaboration artifacts with interdependencies to the System models as shown in Fig. 18.7. Assessments and criteria are different for different product instantiations and are then introduced late in application engineering, using collaboration of distributed stakeholders. In particular, a variation point is resolved for different products differently by using product specific criteria and assessments. This is performed during product instantiation based on a justification matrix (refer Table 18.1), which is constructed using the collaboration of stakeholders. In other words, a justification matrix is the *instantiation view of variability*.

The concepts behind product instantiation are explained based on an example in Fig. 18.7. Here, the Routing variation point (as initially represented in Fig. 18.5) is instantiated for products P1, P2 and P3. The resolutions in these three cases are the variant sets {Traffic congestion routing}, {Traffic congestion routing, Automatic routing} and {Rerouting}. In each case, the variability model is resolved differently, by introducing assessments and criteria that are specific a product instantiation.

The instantiation of the Routing variation point for the product P2 is explained using the justification matrix (refer Table 18.1). The issue of this variation point is on the instantiation of the variations for a new product P2. The optional variants are the variants of Table 18.2. The product specific quality concerns that are obtained from the application engineering teams (who interact with customers) are the criteria. All stakeholders (from domain engineering team, application engineering team and customers) involved in product instantiation process and located in different places give assessments. QOC supports several assessments such as + (supports), ++ (supports strongly), 0 (neutral), – (hinters) and — (hinters strongly). After collecting assessments, resolutions are made on the instantiation of variation points. In case of conflicts on assessments, they can be resolved by starting issues on assessments.

Unlike conventional variability modeling approaches, issue-based variability modeling supports domain and application engineering using the same meta-model. As variability meta-model is viewed as a type of a rhetorical model, issue-based collaboration is supported for product instantiations. Based on these enhancements, conflicts of interests during product instantiation are addressed.

In traditional issue modeling, that is, rationale models such as IBIS, QOC, and DLR [22] as well as rationale management approaches proposed by Dutoit et al. [6]

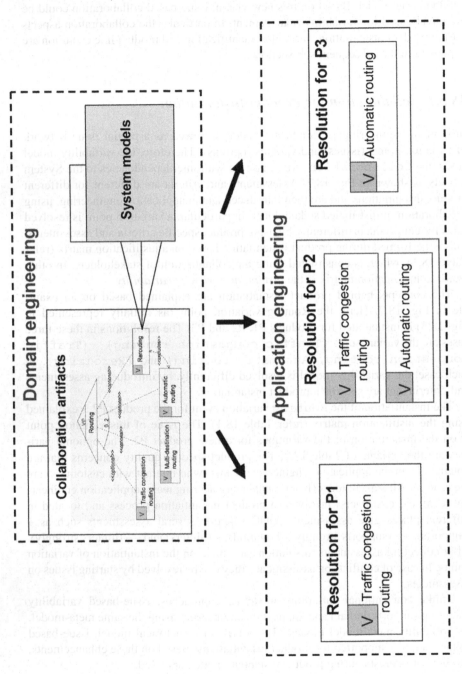

Fig. 18.7 Domain and application engineering, supported by the same meta-model

Table 18.1 Justification matrix, the instantiation view of variability

Variation Point: How to instantiate *Routing management* for P2?

Criteria	Usability	Availability	Reliability	Extensibility	Maintainability	Price
Option 1: Traffic congestion	++	+	+	+	+	+
Option 2: Rerouting	++	−	0	0	0	−−
Option 3: Automatic routing	++	0	+	+	+	0
Option 4: Multi-destination routing	−−	0	−	0	+	−

Resolution: *Traffic congestion* and *Automatic routing* are decided to be instantiated.

Table 18.2 Rationale discussions, supporting collaborative variability identification

1. Issue: What is the variability dependency of the *Automatic routing?*
2. Criteria   *1. Usability*   *1. Availability*   *1. Price*
3. *Option1:* Mandatory   2. ++   2. −−   2. 0
4. *Option2:* Optional   3. 0   3. +   3. +
5. Resolution: Variability dependency of *Automatic routing* is decided to be
   optional because of better assessments in price and availability.

and Gruenbacher and Seyff [9], an issue can have only one resolution. In particular, Harward negotiation model focuses on reaching a single agreement based on the mutual interests of the participants. Unlike the traditional issue modeling and negotiation approaches, in the context of issue-based variability modeling, a variation point can have several resolutions. Each of these resolutions is the instantiation of the variation point for a specific product.

18.5.2 Collaboration for Variability Identification and Product Line Evolution

Rationale discussions could be used for variability identification as well. Discussions are triggered using issues. Options are possible variations (e.g., mandatory, optional or alternative). The distributed stakeholders propose criteria and their arguments in the form of assessments.

Based on the issue-based collaboration, justification matrices are built and decisions are made on the variability identification. This concept of negotiations for

Table 18.3 Updated justification matrix for evolution of variability

1. Issue: What is the variability dependency of the *Automatic routing?*			
2. Criteria	*1. Usability*	*1. Availability_1*	*1. Price_1*
3. *Option1:* Mandatory	2. ++	2. +	2. +
4. *Option2:* Optional	3. 0	3. –	3. 0
5. Resolution: Variability dependency of *Automatic routing* is decided to be mandatory because of better assessments in usability, availability and price.			

variability identification, could be used during reengineering based variability identification as well as during product line maintenance where the variability is added incrementally in order to address the communication problems during variability identification and product line evolution. For example, Table 18.2 is an example of justification matrix for variability identification of the variability dependency of `Automatic routing`. According to issue-based variability modeling, an issue can require several issues (refer meta-model of Fig. 18.6). This means issue of variation point in domain engineering (why do we have a variation point?) is formally linked to issues of variability dependencies and constraints, i.e., justification matrices of variability identification (e.g., Table 18.3). This makes up the knowledge view of variability (Fig. 18.8). The enriched representation of variability also improves the collaboration between distributed stakeholders, by representing and sharing rationale information between distributed stakeholders.

The justification matrices support evolution by a simple update. For example, let us suppose over time the `Availability` and `Price` criteria have changed to `Availability_1` and `Price_1`. By updating the state of the justification matrix (from Table 18.2 to Table 18.3) i.e., redoing the assessments and reevaluating the resolution, we can cope with the evolution of variations.

From this example, we can notice that capturing variability rationale can make product lines evolvable. In case the rationale information (as represented in Table 18.3) is not captured, the variability identification has to be performed again, which is expensive than updating the state of the justification matrices. Furthermore, the relation between variability and criteria is not explicit, in case the variability rationale is not captured.

18.6 Empirical Evaluation

Issue-based variability modeling has been implemented as a plug-in for Sysiphus and have been empirically evaluated based on a series of studies.

The first one is an experimental survey with professionals. In this study 34 professionals were sampled into an experimental group (with 19 professionals) and a control group with (15 professionals) based on stratified random sampling. The experimental group was trained in issue-based variability modeling and the control

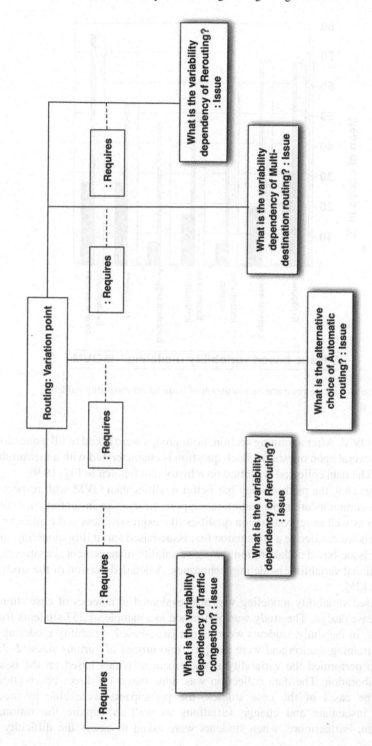

Fig. 18.8   Knowledge view of variability

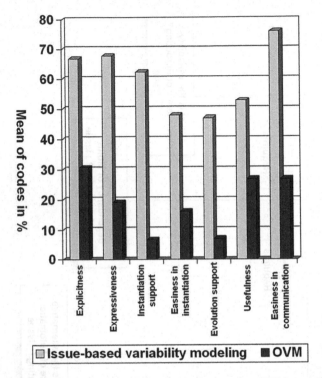

Fig. 18.9 Results from the comparative evaluation of issue-based variability modeling

group used OVM. After a training section, both groups were asked to fill a questionnaire with several open questions. Each question is characterized with a measurable parameter. The data collected is plotted on a histogram (shown in Fig. 18.9).

From Fig. 18.9, the methodology has better qualities than OVM with respect to issue-based communication, instantiation support, easiness in instantiation, evolution support as well as representation qualities like expressiveness and explicitness. Based on this we can derive a conclusion that issue-based variability modeling supports better issue-based collaboration during variability management activities than the conventional variability modeling techniques. A detailed version of the study is available at [25].

Issue-based variability modeling was also evaluated in a series of case studies with muti-case design. The study was performed in a sample of 257 students from TU Munich. In the study, students were taught issue-based variability modeling in a half-day training section and were sampled into groups of various sizes (2–22). Each group performed the variability management activities based on the issue-based collaboration. The data collection was done based on direct observation.

In all the cases of the case studies, the participants were able to model variations, instantiate and change variations as well as capture the rationale behind them. Furthermore, when students were asked to assess the difficulty of

Table 18.4 Results of multiple-regression

1. Independent Variable	1. Dependent Variable	1. N	1. Correlation coefficient	1. p- Value	1. Reject H0
2. Average motivation of group	2. Quality of instantiation	2. 42	2. 0.4295	2. 0.0016	2. Yes
3. Group size			3. –0.0423	3. 0.0695	3. No

issue-based variability modeling on the scale of Very easy, Easy, Fair, Difficult, Very difficult and Don't know the answer, 87.75% of the 258 participants answered with Fair and above. From this, we conclude that issue-based collaboration supported by the methodology is easy to use even in teams with only elementary software engineering knowledge.

We planned to explore the effect of Group size and Average motivation of group on Quality of instantiation. Therefore, we performed multiple regression with Group size and Average motivation of group as independent variables and Quality of instantiation as dependent variable (see Table 18.4). There was a possibility that Average motivation of group was dependent on Group size. In order to check this, we performed linear regression with Group size as independent variable and Average motivation of group as dependent variable as shown in Table 18.5. The p-value for linear regression between Group size and Average motivation of group accepts the null hypothesis (H0), which implies that Group size is independent of Average motivation of group. This enabled us to analyze the results of the multiple regression analysis. From the results (see Table 18.5), the p-value between Group size and Quality of instantiation accepts the null hypothesis.

The correlation coefficient is less ($|{-0.0695}| \ll 1$). So, in the case studies Quality of instantiation is independent of Group size. This gives evidence that the quality of instantiation of issue based variability modeling is independent of Group size, where 2 < Group size < 22.

Table 18.5 Results of linear regression

1. Independent variable	1. Dependent variable	1. N	1. Correlation coefficient	1. p-Value	1. Reject H0
2. Group size	2. Average motivation of group	2. 42	2. 0.2393	2. 0.1269	2. No
3. Quality of rationale	3. Reuse of rationale	3. 55	3. 0.722	3. 0.0000	3. Yes

18.7 Conclusion

Separation of concerns between domain and application engineering could lead to collaboration problems. To address the collaboration problems, this chapter proposes an approach called issue-based variability modeling, by extending traditional variability management based on rationale management. In particular, the meta-model of orthogonal variability modeling is extended with the meta-model of rationale-based unified software engineering model. Issue-based variability modeling supports variability modeling in domain engineering using a partial issue network comprising of issues and options. In application engineering the partial issue-network is resolved during product instantiation, thus enabling variability modeling and product instantiation using the same meta-model. Furthermore, the resolutions are done differently for different products using product specific assessments and criteria. Issue-based variability modeling also enables rationale representation for variability. This supports collaboration for product line evolution.

Issue-based variability modeling has been implemented as a plug-in for an existing RUSE implementation called Sysiphus and was evaluated empirically using several empirical studies. The results show quantitatively that issue-based variability modeling is effective than conventional variability modeling techniques for supporting issue-based collaboration. Further, the issue-based collaboration was tested up to 22 participants.

Acknowledgements I am grateful to Bernd Bruegge, Allen Dutoit and Guenter Boeckle for their support in my research work. Further, my heartily acknowledgements and dedications to my family members mother, Kumari; father, Uma; wife Padmini and sister Padmaja.

References

1. Berenbach B (2006) Impact of organizational structure on distributed requirements engineering processes: Lessons learned. Proceedings of the 2006 international Workshop on Global Software Development for the Practitioner GSD '06, May 23, Shanghai, China, pp. 15–19.
2. Damian D, Marczak S, Kwan I (2007) Collaboration patterns and the impact of distance on awareness in requirements-centred social networks. Proceedings of IEEE RE' 07, New Delhi. IEEE Digital Library, pp. 59–68.
3. Damian D, Zowghi D (2007) Requirements engineering challenges in multi-site software development organizations. Requirements Engineering Journal 8: 149–160.
4. Deelstra S, Sinnema M, Nijhuis J, Bosch J (2004) Experiences in software product families: Problems and issues during product derivation. Software Product Lines, Springer Verlag Lecture Notes on Computer Science Vol. 3154, pp. 65–182.
5. Dutoit A (2002) Rationale management in requirements engineering. PhD. Dissertation, CMU.
6. Dutoit A, McCall R, Mistrik I and Paech B (Eds.) (2006) Rationale Management in Software Engineering. Berlin, Heidelberg, New York: Springer.
7. Fischer R, Ury W (1981) Getting to Yes: Negotiating Agreement Without Giving in, Harward Negotiation Project. Boston, MA: Houghton Mifflin.
8. Gomaa H (2005) Designing Software Product Lines with Uml: From Use Cases to Pattern-Based Software Architectures. Reading, MA: Addison Wesley Longman Publishing Co.

9. Gruenbacher P, Seyff N (2006) Requirements Negotiations. Engineering and Managing Requirements. Berlin, Heidelberg, New York: Springer, pp. 143–162.
10. Hotz L, Krebs T, Wolter K (2004) Using a structure-based configuration tool for product derivation. Proceedings ASE'04 2004 (IEEE Digital Library) pp. 388–391.
11. John I, Dorr J (2003) Elicitation of requirements from user documentation. Proceedings Ninth International Workshop on Requirements Engineering, Foundation for Software Quality (REFSQ#03), pp. 16–17.
12. Kang K, Cohen S, Hess J, Nowak W, Peterson S (1990) Feature-oriented domain analysis (FODA) feasibility study. Technical Report, CMU/SEI-90-TR-21, Software Engineering Institute, Carnegie Mellon University.
13. Kunz W, Rittel R (1970) Issues as elements of information systems, University of California at Berkeley, Institute of Urban and Regional Development.
14. MacLean A, Young RM, Bellotti VME, Moran TP (1991) Questions, options, and criteria: Elements of design space analysis. Human-Computer Interaction 6: 201–250.
15. Paech B, Dorr J, and Koehler M (2005) Improving requirements engineering communication in multiproject environments. IEEE Software 22: 40–47.
16. Paulish DJ (2003) Product line engineering for global development. International Workshop on Product Line Engineering The Early Steps: Planning, Modeling, and Managing, PLEES03.
17. Pohl K, Boeckle G, van der Linder F (2005) Software Product Line Engineering Foundations, Principles, and Techniques, Berlin, Heidelberg, New York: Springer.
18. Santos AL, Koskimies K, Lopes A (2006) A model-driven approach to variability management in product-line engineering. Nordic Journal of Computing 13(3): 196–213.
19. Subrahmanian E, Konda SL, Levy SN, Reich Y, Westerberg AW, Monarch IA (1993) Equations aren't enough: Informal modeling in design. AI EDAM 7(4): 257–274.
20. sysiphus.in.tum.de.
21. Lago P, Van Vliet H (2005) Explicit assumptions enrich architectural models. Proceedings 27th International Conference on Software Engineering, ICSE 2005. ACM Digital Library, pp. 206–214.
22. Lee J (1991) Extending the Potts and Bruns model for recording design rationale. Proceedings ICSE'13, Los Alamitos, CA, pp. 114–125.
23. Thurimella AK (2009) Issue-Based Variability Modeling: Extending Variability Modeling Based on Rationale Management. Saarbrücken, Germany: VDM Dr. Mueller.
24. Thurimella AK, Bruegge B (2007) Evolution in product line requirements engineering: A rationale management approach. Proceedings 15th IEEE RE 07, IEEE Computer Society 2007, pp. 254 257.
25. Thurimella AK, Bruegge B (2007) Empirical evaluation of issue-based variability modeling using the experimental survey technique. Proceedings SEA 2007.
26. Thurimella AK, Bruegge B, Creighton O (2008) Identifying and exploiting the similarities between rationale management and variability management. Proceedings SPLC 2008, Limerick, Ireland. IEEE Computer Society 2008, pp. 99–108.
27. Wolf T (2007) Rationale-based Unified Software Engineering Model. Saarbrücken, Germany: VDM Dr. Mueller.

Chapter 19
Collaborative Software Engineering: Challenges and Prospects

Ivan Mistrík, John Grundy, André van der Hoek, and Jim Whitehead

Abstract Much work is presently ongoing in collaborative software engineering research. This work is beginning to make serious inroads into our ability to more effectively practice collaborative software engineering, with best practices, processes, tools, metrics, and other techniques becoming available for day-to-day use. However, we have not yet reached the point where the practice of collaborative software engineering is routine, without surprises, and generally as optimal as possible. This chapter summarizes the main findings of this book, draws some conclusions on these findings and looks at the prospects for software engineers in dealing with the challenges of collaborative software development. The chapter ends with prospects for collaborative software engineering.

19.1 Introduction

19.1.1 What We Know About Collaborative Software Engineering

Software engineering is naturally a team activity. Software engineers need to collaborate effectively in order to deliver a project on time, on budget and to an appropriate quality level [2]. Traditional software engineering projects have used primarily top-down approaches to team organization and project management, a homogeneous software process and toolset, are co-located enabling regular and proactive face-to-face meetings, and team members usually have the same language and work culture [2, 3, 8].

These projects still face daunting challenges around collaboration. Teams have to be formed and work appropriately delegated, tracked and managed. Specialists within teams or whole specialist teams need to exchange knowledge among themselves and across team boundaries. Evolving requirements and customer needs

I. Mistrík (✉)
Independent Consultant, 69120 Heidelberg, Germany
e-mail: i.j.mistrik@t-online.de

I. Mistrík et al. (eds.), *Collaborative Software Engineering*,
DOI 10.1007/978-3-642-10294-3_19, © Springer-Verlag Berlin Heidelberg 2010

require processes and collaboration support to enable these to be effectively managed [5, 26]. Traditional software tools usually provided limited collaboration support features. A toolset needs mechanisms to support collaboration (e.g., shared workspaces, file repositories, differencing and merging support, configuration, testing, design, process management), communication (email, messages, annotations, video/audio), and co-ordination (locking, versioning, hand-over, auditing) [20, 6]. Many studies of teams, processes, tools and real-world projects [5, 19, 27] have shown the value of appropriate process, project management, technique and tool selection and usage to enable effective and efficient collaboration.

Several recent trends in software engineering have greatly increased the challenges around collaboration on software projects. Agile processes enabling rapid requirements evolution and emergent architectures and documentation demand vastly different team organization, project management and communication strategies [19, 18, 8, 2]. Virtual software organizations with distributed teams, contractual obligations between constituent organizations, and highly distributed teams demand greater support for knowledge sharing, co-ordination and collaboration [13]. Communication may be complicated by time zone, culture and even language differences. Open source software projects exhibit similar challenges but are often characterized by a very wide range of participants, organizations and contributions from teams and individuals with very different motivations and needs. A trend to "global software development" similarly leads us to teams that span country, language, culture, organization, technical tool platform and ultimately software process [18].

In order to address many of these known issues – and discover new issues – in collaborative software engineering, a large number of research and practice projects are taking place. New software processes are being studied to gauge their impact on distributed software projects including open source, global software development and outsourcing projects [2, 8, 17, 24]. These aim to help organizations better understand such contexts for collaboration and formulate the most effective and complementary teams, processes, toolsets and techniques. Communication patterns in open source projects, requirements engineering, coding and testing projects, and projects in agile process, open source and virtual software development organizations, are being analyzed to enhance understanding of needs in these domains [24, 5, 2]. Many face challenges of distance including language, culture and work practice, as well as traditional communication and knowledge management issues. A wide range of new tool support approaches are being developed, deployed and evaluated in various domains. These include but are not limited to improved awareness support, software analysis, configuration management, co-ordination, communication and knowledge management [6, 9, 11, 19].

Sharing knowledge about software engineering projects continues to be a major challenge and best practices for knowledge management in many areas are still unclear [9, 11, 26]. Studies have shown benefits to collaboration of improved knowledge repositories and management practices in requirements, architecture, project management, and software process domains. Communicating rationale about decisions is critical at all levels of software engineering [12, 15, 16].

19.1.2 Objectives of This Chapter

This book makes a case for CoSE as a crucial part of research in software engineering (SE) and as an essential part of future software development and maintenance. In previous chapters, the book has explained what CoSE is, what its potential value is for SE, what its research challenges are and how these challenges might be met. The intention of this concluding chapter is to provide a summary of the previous chapters and a look at prospects meeting the challenges of future CoSE practice.

Section 19.1 summarizes a current status of CoSE. Section 19.2 presents a summary of the book. Section 19.3 reviews some of the present challenges facing collaborative software development and prospects for meeting them.

19.2 Summary of the Book

Software engineering collaboration has multiple goals and means spanning the entire lifecycle of development [27]. Chapters in this book are reporting on advances in achieving some of these goals by presenting their particular means and specific solutions.

Chapter 1 of the book introduces the concepts and tools for CoSE. Part I contains chapters that characterize CoSE. Part II contains chapters that examine various techniques and tool support issues in CoSE. Part III contains chapters addressing organizational issues in CoSE. Part IV contains chapters looking at a variety of related issues in CoSE. Finally, Chapter 19 concludes the book with a summary of the book, current challenges and prospects in CoSE.

As many organizations have discovered to their cost, implementing a global software engineering strategy is a complex and difficult task. Extensive research in this area has identified that this is due to a number of factors which include the nature and impact of geographical, temporal, cultural and linguistic distance. In addition, whether undertaken in a collocated or geographically distributed environment, team based software development is not simply a technical activity. It also has important human, social and cultural implications which need to be specifically addressed. While the technical aspects of software development cannot be underestimated, neither can the importance of establishing and facilitating the effective operation of these teams [18].

Requirements engineering (RE) is an area filled with challenges of a non-technical nature. RE involves activities such as negotiation, analysis and requirements management in subsequent phases of development. RE requires communication from the elicitation phase down to the analysis, implementation and test phases. As such, it involves collaboration among large, often geographically distributed cross-functional teams comprised of requirements analysts, software architects, developers, and testers. This collaboration is driven by coordination needs in software development and relies on communication and awareness. Coordination is a critical aspect in every activity related to a requirement's analysis, implementation or testing. Effective coordination, knowledge management and information sharing among team members with diverse organizational and functional backgrounds is crucial. Collaboration across geographical distance (i.e., different time zones) and socio-cultural distance (i.e., language and culture) creates additional challenges in project members' communication and awareness in the development project [5].

Collaboration can be viewed as the most important lever for achieving high quality, efficient and effective software engineering practices and results in virtually any software developing organization. Although collaboration has been complicated, several trends increase the complexity of managing dependencies between software development teams and organizations. These trends include the increasing adoption of software product lines, the globalization of software engineering and the increasing use of and reliance on 3rd party developers in the context of software ecosystems. The trends share as a common characteristic that the coupling between the software assets as well as between the organizational units is increased. Consequently, decoupling mechanisms need to be introduced to address the increase in coupling [3].

Agile software development is a group of software engineering methodologies, e.g., eXtreme programming (XP), Scrum, Crystal, that became popular in the early 2000s. Agile advocates claim to increase overall software developer productivity, deliver working software on time, and minimise the risk of failure in software projects. While its effectiveness and applicability remain uncertain, it is attracting increasing interest from the software engineering community. The Agile Manifesto emphasises collaboration and interactions, and the reality of XP software development offers evidence that this emphasis is borne out in practice. Observing practice makes it clear to the researcher that the work of an XP team visibly and continually involves collaboration and communication – and that collaboration and communication are part of the technical business of creating working software. There are two key XP practices which illustrate the relationship between the social and technical: pairing and customer collaboration [19].

Ontology captures a shared understanding of a problem domain and is usually specified in a logical language by describing concepts, relationships and additional logical axioms. Knowledge included in ontology is designed for both humans and machines. It can be integrated in development infrastructures and in developed software to support various software project activities. Although ontologies have been around for many years, several factors promote their increasing adoption. First, with a number of W3C standards such as RDF and OWL issued in recent times, tools and methodologies for creating and managing ontologies have matured. Second, the success of the Web enables developers to collaborate in a richer and more dynamic way, instead of working in de facto isolation. Both factors contribute to a slow but growing number of semantic approaches addressing CSD issues. Applications of ontologies in software development can be manifold and so the resulting ontologies will differ in expressivity, scope and purpose [9].

A variety of novel tools have been created to allow software developers to collaborate with each other. There are many approaches how to classify them. One approach classifies them on whether they try to (a) make software developers feel they are co-located, or (b) provide features not found in co-located collaboration.

The result is an overview that relates concepts not linked together earlier, which include not only research tools but also studies that motivate/evaluate them. Each of the surveyed works is described by showing how it builds on or overcomes problems of other research addressed in this chapter. By focusing only on the differences among these works, the chapter covers a large variety of concepts, from over fifty papers. It is targeted mainly at the practitioner familiar with the state of the art, rather than the researcher working on improving current practices. Nonetheless, the interrelationships among the referenced works should be of interest to everyone. In particular, a new researcher in this area should be able to find holes in existing designs and evaluations [6].

In software development the need for coordination among developers generally arises because of the underlying technical dependencies among work artifacts; as well as the structure of the development process. Researchers in the software engineering as well as computer-supported cooperative work communities have recognized this problem and created a host of tools to improve team coordination. However, evaluating the usability and usefulness of such tools has proven to be extremely difficult. One possibility is to focus on different evaluation approaches that are applicable for coordination tools. There exists a diverse range of approaches to evaluating collaborative tools. Adopting a combination of empirical evaluation approaches is perceived as means to meet the challenges typically encountered. The diversity of existing tools and evaluation approaches reflect the many challenges of facilitating coordination in teams. Further, several evaluation frameworks have been proposed to support software tool evaluation [20].

Configuration Management is a discipline responsible for controlling the evolution of products. Since late 1960s, configuration management is considered to be one of the core supporting process to software development and a research field of software engineering. According to IEEE, there are five main functions of configuration management: configuration identification, configuration control, configuration status accounting, configuration evaluations and reviews, and release management and delivery. However, these five functions are traditionally supported by three main subsystems: issue tracking system, version control system, and build management system. Because the primary focus of configuration management is keeping the consistency of products, it is concerned with how people interact to develop and maintain these products. The complexity of software products led to the need of geographically distributed teams composed of a large number of developers with different background. These teams collaborate during software engineering activities, and configuration management can be considered as an enabling technology to allow this collaboration. Collaboration in the context of software engineering encloses different aspects, such as: implicit and explicit communication among developers, awareness regarding other developers' actions, coordination of development tasks to avoid rework and to achieve the project goals, keeping a shared memory with previous development actions history, and providing a shared space where the work made by a developer is available to other developers [15].

The advantages of using explicit software architecture include early interaction with stakeholders, its basis for establishing work breakdown structure and early assessment of quality attributes. Although considerable progress has been made, we still lack techniques for capturing, representing, and maintaining knowledge about software architectures. While much attention has been given to documenting architectural solutions, the rationale for these solutions often remains implicit and is often exchanged in interpersonal, informal communication. The incomplete representation of the needed architectural knowledge leads to several problems that are generally recognized in any software engineering project, and that become just worse in distributed and global software development. When software engineering projects are distributed or global, the problems above are aggravated. Knowledge transfer is a communication process requiring strict interaction and agile information exchange. In local software development, it is already difficult to rationalize the type and amount of knowledge we need to exchange. If in addition exchanges occur remotely and via a technological infrastructure, we have to make this knowledge explicit, and we need to identify agile means to render this process as dynamic and powerful as possible [11].

Software development is in essence information-intensive collaborative knowledge activity. It is about using information, generating information, and making information artifacts. The wide acceptance of agile processes and the success of many open source projects provide strong evidence that human aspects do matter in software development; cognitive and social processes play essential roles in successful software projects in which individuals' creative thinking in using and generating information are nurtured. There is an argument that software engineering environments must be designed to foster such individuals' creative knowledge processes, and that collaboration must be supported in the context of individuals' development activities. Collaborative software development environments should be designed to facilitate and nurture individuals' creative knowledge processes. Collaboration takes place with or without explicit communication. On the one hand, software developers regularly engage in collaboration through artifacts without explicit communication (e.g., by writing comments in code to be read by others). On the other hand, explicit communication becomes necessary when developers must ask their peers for information that is otherwise not obtainable. Existing studies have provided ample evidence that both collocated and distributed software development teams frequently engage in communication to acquire necessary information from peer developers [16].

A common feature of many software analysis tools is that they focus on just a particular kind of analysis to produce the results wanted. If different analyses are required, an engineer needs to run several tools, each one specialized on a particular aspect, ranging from pure source code analysis, duplication analysis, co-change analysis, bug prediction, to bug fixing patterns and visualization. All these techniques have their own explicit or implicit meta-model which dictates how to represent the input and the output data. Thus the sharing of information between tools is only possible by means of a cumbersome export towards files complying with a specified exchange format. Also, if there are several analyses of the same kind (*e.g.*, code duplication analysis) there is hardly any way to compare the results or integrate them other than manual investigation. Tool interoperability is hampered even more by their stand-alone nature as well as their platform and language dependence. As a consequence, distributed and collaborative software analysis scenarios are severely limited. The combination and integration of different software analysis tools is a challenging problem when we need to gain a deeper insight into a software system's evolution. For every required analysis a specialized tool, with its own explicit or implicit meta-model dictating how to represent the input and output, has to be installed, configured and executed. Even if different analyses of the same kind exist, the only way to compare them is to do it manually [8].

Communication and collaboration among team members are key success factors for large, complex software projects. In addition to industry, examples of such projects can be found in the Open Source Software (OSS) community, for example, the Mozilla, Apache, Eclipse projects. OSS projects are of particular interest for communication and collaboration research because their developers rarely or never meet face-to-face. Findings of previous research showed that OSS developers coordinate their work almost exclusively by three information spaces: the implementation space, the documentation space, and the discussion space. Typically, in OSS projects a versioning system, such as the concurrent versions system, provides the backend of the implementation space. It keeps track of changes made to projected related files and corresponding versions. The World Wide Web is used as the primary documentation space. Because of the distributed and informal nature of OSS projects, discussions between project members, project associates, and users are done and tracked in mailing lists and bug reporting systems. This results in a representative data set that enables communication and collaboration analysis [17].

For the past few years, Siemens has been experimenting with software development processes and practices for globally distributed projects using student-based development teams located at different universities around the world. The students who make up the Global Studio Project (GSP) simulate an industrial software development project using common practices for collaboration among distributed sites. Experiences with this project have been reported in a number of papers, and it has been documented as a case study (GSP 2005). The motivation for studying multi-site software development processes is driven by the business needs. A number of questions were raised, and they are still being investigated [2].

Free/open source software development (FOSSD) is a way for building, deploying, and sustaining large software systems on a global basis, and differs in many interesting ways from the principles and practices traditionally advocated for software engineering. Hundreds of FOSS systems are now in use by thousands to millions of end-users, and some of these FOSS systems entail hundreds-of-thousands to millions of lines of source code. So what's going on here, and how are collaborative FOSSD processes used to build and sustain these projects, and how might differences with SE be employed to explain what's going on with FOSSD? One of the more significant features of FOSSD is the formation and enactment of collaborative software development practices and processes performed by loosely coordinated software developers and contributors. These people may volunteer their time and skill to such effort, and may only work at their personal discretion rather than as assigned and scheduled. Further, FOSS developers are generally expected (or prefer) to provide their own computing resources (e.g., laptop computers on the go, or desktop computers at home), and bring their own software tools with them. FOSS developers often work on global software projects that do not typically have a corporate owner or management staff to organize, direct, monitor, and improve the software development processes being put into practice on such projects [24].

The outsourcing of software development implies that an organization wholly or partially contracts out software development to another organisation. If the partner organization is located abroad, this might be termed "an offshore outsourcing of software development". If the development takes place in physically far-flung locations, it is called "global software development" or "distributed software development". Whether domestic or foreign, outsourcing can be an uncertain undertaking. Nonetheless many companies use offshore outsourcing to reduce time-to-market, to tap global resources, to profit from round-the-clock development, and to reduce costs. The goal of "offshore outsourcing software development" is to uphold competitiveness in the global market. This goal should be promoted by the concise and purposeful employment of every resource – information technology, talent and competence to assure a thriving offshore outsourcing project. All of which helps the company maintain ongoing global penetration. However, global distribution of the development raises a number of knotty questions concerning accomplishment and implementation. Often there is a huge disparity between targets and the results attained [13].

According to a recent paradigm shift in the field of software architecture, the product of the architecting process is no longer only the models in the various architecture views, but the broader notion of Architectural Knowledge (AK): the architecture design as well as the design decisions, rationale, assumptions, context, and other factors that together determine architecture solutions. Architectural (design) decisions are an important type of AK, as they form the basis underlying software architecture. Other types of AK include concepts from architectural design (e.g., components, connectors), requirements engineering (e.g., risks, concerns, requirements), people (e.g., stakeholders, organization structures, roles), and the development process (e.g., activities). The entire set of AK needs to be iteratively produced, shared, and consumed during the whole architecture lifecycle by a number of different stakeholders as effectively as possible. The stakeholders in architecture may belong to the same or different organization and include roles such as: architects, requirements engineers, developers, maintainers, testers, end users, and managers etc. Each of the stakeholders has his/her own area of expertise and a set of concerns in a system being developed, maintained or evolved. The architect needs to facilitate the collaboration between the stakeholders, provide AK through a common language for communication and negotiation, and eventually make the necessary design decisions and trade-offs. However, in practice, there are several issues that hinder the effective stakeholder collaboration during the architecting process, which diminishes the quality of the resulting product. One of these problems is the lack of integration of the various architectural activities and their corresponding artifacts across the architecture lifecycle. The different stakeholders typically have different backgrounds, perform discrete architectural activities in a rather isolated manner, and use their own AK domain models and suite of preferred tools. The result is a mosaic of activities and artifacts rather than a uniform process and a solid product [12].

Software product line engineering enables customization of products for various market-segments from an abstraction called a product line platform. The set of products are developed from a product line platform is termed as a software product line. Software product line engineering provides several advantages based on reuse; quicker time-to market, improved cost savings and defect rates. Using software product lines several companies have recorded success stories. A product line platform is made up of several assets. An asset could be a system model element (artifacts that are used in software development such as use cases, classes, test cases etc) or a variability model element, an abstraction for variability. Variability is introduced in a product line platform as an abstraction to allow customization and reuse of artifacts to address the needs of different market segments. Variability management involves several activities. Variability identification covers identification and representation of variability; product instantiation which deals with the resolution of variability for individual products of a product line; and variability evolution, which addresses the change of variability itself. Product line evolution includes the evolution of system model elements and variability model elements. Software product line engineering involves two activities, domain engineering and application engineering. Domain engineering is an activity in which assets of a product line platform are identified, implemented and maintained. Another activity, application engineering is responsible for instantiating products from a product line platform. In product line requirements engineering, the activities of variability management are to be performed based on collaboration of domain and application engineering. Therefore, supporting collaboration between domain and application engineering is critical. The communication problem between conflicting views exists from the level of single system requirements engineering. To address the collaboration between domain and application engineering, in this contribution, variability management is extended using rationale management in order to enable issue-based collaboration between domain and application engineers. The collaboration supported by a rhetorical model is termed as issue-based collaboration. Rationale is defined as the reasoning that leads to a system model. Rationale management is viewed as a special branch of collaborative software engineering [26].

19.3 Today's Challenges

As should be clear from the collected chapters in this book, much work is presently ongoing in collaborative software engineering research, work of a broad variety and often great amount of depth. This work is beginning to make serious inroads into our ability to more effectively practice collaborative software engineering, with best practices, processes, tools, metrics, and other techniques becoming available for day-to-day use. However, we have not yet reached the point where the practice of collaborative software engineering is routine, without surprises, and generally as optimal as possible. Partly, this is unavoidable, as the fundamental tensions discussed in Section 1.7 make achieving the optimum very difficult, if not impossible. At the same time, we should acknowledge that, while the research has advanced greatly over the past decade, many difficult challenges still exist when it comes to understanding and practicing collaborative software engineering. In the below, we highlight several key such challenges that we believe are among the most pressing and at the same time most promising to address at this moment in time.

Building a theoretical understanding of COSE. In any research field, one of the keys to advancement is to build an understanding of its underlying truths and phenomena. So it is in software engineering, and in the case of this book, collaborative software engineering. We need to build an understanding of what factors influence collaborative work and how those factors together determine the overall effectiveness of a given collaborative effort. This not only requires identifying each of the factors at play, but also how those factors influence one another. As one example, the role of awareness has been recognized for some time now [6]. As another example, trust has recently come forward as a crucial factor in distributed projects [1]. While each of these factors must be studied in depth, they cannot be studied in isolation; they are closely interrelated and must be understood as a collective. The notion of congruence is appealing in this regard, having recently been proposed as foundational and theoretical approach to contextualizing coordination needs versus coordination capabilities [4, 21]. It remains to be seen whether all necessary data can be gathered, but the concept represents an intriguing look at collaborative work.

Designing assessment methods for specific situations. Having an overall understanding of the factors at work in collaborative software engineering is not sufficient. We should also be able to assess specific situations and circumstances in which collaborative individuals, teams, and organizations find themselves. Are there any coordination problems presently? Are there latent issues that may lead to future coordination problems? If there are issues, what are some potential solutions to them? How will those solutions affect other collaborative factors in the organization? These are key questions for which we do not have good answers at this time. Social-technical network analysis with respect to the presence or absence of communication with respect to pieces of code that depend on one another is an example of a promising direction of research in this regard [22], though even there it is still unproven whether it is actually the presence or absence of communication that indicates good collaboration. Advocates of "presence" argue that such communication indicates that people talk and presumably resolve issues. Advocates of "absence" argue that if every technical dependency had to give rise to communication between developers, excess communication would take place. Moreover, they argue that other strategies, such as properly partitioning and scheduling the work, should actually prevent communication from being needed. At this time, there is no clear answer, other than that both sides of the argument are right at different times, but that we have no way of distinguishing yet when those times are. Similarly open-ended question pertain to assessing given situations with respect to a whole host of different factors – the field has not matured sufficiently yet in this regard.

Implementing tool support. Many recent advances in collaborative software engineering have to do with the creation of new tools in support of particularly collaborative practices. A host of tools has emerged, with various purposes behind them. Mylyn focuses on providing task context [10], CollabVS [7] and Palantír [23] on mitigating risks of parallel work, and Expertise Browser [14] on finding experts on particular areas of the code base. Many others exist, as the survey by Dewan in Chapter 7 shows [6]. Some tools are designed to help the researchers themselves, in efforts to understand collaborative practices and situations. Social-technical network analysis tools such as Ariadne [25], for instance, serve this purpose. But today's tools have only brought us "so far"; as new situations are investigated and hypotheses formed, new tools can be developed. One could think of tools that explicitly represent and work with trust, tools that prevent to just direct conflicts but also indirect conflicts, tools that better help identify necessary communications across team or organizational boundaries, awareness tools that cross phases of the life cycle, and so on. Much work remains to be done.

Beyond these three overarching categories, several challenges of "smaller" scale are presently at the forefront of the community. That is, within and across the above three categories in-depth investigations are needed regarding a variety of subjects. We mention such questions as: How could closed-source development benefit from open-source practices, and vice versa? How can knowledge better be preserved as it arises from and spreads to various teams in a collaborative environment? How can wikis be streamlined to more effectively support collaborative work? How can cultural barriers be bridged more smoothly? What other forms of awareness can be supported with tools? How can we better predict future coordination needs, and bottlenecks? Answers to these and other questions like it stand to improve the practice of collaborative software engineering, but will require a broad and deep research effort for years to come.

19.4 Prospects

This book has emphasized how collaboration is an integral part of software engineering project work, making it seem that the problems of collaboration are eternal, a form of status quo. This couldn't be further from the truth, as software engineering collaboration is a clear example of tangible forward progress. Technologies such as wikis, software forges, discussion lists, web sites, social network sites, email, instant messaging, mobile phones (and many others) combined with improved conceptual understanding of the collaborative goals and practice have created a golden age for project collaboration.

Consider the difference between collaboration practice today and 20 years ago, just prior to the widespread adoption of the Internet. Today, open source projects routinely gather project participants from around the world, use project forges for project collaboration (including mailing lists, SCM repositories, bug tracking systems, project web pages, etc.) and gather bug reports from users of their software.

Twenty years ago there were open source projects, but it was very challenging to create the collaboration infrastructure needed (you typically needed to be in an academic environment), the number of people on the Internet was much smaller than today, and knowledge of how to use tools such as CVS was thinly spread.

Today, commercial projects often involve multiple groups, located at different geographic sites. Collaboration technologies, combined with an improving conceptual understanding of how to manage and foster collaboration across wide geographic and cultural distance make these wide-area collaborations work, with comparatively little impact on project speed and quality. Twenty years ago, such wide-area collaboration was rare, modularized at the level of system-components, and extremely expensive. It is unclear whether it was even possible to perform the kind of fine-grain global software engineering that is commonplace today.

Today, a project web site is a common tool for collecting project documents such as requirements, designs, test plans, user interface sketches, and so on. While simple, such web sites are a huge improvement in recording and finding project knowledge over 20 years ago, when finding and copying project documents was major challenge.

It is commonplace today for software to report back to the manufacturer when it experiences a crash. Web sites with end-user submitted questions, workarounds for problems, and suggestions for future features are now typical. Even the most obscure discussion forum can potentially be critically useful if it holds discussion relevant to a specific user's problem. Twenty years ago, users were able to exchange this type of knowledge via Netnews, if they were lucky enough to be on the Internet. Computer user groups, software magazines, and software retail outlets also helped, but the knowledge could not be easily stored and searched.

Finally, today computer games such as Little Big Planet allow players to create and contribute new game levels for others to play... over one million of them so far. This type of user generated content was just not feasible before the internet, combined with low-cost storage and servers.

Dramatic as the past 20 years have been, the future of collaboration in software engineering promises to be even brighter. For starters, the widespread integration of the internet into most facets of life is just beginning. Mobile internet access, now very expensive, will become less expensive over time, promoting the spread of networks out of the first world, making it possible to tap the potential of many billions more people. There are many smart people in the world with time on their hands. Some simply wish to find some way they can make a positive contribution, and thereby generate meaning and create community in their lives.

Collaboration tools will become more sophisticated. Following the trend of desktop applications migrating to the web, software development environments will increasingly be web-based, allowing all project documents to live in the cloud. This, in turn, makes it possible to add social network site capabilities to projects, which should make it easier to build collaborations. With project data in the cloud, it should become easier to combine together various types of software project models, thereby finding errors and inconsistencies, but also recording richer networks of interrelationships among the artifacts. Awareness of the work of others should also be easier in web-based environments, where all work, down to the keystroke level, is available.

As the amount of code available on the web continues to grow, so does the potential for finding existing source code to use in an existing project. Once key issues in the formation of searches and adoption of found code are resolved, this kind of anonymous collaboration via code repositories could result in substantial improvement in coding productivity.

During the first phase of internet adoption (c. 1990–2010) advances in software project collaboration generally were the result of being able to communicate cheaply with people at a distance, and having a universal viewer for documents (the web). Future advances will be more sophisticated, explicitly modeling interpersonal and project relationships, providing deeper integration of software project data, leveraging deeper understanding of code structure and meaning, and combining collaboration services in unique configurations.

The many chapters in this volume speak to the broad array of potential futures in software engineering collaboration. Though not all of these ideas will be widely adopted, together they make a compelling case that the future of collaboration in software engineering is bright, with much potential for further unleashing the potential of software engineers working in teams.

References

1. Al-Ani B, Redmiles D (2009). In strangers we trust? Findings of an empirical study of distributed development. IEEE International Conference on Global Software Engineering, 13–16 July, Limerick, Ireland, 2009.
2. Avritzer A, Paulish DJ (2009) A comparison of commonly used processes for multi-site software development. In: Mistrík I, Grundy J, van der Hoek A, Whitehead J (eds.) Collaborative Software Engineering. Springer.
3. Bosch J, Bosch-Sijtsema P (2009) Softwares product lines, global development and ecosystems: collaboration in software engineering. In: Mistrík I, Grundy J, van der Hoek A, Whitehead J (eds.) Collaborative Software Engineering. Springer.
4. Cataldo M et al. (2006) Identification of coordination requirements: Implications for the design of collaboration and awareness tools. ACM Conference on Computer Supported Cooperative Work, pp. 353–362.
5. Damian D, Kwan I, Marczak S (2009) Requirements-driven collaboration: Leveraging the invisible relationships between requirements and people. In: Mistrík I, Grundy J, van der Hoek A, Whitehead J (eds.) Collaborative Software Engineering. Springer.
6. Dewan P (2009) Towards and beyond being there in collaborative software development. In: Mistrík I, Grundy J, van der Hoek A, Whitehead J (eds.) Collaborative Software Engineering. Springer.
7. Dewan P, Hegde R (2007) Semi-synchronous conflict detection and resolution in asynchronous software development. European Computer Supported Cooperative Work, pp. 159–178.
8. Ghezzi G, Gall HC (2009) Distributed and collaborative software analysis. In: Mistrík I, Grundy J, van der Hoek A, Whitehead J (eds.) Collaborative Software Engineering. Springer.
9. Happel HJ, Maalej W, Seedorf S (2009) Applications of ontologies in collaborative software development. In: Mistrík I, Grundy J, van der Hoek A, Whitehead J (eds.) Collaborative Software Engineering. Springer.

10. Kersten M, Murphy GC (2006) Using task context to improve programmer productivity. Proceedings of the 14th ACM SIGSOFT International Symposium on Foundations of Software Engineering (Portland, OR, USA, 05–11 November 2006). SIGSOFT '06/FSE-14. ACM, New York, pp. 1–11.

11. Lago P, Farenhorst R, Avgeriou P, de Boer RC, Clerc V, Jansen A, van Vliet H (2009) The GRIFFIN collaborative virtual community for architectural knowledge management. In: Mistrík I, Grundy J, van der Hoek A, Whitehead J (eds.) Collaborative Software Engineering. Springer.

12. Liang P, Jansen A, Avgeriou P (2009) Collaborative software architecting through knowledge sharing. In: Mistrík I, Grundy J, van der Hoek, Whitehead J (eds.) Collaborative Software Engineering. Springer.

13. Mäkio J, Betz S, Oberweis A (2009) OUTSHORE maturity model: Assistance for software offshore outsourcing decisions. In: Mistrík I, Grundy J, van der Hoek A, Whitehead (eds.) Collaborative Software Engineering. Springer.

14. Mockus A, Herbsleb J D (2002) Expertise browser: A quantitative approach to identifying expertise. Proceedings of the 24th international Conference on Software Engineering (Orlando, FL, 19–25 May 2002). ICSE '02. ACM, New York, pp. 503–512.

15. Murta LGP, Werner CML, Estublier J (2009) The configuration management role in collaborative software engineering. In: Mistrík I, Grundy J, van der Hoek, Whitehead J (eds.) Collaborative Software Engineering. Springer.

16. Nakakoji K, Ye Y, Yamamoto Y (2009) Supporting expertise communication in developer-centered collaborative software development environments. In: Mistrík I, Grundy J, van der Hoek A, Whitehead J (eds.) Collaborative Software Engineering. Springer.

17. Pinzger M, Gall HC (2009) Dynamic analysis of communication and collaboration in OSS projects. In: Mistrík I, Grundy J, van der Hoek A, Whitehead J (eds.) Collaborative Software Engineering. Springer.

18. Richardson I, Casey V, Burton J, McCaffery F (2009) Global software engineering: A software process approach. In: Mistrík I, Grundy J, van der Hoek A, Whitehead J (eds.) Collaborative Software Engineering. Springer.

19. Robinson H, Sharp H (2009) Collaboration, communication and coordination in agile software development practice. In: Mistrík I, Grundy J, van der Hoek A, Whitehead J (eds.) Collaborative Software Engineering. Springer.

20. Sarma A, Al-Ani B, Trainer E, Sila Filho RS, da Silva I, Redmiles D, van der Hoek A (2009) Continuous coordination tools and their evaluation. In: Mistrík I, Grundy J, van der Hoek A, Whitehead J (eds.) Collaborative Software Engineering. Springer.

21. Sarma A, Herbsleb J, van der Hoek A (2008) Challenges in measuring, understanding, and achieving social-technical congruence. Technical Report CMU-ISR-08-106, Carnegie Mellon University, Institute for Software Research International, Pittsburg.

22. Sarma A, Maccherone L, Wagstrom P, Herbsleb J (2009) Tesseract: Interactive Visual Exploration of Socio-Technical Relationships in Software Development, Proceedings of the Thirty-first International Conference on Software Engineering, Vancouver, Canada.

23. Sarma A, Bortis G, van der Hoek A (2007) Towards supporting awareness of indirect conflicts across software configuration management workspaces. Twenty-second IEEE/ACM International Conference on Automated Software Engineering, November 2007, pp. 94–103.

24. Scacchi W (2009) Collaborative practices and affordances in free/open source software development. In: Mistrík I, Grundy J, van der Hoek A, Whitehead J (eds.) Collaborative Software Engineering. Springer.

25. de Souza C, Quirk S, Trainer E, Redmiles DF (2007) Supporting collaborative software development through the visualization of socio-technical dependencies. 2007 International ACM SIGGROUP Conference on Supporting Group Work (Sanibel Island, FL), November 2007, pp. 147–156.

26. Thurimella AK (2009) Collaborative product line requirements engineering using ratio-nale. In: Mistrík I, Grundy J, van der Hoek, Whitehead J (eds.) Collaborative. Software Engineering. Springer.
27. Whitehead EJ (2007) Collaboration in software engineering: a roadmap. Future of Software Engineering (FOSE 2007), 23–25 May 2007, Minneapolis, MN, pp. 214–225.

Editor Biographies

John Grundy is Professor of Software Engineering at the University of Auckland, New Zealand. He has published over 170 refereed papers on software engineering tools and methods, automated software engineering, visual languages and environments, collaborative work systems and tools, aspect-oriented software development, user interfaces, software process technology and distributed systems. He has made numerous contributions to the field of collaborative software engineering including developing novel process modeling and enactment tools; collaborative editing tools, both synchronous and asynchronous; thin-client project management tools; software visualization tools for exploratory review; sketching-based UML and software design tools providing hand-drawn diagram support for collaborative review and annotation; and numerous event-based collaborative software architectures for building collaborative software engineering tools. He has been Program Chair of the IEEE/ACM Automated Software Engineering conference, the IEEE Visual Languages and Human-Centric Computing Conference, and has been a PC member for the International Conference on Software Engineering.

André van der Hoek is an associate professor in the Department of Informatics of the Donald Bren School of Information and Computer Sciences and a faculty member of the Institute for Software Research, both at the University of California, Irvine. He holds a joint B.S. and M.S. degree in Business-Oriented Computer Science from the Erasmus University Rotterdam, the Netherlands, and a Ph.D. degree in Computer Science from the University of Colorado at Boulder. His research focuses on understanding and advancing the role of design, co-ordination, and education in software engineering. He has authored and co-authored over 80 peer-reviewed journal and conference publications, and in 2006 was a recipient of an ACM SIGSOFT Distinguished Paper Award. He is a co-author of the 2005 Configuration Management Impact Report as well as the 2007 Futures of Software Engineering Report on Software Design and Architecture. He has served on numerous international program committees, is a member of the editorial board of ACM Transactions on Software Engineering and Methodology, and is program chair of the 2010 ACM SIGSOFT International Symposium on Foundations of Software Engineering. He is the principal designer of the B.S. in Informatics at UC Irvine

I. Mistrík et al. (eds.), *Collaborative Software Engineering*,
DOI 10.1007/978-3-642-10294-3, © Springer-Verlag Berlin Heidelberg 2010

and was honored, in 2005, as UC Irvine Professor of the Year for his outstanding and innovative educational contributions.

Ivan Mistrík is an independent consultant and researcher in software-intensive systems engineering. He is a computer scientist who is interested in software engineering (SE) and software architecture (SA), in particular: life cycle software engineering, requirements engineering, relating software requirements and architectures, knowledge management in software development, rationale-based software development, and collaborative software engineering. He has more than forty years' experience in the field of computer systems engineering as an information systems developer, R&D leader, SE/SA research analyst, educator in computer sciences, and ICT management consultant. In the past 40 years, he has been primarily working at various R&D institutions and has done consulting on a variety of large international projects sponsored by ESA, EU, NASA, NATO, and UN. He has also taught university-level computer sciences courses in software engineering, software architecture, distributed information systems, and human-computer interaction. He is the author or co-author of more than 80 articles and papers in international journals, conferences, books and workshops, most recently a chapter Capture of Software Requirements and Rationale through Collaborative Software Development and a paper Knowledge Management in the Global Software Engineering Environment. He has also written over 90 technical reports and presented over 70 scientific/technical talks. He has served in many program committees and panels of reputable international conferences and organized a number of scientific workshops, most recently the workshop Knowledge Engineering in Global Software Development at International Conference on Global Software Engineering 2009. He has been a guest-editor of IEE Proceedings Software: A special Issue on Relating Software Requirements and Architectures published by IEE in 2005 and a lead-editor of the book Rationale Management in Software Engineering published by Springer-Verlag in 2006. He has been a co-author of the book Rationale-Based Software Engineering published by Springer-Verlag in May 2008. Currently, he is a lead-editor of the book Collaborative Software Engineering to be published in 2009.

Jim Whitehead is Associate Professor of Computer Science at the University of California, Santa Cruz. Jim received the Bachelor of Science in Electrical Engineering from the Rensselaer Polytechnic Institute in 1989, and a PhD in Information and Computer Science from the University of California, Irvine in 2000. From 1996–2004, he created and led the Internet Engineering Task Force Working Group on Web Distributed Authoring and Versioning (WebDAV), and participated in the creation of the DeltaV follow-on standard for versioning and configuration management. In 2005–2006, he led efforts to create a new major at UC Santa Cruz, the Bachelor of Science in Computer Science: Computer Game Design.

Index